ANTI-ZIONISM AND
ANTISEMITISM

STUDIES IN ANTISEMITISM
Alvin H. Rosenfeld, editor

ANTI-ZIONISM AND ANTISEMITISM

The Dynamics of Delegitimization

—ɯ—

EDITED BY

ALVIN H. ROSENFELD

INDIANA UNIVERSITY PRESS

This book is a publication of

Indiana University Press
Office of Scholarly Publishing
Herman B Wells Library 350
1320 East 10th Street
Bloomington, Indiana 47405 USA

iupress.indiana.edu

Manufactured in the United States of America

Cataloging information is available from the Library of Congress.

ISBN 978-0-253-03869-2 (cloth)
ISBN 978-0-253-04002-2 (paperback)
ISBN 978-0-253-03872-2 (ebook)

1 2 3 4 5   23 22 21 20 19

This book is dedicated to the memory of
Erna Rosenfeld
(1939–2016),
whose love and support made possible
virtually everything I have done over the years.

Contents

Introduction

ALVIN H. ROSENFELD

IN EXAMINING THE links between anti-Zionism and antisemitism, the chapters of this book address issues that date back decades but have taken on a new urgency in our own day. Frans Timmermans, a former Dutch foreign minister and first vice president of the European Commission, recognized as much when, speaking at a EU meeting in Brussels on October 1, 2015, he noted a sharp increase in openly displayed hatred in today's Europe. "Europe," he said, "is going through a period of crisis and turmoil, which is challenging the very fabric of European society." He saw the rise in antisemitism as symptomatic of this turmoil and acknowledged the threats it poses: "When you know about European history, you know that the darker, uglier forces in our societies always turn first against minorities. Always turn first against Jews . . . Antisemitism is not just terrible for the Jewish community, it is like a fever in an infected body . . . Left unchallenged, [it] will create a much, much bigger problem . . . So tackling antisemitism is an essential operation to save what we cherish in our society."

Timmermans concluded his reflections by observing that, far from having been eradicated, "antisemitism is still a reality, and that it is in fact on the rise—old antisemitism that we have known for centuries, and [a] new antisemitism, that sometimes tries to hide itself behind anti-Zionism."[1]

If matters in Europe were bad when Timmermans spoke—and they were—they have since become worse, and on various fronts. In both its older and newer forms, a resurgent antisemitism has come powerfully to the fore and is now widespread. That is especially so with regard to hostility to Israel, which, in its most extreme forms, impels its adherents to denounce the Jewish state as a criminal entity and to vilify and attack those identified with it. References to Israel as a successor state to apartheid South Africa or to Nazi Germany are typical of the rhetoric of this obsession at its most overwrought. But lesser gradations of vilification are also in wide circulation today—and not just on the margins of society but increasingly within the mainstream. Such hostile passions fuel much of the animus that calls itself anti-Zionism.

Most arguments against Zionism formulated in the prestate period would find few supporters today. The destruction of most of European Jewry during World War II and the establishment of Israel a few years later changed history in decisive ways and brought most Jews and others to recognize the need for and validity of a sovereign Jewish state. Nevertheless, seven decades after Israel's establishment, public calls for its end are becoming more prevalent. Those who align themselves with radical anti-Zionist agendas frequently advance the goals of delegitimization. And the ultimate end point of delegitimization is the dissolution of Israel as a sovereign Jewish state and, for some, the nullification of the notion of the Jewish people as such.

Those who hold these aggressive views may, as Timmermans notes, hide behind the facade of anti-Zionism, but the issue here is not Zionism. Most of today's fervent anti-Zionists probably know little, if anything, about Zionism and simply do not like Jews or the Jewish state. As examples, recall the former French ambassador to London, Daniel Bernard, who referred to Israel as "that shitty little country,"[2] and the Irish poet Tom Paulin, who equated Israeli soldiers with the SS and declared that "Brooklyn-born Jews" living on the West Bank are "Nazis" and should "be shot dead" ("I feel nothing but hatred for them").[3] Most people in Western societies know it is unacceptable after the Holocaust to say such things outright, so they take cover behind labels such as anti-Zionism that are considered safe enough to distance them from any embarrassing connection to the older forms of Jew hatred.

Anti-Zionism, though, is often a camouflage term, as Stephen Harper, the former Canadian prime minister, recognized when he called anti-Zionism "the face of the new antisemitism. It targets the Jewish people by targeting Israel and attempts to make the old bigotry acceptable for a new generation."[4] In 2014, Manual Valls, the French interior minister at the time, spoke out against such bigotry by denouncing anti-Zionism as "an invitation to antisemitism."[5] In June 2017, Emmanuel Macron, the current French president, spoke out strongly against anti-Zionism, calling it "a reinvention of antisemitism" and pledged that his government to "not surrender" to it.[6] Pope Francis, speaking in October 2015, was equally emphatic: "To attack Jews is antisemitism, but an outright attack on the State of Israel is also antisemitism."[7]

Despite such denunciations by prominent world figures, anti-Zionism not only persists but also now has global reach and, to quote the late eminent scholar Robert Wistrich, "has become the most dangerous and effective form of antisemitism in our time." Underwritten by an ideology that aims at the elimination of Israel, and sometimes accompanied by a radical vision of "a world liberated from the Jews," it is "a totalist form of antisemitism."[8] Attracting supporters among people on the political left, the political right, and those with no particular political affiliation, as well as among large numbers of Muslims, it is a potent force and shows up in street-level acts of anti-Jewish violence as well as intellectual and political denunciations of Israel and the Jews, often by people who claim to hold progressive views. They routinely charge Israel with the worst of sins—among them, racism, apartheid, crimes against humanity, ethnic cleansing, and even genocide. The ritual repetition of these accusations has developed into an emotionally charged litany that demonizes the Jewish state and its supporters in ways that may recall the antisemitism that preceded the persecution and destruction of the Jews during World War II.

To explore these troubling developments in their historical, political, social, and ideological dimensions, Indiana University's Institute for the Study of Contemporary Antisemitism (ISCA) brought together seventy scholars from sixteen countries for four days of intensive deliberation on the links between anti-Zionism and antisemitism. The meetings took place April 2–6, 2016, on Indiana University's Bloomington campus and were marked by vigorous discussion and debate on some of the most pressing questions of the day. For instance, publicly voiced calls for the end of Israel are becoming more prevalent at a time when antisemitism is on the upsurge in Europe and elsewhere. How, if at all, are these phenomena related? What does Zionism signify to its present-day opponents? What motivates them to fixate, often passionately, on what they see as the singular "injustices" and even "evil" of Zionism and Israel? Of what irredeemable sin do they find Israel to be uniquely guilty? Why, alone among all the world's countries, is Israel judged to be unacceptable as a state and unworthy of a future? No other nation, after all, is targeted for elimination. Why is Israel?

These and related questions are explored in depth in the pages of this book. All the chapters are revised versions of papers that were presented at the April 2016 gathering in Bloomington, which was the third international scholars' conference on antisemitism that ISCA has convened since its inaugural conference in 2011.

I wish to thank the conference participants for their tireless and collegial engagement with the difficult subject matter before us. Their insights and ideas, developed over the course of our deliberations and now displayed in the pages of this book, will help readers better understand the nature of today's antisemitism, especially in its anti-Zionist manifestations.

I am particularly grateful to professors Doron Ben-Atar, Bruno Chaouat, Günther Jikeli, and Elhanan Yakira, all of whom served on the conference's Academic Advisory Committee and provided early and invaluable input into the conceptualization of the conference theme and the selection of speakers.

I am also deeply appreciative of the many ways that M. Alison Hunt and Melissa Deckard assisted me in organizing the conference and looked after its innumerable logistical details. To host an international gathering of this size and length is demanding, and Alison and Melissa measured up to the task with a rare degree of expertise and goodwill throughout. Tracy Richardson, Melissa Hunt, David Axelrod, Tova Zimm, and Shayna Goodman also helped with a range of conference-related details. I thank them as well.

Special thanks go to Janet Rabinowitch for reading and carefully editing the book's chapters. I could not ask for a more professionally skilled editorial partner than Janet, nor a more personally gracious, collegial, and cooperative one. I am hugely appreciative of all her efforts on this volume's behalf. I likewise am grateful to my research assistant, Katelyn Klingler, who helped me prepare the final version of the book's manuscript and did so in her usual meticulous and cheerful fashion.

My deepest gratitude goes to the following benefactors, without whose generous support this book and the conference that preceded it would not have been possible: the Justin M. Druck Family (sponsoring benefactor), the Bodman Foundation, Leslie Lenkowsky, Hart and Simona Hasten, Robert A. and Sandra S. Borns, Monique Stolnitz, Tom Kramer, Marija Krupoves-Berg, Sandra and Norman Berg, Gale Nichols, Roger and Claudette Temam, and Irwin Broh. Special thanks go to Kenneth Waltzer and the Academic Engagement Network for the award of a microgrant for the publication of this volume. In addition to being of vital practical help, the support of all these friends has been the best vote of confidence in our work that I could possibly hope for.

Intensive study of antisemitism is an important but often disheartening endeavor, and we were fortunate, at the end of the conference, to have our spirits lifted by an inspiring concert of Jewish music given by Marija Krupoves-Berg, Svetla Vladeva, Tomas Lozano, Diederik van Wassenaer, and Shaun Williams. It is a pleasure to acknowledge their extraordinarily rich and most welcome contribution to our work.

Finally, I am most grateful to President Michael McRobbie, Provost Lauren Robel, and Dean of the College of Arts and Sciences Larry Singell for their ongoing support of the work of the Institute for the Study of Contemporary Antisemitism. Indiana University is one of only two institutions of higher learning in the United States that houses a research institute of this kind. It is both a privilege and a pleasure to work at a university whose administrative leadership is as understanding, cooperative, and supportive of the initiatives that ISCA undertakes as these distinguished colleagues are. I feel fortunate to work with them these many years.

NOTES

1. "European Union Steps Up Fight against Growing Hate against Jews and Muslims," World Jewish Congress, October 1, 2015, http://www.worldjewishcongress.org/en/news/european-union-steps-up-fight-against-growing-hate-against-jews-and-muslims-10-5-2015.

2. Ewan MacAskill, "Israel Seeks Head of French Envoy," *Guardian,* December 19, 2001, http://www.theguardian.com/world/2001/dec/20/israel2.3

3. Robert Worth, "Poet Who Spoke against Israel Is Reinvited to Talk at Harvard," *New York Times,* November 21, 2002, http://www.nytimes.com/2002/11/21/education/21POET.html.

4. Barak Ravid, "Harper Tells Knesset: Anti-Zionism Is the New Face of Anti-Semitism," *Haaretz*, January 20, 2014, http://www.haaretz.com /israel-news/1.569559.

5. "French Interior Minister: Anti-Zionism Is New Anti-Semitism," *Haaretz*, March 20, 2014, http://www.haaretz.com/jewish/news/1.581034.

6. Benjamin Kentish, "Emmanuel Macron Says Anti-Zionism Is a New Type of Anti-Semitism," *Independent*, July 17, 2017, http://www .independent.co.uk/news/world/europe/emmanuel-macron-anti -zionism-anti-semitism-israel-jewish-state-france-president-racism -attacks-a7844711.html.

7. Jonathan S. Tobin, "The Pope's Lesson on Anti-Semitism," *Commentary*, October 30, 2015, https://www.commentarymagazine.com /foreign-policy/middle-east/israel/pope-francis-anti-semitism/.

8. Robert Wistrich, "Anti-Zionism and Anti-Semitism," *Jewish Political Studies Review* 16, no. 3–4 (Fall 2004).

ALVIN H. ROSENFELD holds the Irving M. Glazer Chair in Jewish Studies and is Professor of English and Founding Director of the Institute for the Study of Contemporary Antisemitism at Indiana University–Bloomington. He is editor of *Deciphering the New Antisemitism* (IUP) and *Resurgent Antisemitism: Global Perspectives* (IUP) and author of *The End of the Holocaust* (IUP).

ANTI-ZIONISM AND ANTISEMITISM

PART I

Ideological and Theoretical Sources and Implications

The New Replacement Theory

Anti-Zionism, Antisemitism, and the Denial of History

JAMES WALD

ANTISEMITISM HAS HISTORICALLY tended to focus on the most prominent manifestation of Judaism in a given era: originally, religion; in modern times, race; and today, Jewish nationhood in the form of Zionism and Israel.[1] As a result, the relation between anti-Israel discourse and antisemitism has become increasingly contested. At the center of this issue is the debate over not just the definition but the very existence of the so-called new antisemitism.[2] Anthropologists tell us that such liminal areas—in this case, between the boundaries of legitimate and illegitimate criticism, academic and popular debate, and innocent or insidious use of antisemitic memes—are dangerous territory, but it is there that this chapter deliberately ventures.[3]

I examine the intersection of traditional antisemitic thinking with denial or radical revision of the historical record, aimed at or tending toward delegitimization of the Jewish state. Ironically, the complexity of the task is in some ways the result of *progress* in three areas:

1. Today, in contrast to the past, no respectable person openly admits to being an antisemite or harboring antisemitic views.[4]
2. With the scientization of discourse, even extremists now feel compelled to argue on rational grounds of science and

scholarship (or at least appear to). Rather than simply asserting that the biblical narrative trumps Darwin's theory,
opponents of evolution have invented "creation science" to
cloak their fundamentally unscientific views in the mantle
of modern knowledge. Holocaust deniers, rather than simply dismissing the event as a fantastic lie, cite arcane historical details and evidence from physics and chemistry in their
attempt to prove that the genocide could not have occurred.
Even some of the cruder popular anti-Zionist and anti-Israel
discourse now avails itself of vocabulary and concepts bor-
rowed from academe.[5]

3. With increasing public sophistication comes a welcome
skepticism toward received wisdom and "standard narratives," but the negative corollary is a willingness to lend credence even to deeply flawed alternatives.[6] Reflexive doubt
thus becomes the ironic doorway to new certainty.

In the present case, the received wisdom is that (1) the Jews
were a people indigenous to the ancient Near East; (2) the Jewish
national movement, Zionism, was morally as well as substan-
tively comparable to any other; and (3) the reestablishment of a
Jewish commonwealth was therefore an act of restoration rather
than usurpation (its unfortunate distinction, as Mark Lilla observes, being that the suffering or injustices inherent in its creation occurred within living memory rather than in the mists of
antiquity).[7] The negation of these three postulates increasingly
takes the form of calls for the end of the Jewish state. It is a stunning development. In 1922, the fifty-one members of the League
of Nations unanimously approved the Palestine Mandate, whose
preamble includes the rationale: "Whereas recognition has been
given to the historical connection of the Jewish people with
Palestine and to the grounds for reconstituting their national
home in that country."[8] Today, not just the reconstitution but
even the once self-evident "historical connection" on which it
was premised is called into doubt. That a view once "marginal

and unworthy of serious refutation" is now "commonly held" and "increasingly seen as legitimate" commands the attention of the historian, not least when world leaders such as the pope feel the need to intervene.[9] After all, contemporaneous upheavals arising from the redrawing of borders and state formation—expulsion of the ethnic Germans and Indian Partition—were far bloodier.[10] We may, as academics or citizens, reflect on the necessity or ethicality of the action; only the founding of Israel moves respectable voices to demand its reversal.

The past, as well as the present, has thus become a battleground. This chapter focuses on three such historical areas hitherto not treated together: the Holocaust, archaeology, and genetics and ethnicity.[11] What renders these discourses so insidious is the fact that (1) each exists in "extreme" and "soft" versions—the former preposterous, pseudoscientific, and antisemitic, and the latter straddling the boundary between legitimate academic debate and the inherently or potentially antisemitic (ironically, the existence of the former adds to the credibility of the latter, causing it to appear more acceptable by comparison); (2) they often entail an explicit assault on Israeli and Jewish scholarship; and (3) they are moreover linked in what I call the new replacement theory. In church doctrine, supersessionism or replacement theology asserted that the New Covenant had superseded the old, and Christianity thus replaced Judaism as the new or true Israel (*verus Israel*).[12] In the new replacement theory, Palestine replaces Israel as the sole moral and practical heir to the land. Not coincidentally, the involvement of the churches in anti-Israel activism has led to a revival of literal replacement theory in some quarters.[13]

THE HOLOCAUST AND THE NEW
DISCOURSE OF REMORSE

Holocaust denial has flourished in some sectors of Arab and Muslim society because attacking the historicity of the presumed cause of Israel's creation is seen as a way to undermine the legitimacy of the state.[14] In contrast to Holocaust denial, the soft instrumentalization of the Holocaust in anti-Israel arguments enjoys growing academic as well as popular acceptance, though on closer scrutiny, it proves to be built on false premises and false analogies. A new discourse of remorse holds that the creation of Israel was a mistake founded on an injustice, with further proof retroactively adduced through denunciations of current Israeli policy that often assume an antisemitic character. The argument may be summarized as follows: (1) Israel's purported right to exist derives from the Holocaust; (2) Europe created Israel based on emotions of guilt rather than reason and fairness; (3) Palestinians thus paid the price for the crimes of Europeans; (4) Israel has failed to learn the lessons of the Holocaust and has itself become an oppressor; and (5) in the most extreme instances of Israel acting as an oppressor, Israelis become latter-day Nazis.

The first and second parts of the argument assert not just that the great powers created a Jewish state out of Holocaust guilt (although this factor played no role) but that the Jews sought statehood *because of* the Holocaust. Of the five points, this one seems the most innocuous;[15] yet it is in some ways the most insidious because it is untrue *and* sets almost all the others in motion. By fixing the starting point as the Holocaust, this view conflates immediate circumstances with ultimate causes. It telescopes Jewish attachment to the land of Israel by both modernizing and secularizing it, thereby rendering invisible the entire history of political and religious Zionism, not to mention the centrality of the land in the Hebrew Bible, liturgy, Talmud, and Jewish tradition. In the process, it implicitly defines or recontextualizes Israelis as Europeans rather than indigenes (even though antisemites historically saw Jews as Asiatic aliens) and makes the right of self-determination for the Jews alone contingent on having suffered a world-historical tragedy rather than possession of intrinsic peoplehood.[16] Einat Wilf refers to the phenomenon as "Zionism denial."[17]

If the first two points of the argument are accepted, then the third necessarily follows. If Europe created Israel out of guilt over the Holocaust, then Palestinians are not just the unfortunate losers in a tragic conflict but the doubly blameless victims, defeated in one because of what happened to their adversary in another. It is a concept captured in Edward Said's seductive phrase, "the victims of the victims, the refugees of the refugees."[18] Rather than serving as a call for Israelis to heed the narrative of the other side, this notion serves to negate the Israeli narrative. The injustice entailed in or arising from the creation of Israel could occur only because the Jews failed to learn the lessons of their own history (the fourth part of the argument). British member of Parliament David Ward, on Holocaust Memorial Day, said, "Having visited Auschwitz twice—once with my family and once with local schools—I am saddened that the Jews, who suffered unbelievable levels of persecution during the Holocaust, could within a few years of liberation from the death camps be inflicting atrocities on Palestinians in the new state of Israel and continue to do so on a daily basis in the West Bank and Gaza."[19]

Portuguese Nobel laureate José Saramago saw the cruelty as deliberate: "Living under the shadows of the Holocaust and expecting to be forgiven for anything they do on behalf of what they have suffered. . . . They didn't learn anything from the suffering of their parents and grandparents."[20] The notion of "the victims of the victims" of course carries with it not just an irony but an accusation: the Jews—of all people—should have known better, and it is here that a clearly supersessionist element creeps in. Supersessionism, we need to remind ourselves, was not just a matter of a new doctrine arising to replace an old one. Rather, the Jews, through their errors, actively brought about the abrogation of their covenant. Blind to the meaning of their own scripture, they rejected their prophets and the prophecy of salvation. The resultant crime of deicide was punished by loss of sovereignty and humiliating subjugation.[21] The anti-Zionist version charges

Israelis with both failure to learn the lessons of Auschwitz and blindness to the secular gospel of human rights.

The inevitable conclusion of this new discourse of remorse is that the creation of Israel was a mistake, the only debate revolving around whether it is to be reversed or merely regretted. This view has the added psychological advantage of permitting Europeans to engage in moral preening by acknowledging their guilt while absolving themselves of any sin worse than an excess of misdirected humanitarianism. Poet Tom Paulin called Israel "a historical obscenity" that "never . . . had the right to exist," while novelist and historian A.N. Wilson, more in sorrow than in anger, called "the 1948 experiment" "lazy thinking."[22] If such views are no longer marginal, the stalled peace process may be partly to blame, but so, too, is the fact that, as Andrei Markovits puts it, "the post-Auschwitz moratorium is gradually coming to an end. The Jews are not 'off limits' anymore in Europe."[23]

What has been called "Holocaust inversion" (Manfred Gerstenberg) or "Holocaust reversal" (Einat Wilf) takes the foregoing to its ultimate conclusion in the fifth point of the argument and holds that the Israelis not only have forgotten the lesson of the Nazis but also have even become the new Nazis, doing to others what was done to them.[24] From the panoply of examples, we may bracket the many vulgar manifestations in popular discourse and social media and instead focus on a few cases from presumably more sophisticated quarters.[25] What is striking is that a viewpoint formerly confined to the domain of Soviet Cold War propaganda, right-wing extremism, and Arab popular media is increasingly found in the mainstream of "sophisticated" Western discourse. This view began to surface at the time of the First Lebanon War, gained currency during the second Intifada, and seems to have become *salonfähig* (socially acceptable) in the wake of the several Gaza conflicts.[26] Typical manifestations include the likening of Israelis to Nazis and the invocation of sites of Holocaust atrocities such as concentration camps and ghettos.

In 2001, Tom Paulin created a furor when, in a poem reflecting on the death of the Palestinian boy Mohammed al-Dura, said to have been killed in a cross fire during the second Intifada, he called the Israel Defense Forces (IDF) soldiers the "Zionist SS."[27] Yet such language was already not unique, even in respectable quarters. The Vatican's *Osservatore Romano* condemned Israel's Operation Defensive Shield in language harsher than it applied to any actual genocide, speaking of "an aggression that has become an extermination." The bishop of Eichstätt, just after visiting the Holocaust memorial at Yad Vashem, likened Ramallah to the Warsaw ghetto.[28] José Saramago became notorious for comparing "what is happening in Palestine . . . to what happened in Auschwitz," but he in fact went further, calling Israelis and IDF "rentiers of the Holocaust."[29] Moreover, he made clear that the real culprit was Judaism: "Contaminated by the monstrous and rooted 'certitude' that in this catastrophic and absurd world there exists a people chosen by God . . . the Jews endlessly scratch their own wound to keep it bleeding, to make it incurable, and they show it to the world as if it were a banner. Israel seizes hold of the terrible words of God in Deuteronomy: 'Vengeance is mine, and I will be repaid.'"[30]

Cartoons likening Israel to Nazi Germany, once a staple only in the Soviet and Arab press, have become "standard operating procedure . . . among the British and Continental left-liberal milieu."[31] A typical piece appeared in the respected *Guardian* following the clash between IDF commandos and Turkish Islamists aboard the *Mavi Marmara* attempting to break the Gaza blockade in 2010.[32] The cartoon shows an Israeli naval boat whose flag is composed of emblems of death: bones form the Star of David (with a skull in the center for good measure) and barbed wire forms the horizontal stripes. Significantly, we see only the commando boats and not the victims. Without the accompanying articles, one would not know the subject, but then, one does not need to. The IDF is a mobile death camp; what else could one possibly add?[33]

It should be disturbing that the Holocaust-Auschwitz linkage is by far the most common analogy employed in English-language coverage of the Israel-Palestine conflict. Tellingly, those who use it—unlike some who invoke "apartheid," the second-most prevalent analogy—do not bother to articulate the implied resemblance, which presumably speaks for itself.[34] Because it is difficult, if not impossible, to imagine a rigorous rather than polemical-emotional use of the Nazi analogy, it almost always fits the International Working Definition of Antisemitism.[35] The more it occurs, the more we should be on our guard. Nazism is figured as pure evil, and Paulin pursued the idea to its logical conclusion, saying of settlers, "They should be shot dead. I think they are Nazis."[36] Others do not go quite so far but feel that Israel has forfeited the right to empathy, if not existence.

ARCHAEOLOGY

With the publication of the article "Historical Certainty Proves Elusive at Jerusalem's Holiest Place," the *New York Times* found itself embroiled in controversy in 2015. Noting that the two biblical "temples are integral to Jewish religious history and to Israel's disputed assertions of sovereignty over all of Jerusalem," it added, "Palestinians, suspicious of Israel's intentions for the site, have increasingly expressed doubt that the temples ever existed—at least in that location. Many Israelis regard such a challenge as false and inflammatory denialism."[37] Because the article seemed to endorse the view that, absent 100 percent certain physical proof, the existence of at least the first temple could not be affirmed, the paper, facing a torrent of criticism, backtracked, insisting that the uncertainty applied only to the exact location rather than existence of the edifices. Why Palestinians, however concerned they might be about Israeli policies, should deny universally accepted facts regarding Jewish history and the Temple Mount was left unexplained. The article was laconically alluding to a trend prominent in Palestinian discourse but largely unreported in the Western press. In 2001, the mufti of Jerusalem issued a fatwa declaring, "No stone of the Western Wall has any connection to Hebrew history." And in 2015, he asserted, Al Aqsa "was a mosque '3,000 years ago, and 30,000 years ago' and has been 'since the creation of the world.'"[38] Palestinian media deny the "fabrications" supporting "the Zionist assumption" of the existence of the temple (a "myth") and even "any connection between the Jews and Jerusalem."[39] Arab and Muslim commentators throughout the region increasingly append an adjective equivalent to "alleged" to mentions of the Jewish temple.[40]

It was not always so. Under the early Palestine Mandate, despite frictions over the holy places, the historicity of the Jewish presence and existence of the temples was not seriously called into question.[41] That said, there are some disturbing continuities: (1) a tendency to expand exclusive Arab/Muslim claims over holy sites of mutual significance (sometimes entailing distortion of the historical record) in tandem with (2) charges of a Jewish conspiracy to take over or destroy the sites. In 2014, Arab states temporarily blocked an exhibition by the Simon Wiesenthal Center in cooperation with UNESCO on "the 3,500-year relationship between the Jewish people and the land of Israel" on the grounds that it was "highly political" and would "cause damage to the peace negotiations."[42] In 2015–16, the head of UNESCO twice deplored an Arab draft resolution that (echoing disputes under the Mandate) classified the Western Wall solely as the Muslim Al Buraq Wall, noting the draft resolution's inflammatory character and its disrespect for the shared sacredness of Jerusalem.[43] The UNESCO tendency to condemn all Israeli archaeological activity beyond the Green Line as a violation of international law also increasingly appropriates, in substance and spirit, popular Arab charges of plots to "Judaize" the area (especially Jerusalem). Now, as during the bloody clashes of 1929, conspiracy theories regarding Jewish violations of the status quo and threats to Muslim holy sites serve to mobilize Arab religious and nationalist sentiment.[44] Zionists are said to plant false evidence of Jewish historical presence while (ever since 1897) destroying Arab heritage.[45] We are here in the realm of myth, paranoia, and pseudoscience, but lest one dismiss such pronouncements as pandering to an internal audience, one would do well to recall that Yasser Arafat's dogged insistence that a Jewish temple never stood in Jerusalem was one of the factors that destroyed the already fragile trust of the parties in the Camp David peace talks at the end of the Clinton administration.[46]

The *New York Times* presumably committed its embarrassing faux pas out of a misguided journalistic sense of evenhandedness, according to which both narratives deserve coverage. Yet even equal coverage does not require equal credence.[47] We reject what has come to be called temple denial, like Holocaust denial, as an intellectual embarrassment possessing no more merit than the belief that alien astronauts built the pyramids. There are reasons. One hallmark of the academic profession is the ability to *articulate criteria* for distinguishing between pseudohistory and legitimate revision of established opinion and for assessing the merits of the latter.[48] As Peter Kosso explains, "The responsibility for accepting a challenge comes with the right to claim knowledge. But this does not mean that theorizing in science, archaeology, or history is a free-for-all of skepticism where nothing can be known because everything can be challenged. There are definite standards of appropriate challenge and standards for evaluating how well a challenge has been met."[49]

The ground for the *Times*'s combination of criticism and credulity was prepared by trends in academia that apply this skepticism to the history of "ancient Israel" in particular. Biblical archaeology originated in the Christian West as an attempt not just to explore the past but also to confirm the scriptural verities. In the twentieth century, new orientations and evidence revealed irreconcilable gaps between elements of the biblical narrative and the archaeological record, particularly in the formative phases of Jewish history from the Patriarchs to the monarchies of David and Solomon. The most radical revisionists have been the "biblical minimalists" associated with the Copenhagen (Thomas Thompson, Niels Peter Lemche) and Sheffield (Philip R. Davies, Keith Whitelam) schools. They are not schools in the sense of possessing a unified agenda, but, going well beyond the consensus that the Bible is an essentially literary-religious work containing some historical evidence, they are united in the view that it was written much later than commonly accepted—in the Persian or even Hellenistic period—and is a self-referential mythological book largely devoid of historical value.[50] As biblical scholars at home with texts rather than test pits, they nonetheless claim support from archaeology. Both their method and findings are controversial.[51] Ruling out the Bible as a source of insight into earlier eras, they also reject as merely conjectural the wealth of material evidence that, in combination with robust explanatory models, is the essence of archaeological interpretation. The result, as Brad Kelle and Megan Moore put it, is that ancient "'Israel' itself" becomes "a problematic historical subject."[52]

Some see the denial of the knowability as well as the existence of an Israelite past as antisemitic—a charge the minimalists hotly deny.[53] According to Philip Davies, they do, however, assert that given that biblical scholarship focuses "on the Israelite identity of a land that has actually been non-Jewish in terms of its indigenous population for the larger part of its recorded history," "the danger" is "that [it] is 'Zionist' and that it participates in the elimination of the Palestinian identity . . . a kind of retrospective colonizing of the past."[54] Davies calls this result "inevitable" and denies any hostility to Judaism or the existence of Israel.[55] In the hands of Keith Whitelam, the critique acquires an explicit political coloring. The title of his 1996 book, *The Invention of Ancient Israel: The Silencing of Palestinian History*, encapsulates his argument: "Biblical studies has formed part of a complex arrangement of scholarly, economic, and military power by which Palestinians have been denied a contemporary presence."[56] Western scholarship, Zionist doctrine, and archaeology created out of Canaanites a mythical biblical Israel whose history needs to be moved from the center to the margins of a discourse rewritten as the history of ancient Palestinians.

Anthropologist Nadia Abu El-Haj continued this line of argumentation in *Facts on the Ground: Archaeological Practice and Territorial Self-Fashioning in Israeli Society* (2001). Her theoretical sophistication and avowedly postmodern methodology helped the book win plaudits from social scientists as well as scholars in the humanities who were sympathetic to its political stance.[57] By contrast, it received low marks from those conversant with both field archaeology and the specialized literature.[58] She portrays Israeli archaeology as "colonizing the terrain of 'Palestine,' remaking it into 'Eretz Yisrael' (the Land of Israel) . . . assembl[ing] material-symbolic facts that rendered *visible* the land's identity as Jewish, *by definition* [emphasis in the original]." For Abu El-Haj, as for the minimalists, there is no objectively identifiable ancient Israelite culture; there is only a subjective naming of objects assigned to that culture (viewed through the prism of the Bible), the repeated invocation of which in turn retroactively affirms the existence of the culture. From this intellectual sleight of hand, "a settler-colonial community emerged as a national, an original, and a native one."[59]

Whitelam and Abu El-Haj challenge the legitimacy of Israel itself by ascribing to the putative flaws of Israeli archaeology a uniquely nefarious character and set of consequences, drawing a parallel between the usurpation of the past and the land and suppression of memory and culture on one hand and human rights on the other. Abu El-Haj was one of the sponsors of the American Anthropological Association's Israel boycott resolution, which cited alleged suppression of Palestinian archaeology as one of its grievances.[60] In the ethnic-genetic realm, too, academic arguments assume an increasingly political stance (eventuating in the critique of an entire body of Israeli/Jewish scholarship) and then, in simplified form, serve as tools in the popular discourse of delegitimization.

ETHNICITY AND GENETICS

If the congeries of traditional European Jew haters over the centuries agreed on one thing, it was that Jews were Levantine aliens. For the church, the whole point of supersessionism and its social consequences was that the Jews were "physical Israel," descendants of the deicides of Judea. Many skeptics of emancipation saw in the particularistic Mediterranean religion of the Jews the major obstacle to full membership in modern society. For racists, the Jew was the biological as well as cultural Other: the "Semite." Ironically, the most potent ethnobiological weapon in today's antisemitic arsenal is the charge that Jews are not really Jews at all.

Those who deny the Middle Eastern origins of the Jews have until recently belonged to an extreme fringe. Chief among them were the British Israelites and related groups, who held that the Anglo-Saxons or other northern Europeans were the descendants of the Ten Lost Tribes of ancient Israel. Under the influence of American racism and the conflict over Mandatory Palestine, the once paternalistically philosemitic movement denounced putative Jews as impure or false: the remnant of Judah had debased itself through intermarriage with pagans, while Ashkenazim were Khazars, a Turkic tribe of the Pontic-Caspian steppe that converted to Judaism in the early Middle Ages. Antisemitism, anti-Zionism, and anti-Bolshevism coalesced; the thought that control of the Holy Land might pass from Britain to socialist Ashkenazi imposter Jews was anathema.[61]

The hypothesis of the Khazar origins of Ashkenazi Jews began as a legitimate one with the potential to address three questions: the fate of the converts, the "demographic miracle" by which

Eastern Europe replaced the Middle East as the center of world Jewry, and the physical differences between Ashkenazim and Sephardim.[62] Antisemites appropriated it, however, as an explanation for the barbarous character and communist proclivities of the Jews. Prominent in strands of Cold War extremism and the Christian identity movement, this Khazar myth has resurfaced to become ubiquitous on the international far right—and increasingly common in anti-Israel discourse.[63] The book that did the most to popularize the legitimate thesis was Arthur Koestler's *The Thirteenth Tribe* (1976). His findings, he thought, rendered the notion of religious and racial antisemitism meaningless. Acknowledging their potential misuse in attacks on Israel's legitimacy, he concluded reassuringly that the right of the state to exist was "based on international law . . . and cannot be undone, except by genocide."[64] Posterity has adjudged him naive.

Arab refutations of the Zionist claim to Palestine were, for the most part, based not on denial of the Jews' original residency there but rather on its short duration, coupled with the insistence that the Jews were a religious rather than national community. In other words, indigeneity was acknowledged, but its precedence was denied. George Hourani's 1968 presidential address to the Middle East Studies Association characterized the Palestinian claim as rooted in the "overwhelming fact . . . that they were the majority there from the seventh century A.D. (if not before) to the twentieth."[65] Even then, however, the "if not before" was gaining in prominence. Rashid Khalidi noted an anachronistic tendency to discern the roots of a presumed Palestinian national consciousness ever further in the past with a corollary "predilection for seeing in peoples such as the Canaanites, Jebusites, Amorites, and Philistines the lineal ancestors of the modern Palestinians." Today it has become the norm.[66] Bad history it may be for multiple reasons, but like the assault on the archaeological evidence, it serves to rebut Jewish claims of chronological primacy and cultural continuity. The Jews thus become but one of a series of fleeting conquerors, a view epitomized by Mohammed Abbas's defiant and revealing declaration: "When he claims—that they [Jews] have a historical right dating back to 3,000 years BCE—we say that the nation of Palestine upon the land of Canaan had a 7,000 year history BCE. . . . 'Netanyahu, you are incidental in history. We are the people of history. We are the owners of history.'"[67]

The Arab national movement has, however, periodically flirted with forms of more flagrant historical denial. In 2015 alone, articles in the official Palestinian daily explained (in several variations) that the ancient Israelites were in fact a vanished Arab Yemenite tribe that had "never ruled" or left behind "antiquities" in Palestine.[68] Another line of argument denies the Middle Eastern origins of the Jews altogether. One article called the idea of a four-thousand-year-old Jewish connection to the land "made-up history, written by thieves who fled the Caucasus mountains into Eastern and then Central Europe, . . . claiming to be Jews." Another declared, "Most of the Jews today are of Khazar origin," who "became Zionists, or Ashkenazis." Still another, in the same vein, cited the work of "two fair Jews": Arthur Koestler and Shlomo Sand.[69] The rise and fall and rise of the Khazar myth in Arab anti-Zionism and antisemitism is revealing. Several Arab spokesmen invoked it in the United Nations Partition debate, as when the Syrian representative, citing the *Jewish Encyclopedia*, declared, "We have been able to prove that the Jews of Eastern Europe are not related in any way to Israel and that they are purely of Russian Khazar origin."[70] By the late twentieth century, the thesis seemed to have disappeared from mainstream Arab discourse. Its recent revival reflects new debates in the academy.

In his *The Invention of the Jewish People* (Hebrew 2008; English 2009), Israeli historian Shlomo Sand argues that Jews were only members of a religious community, which was moreover the product of centuries of conversions consigned by today's intellectual and political establishment to "realms of silence." The notion of a collective national identity was an invention of nineteenth-century historians, seized on by Zionists.[71] The story of the Khazars is exhibit A.[72] Sand also ventures into the field of DNA and genetics. It is one of the ironies of history that, half a century after their near extermination mandated by the racial pseudoscience of the Nazis, Jews of European descent proved (by virtue of their historic isolation) an ideal subject for legitimate genetic research.[73] For scientists, it was a unique opportunity to recover the story of a people deprived of its history, from marriage and migration patterns to heritable disease. A complex and dynamic field that has yielded stunning results becomes, in Sand's caricature, just a variation on his theme of the search for preconceived results and suppression of inconvenient ones.[74] Just as the need to counter Palestinian nationalism by proving that the Jews were "descendants of the kingdoms of David and Solomon" (321) required the silencing of the Khazar story, so Jewish genetics became simply the modern incarnation of "the Zionist idea of the Jewish nation-race" (275). "After exhausting all the historical arguments" (318) for Jewish peoplehood, there remained only a quixotic quest: "the last resort: a Jewish DNA" (321). "Hitler," he concludes, "would certainly have been very pleased!" (319).[75] Surprisingly, Sand did not engage the genetic speculation on Jews and Khazars, but when Israeli scientist Eran Elhaik claimed to have proven the Khazar-Ashkenazi connection, Sand proclaimed himself vindicated, even though most scientists rejected the research as severely flawed.[76] Anti-Zionists as well as antisemites eagerly seized on both Sand's and Elhaik's findings.

Abu El-Haj picked up where Sand left off, devoting an entire book to Jewish *Genealogical Science* (2012).[77] It is the logical corollary of her earlier book. A reviewer's summary of her critique of the genetic discourse could be turned back on the two books themselves: "a circular logic of discovery, interpretation, and proof."[78] Both combine a sophisticated theoretical framework with a monochromatic reading of a variegated body of literature. Both archaeology and genetics thus appear to be futile attempts to demonstrate that the Jews are one people with historical and cultural continuity traceable to a common origin in the Middle East. Notable, too, is the implication of a deep anxiety on the part of the practitioners, as if they themselves doubt the rectitude of their cause.[79]

TOWARD SOME CONCLUSIONS

The ultimate irony of the new replacement theory is that no one admits to being an antisemite and that everyone is Jewish but the Jews. The church made Jesus into a Christian. In today's discourse, Jesus is a Palestinian; Gaza is the Warsaw ghetto—or a "concentration camp" (it seems that everyone but the Jews wants to have suffered a Holocaust); and Palestinians, rather than Jews, are the descendants and true heirs of biblical Israelites.

If one needed proof that the "new antisemitism" indeed constitutes a qualitatively new phenomenon, it might be this: not just that the sinister characteristics once attributed to Jews are now applied to Israel as a Jewish collectivity but,[80] further, that so much of the assault on Israel and Zionism now entails the denial or appropriation of Jewish history. In the past, Jews were rendered alien to the West by being orientalized. Today, Jews are rendered alien to the Middle East by being redefined as European (this, although over half of Israelis are of Sephardi or Mizrachi descent). Amos Oz famously summarized the reversal: "Out there, in the world, all the walls were covered with graffiti: 'Yids, go back to Palestine,' so we came back to Palestine, and now the worldatlarge shouts at us: 'Yids, get out of Palestine.'"[81] Israel's declaration of independence in 1948 justified statehood on three chief grounds: the historical connection to the land (affirmed by the Mandate), the universal right of self-determination, and the Holocaust as proof of the need for a national home.[82] The discourses described in this chapter negate all three and dovetail with a nominally more positive one, according to which the diasporic condition is a noble one—and the only appropriate one for the Jews.[83]

This situation should be of concern. First, to be able to distinguish legitimate historical revision from bad history and outright pseudohistory is an intellectual imperative, and the debate over Jewish indigeneity can serve as a textbook example of the use and abuse of history. Second, appropriating the Holocaust and denying the Jewish historical presence in the Middle East will hardly make Israelis more amenable to compromise.[84] To attempt to relitigate the conflict based on competing claims of origins is to return to the apologetics of the pre-Partition era or at least pre-Oslo era: pure regression. Achieving peace in the present is difficult enough without distorting the past.

NOTES

1. Meir Litvak and Esther Webman, "Israel and Antisemitism," in *Antisemitism: A History,* ed. Albert S. Lindemann and Richard S. Levy (Oxford: Oxford University Press, 2010), 237–49.

2. Alvin H. Rosenfeld, ed., *Deciphering the New Antisemitism* (Bloomington: Indiana University Press, 2015).

3. Kenneth Marcus, *The Definition of Anti-Semitism* (Oxford: Oxford University Press, 2015), 10–12, 146–69.

4. See, e.g., Marcus, *Definition of Anti-Semitism,* 10–12, 148–50.

5. Leon H. Albert, "'Scientific' Creationism as a Pseudoscience," *Creation Evolution Journal* 6, no. 2 (Summer 1986): 25–34, https://ncse .com/cej/6/2/scientific-creationism-as-pseudoscience. On Holocaust denial and science, see Robert Wistrich, *A Lethal Obsession: Anti-Semitism from Antiquity to the Global Jihad* (New York: Random House, 2010), 640–44; Michael Shermer and Alan Grobman, *Denying History: Who Says the Holocaust Never Happened and Why Do They Say It?* (Berkeley: University of California Press, 2000), esp. 1–35, 99–172, 231–56; and John C. Zimmerman, *Holocaust Denial: Demographics, Testimonies, and Ideologies* (Lanham, MD: University Press of America, 2000), 173–201.

6. Alan Sokal, "Pseudoscience and Postmodernism: Antagonists or Fellow Travelers?" in *Archaeological Fantasies: How Pseudoarchaeology Misrepresents the Past and Misleads the Public,* ed. Garret G. Fagan

THE NEW REPLACEMENT THEORY

(London: Routledge, 2006), 286–361. On postmodernism and the past, see Richard J. Evans, *In Defense of History* (New York: W. W. Norton, 1999).

7. "The End of Politics," *The New Republic,* June 23, 2003.

8. "The Palestine Mandate," *The Avalon Project: Documents in Law, History and Diplomacy,* 2008, http://avalon.law.yale.edu/20th_century /palmanda.asp.

9. Ruth Gavison, "The Jews' Right to Statehood: A Defense," *Azure,* Summer 2003, 70–108, 70–71; Yair Rosenberg, "Pope Francis: Anti-Zionism Is Anti-Semitism," *Tablet,* October 29, 2015, http://www .tabletmag.com/scroll/194614/pope-francis-anti-zionism-is-anti-semitism.

10. See, for convenient overviews, Norman N. Naimark, *Fires of Hatred: Ethnic Cleansing in Twentieth-Century Europe* (Cambridge, MA: Harvard University Press, 2001), and Nisid Hajari, *Midnight's Furies: The Deadly Legacy of India's Partition* (Boston: Houghton Mifflin Harcourt, 2015).

11. What I discuss here has been treated elsewhere but not, I think, together and in this framework. What follows is necessarily suggestive rather than exhaustive.

12. Rosemary Radford Ruether, *Faith and Fratricide: The Theological Roots of Anti-Semitism* (New York: Seabury Press, 1979); Norman A. Beck, *Mature Christianity in the 21st Century: The Recognition and Repudiation of the Anti-Jewish Polemic in the New Testament,* rev. ed. (New York: Crossroad, 1994). The persistence of supersessionistic thinking is a subject I am pursuing in other research.

13. Even deicide, which most churches have repudiated. "Sabeel Ecumenical Liberation Center," *NGO Monitor,* May 1, 2018, http://www .ngo-monitor.org/ngos/sabeel_ecumenical_liberation_theology_center/; Dexter van Zile, "Updating the Ancient Infrastructure of Christian Contempt: Sabeel," *Jewish Political Studies Review* 23, no. 1–2 (Spring 2011), http://jcpa.org/article/updating-the-ancient-infrastructure-of-christian -contempt-sabeel/; Central Conference of American Rabbis Resolution on the 2009 Kairos Document, April 14, 2012, http://ccarnet.org/rabbis -speak/resolutions/2010/ccar-resolution-2009-kairos-document/.

14. See, e.g., Wistrich, *A Lethal Obsession,* 649–61.

15. Herb Keinon, "Obama's Agenda Aimed to Combat Holocaust Denial," *Jerusalem Post,* March 18, 2013, http://www.jpost.com /International/Oren-Obamas-agenda-aims-to-combat-Jewish-history -deniers-306750.

16. For information on the historical characterization of Jews as Asiatic aliens, see S. Ilan Troen, "De-Judaizing the Homeland: Academic Politics in Rewriting the History of Palestine," *Israel Affairs* 13, no. 4 (October 2007), 877.

17. Einat Wilf, "Zionism Denial," *Daily Beast*, April 17, 2012, http://www.thedailybeast.com/articles/2012/04/17/zionism-denial.html.

18. Edward Said, "The One State Solution," *New York Times Magazine*, January 10, 1999, http://www.nytimes.com/1999/01/10/magazine/the-one-state-solution.html?pagewanted=all&_r=0.

19. Leslie Klaff, "Holocaust Inversion and Contemporary Antisemitism," *Fathom*, Winter 2014, http://fathomjournal.org/holocaust-inversion-and-contemporary-antisemitism/.

20. Cited in David Frum, "Death of a Jew-Hater," *National Post*, June 19, 2010, http://news.nationalpost.com/full-comment/david-frum-death-of-a-jew-hater.

21. Robert Bonfil, "Aliens Within: The Jews and Antijudaism," in *Handbook of European History, 1400–1600: Late Middle Ages, Renaissance, and Reformation*, ed. Thomas A. Brady Jr., Heiko A. Oberman, and James D. Tracy, vol. 1, *Structures and Assertions* (Grand Rapids, MI: Eerdmans, 1996), 263–302; Nina Rowe, *The Jew, the Cathedral and the Medieval City: Synagoga and Ecclesia in the Thirteenth Century* (New York: Cambridge University Press, 2011).

22. "That Weasel Word," interview with Tom Paulin, *Al Ahram Weekly Online*, April 4–10, 2002, http://weekly.ahram.org.eg/Archive/2002/580/cu2.htm; Wilson, quoted in David Landau, "Jewish Angst in Albion" August 13, 2007, http://www.jewishagency.org/antisemitism/content/24092 (originally in *Haaretz*, January 2002).

23. Andrei Markovits, *Uncouth Nation: Why Europe Dislikes America* (Princeton, NJ: Princeton University Press, 2007), 184.

24. Manfred Gerstenfeld, "The Multiple Distortions of Holocaust Memory," *Jewish Political Studies Review* 19, no. 3/4 (Fall 2007): 35–55; Manfred Gerstenfeld, *The Abuse of Holocaust Memory: Distortions and Reponses* (Jerusalem: Jerusalem Center for Public Affairs, Institute for Global Jewish Affairs, Anti-Defamation League, 2009).

25. For more on manifestations of Holocaust inversion in popular discourse and social media, see Andre Oboler and David Matas, eds., "Online Antisemitism: A Systematic Review," Report of the Online Antisemitism Working Group of the Global Forum to Combat Antisemitism (Ministry of Foreign Affairs of the State of Israel, May 30, 2013).

26. See, e.g., Wistrich, *A Lethal Obsession*, 138–58, 494–514; Markovits, *Uncouth Nation*, 164–67.

27. Tom Paulin, "Killed in the Crossfire" (2001), cited in Wistrich, *A Lethal Obsession*, 410–11.

28. *Osservatore Romano*, cited in Richard L. Rubenstein, "The Witness-People Myth, Israel, and Anti-Zionism in the Western World," in *Not Your Father's Antisemitism: Hatred of the Jews in the 21st Century*, ed. Michael Berenbaum (St. Paul, MN: Paragon House, 2008), at 308. Fania Oz-Salzberger reacts to the Bishop of Eichstätt, "The Obligation to Cry Out," *Haaretz*, March 19, 2007, http://www.haaretz.com/the-obligation -to-cry-out-1.216009.

29. Jerome Bourdon, "Outrageous, Inescapable? Debating Historical Analogies in the Coverage of the Israeli-Palestinian Conflict," *Discourse and Communications* 9, no. 4 (2015): 411, 414.

30. Frum, "Death of a Jew-Hater."

31. For more on anti-Israel cartoons in Soviet and Arab media, see "Major Anti-Semitic Motifs in Arab Cartoons," interview with Joël Kotek, Jerusalem Center for Public Affairs, June 1, 2004, http://jcpa.org/article /major-anti-semitic-motifs-in-arab-cartoons. For more on the increasing frequency of these cartoons in other parts of the world, see Markovits, *Uncouth Nation*, 164, 169.

32. CiFWatch, "Guardian Publishes Antisemitic Cartoon," June 1, 2010, https://ukmediawatch.org/2010/06/01/guardian-publishes-antisemitic -cartoon/.

33. Harriet Sherwood, "Israeli Commandos Kill Activists on Flotilla Bound for Gaza," *Guardian*, May 31, 2010, https://www.theguardian.com /world/2010/may/31/israel-kills-activists-flotilla-gaza. Reader comments can be found at "Open Thread: IDF Attacked by 'Peace Activists' Upon Boarding," May 31, 2010, https://ukmediawatch.org/2010/05/31 /open-thread-idf-navy-warns-flotilla/.

34. Using the LexisNexis database, Bourdon found 641 examples between 1977 and 2014. *Auschwitz-Holocaust* accounted for 312; *apartheid*, for 222; *Northern Ireland, Native American*, and *civil rights* together accounted for only 107. Statistics from p. 410.

35. For this working definition, as well as examples of its many possible manifestations, see "Working Definition of Antisemitism," International Holocaust Remembrance Alliance, December 12, 2016, https://www.holocaustremembrance.com/media-room/stories /working-definition-antisemitism-0.

36. Paulin, in "That Weasel Word."

37. Rick Gladstone, "Historical Certainty Proves Elusive at Jerusalem's Holiest Place," *New York Times*, October 8, 2015, http:// www.nytimes.com/2015/10/09/world/middleeast/historical

-certainty-proves-elusive-at-jerusalems-holiest-place.html?_r=0; responses, e.g., Liel Leibovitz, "'The New York Times' Goes Truther on the Temple Mount," *Tablet*, October 9, 2015, http://www.tabletmag.com /scroll/194092/the-new-york-times-goes-truther-on-the-temple-mount; "NY Times Amends Article Questioning Jewish Temples' Existence on Temple Mount," *Jewish Telegraphic Agency*, October 11, 2015, http://www .jta.org/2015/10/11/news-opinion/israel-middle-east/ny-times-amends -article-questioning-jewish-temples-existence-on-temple-mount.

38. Itamar Marcus, "Lies, Libels and Historical Revisionism in the Palestinian Authority," *Palestinian Media Watch*, February 22, 2001, http://www.palwatch.org/main.aspx?fi=155&doc_id=2322; Ilan Ben Zion, "Jerusalem Mufti: Temple Mount Never Housed Jewish Temple," *Times of Israel*, October 25, 2015, http://www.timesofisrael.com /jerusalem-mufti-denies-temple-mount-ever-housed-jewish-shrine/.

39. Palestine News Network, April 8, 2007, reproduced in *PaleoJudaica*, April 10, 2007, http://paleojudaica.blogspot.com/2007_04_08_archive .html#117619486372387752; "Jewish History in Land of Israel Erased," PATV, June 23, 2009, *Palestinian Media Watch*, http://palwatch.org/main .aspx?fi=490&all=1; "Op-ed in Official PA Daily: 'Religious, Historical, and Even Biblical Facts Deny Any Connection between the Jews and Jerusalem' or to 'Historic Palestine,'" *Palestinian Media Watch*, December 13, 2015, http://palwatch.org/main.aspx?fi=490&all=1.

40. Nadav Shragai, "In the Beginning Was Al-Aqsa," *Haaretz*, November 27, 2005; and in greater detail, Shragai, *The "Al-Aksa Is in Danger" Libel: The History of a Lie* (Jerusalem: Jerusalem Center for Public Affairs, 2012), http://jcpa.org/al-aksa-is-in-danger-libel/.

41. *A Brief Guide to Al-Haram Al-Sharif Jerusalem* (Jerusalem: Supreme Moslem Council, 1925), 4, 6.

42. Raphael Ahren, "UNESCO Deletes 'Israel' from Title of Its Exhibit on Jewish Ties to Israel," *Times of Israel*, June 11, 2014, http://www .timesofisrael.com/embargoed-until-wed-7pm-unesco-where-the-land-of -israel-needs-to-be-the-holy-land/.

43. Noga Tarnopolsky, "UNESCO Says No Jewish History on Temple Mount," *Media Line*, April 17, 2016, http://www.themedialine.org/news /unesco-says-no-jewish-history-on-temple-mount-hebron-and-bethlehem -integral-part-of-palestine/.

44. Avraham Sela, "The 'Wailing Wall' Riots (1929) as a Watershed in the Palestine Conflict," *The Muslim World* 84, no. 1–2 (January–April 1994): 60–94; Shragai, *"Al-Aksa Is in Danger" Libel*; Yitzhak Reiter, *Jerusalem and Its Role in Islamic Solidarity* (New York: Palgrave Macmillan,

2008). See further "Jerusalem's Temple/Jewish History Denied,"
Palestinian Media Watch, accessed September 16, 2016, http://palwatch
.org/main.aspx?fi=487#489.

45. "Israel 'Attempts to Erase the Real Arab History' in Jerusalem 'and
Replace It with a Fake Jewish History Which Has No Roots in This Land,"
Official Palestinian Authority TV, October 21, 2014, *Palestinian Media
Watch*, http://palwatch.org/main.aspx?fi=490&all=1; "PA TV Libel: Israel
'Implant[s] Fake Jewish Graves' in Jerusalem 'to Support . . . [Their] Fake
Judaization Stories,'" Official Palestinian Authority TV, October 27, 2014,
Palestinian Media Watch, http://palwatch.org/main.aspx?fi=490&all=1.
Charges of forgery appear in United Nations Educational, Scientific
and Cultural Organization, Executive Board Decision 199 EX
/PX/DR.19.1 Rev., Paris, April 11, 2016, http://unesdoc.unesco.org
/images/0024/002443/244378e.pdf. On Zionist conspiracy, see Samuel
Thorpe, "Magic Bowls of Antiquity," *Aeon*, May 24, 2016, https://aeon.co
/essays/what-should-be-done-with-the-magic-bowls-of-jewish-babylonia.

46. Dennis Ross, *The Missing Peace: The Inside Story of the Fight for
Middle East Peace* (New York: Farrar, Straus and Giroux, 2004), 694–722,
esp. 694, 718.

47. James Davila says, "There are 'competing narratives' here only in the
sense that there are 'competing narratives' between evolutionary theory
and creationism." *PaleoJudaica*, June 2, 2009, http://paleojudaica.blogspot
.com/2009_05_31_archive.html#5447067653996419892.

48. See, e.g., Shermer and Grobman, *Denying History*, xv–xvi, 19–38,
99–119, 231–56.

49. Peter Kosso, "Introduction: The Epistemology of Archaeology," in
Fagan, *Archaeological Fantasies: How Pseudoarchaeology Misrepresents the
Past and Misleads the Public*, ed. Garret G. Fagan (London: Routledge,
2006), 3.

50. For overviews of the field, see Thomas W. Davis, *Shifting Sands: The
Rise and Fall of Biblical Archaeology* (New York: Oxford University Press,
2004); Brad Kelle and Megan Bishop Moore, *Biblical History and Israel's
Past: The Changing Study of the Bible and History* (Grand Rapids, MI:
Eerdmans, 2011).

51. The sharpest centrist critique has come from William G. Dever:
e.g., "Review: 'Will the Real Israel Please Stand Up?' Archaeology and
Israelite Historiography: Part I," *Bulletin of the American Schools of Oriental
Research* 297 (February 1995): 61–80; "Archaeology, Ideology, and the
Quest for an 'Ancient' or 'Biblical Israel,'" *Near Eastern Archaeology* 61, no.
1 (March 1998): 39–52.

52. Marc Brettler, "The Copenhagen School: The Historiographical Issues," *AJS Review* 27, no. 1 (April 2003): 1–21. Kelle and Moore, *Biblical History*, 33.

53. Among serious rather than histrionic critics is William Dever, "Archaeology, Ideology," 45–46. Thompson defended himself in "A View from Copenhagen: Israel and the History of Palestine," accessed September 16, 2016, http://www.bibleinterp.com/articles/copenhagen .shtml.

54. Philip Davies, "Minimalism, 'Ancient Israel,' and Anti-Semitism," accessed September 16, 2016. http://prophetess.lstc.edu/~rklein /Documents/Minimalism.htm.

55. Davies, "Minimalism, 'Ancient Israel,' and Anti-Semitism."

56. Keith W. Whitelam, *The Invention of Ancient Israel: The Silencing of Palestinian History* (New York: Routledge, 1996), 226.

57. Nadia Abu El-Haj, *Facts on the Ground: Archaeological Practice and Territorial Self-Fashioning in Israeli Society* (Chicago: University of Chicago Press, 2001). Among positive reviews is Elia Zureik's in *MIT Electronic Journal of Middle East Studies* 2 (October 2002), http://www.mafhoum .com/press4/137C31_fichiers/zureik.htm.

58. Among the main critiques by those familiar with the archaeological discipline and scholarship are Aren M. Maier, *ISIS* 95, no. 3 (2004): 523–24; Alexander H. Joffe, *Journal of Near Eastern Studies* 64, no. 4 (October 2005): 297–304; Diana Muir and Avigail Appelbaum, *History News Network*, October 24, 2007, http://historynewsnetwork.org /blog/25976.

59. Abu El-Haj, *Facts on the Ground*, 18, 242, 118–21. Troen, "De-Judaizing the Homeland," 880–82, pointedly notes that the historians who developed the settler-colonial model did not include Israel in it.

60. For more on the uniquely nefarious character ascribed to Israeli archaeology, compare with the nuanced picture in Rachel S. Hallote and Alexander H. Joffe, "The Politics of Israeli Archaeology: Between 'Nationalism' and 'Science' in the Age of the Second Republic," *Israel Studies* 7, no. 3 (2002): 84–116; Steven Rosen, "Coming of Age: The Decline of Archaeology in Israeli Identity," *Ben Gurion University Review* 1 (2005): 43–58; Amnon Ben-Tor, "An Archaeological Stain" January 2, 2007, http:// blog.bibleplaces.com/2007/01/response-to-rafi-greenberg.html (originally in *Haaretz*, December 29, 2006, in Hebrew). And even minimalist Thompson affirms the objectivity of the West Bank archaeological survey. For more on the boycott of Israel on archaeological grounds, see "American Anthropological Association (AAA) Resolution to Boycott

Israeli Academic Institutions," accessed September 16, 2016, https://anthroboycott.wordpress.com/the-resolution/. Boycott supporters also invoked Abu El-Haj's work: Isaiah Silver, "Digging the Occupation: The Politics of Boycotts and Archaeology in Israel (BDS pt. 3)", *Savage Minds*, July 6, 2014, http://savageminds.org/2014/07/06/digging-the-occupation-the-politics-of-boycotts-and-archeology-in-israel-bds-pt-3/.

61. This is part of my larger research project on both the Khazars and antisemitic discourse. Michael Barkun is one of the few scholars who has explored this murky history, in *Religion and the Racist Right: The Origins of the Christian Identity Movement* (Chapel Hill: University of North Carolina Press, 1994), 121–42.

62. Kevin Brook surveys the literature on a wide range of topics in *The Jews of Khazaria*, 2nd ed. (Lanham, MD: Rowman and Littlefield, 2006).

63. Victor Shnirelman, *The Myth of the Khazars and Intellectual Antisemitism in Russia, 1970s–1990s* (Jerusalem: Vidal Sassoon International Center for the Study of Antisemitism, Hebrew University of Jerusalem, 2002). Not only Internet hate sites but even the "talkbacks" on articles involving Israel in mainstream media invariably contain references to "Khazars" as shorthand for Jews, Israelis, Zionists.

64. Arthur Koestler, *The Thirteenth Tribe: The Khazar Empire and Its Heritage* (New York: Random House, 1976), 17 on antisemitism, 223 on Israel.

65. George F. Hourani, "Palestine as a Problem of Ethics," *Middle East Studies Association Bulletin* 3, no. 1 (February 15, 1969): 15–25, 17.

66. David Wenkel, "Palestinians, Jebusites, and Evangelicals," *Middle East Quarterly* 14, no. 3 (Summer 2007), http://www.meforum.org/1713/palestinians-jebusites-and-evangelicals. A few years later, Khalidi espoused those very views.

67. "Mahmoud Abbas," Official Palestinian Authority TV, May 14, 2011, http://palwatch.org/main.aspx?fi=709&doc_id=5043.

68. "Jewish History in Land of Israel Erased," *Palestinian Media Watch*, December 6, 2015; October 28, 2015; October 14, 2015; August 28, 2015; December 13, 2015; and many more, http://palwatch.org/main.aspx?fi=490&all=1.

69. All from Official PA Daily, "Jewish History in Land of Israel Erased," *Palestinian Media Watch*, February 14, 2016; September 16, 2015; October 14, 2015, http://palwatch.org/main.aspx?fi=490&all=1.

70. Amir Arslan (Syria), United Nations General Assembly, A/PV.125, November 26, 1947, https://unispal.un.org/DPA/DPR/unispal.nsf/0/8E9EACABC8A7E3D185256CF0005BA586.

71. Shlomo Sand, *The Invention of the Jewish People*, trans. Yael Lotan (London: Verso, 2009). Among the most substantive critiques are Israel Bartal's in *Haaretz*, July 20, 2008, reproduced at "Israel Bartal's Response to Shlomo Sands' Invention of the Jewish People (Haaretz 7/2008)," *ce399 | research archive: (anti)fascism*, June 29, 2010, https://ce399fascism.wordpress.com/2010/06/29/israel-bartals-response-to-shlomo-sands-invention-of-the-jewish-people-haaretz-72008/; Anita Shapira, "The Jewish-People Deniers," *Journal of Israeli History* 28, no. 1 (March 2009): 63–72; and Derek J. Penslar, "Shlomo Sand's *The Invention of the Jewish People* and the End of the New History," *Israel Studies* 17, no. 2 (Summer 2012): 156–68.

72. Sand, *The Invention of the Jewish People*, particularly chapter 2, "Realms of Silence: In Search of Lost (Jewish) Time," 190–249 (especially 210–49), and in the 2010 afterword, especially 319–21.

73. David B. Goldstein, *Jacob's Legacy: A Genetic View of Jewish History* (New Haven: Yale University Press, 2008); Harry Ostrer, *Legacy: A Genetic History of the Jewish People* (Oxford: Oxford University Press, 2012).

74. Sand, *Invention of the Jewish People*, 256–80, 318–21.

75. Sand, *Invention of the Jewish People*.

76. The potential smoking gun was a genetic marker found among Ashkenazi but not Sephardic Levites, suggesting Slavic or Central Asian origin. Goldstein conveniently summarizes in *Jacob's Legacy*, 61–74. Elhaik's work is presented in popular form by Ofer Aderet, "The Jewish People's Ultimate Treasure Hunt," *Haaretz*, December 28, 2012, http://www.haaretz.com/israel-news/the-jewish-people-s-ultimate-treasure-hunt.premium-1.490539. Among critiques is Razib Khan, "Ashkenazi Jews Are Probably Not Descended from the Khazars," *Gene Expression*, August 8, 2012, http://blogs.discovermagazine.com/gnxp/2012/08/ashkenazi-jews-are-probably-not-descended-from-the-khazars/#.V9zcrLWTFEQ. Subsequent research has also refuted the Levite thesis: S. Rootsi, D. M. Behar, M. Järve, et al., "Phylogenetic Applications of Whole Y-Chromosome Sequences and the Near Eastern Origin of Ashkenazi Levites," *Nature Communications* 4, article no. 2928 (December 17, 2013), doi:10.1038/ncomms3928. Doron M. Beharl, Lauri Saag, Monika Karmin, et al., "The Genetic Variation in the R1a Clade among the Ashkenazi Levites' Y Chromosome," *Nature Scientific Reports* 7, Article number: 14969 (November 2017), DOI: https://doi.org/10.1038/s41598-017-14761-7.

77. Nadia Abu El-Haj, *The Genealogical Science: The Search for Jewish Origins and the Politics of Epistemology* (Chicago: University of Chicago Press, 2012).

78. Susan Maratha Khan, "Who Are the Jews? New Formulations of an Age-Old Question," *Human Biology* 85, no. 6 (December 2013), 921.

79. Contrary to the implications by Sand and Abu El-Haj, Israeli and Jewish genetic scholarship has not been driven by patently political agendas. Diana Muir and Paul Appelbaum incisively survey the pitfalls of instrumentalizing genetics in "The Gene Wars: What Can Science Teach Us About the Validity of Nationalist Claims?" *Azure* 27 (Winter 2007): 51–79, http://www.dianamuirappelbaum.com/?page_id=389#.V83clLWTGbc.

80. Marcus, *Definition of Anti-Semitism*, 11.

81. "*A Tale of Love and Darkness*—Growing Up with Israel: Writer Amos Oz," National Public Radio, December 1, 2004, http://www.npr.org/templates/story/story.php?storyId=4195061.

82. "Declaration of Israel's Independence 1948," *The Avalon Project: Documents in Law, History and Diplomacy,* accessed September 16, 2016, http://avalon.law.yale.edu/20th_century/israel.asp. Chaim Gans argues that acceptance of the three claims in the framework of an "egalitarian Zionism" allows for "self-determination of the Jews and Arabs . . . mainly in two separate states"; see Chaim Gans, *A Political Theory for the Jewish People* (New York: Oxford University Press, 2016), 82–84.

83. A tendency notably embodied by the work of Judith Butler.

84. Susan Maratha Khan, "Who Are the Jews?," 922, notes the book's aim of "casting doubt on the foundational assumption on which the Zionist enterprise is predicated (that Jews are not simply adherents to a faith but are a people, a nation, a 'race,' with attendant rights to national self-determination)."

JAMES WALD is Professor of Modern European History at Hampshire College in Amherst, Massachusetts. His research interests in antisemitism include Nazi and racist ideology, the persistence and secularization of traditional Christian supersessionism historical denial, and the Khazar myth. He is coeditor, with Mark Weitzman (Simon Wiesenthal Center) and Robert Williams (US Holocaust Memorial Museum), of the forthcoming *Routledge History of Antisemitism*.

TWO

—ᵐ—

From Wilhelm Marr to *Mavi Marmara*

Antisemitism and Anti-Zionism as Forms of Anti-Jewish Action

THORSTEN FUCHSHUBER

WILHELM MARR, THE German journalist who popularized the term *antisemitism* in the late nineteenth century, did so because he wanted to move away from Christian anti-Judaism and transform Judeophobia into a kind of modern political concept. He argued that antisemitism is based on rational arguments and proudly called himself an antisemite. Marr claimed that he had nothing against Jews as individuals—only against Judaism, which he saw as a destructive social concept. He developed his understanding of antisemitism at the dawn of the liberal era and was therefore forced to resort to seemingly rational arguments in order to avoid lawsuits and comply with accepted forms of public debate.

Today the term *anti-Zionism* fulfills a similar function: it serves as a socially accepted form for the expression of antisemitic attitudes, and for their rationalization and legitimization as political arguments. Again, these arguments are supposedly not directed against the Jews but against the state of Israel. Now, however, they are based on a postmodern understanding of universalism rather than on a concept of rationalism that is considered part of the colonialist legacy. In 1862, Marr wrote that "Judaism must end if humanity is to begin" in his first antisemitic pamphlet, *Der Judenspiegel*; today, some 150 years later, the

French philosopher Alain Badiou informs us that contemporary universalism requires everyone to disassociate himself or herself from Israel and to denounce its identity as a Jewish state.[1]

I argue that both anti-Zionism and antisemitism must be understood as a means to rationalize hatred against Jews. Looking back at Marr reminds us that the term *antisemitism* was not coined as a result of any objective analysis of the specifics of Jew hatred in modernity. It was instead a catchword used as a propaganda tool to rally the like-minded around the flag, so to speak.

Therefore, when discussing various historical forms of Jew hatred, one should look at these concepts not merely in terms of the changes to an anti-Jewish mind-set or ideology. Although that is also important, it must be kept in mind that Jew haters have always seen the practical necessity of restructuring their anti-Jewish strategy and actions in response to changing social realities. This practical necessity can be summarized in one question: How can we harm our enemy—the Jew—in the most striking and most destructive way but also in a way that is the most acceptable to and convincing for the rest of society? This chapter discusses the antisemitic quest for effective forms of action against Jews by taking a brief look into the past as well as a more detailed look at the present.

Marr sought to create an anti-Jewish strategy that accounted for the fact that the German Jews had attained legal emancipation. In the next section, I present Marr's concept of antisemitism. I later argue that anti-Zionism can be analyzed as an anti-Jewish strategy responding to the fact that Jewish emancipation led to a Jewish nation-state. Last, I analyze anti-Zionism as a practical answer to this antisemitic quest for efficient anti-Jewish action.

WILHELM MARR'S CONCEPT OF ANTISEMITISM

Wilhelm Marr was probably among the first antisemitic authors who formulated a "clearly post-emancipatory argument" with regard to the legal and political status of the Jews in Germany.[2] In his 1879 book *Der Sieg des Judenthums über das Germanenthum* (The Victory of Judaism over German Identity and Culture), Marr stressed the need to oppose the Jewish people from a nonconfessional perspective. Consider, too, for example, the philosopher-historian Bruno Bauer: in 1843, he was living at a time when Jews were still denied equal rights in Germany. Thus, Bauer stressed the need to further bar their emancipation by referring to what he understood as the Jewish "essence," which he still saw as largely defined by religion.[3] Marr, writing when Jewish emancipation had finally been accomplished, regarded such arguments as simply "nonsensical."[4] By emphasizing the religious aspect, Marr argued, the German people had been blinded to the real danger posed by Jewish emancipation. "It did not occur to anyone," he wrote, "that the Jewish question was a sociopolitical one. . . . Judaism's sociopolitical invasion of German society achieved legal status. A foreign dominion that factually had already existed was legally recognized."[5]

Now that the legal and political emancipation of the Jews had been accomplished, Marr declared, they would further usurp power over the German state. He saw the law merely as an instrument in the Jews' hands that gave them power over the state, just as did Nazi jurist Carl Schmitt, who, fifty years later, coined the slogan "The masters of the lex subjugate the rex."[6] The Jew haters had lost the legal sphere as a tool to be used against the Jews and now saw the law as having become the Jews' weapon in their struggle for dominance. Marr thus recognized the need for a new strategy against the Jews—namely, a more general political attack against them.

In his biography of Marr, Moshe Zimmermann writes in depth about the function of the term *antisemitism* and whether it was truly invented by Marr in 1879. Zimmermann concludes that the term *antisemitism*, compared to *anti-Jewish*, became popular in particular among writers and scholars because of its scientific pretentions. The term was also somewhat vague and thus "good cover" against "legal suits," casting "a cloak of uncertainty over the intent of the hatred against the Jews (which people still avoided mentioning explicitly)."[7] As Zimmermann wrote in 1986, the term *antisemitism* served the same "purpose which the term 'anti-Zionism' serves today—evading the accusation of engaging in something improper."[8]

While that is worth considering, according to Richard S. Levy, Zimmermann still misses the crucial point. In his critical review of the Marr biography, Levy wrote that the "designations 'anti-Semite' and 'anti-Semitism' gained immediate currency all over Europe" because they answered a "need for new terms, terms that better described a *new and . . . necessary form of action against Jews.* Marr . . . had understood that once Jews gained legal emancipation, the old sorts of anti-Jewish behavior . . . were no longer adequate. Now it was too late for such defensive gestures. A continuous political effort would have to be mounted, institutionalized in parties, propaganda associations, and newspapers."[9]

This continuous political effort is exactly what Marr pursued. He founded a variety of antisemitic newspapers, such as the *Deutsche Wacht* (German Guard) and the *Antisemitische Flugblätter* (Antisemitic Leaflets). Arguing that antisemitism is based on rational arguments, he claimed that he had nothing against Jews as individuals; what he opposed was Judaism itself, which he considered a destructive social concept.

Although Marr had begun with proposals for measures such as assimilation, baptism, and mixed marriages between Jews and non-Jews in 1862, by 1879 the forms of action he was proposing had become more radically exclusionary.[10] As Zimmerman writes, they "included a ban on business dealings with Jews, the severance of social relations with Jews, withdrawing support from the Jewish press and Jewish candidates, and the separation of Jewish from non-Jewish education; in short—'the isolation of Jewry within the state and society.'"[11]

Clearly, after the legal sphere had been lost as a weapon against the Jews, Marr sought new ways to mobilize for their total exclusion from society—politically, socially, and economically—all in the name of a "noble" antisemitism. As Marr wrote, a "'bulwark' must be erected against the Semitic flood, since the educated person must certainly reject barbaric measures."[12] Some 150 years after Marr, we know that the National Socialists used precisely this strategy of social exclusion before taking the next step toward their policy of extermination. Thus, what Marr had previously proposed was a new form of practice rather than a new anti-Jewish ideology.

ANTI-ZIONISM AS AN ANTI-JEWISH STRATEGY

Insofar as Marr's concept of antisemitism was a response to Jewish emancipation, anti-Zionism is a response to the foundation of the state of Israel. Just as Marr was confronted with formal law as a social institution that protected Jews equally as citizens, Judeophobes today are confronted with the Jewish state as a social and political institution that protects Jews, and not only in Israel. And just as Marr sought forms of action to undermine the social status of Jews as citizens, anti-Zionism attempts to find strategies to undermine the sovereignty of Israel. Below, I discuss some of these strategies and their implied forms of action.

When we speak of the sovereignty of a nation-state, we can focus on its internal sovereignty and political constitution; we can discuss the relationship between the sovereign and the subjects protected and governed by the sovereign, or we can enter into the long-standing discussion on what sovereignty means externally—that is, the relationships between sovereign states.[13] What makes Israeli sovereignty exceptional, among other factors, is that the question of its subjects' identity cannot be answered simply by referring to its citizens; it is also necessary to take the Israeli law of return into consideration. Israeli sovereignty implies a guarantee to protect the life and liberty of Jews and their families globally.

That is why after 1948 the antisemitic question of how can we harm our Jewish enemy in the most striking, most destructive, and most acceptable way found this response: by finding strategies and forms of action to deny, undermine, and directly attack Israeli sovereignty. Anti-Zionism is antisemitism on a global level in that anti-Zionism is the materialization of antisemitism as an international movement, and, according to Hannah Arendt, that is what it was supposed to be from the very beginning.[14] It uses all the instruments at its disposal on an international level with the goal of destroying Jewish sovereignty and ultimately Jewish existence itself.

From this perspective, we are able to understand that anti-Zionism is a new form of Judeophobia only in the sense that what stands between the Jew haters and their enemy (the Jew) has changed. In other words, while the transition from antisemitism to anti-Zionism signals a particular change in the sociohistorical determination of the form (or as Hegel puts it, the *Formbestimmung*) of anti-Judaism, it is not the object of Jew hatred that has changed.[15] Israel is merely the new obstacle that stands between Judeophobes and the fulfillment of their unsubstantiated hatred against the Jews. Moreover, the change in form (Hegel's *Formwandel*) in question here is a rather minor one compared with the transformation of Christian anti-Judaism into what we now call antisemitism.[16]

Modern antisemitism emerged with the ground-shaking social changes that accompanied the development of the capitalist mode of production. It was at this particular historical stage, when antisemitism became systematic, as sociologist Detlev Claussen has pointed out, that it became a method of explaining all the abstract and frightening phenomena of society, and therefore truly a religion of everyday life: "It was only bourgeois society that developed into the antisemitic society par excellence."[17]

Anti-Zionism, by contrast, did not emerge in the wake of a comparable fundamental global change. Rather, the anti-Zionist form of Jew hatred arose in response to the more recent emancipation of Jews as citizens: as citizens of a Jewish state equal among other states. And it is only in reference to the historical Jewish critics of Jewish emancipation that it makes any sense to label contemporary anti-Zionism as antisemitic anti-Zionism in order to differentiate between Jewish anti-Zionism before the Shoah and the global antisemitic anti-Zionism observed since the foundation of the state of Israel and especially since the Six-Day War. While historical anti-Zionism stood for a specific perspective on how best to achieve Jewish emancipation—and, moreover, the universal emancipation of all humans—contemporary anti-Zionism aims to destroy the Jewish state and along with it the successful Jewish emancipation that has enabled Jews to defend themselves— socially, politically, and militarily—against antisemitism within and beyond Israel.[18] Anti-Zionism should therefore be considered a new form of anti-Jewish action rather than a new form of Judeophobia.

ANTI-ZIONISM AS ANTI-JEWISH ACTION

In the last ten years, the so-called one-state solution has gained much ground within the anti-Zionist movement.[19] Arguments in favor of a binational state where Palestinians and Jews would live together in a "shared and secular democratic state" usually insinuate that Israel as a *Jewish* state is not democratic— which basically means that Palestinian Israeli citizens are not granted the same rights as Jewish Israeli citizens.[20] Contrary to that claim, the Israeli Basic Law on Human Dignity and Liberty states that the state of Israel is a Jewish *and* democratic state.[21] Nonetheless, self-proclaimed anti-Zionists in favor of a one-state solution remind their audience that prior to the foundation of the state of Israel, Jewish intellectuals such as Hannah Arendt and Martin Buber argued in favor of some sort of democratic, binational solution to the conflict between Palestinians and the Jewish inhabitants of Palestine.[22] While this is true, these anti-Zionists usually ignore the fact that neither Buber nor Arendt considered themselves to be anti-Zionist. In fact, Buber was a passionate Zionist, and, despite all her criticism, Arendt stayed close to the Zionist movement throughout her life as well. Thus, even though it may sound like a *contradictio in adjecto* to the anti-Zionists, the concept of Zionism and the argument for a binational state (however critical toward the latter one may be) have been at least for some Zionists just as reconcilable historically as is the reality of the state of Israel as a Jewish and, at the same time, democratic state today.

Hannah Arendt's pro-Zionist perspective led her to argue against Jewish sovereignty in May 1948, because she thought it would threaten the goal of a Jewish homeland, endanger the lives of Palestinians and Jews, and therefore ultimately leave "the unique possibilities and the unique achievements of Zionism in Palestine destroyed."[23] Apart from her general criticism of the concept of sovereignty, she was concerned above all that a sovereign Jewish state would not be capable of defending itself and its citizens. Thus, she warned of the "pseudo-sovereignty of a Jewish state."[24]

In contrast, the anti-Zionist perspective focuses not on the lack but on the full effect of Jewish sovereignty, which has rendered the state of Israel fully capable of self-defense. To deny the importance of Jewish sovereignty and ultimately destroy its very existence, anti-Zionists pretend to make the case for universalism and democracy and label Israel an obsolete relic built on outmoded political concepts such as the nation-state and national sovereignty. This view was represented by Richard Falk at the Second Palestine Solidarity Conference in Stuttgart in May 2013 under the title "Working for One Secular, Democratic State for All Its Citizens." Falk, professor emeritus for international law at Princeton University and former United Nations special rapporteur in the disputed territories, argued that "the idea of an ethnic Palestinian state right next to a Jewish state is also not reconcilable with the contemporary affirmation of human rights, the dignity of the individual, and the equality of all human beings. In the light of such fundamental, ethical and political concepts by a legitimate form of government, notions of a Jewish state and a Palestinian state in the 21st century not only seem unfavorable, but a serious violation of the rights of all that are living there."[25]

According to Falk, Jewish sovereignty should be dismissed in the name of human rights, equality, and the dignity of the individual. But not a word was said from this supposed expert on the situation in Palestine about the lethal threat of antisemitism to Israel's Jews.[26] The case he opened against Israel can be radicalized in any way desired, and can be observed in various contributions to the same conference. Joseph Massad, professor of modern Arab politics and intellectual history at New York's Columbia University, for example, suggested that Zionism fully espouses all the ideas of "Marr's anti-Semitic program."[27] According to Massad, Zionism supports the antisemitic assertion that "Jews did not fit in the new national configurations, and disrupted national and racial purity essential to most European nationalisms," and therefore Zionism itself is inherently racist and antisemitic. However, most European Jews, as Massad explained further, saw through this. That is why they stayed in Europe and exposed themselves to the lethal threat of Nazi Germany's antisemitic policy. "While the majority of Jews continued to resist the anti-Semitic basis of Zionism and its alliances with anti-Semites," Massad declared, "the Nazi genocide not only killed ninety percent of European Jews but in the process also killed the majority of Jewish enemies of Zionism, who died precisely because they refused to heed the Zionist call of abandoning their countries and homes."[28] Not only does Massad add a new version of the libel about a full-fledged collaboration of Nazis and Zionists prior to the Shoah,[29] but he also implies that the Shoah played well into the hands of the Zionists as the Nazis helped them get rid of their "Jewish enemies" when the "holocaust killed off the majority of Jews who fought and struggled against European anti-Semitism, including Zionism."[30]

The consequences that anti-Zionism draws from all this are evident: supporting the existence of Jewish sovereignty means supporting "Nazi pro-Zionism" and "Zionism's anti-Semitic program of assimilating Jews into whiteness in a colonial settler state" is, in short, "a direct continuation of anti-Semitic policies prevalent before the war" and is now, of course, "directed at Arabs and Muslims."[31] By contrast, according to this perfidious logic, fighting against Israel is fighting against Nazism, antisemitism, colonialism, and (anti-Muslim) racism, all at the same time. Or, as another speaker put it in his account of the conference, if one really wants to invoke "antifascist values and lessons drawn from the crimes of the Nazis as condensed in universal human rights, one had to fight against Zionist colonialism."[32]

Statements like these show how anti-Zionists aim to transform elements of postmodern discourse such as postnational universalism and postcolonial antiracism into a postmodern anti-Jewish action strategy in order to attain acceptance and attract followers. But in the search for such a strategy, why has the one-state solution only recently gained such popularity? The answer is provided by John Rees, cofounder of the Stop the War Coalition. In a July 2014 article for the journal *Counterfire,* Rees asks "what strategy can bring the Palestinians victory" and informs us that the "rise of the two-state solution was in part a result of the decay of Arab nationalism."[33] Once the "heroic phase of Arab nationalist resistance to European colonialism" lay in the past and had become a quagmire of neoliberalism and corruption, "another force [political Islam] arose" and displaced "Arab nationalism as a vehicle for anti-imperialist sentiment in the Middle East. . . . Its primary appeal has been its relative willingness to fight imperialism just at the moment when the previous generation of Arab nationalists were colluding with it."[34] Rees's assessment of this newfound force is crystal clear: "All this returns us to the possibility of a one-state solution: a single, democratic, multi-faith state running from the River Jordan to the Mediterranean Sea," governed by the "Palestinians and *others* that live within the borders of historic Palestine."[35]

At least some of the attendees of the Stuttgart conference hold views similar to these. They vehemently advocate drawing closer to political Islam and even actively invite Islamists to join forces with them.[36] At the same time, although these anti-Zionists are supposedly in favor of a "secular, democratic state," they reveal that their claims for secularism are just a bluff when they demand that their fellow combatants dispense with the "epithet 'secular.'"[37] Even while many Islamists stand in favor of democracy, as Wilhelm Langthaler assumes, "secularism remains a bogeyman to them."[38]

What the anti-Zionists are denying is that a Jewish sovereign state exists and must exist. This denial is part of a strategy seeking to deprive the Jewish people of the only sovereign force uncompromisingly ready to defend Jews worldwide against antisemitism and the forces of political Islam—the same forces John Rees and his kind promote as a model for their "democratic," but hardly secular, solution.

Although the promotion of a one-state solution may be regarded as a rather propagandistic aspect of contemporary forms of anti-Jewish action, not least because it is designed to attract new followers, attempts to use international law as a weapon against Israel are among the more practical efforts to take action against Jewish sovereignty. So-called lawfare against Israel does not merely attempt to delegitimize the Jewish state in the public perception. As Jeremy Rabkin clearly defines it, *lawfare* is a "strategy of using or misusing law as a substitute for traditional military means *to achieve military objectives*."[39] The anti-Zionist movement has clearly understood that international law, in cases where it has a binding impact, can actually undermine the sovereignty of a state.

There is, of course, an ongoing discussion in political theory regarding whether the concept of sovereignty really implies that a state is responsible to no one and not bound by international and humanitarian law. But the fact is that international law is a negotiated set of rules that results from power relations and not from a supreme political body equipped with the executive authorities of a state. Thus, when a sovereign nation-state can be forced from the outside to comply with international law or an international set of rules, instead of doing so of its free general will, its sovereignty is effectively diminished. And trying to impose this force on Israel is part of the strategy of the BDS (Boycott, Divestment, Sanctions) movement and the initiatives attempting to drag Israel before the International Criminal Court (ICC).

Clearly, the reason for the Palestinian Authority's decision to sign the Rome Statute and to submit itself to the jurisdiction of the ICC was not to strengthen the rule of law in Israel or a future Palestine. As Mazen Mazri of London's City Law School puts it, despite "its characterization as a court, the ICC is essentially a political institution, and international criminal justice is essentially a contested political framework."[40] However, he adds, "International law is part of the fabric of international relations, and to ignore it would be to forfeit a potentially useful tool."[41]

Mazri's colleague Noura Erakat, a law professor at George Mason University, elaborates on how this tool can be used most effectively: "The challenge ahead is to innovate not simply litigation strategies but to put them in conversation with radical popular mobilization."[42] As a part of this radical mobilization, she envisions "primarily but not exclusively the global BDS campaign," as well as Hamas.[43] The latter she hopes to see in "a more realistic unity government . . . one that envisions the possibility of ICC prosecution *against* Palestinian groups and prepares for the attendant fallout."[44] Erakat advises the Palestinian Authority to limit its engagement with the ICC to the question of settlements to minimize the risks of Palestine itself being prosecuted "for suicide bombings launched from the West Bank and other alleged crimes under the Rome Statute."[45]

The strategy of using international law as a battering ram against Israeli sovereignty includes creating "innovative claims within the International Court of Justice (ICJ) as well as foreign national courts" while protecting Islamist terrorist groups from being prosecuted.[46] As Erakat points out, it has been a wise decision for the Palestinian leadership not to refer any specific situation or case to the office of the prosecutor of the ICC. According to her, the main benefit that one can hope to extract from the ICC is deterring Israel from using reasonable military force in any future conflict in the West Bank or the Gaza Strip—that is, as a tool to undermine Israel's self-defense capabilities.

Having come to no legal conclusion, the ICC is still involved in the aftermath of the so-called Gaza Freedom Flotilla. It is probably the most interesting example of anti-Jewish action, because it includes both direct action and lawfare against Israel.

The Freedom Flotilla sailed in May 2010 and consisted of six ships, including the passenger vessel *Mavi Marmara* that served as the flagship of the convoy. According to official claims by the organizers, the flotilla was supposed to carry humanitarian aid and construction material to Gaza in May 2010. However, the main groups behind the flotilla—the Free Gaza Movement and the Turkish Foundation for Human Rights and Freedoms and Humanitarian Relief—deliberately planned to break the Israeli-Egyptian blockade of the Gaza Strip, refusing the Israeli offer to check the cargo in Ashdod harbor and deliver the goods—including materials banned for import, such as cement—to Gaza via land. This refusal underlines that the purpose of the flotilla was not humanitarian but political, and its aim was to directly violate Israeli sovereignty. Adam Shapiro, one of the board members of the Free Gaza Movement, summed up its goals: "Free

Gaza is but one tactic of a larger strategy, to transform this conflict from one between Israel and the Palestinians . . . to one between the rest of the world and Israel."[47]

The anti-Zionist movement is clearly engaged in actions that constitute attempts to maneuver Israel into a lose-lose situation: either it accepts the impingement on its sovereignty, or it risks international isolation. Furthermore, the Gaza flotilla was characterized by a specific division of labor. On one hand, Israeli sovereignty was directly tested by the flotilla's attempt to break through Israel's "naval blockade" and by Islamist hardcore activists physically attacking Israel Defense Forces (IDF) soldiers; on the other hand, so-called human rights activists such as two members of the German federal parliament, Annette Groth and Inge Höger, as well as the popular German international law scholar Norman Paech (also from Die Linke), presenting themselves as more moderate and respectable, tried to maximize the anti-Israel fallout in the media, in international relations, and with regard to international law.[48]

CONCLUSION

The changes we are observing in the expression of Jew hatred are not only the result of social changes reflected in an unconscious process of antisemitic projections. They are also based on the haters' need, through new forms of anti-Jewish action, to adequately respond to sociohistorical changes—above all, the creation of the state of Israel—insofar as they affect the antisemitic worldview. The contemporary anti-Jewish mind-set and form of action we know as anti-Zionism allows for the global unification of Jew haters based on their common enemy.

Whereas Wilhelm Marr opposed the Jews in the name of humanism, the anti-Zionists oppose Israel in the name of a universalism that is no less toxic than Marr's humanism, which itself paved the way for the race theorists to exclude the Jews from the human race. This is perfectly illustrated by the understanding of universalism proposed by Alain Badiou. As Shira Wolosky explains, for Badiou, the "figure of the Jew emerges as the very essence of particularism, the betrayer of saving universalism."[49] Badiou's universalism is an empty and destructive one, without any room for the Jews; its aim is to erase every distinction. His philosophical concept of universalism is one in which even the words that allow for distinction have to be erased.[50] But if the Jew is the essence of particularism, it is the universalist antisemite who intuitively understands what this requires on a practical level. In contrast, Theodor W. Adorno, whose thinking aimed at the prospect of allowing difference without fear, knew that only a concept of universalism that is able to reconcile the individual, the particular, and the universal deserves to be called universalism: "The totality of the universal expresses its own failure. What tolerates nothing particular is thus revealing itself as particularly dominant. The general reason that comes to prevail is already a restricted reason."[51]

Thus, anti-Zionist universalism is an antisemitic universalism, because it sees the Jewish state and the Jews as outdated forms of particularism, preventing universalism from its fulfillment, just as Marr had felt that the Jews had prevented human emancipation.[52] Anti-Zionists are, as Vladimir Jankélévitch wrote, antisemites in the name of democracy.[53] While Marr's primary goal was to isolate German Jews on the social stage even after their emancipation, today's anti-Zionists are attempting to isolate Israel on the international stage through all forms of boycott— cultural, academic, and economic. At the same time, they are working to curtail and finally destroy Israeli sovereignty. Ultimately, all anti-Jewish action represents an attempt to attain a consistent goal: the destruction of the legal, political, and social institutions that serve as guarantors of contemporary Jewry in all its forms.

NOTES

1. For more on *Der Judenspiegel*, see "Das Judenthum muß aufhören, wenn das Menschenthum anfangen soll." Wilhelm Marr, *Der Judenspiegel* (Hamburg, 1862), 54.

From Alan Badiou, *Circonstances 3: Portées du mot juif* (Paris: Léo Scheer, 2008), 14, 15:

> Il est clair qu'aujourd'hui l'équivalent de la rupture religieuse de Paul avec le judaïsme établi, de la rupture rationaliste de Spinoza avec la Synagogue, ou de la rupture politique de Marx avec l'intégration bourgeoise d'une partie de sa communauté d'origine, est la rupture subjective avec l'État d'Israël, non dans son existence empirique, ni plus ni moins impure que celle de tous les États, mais dans sa prétention identitaire fermée à être un « État juif » et à tirer de cette prétention d'incessants privilèges, singulièrement quand il s'agit de fouler aux pieds ce qui nous tient lieu de droit international. Un État et un pays vraiment contemporains sont toujours cosmopolites, parfaitement indistincts dans leur configuration identitaire.

> [It is obvious that today's equivalent to Paul's religious separation from established Judaism, to Spinoza's rationalist separation from the Synagogue, or to Marx's political separation from the bourgeois integration of a part of his native community, is the subjective separation from the State of Israel, not from its empirical existence, which is no more or less impure than any other state, but from its exclusive identitarian claim of being a "Jewish State" and from the policy of drawing on unending privilege based on that claim; and remarkably, by trampling on what serves as international law. A truly contemporary state and country are always cosmopolitan, perfectly indistinguishable in the configuration of their identity.]

Not only does Badiou deny the role of the Shoah in the foundation of the state of Israel, but also he is indifferent to the fact that only a Jewish state can reliably guarantee the safety and protection of Jews in Israel and all over the world in the face of antisemitism. As discussed toward the end of this chapter, Badiou's proposal on how to best fight antisemitism is indeed for the Jews to abandon their "particularistic" Jewish identity, a proposal well known from older antisemitic writings, such as Bruno Bauer's *Die Judenfrage* [The Jewish question] (Brunswick, Germany: Friedrich Otto, 1843).

2. Moshe Zimmermann, *Wilhelm Marr: The Patriarch of Antisemitism* (New York: Oxford University Press, 1986), 45.

3. "Seine Religion und Lebensart verpflichten ihn [den Juden; T.F.] zu ewiger Absondrung: warum? Weil sie sein Wesen sind. . . . Die Emancipation der Juden ist auf eine grundliche, erfolgreiche und sichre Weise erst möglich, wenn sie nicht als Juden, d.h. als Wesen, die den Christen immer fremd bleiben müssen, emancipirt werden, sondern wenn sie sich zu Menschen machen, die durch keine, auch durch keine fälschlich für wesentlich gehaltne Schranke mehr von ihren Mitmenschen getrennt sind" (Bauer, *Die Judenfrage*, 19, 60).

[His (the Jew's; T.F.) religion and his way of life force him into eternal isolation: why? Because they are his essence. . . .The emancipation of the Jews in a thorough, successful, and reliable way will only be possible if they are not emancipated as Jews, that is as beings that must forever remain foreign to Christians, but rather if they turn themselves into humans no longer separated from their fellow humans by any barriers, including barriers mistaken as essential.]

4. "Wie blödsinnig die religiöse Seite dieses Hasses [gegen die Juden; T.F.] war, erhellt schon daraus, dass man die Juden verantwortlich für die Kreuzigung Christi machen wollte; eine Prozedur, welche bekanntlich die römischen Autoritäten, dem Geschrei eines jerusalemitischen Pöbels feige nachgebend, in Scene gesetzt hatten." Wilhelm Marr, *Der Sieg des Judenthums über das Germanenthum: Vom nicht confessionellen Standpunkt aus betrachtet* (Bern: Rudolp Costenoble, 8. Auflage, 1879), 7.

[The mere fact that one wanted to hold the Jews responsible for the crucifixion of Christ—after a trial known to have been staged by the cowardly Roman authorities who gave into the cries of a Jerusalemite mob—demonstrates how nonsensical the religious aspect of this hatred (against the Jews; T.F.) was.]

5. Marr, *Der Sieg des Judenthums*, 21.

6. Carl Schmitt, *Über die drei Arten des rechtswissenschaftlichen Denkens* (Hamburg: Hanseatische Verlagsanstalt, 1934), 15. Quoted in Raphael Gross, *Carl Schmitt und die Juden: Eine deutsche Rechtslehre. Erweiterte Ausgabe* (Frankfurt: Suhrkamp, 2000), 79. Gross points out that this quote has to be seen against the charge of the "allegedly 'soil-less' Jewish nation" that only exists in law and that with this idea Schmitt actualized a popular antisemitic tradition, suggesting that "the Jews" strive for the *rule of law* instead of the *rule of man*, struggling against the king ("rex") or the *Führer* in order to subjugate him (80). As Shira Wolosky notes, the identification of Jews and law is also at the core of Alain Badiou's anti-universalist universalism. Shira Wolosky, "Badiou, Paul,

and Anti-Judaism: Post-Identity and the Abuse of Ethics," *Telos*, no. 175 (Summer 2016), 43, 44, 45.

7. Zimmermann, *Wilhelm Marr*, 90, 94.

8. Zimmermann, *Wilhelm Marr*, 94.

9. Richard S. Levy, review of *Wilhelm Marr: The Patriarch of Anti-Semitism*, by Moshe Zimmermann, *Commentary*, April 1, 1987, https:// www.commentarymagazine.com/article/wilhelm-marr-the-patriarch-of -anti-semitism-by-moshe-zimmermann (emphasis added).

10. Zimmermann, *Wilhelm Marr*, 48.

11. Zimmermann, *Wilhelm Marr*, 88. As Zimmermann writes, Marr even proposed sending the Jews to Palestine in his later days. In January 1889, he sent a letter to Baron Hirsch stating, "I will guarantee that our anti-Semitic movement will agree to obtain Palestine a second time for the Jews" (87).

12. Wilhelm Marr, "Der Gesellschaftsvertrag mit den Juden," in *Deutsche Wacht* (1879), 78, quoted from Zimmermann, *Wilhelm Marr*, 88. Zimmermann adds: "The tone of the statements of the bourgeois Marr evokes a feeling of sorrow that his education prevented him from wholeheartedly proposing such a [barbaric; T.F.] solution."

13. In various analyses, the social critic Gerhard Scheit has pointed out that international law is only meant to apply but does not apply in an effective way because there is no sovereign body that guarantees the rule of international law. International law is a set of conventions that are based on arrangements between states, and as such it is not guaranteed by a superordinate power. See Gerhard Scheit, *Der Wahn vom Weltsouverän: Zur Kritik des Völkerrechts* (Freiburg: ça ira, 2009), 10. Scheit further explains that it is precisely Israel that is continually forced to lend credence to this, as antisemitic attacks against its existence are not repelled by international law but only by the sovereignty of the Jewish state, as exercised by the Israel Defense Forces (14, 15).

14. Hannah Arendt, "Antisemitismus und faschistische Internationale," in *Nach Auschwitz: Essays und Kommentare 1* (Berlin: Tiamat, 1981), 32.

15. In fact, the final goal of every historical form of anti-Judaism has never changed: despite all the transformations, rationalizations, and justifications, the ultimate aim of all forms of anti-Judaism is the physical harm and annihilation of specific persons designated as Jewish, whether they actually are or not.

16. And we generally do not have Marr and his strategy in mind when we refer to the concept of modern antisemitism.

17. Detlev Claussen, *Aspekte der Alltagsreligion: Ideologiekritik unter veränderten gesellschaftlichen Verhältnissen* (Frankfurt: Neue Kritik, 2000), 125.

18. The argument that not everyone who considers himself or herself an anti-Zionist has the goal of destroying the state of Israel but is merely criticizing a certain policy is unconvincing: people who argue against Israel as a Jewish state in favor of a one-state solution are at the very least ignoring the destructive force of antisemitism and therefore opting for a development that would leave Jews defenseless. Further, criticism of the policy of a certain state or government does not imply the necessity to constitute one's own political identity in negation of this specific policy. In fact, it would be difficult to find a comparable terminological construction without regard to ideological movements of global significance (antifascism, anticommunism, etc.). And the perceived global significance of Judaism, no matter how large its contribution to civilization may be in reality, has all too often been dominated by the hallucination of the power and influence of "the Jews." Today's concept of anti-Zionism is founded on that delusion.

19. Among the more prominent attempts to promote it was the Palestine Solidarity Conference titled "Separated in the Past—Together in the Future" that took place in Stuttgart, Germany, in November 2010. The more than two hundred participants included scholars such as Ilan Pappe, Haidar Aid from Al Aqsa University in Gaza, Mazin Qumsiyeh from Birzeit University in Ramallah, the prominent German international law professor Norman Paech, activists such as *Electronic Intifada* founder Ali Abunimah, journalists, and politicians. The final declaration of the conference states that Israel is a racist state that treats Israeli Palestinians like second-class citizens and denies Palestinian refugees the internationally acknowledged right to return. It calls for the creation of a "common, secular and democratic state on the terrain of the historical Palestine," which naturally "includes the displaced Palestinians." See "Stuttgart Declaration: Closing Document of the Palestine Solidarity Conference 'Separated in the Past—Together in the Future,'" (Palestine Solidarity Conference, Stuttgart, Germany, November 26–28, 2010), https://senderfreiespalaestina.de/petition/Stuttgart_Declaration_EN _final.pdf.

The conference was followed by another three-day conference under the abbreviated title One Democratic State. It took place in May 2013 and was broadcast live by TV station Al Jazeera. According to the organizers, more than three hundred people attended the event. Palästinakomitee

Stuttgart, "Ein demokratischer Staat," December 9, 2015, https://
senderfreiespalaestina.de/ods_konferenzen.htm.

20. For more on propositions for a binational state, see "Stuttgart
Declaration: Closing Document."

21. "Basic Law: Human Dignity and Liberty," The Knesset, accessed July
25, 2018, https://www.knesset.gov.il/laws/special/eng/basic3_eng.htm.

22. For more on those in favor of a two-state solution, see Edward
Said, "The One-State Solution," *New York Times*, January 10, 1999,
http://www.nytimes.com/1999/01/10/magazine/the-one-state-solution.
html?pagewanted=all. For more on Buber's proposition for a binational
state, see Martin Buber, *A Land of Two Peoples: Martin Buber on Jews
and Arabs*, ed. Paul Mendes-Flohr (Chicago: University of Chicago
Press, 2005).

23. The article was published just days before the Israeli declaration of
independence. Hannah Arendt, "To Save the Jewish Homeland: There Is
Still Time," *Commentary*, May 1, 1948, https://www.commentarymagazine
.com/articles/to-save-the-jewish-homelandthere-is-still-time/.

24. Arendt argues in favor of a federated state, referring to a proposition
made by Judah Magnes that would allow one to "avoid the troublesome
majority-minority constellation" by transferring decision making and
conflict solution largely to "Jewish Arab community councils" (Arendt
had always been sympathetic to the idea of council democracy). In 1948,
these ideas of a common state did not sound any less idealistic than
they do today, and Hannah Arendt was well aware that this was merely
wishful thinking. She knew that her ideas would find no sympathy among
the majority of Jews or the Arabs, the national movements of the latter
taking on an "increasingly fascist coloration," according to her. Thereby
dismissing any realization of a federated state in the near future, she still
called for refraining from declaring a Jewish state. A Jewish state, she
argued, "at this moment and under present circumstances . . . can only be
erected at the price of a Jewish homeland." Clearly, Arendt's concern was
genuinely a Zionist one. Not only does she point out that the declaration
of a Jewish state would require its people to live in a constant state of
belligerence with disastrous effects on society, but more importantly, in
"the light of political, military, and geographic realities," she also presumed
that such a state would face military force from its enemies on a level that
would ultimately be too much for the newly founded state to endure. In
her albeit very critical understanding of the concept of sovereignty, Arendt
was well aware that the latter is defined and proven primarily through
external relations and the capability of the sovereign state to defend itself

against external enemies. And because her assessment of this capability of a prospective Jewish state was a negative one, she considered its sovereignty only "pseudo-sovereignty": a defenseless Jewish state would ultimately destroy the Zionist achievement of "a Jewish homeland" in Palestine. While the cost of a more or less constant state of belligerence that Israeli society is forced to bear is indeed substantial in various ways, Arendt has been fortunately proven wrong concerning its defensive capabilities. All quotes from Arendt, "To Save the Jewish Homeland."

25. "Erscheint die Idee eines ethnisch palästinensischen Staates an der Seite eines jüdischen Staates auch nicht vereinbar mit der heutigen Bejahung von Menschenrechten, der Würde jedes Einzelnen, der Gleichheit aller Menschen. Solche grundlegenden ethischen und politischen Ideen von einer legitimen Regierungsform lassen die Vorstellungen eines jüdischen Staates und eines palästinensischen Staates im 21. Jahrhundert nicht nur unvorteilhaft erscheinen, sondern vielmehr als gravierende Verletzung der Rechte all jener, die dort leben." Richard Falk, "BDS und die Perspektiven für einen gemeinsamen, demokratischen Staat in Palästina: Rede von Richard Falk, auf der 2. Palästina-Solidaritätskonferenz (paper, Palestine Solidarity Conference, Stuttgart, Germany, May 10–12, 2013), https://senderfreiespalaestina.de /pdfs/richard-falk-bds-gemeinsamer-staat.pdf.

26. Falk, Said, and others with their vision of a one-state solution could have learned a lot from Hannah Arendt and her perspective on the future of Jews and Arabs in Palestine. With her pessimistic outlook on the future, she saw the elimination "of all terrorist groups" as an "axiomatic" criterion for any exit from the status quo. Speaking of terrorist groups, she, of course, had Jewish groups in mind when calling for "swift punishment of all terrorist deeds (and not merely protests against them)," stating that only these decisive measures will be the "valid proof that the Jewish people in Palestine has recovered its sense of political reality." What Arendt wrote with regard to Irgun, Lehi, and others in 1948 can and must be applied to Palestinian terror today: The "elimination of all terrorist groups (and not agreements with them)"—as in the case of Hamas with its antisemitic agenda—should be considered as the minimum requirement to exit from the present status quo. Only this, one might add, would be valid proof that the Palestinian people have recovered some sense of political reality and are no longer blinded by antisemitic rants and delusions. All quotes from Arendt, "To Save the Jewish Homeland."

27. Joseph A. Massad, "The Last of the Semites: Speech of Joseph A. Massad at the Second Palestine Solidarity Conference" (paper, Palestine

Solidarity Conference, Stuttgart, Germany, May 10–12, 2013), https://senderfreiespalaestina.de/pdfs/joseph-massad-last-of-semites-en.pdf.

28. Massad, *Last of the Semites.*

29. Francis R. Nicosia, *Zionism and Anti-Semitism in Nazi Germany* (Cambridge: Cambridge University Press, 2008).

30. Massad, *Last of the Semites.*

31. Massad, *Last of the Semites.*

32. Wilhelm Langthaler, *Deutsche Staatsraison gegen Demokratie,* May 25, 2013,

https://senderfreiespalaestina.de/meinung.htm. The author, Wilhelm Langthaler, goes on to quote historian Ilan Pappe, according to whom the two-state solution was a "purely Zionist invention" anyway, "to sell the 19th century's colonial principles in the 21st century to a world longing for democracy and that has had bitter experiences with nationalism in the 20th century."

33. John Rees, "Palestine: The Only Solution Is Now the One-State Solution," *Counterfire,* July 23, 2014, http://www.counterfire.org/articles/analysis/17339-palestine-the-only-solution-is-now-the-one-state-solution.

34. Rees, "Palestine."

35. Rees, "Palestine," emphasis added.

36. Langthaler, *Deutsche Staatsraison.*

37. Langthaler, *Deutsche Staatsraison.*

38. Langthaler, *Deutsche Staatsraison.*

39. Jeremy Rabkin, "Lawfare: The International Court of Justice Rules in Favor of Terrorism," *Wall Street Journal,* September 17, 2004; quoted in Anne Herzberg, *NGO "Lawfare": Exploitation of Courts in the Arab-Israeli Conflict,* 2nd ed. (Jerusalem: NGO Monitor, 2010), 2, emphasis added.

40. Middle East Research and Information Project, *Palestine and the ICC,* January 8, 2015, http://www.merip.org/palestine-icc.

41. Middle East Research and Information Project.

42. Middle East Research and Information Project.

43. Middle East Research and Information Project.

44. Middle East Research and Information Project, emphasis added.

45. Noura Erakat, "Who Is Afraid of the International Criminal Court?" *Beta,* January 12, 2015, http://www.jadaliyya.com/pages/index/20523/who-is-afraid-of-the-international-criminal-court.

46. Erakat, "Who Is Afraid of the International Criminal Court?"

47. Melanie Phillips, "The Flotilla and the Third Intifada," *Jerusalem Connection,* June 29, 2011, http://thejerusalemconnection.us/blog/2011/06/29/the-flotilla-and-the-third-intifada/.

48. When the flotilla's six civilian ships were stopped en route to Gaza while still in international waters on May 31, 2010, seven IDF soldiers were injured in the clash that ensued on one of them, the *Mavi Marmara*, and nine activists of the Turkish Foundation for Human Rights and Freedoms and Humanitarian Relief were killed. The activists attacked the IDF commandos with, at a minimum, metal pipes and bats as they came down from the helicopter. Videos show activists beating one of the soldiers and trying to kidnap him.

49. Shira Wolosky, "Badiou, Paul, and Anti-Judaism: The Abuse of Ethics," *Telosscope*, June 27, 2016, http://www.telospress.com/badiou-paul -and-anti-judaism-the-abuse-of-ethics/. Wolosky explains this in depth in her article of the same name in the printed version of *Telos*, no. 175; see pages 35–56 of that version.

50. For more on Badiou's universalism, see Wolosky, "Badiou, Paul," in *Telos*, 52. As Wolosky states, Badiou's concept of universalism opposes any social order as oppressive, and as such it is perfectly compatible with hatred against civilization and thus with what can be considered the core of the antisemitic delusion.

51. Theodor W. Adorno, *Negative Dialectics* (New York: Bloomsbury, 2014), 317.

52. "Es ist daher hohe, vielleicht die höchste Zeit, auch diese 'Errungenschaft' [die Judenemanzipation; T.F.] zu revidiren. Oder sollte man an maßgebender Stelle wirklich der Ansicht sein, vor allem Irren, vor allen Wirren der Revolution die Flagge zu streichen, weil diese Revolution—die Gesellschaft der Gefahr der Verjudung überliefert hat?" Wilhelm Marr, An die Adresse des hohen Bundesrathes und des deutschen Reichstages, November 1879 in Deutsche Wacht, Monatsschrift für nationale Kulturinteressen (Organ der antijüdischen Vereinigung) (Berlin: Otto Hentze, 1879), 4.

53. Vladimir Jankélévitch, *Das Verzeihen. Essays zur Moral und Kulturphilosophie.* (Frankfurt: Suhrkamp, 2003), 245.

THORSTEN FUCHSHUBER is a research associate at the Centre Interdisciplinaire d'Etude des Religions et de la Laïcité, Université libre de Bruxelles. His research interests concentrate on critical theory, legal philosophy, Jewish philosophy, and antisemitism.

THREE

Social Criticism and the "Jewish Problem"

BALÁZS BERKOVITS

MANY SIGNS INDICATE that in Western Europe, social criticism and political action aimed at promoting change are closely intertwined with critiques of Israel. This is the case even if the subject of the action, demands, or demonstration is not even remotely linked to the Israeli-Palestinian conflict. Associations dedicated to various humanitarian and legal causes—for example, human rights nongovernmental organizations, labor unions, pacifist organizations, and advocates for the homeless—often share a virulent anti-Zionism that denigrates Israel and denies its right to exist. This is also the case with many university organizations and scientific associations that promote various calls for boycotts of Israel. These days, progressives and intellectuals attack Israel on an almost daily basis. What are the reasons for this phenomenon? Why is social criticism so often linked to critiques of Israel? How does leftist social and political criticism relate to popular understandings of the Holocaust and of contemporary Israel, and how is it that the "Jewish question," or even the "Jewish problem," has been reformulated on the progressive side of the political spectrum?

In Western Europe, traditional antisemitism has gradually given way to a new kind of Judeophobia.[1] In this new anti-Jewish discourse and action, Jews are no longer taken to be an inferior race; rather, the Jews are seen as treating other peoples as inferiors. Now it is the Jews who are the racists—some even liken them to the Nazis—and the notion that they intend to rule the world, which originated in traditional antisemitic discourse, persists. Jews are the agents not only of big capital, capitalism, or communism but also of "international Zionism," which is understood to be an influence on imperialist and especially American politics. These developments have been summarized succinctly by Jean-Claude Milner: "We can expect Europe to become the privileged territory for anti-Judaism. We can even expect it to become such in exact proportion to its proclaimed rejection of antisemitism."[2] Or, as Rusi Jaspal has noted, "Antisemitism evokes imagery of fascism, extremism, death and genocide, while anti-Zionism evokes imagery of anti-capitalism, anti-racism and minority rights. The former has a malevolent action orientation, while the latter is understood to have a benevolent one."[3]

As Pierre-André Taguieff, Alain Finkielkraut, and many others have noted, in our epoch, the political socialization of critical intellectuals often includes anti-Zionism.[4] These intellectuals have recourse to humanist social criticism and stand up against nationalism and oppression in favor of the excluded, the poor, and immigrants. Therefore, anti-Zionism (and probably also left-wing antisemitism) cannot simply be dismissed as racism and prejudice. In fact, it seems that standing up for good causes is intertwined with a sort of mechanical critique of Israel, against which rational arguments seem to be useless (just as they are against traditional antisemitism). However, Taguieff and Finkielkraut cannot determine how and why "the Israeli" (but sometimes also "the Jew") has become an important figure, a symbol of oppression and exploitation in this kind of imagery, contrasted not only with the "colonized, exploited, and assassinated Palestinian" but also with everybody who suffers from social exclusion. Why are Israel and the exceptionality of the Holocaust among critical intellectuals' main targets? Finkielkraut upholds an explanation originally advanced by the philosopher Vladimir Jankélévitch that this inverted figure of the victim emerged from Europe's bad conscience, from its will to get rid of latent remorse.[5] Therefore, said Jankélévitch and then Finkielkraut, anti-Zionism as a "justified antisemitism" is instrumental in this respect.

In France, Eric Marty and Danny Trom, in the wake of Jean-Claude Milner, have been the most perspicacious detractors of anti-Zionist and sometimes antisemitic discourse in contemporary European social-scientific and philosophical works considered progressive and critical.[6] These authors do not turn to social-psychological hypotheses or the collective unconscious to explain the phenomenon; their analyses are more philosophically informed and conceptual.

The French sociologist Danny Trom, in a seminal book that is unfortunately not widely known, analyzes the emergence of anti-Zionism and, more generally, of the "Jewish problem" (which he contrasts with the Jewish question) in sociological and philosophical works of the radical left that aim to restore or reinvigorate social and political criticism.[7] The idea that the Jewish problem has been reformulated in our era comes from Milner.[8] In Milner's view, to describe a problem is to diagnose an objectively existing issue in need of resolution; the problem therefore demands a definitive solution. Ever since the Enlightenment, Europeans have thought in these terms: society is the realm where problems emerge, and politics is the mode of action that should resolve them. Now this set of problems contains the word *Jewish*. Proposed solutions can vary, but the problem remains essentially the same as long as it is not resolved. In contrast, the question is not located in objective reality but formulated in language, and thus does not require a definitive answer. Furthermore, the Jewish question corresponds to the "anti-Semite question," which was posed, for example, by Jean-Paul Sartre in his famous essay on antisemitism, whereas when this issue is formulated as a problem, it can no longer be treated as a question.[9]

According to Trom, the "Jew" as a "problem," as an obstacle to be overcome, has reemerged in progressive thought, and theoreticians have even proposed solutions to it. It is precisely these solutions that one should fear, because they are aimed at the annihilation of Jewish memory and "exceptionality" (understood as particularism and as the thesis of the uniqueness of the Holocaust), of the word *Jewish* (sometimes stigmatized as a "transcendental signifier"), and even of Israel. These solutions could take the form of even more radical demands in the future. Trom explores these reformulations in mainstream and well-known sociological and philosophical texts with the intention of unearthing the theoretical foundations of contemporary anti-Judaism. Eric Marty, who also deals with philosophical works, emphasizes the instrumentalization of the Holocaust (and its ensuing neutralization and relativization) as well as the denial of its Jewishness, especially in his essays on Genet, Agamben, and Badiou.[10]

Drawing on these authors and rereading some of the materials they have used, I identify the topics through which the "Jewish problem" emerges in critical—both theoretical and empirical—social-scientific, philosophical, and political works. The problem I address emerges at the confluence of four different but related issues linked to the interpretation of the Holocaust: the crisis of social and political critique, which has resulted in the search for novel types of criticism; the relationship between the interpretation of the social question, suffering, and domination and the metaphorization of the Holocaust; the paradoxes of the universality and uniqueness of the Holocaust; and the nature of some of its social-scientific explanations.

THE CRISIS OF SOCIAL CRITICISM

According to Danny Trom's diagnosis, in most cases, the Jewish problem arises when there is an intention to renew social and political criticism. We have been hearing about the crisis of criticism for at least five decades now; it no longer seems possible to attribute social injustice to the activities of particular groups of people or to clear-cut social mechanisms. So the root of the crisis is not only that the agents of social change—that is, the proletariat or the working class—seem to be missing (the lack of which has been amply thematized by critical theory after the war) but also that the dominators and oppressors themselves seem to be absent. Therefore, the new social question is formulated in terms of exclusion, the basis of which is subjective suffering, which needs to be made objective—that is, acknowledged. However, the utmost suffering is the Holocaust, which thereby becomes the standard; all suffering is then compared to the Holocaust to make a dramatic impression and arouse pity. In this respect, we can cite, for example, the following formulations: "the firm is like a concentration camp," "refugees are treated like the Nazis treated the Jews," and "shelters for the homeless are like camps."

Therefore, according to Trom, a relationship is constructed between the Holocaust and the social question: on one hand, victims are presented as if their suffering is equivalent to that of the Jewish victims of the Holocaust; on the other, there is an intention to combat the so-called privilege attributed to the Holocaust, for the limits of the analogy are clearly delineated by the Holocaust as a historical event, and the thesis of its uniqueness. It is as if the Holocaust denies the suffering of other people, as if there is only a limited amount that could be distributed. So far, the Holocaust has won the discursive competition between victims, writes, for example, Jean-Michel Chaumont, and this is the reason why the Jews ultimately cannot be criticized for "anything they do or don't do"; they aspire to the "privilege of impunity."[11] The monopoly of the Jews on the market of suffering is evident, Chaumont continues elsewhere, because they have relegated to the background political resisters as well as other victims of the death camps: homosexuals, gypsies, the mentally ill, and, generally speaking, all the victims of any genocide.[12]

Political interpreters of the Holocaust consider the notion of its uniqueness to be their enemy and prescribe for themselves the task of deconstructing what they call the "uniqueness thesis" in an effort to "democratize" and universalize suffering and to deprive Jews of what they consider an "undue monopoly."[13] More radical approaches assert that this monopoly is maintained by the social privilege many Jews enjoy in contemporary society.[14]

It should be noted, though, that few theoreticians have advocated a strong theological or metaphysical version of the uniqueness thesis. This strong version would entail incomparability and resistance to all historical explanation, which is far from the intentions of even those who employ the term.[15] And there are others who absolutely avoid it. For example, to preclude all misunderstanding, Yehuda Bauer explicitly abandons the term *uniqueness*, instead employing *unprecedentedness* in the hope of highlighting the essential comparability of the Holocaust with other genocides. According to Bauer, whose position could be termed as "weak uniqueness," the Holocaust "not only can, but must, be compared with other genocidal events of a similar nature or quality," while it should be considered as the first in the series in time and, to date, also in gravity. However, he intends to preserve its particular, historical-empirical traits, which single it out, and assign it a paradigm status.[16] Also, as it strives for empirical precision, Bauer's analysis can totally be opposed to procedures of reductive universalization, banalization, or metaphorization of the Holocaust (see *infra*). This means that the critics' argument against uniqueness is a straw man, while what they actually mean to attack under this misleading heading is the paradigm status of the Holocaust, which nevertheless retains many aspects of exceptionality. Therefore, the real, if unavowed, problem for the leftist critics is not that the Holocaust is perceived as incomparably unique or exclusionary but quite the contrary (even if they also argue that the Holocaust as the standard for evil is being maintained by the power relations between different groups).

All this is in line with the interpretation of Trom, according to whom the uniqueness thesis of the Holocaust is perceived by radical social critics as something to be overcome for two reasons: first, because it represents the unreachable summit of suffering, which makes it exceptional and incomparable; and second, because it manifests the illegitimate monopolization of suffering, a certain symbolic violence inflicted on other forms of suffering. However, one might conclude that these two aspects eventually merge, which is made possible by the implication that privileging the Holocaust as the utmost suffering is about placing it above others of equal value, and its evaluation as such is altogether due to the dominant position of Jews.[17] A third reason should be added: leftist discourses promote the idea of universal human suffering, whereas the Holocaust tends to particularize it while still asserting its universal value. Therefore, the notion of Holocaust as the dominant but particularized form of suffering should be combated, overcome, and obliterated, as should the Jew hidden behind it, for he or she is the one who promotes the uniqueness thesis and, of course, has the power to do so.[18] Therefore, the key aspect of this combat seems to be an operation of "reductive universalization," the instances of which are important to highlight.

UNIQUENESS AND UNIVERSALIZATION

Many studies have examined the metaphorization of the Holocaust in the realm of popular culture, history writing, and politics.[19] These approaches are either critical or neutral/descriptive (and the latter often turn out to be apologetic). Critics whose approaches tend toward uniqueness (usually in the weak sense) sometimes find it hard to establish a normative position. What is the basis of their critique? And what would be an ideal situation with regard to the memory of the Holocaust? How should it be transmitted and used without instrumentalizing it? In turn, neutral/descriptive approaches often turn a blind eye to politics, while "cultural factors" and "narrative constraints" play a key role in their reasoning.[20] Thus, not only are they incapable of analyzing the political stakes of Holocaust metaphorization (or they are unwilling to do so), but also they open the door to various kinds of (re)politicizations of the issue. In fact, interestingly enough, characteristic political usages and interpretations of the Holocaust—as figures of reductive universalization—play a key role in contemporary critical theories. Therefore, the political usages of the Holocaust as a "free-floating signifier" and the motives for such usages still need to be highlighted. Certainly, there is the cultural phenomenon, the spreading of the Holocaust metaphor, which testifies to its exceptionality and simultaneously renders it banal. Its existence and importance should not be overlooked, denied, or critically dismissed. But the political usage should be at least partly distinguished from it. These usages cannot be judged outright normatively, for there is no clear basis on which one could establish this criticism. However, motives and methods should be highlighted in the hope of conducting an immanent critique.

Universalization as a Cultural Phenomenon

Neutral accounts of these universalizing processes are epitomized by Jeffrey C. Alexander's essay.[21] However, Alexander's description of "universalizing tendencies" includes both the discourse that preserves the uniqueness of the Holocaust and that which expands the use of the Holocaust as a broad signifier of evil and suffering—thereby blurring some important boundaries (especially with regard to the term *universal*) while depoliticizing all narrative constructions and forms of memory. Although this view is necessary for enlarging the perspective on the issue, due to its depoliticized nature, it falls short of addressing the issue's core problems. I therefore turn to other authors, who, in contrast to Alexander, not only engage with the political aspects of these universalizing discourses but also detect the emergence of a novel formulation of the so-called Jewish problem.

The emergence of the Jewish problem becomes evident if we consider closely, for example, the works of Alain Badiou and Giorgio Agamben, who, besides constructing metaphorical extensions of the Holocaust, intend to eradicate the memory of genocide as well by muting its surviving victims in order to be able to construct a revolutionary politics. Badiou links the Pauline universalist message to the communist enterprise while advocating the forgetting of the "particularist" message of the Holocaust and even the word *Jewish*; he holds the Jews themselves responsible for their suffering.[22] Agamben constructs a deterministic political ontology (and mythology) from the camp metaphor while denying the possibility of bearing witness to the death camp in an authentic way at all, by exalting the figure of the "Muselmann."[23]

Discussing the "social construction of moral universals," Alexander has provided a supposedly value-free account of the process of universalization of the Holocaust as an "archetypal trauma."[24] According to Alexander, the now dominant narrative of the Holocaust is the "tragic narrative," in which it appears as the symbol of universal suffering and universal evil. The predominance of this narrative, which followed the "progressive" one (as he calls it), has resulted in "a decided increase in moral and social justice."[25] This can be shown by pointing to very palpable consequences in the legal domain, such as the Universal Declaration of Human Rights, or the reduced significance of national sovereignty in "rogue states" that commit genocide against their own people. And there are less concrete outcomes as well, linked to the "free-floating Holocaust symbol" or its analogical usage, which have, however, an important discursive significance. For example, war crimes, national tragedies, and genocides could be compared to the Holocaust, thereby helping some groups of people earn recognition or sue for compensation; furthermore, it is now possible to describe Hiroshima or

Dresden or atrocities committed during the Vietnam War or even the Israeli-Palestinian conflict as "holocausts."

While Alexander's interpretation is mostly descriptive and utterly depoliticized—or, rather, is silent about the political stakes concerning the universalization and/or relativization of the Holocaust—it can be fruitfully contrasted to other approaches. These approaches, in turn, attempt to grasp both the depoliticization of the Holocaust—for example, its reduction to pure human suffering or the tendencies to blur the distinction between victims and perpetrators—and its (re)politicization, including the competition of victims in the fight for recognition of their suffering and the intention of overcoming its Jewishness. In fact, from the perspective of these approaches, Alexander, rather than merely interpreting the discursive figures, would seem to be partaking unconsciously in the very depoliticization of the issue by endorsing without reflection the instrumentalization of the Holocaust metaphor in cases that are highly dubious or controversial and by opening the door to diverse and often doubtful repoliticizations.

This tendency is also clear from Alexander's formulation of the paradox of uniqueness and universality. In this respect, he makes an interesting point, though a merely logical one: "The trauma could not function as a metaphor of archetypal tragedy unless it were regarded as radically different from any other evil act in modern times. Yet, it was this very status—as a unique event—that eventually compelled it to become generalized and departicularized. . . . By providing . . . a standard for comparative judgment, the Holocaust became a norm, initiating a succession of metonymic, analogic, and legal evaluations that deprived it of its 'uniqueness' by establishing its degrees of likeness or unlikeness to other possible manifestations of evility."[26] However, Alexander fails to develop a political account of the struggles of differential victimhood, of the accusation that Jews monopolize suffering, or of the instrumentalization and symbolic inversion of Holocaust talk by anti-Zionists.

Another example of a value-free account of universalization is found in chapter ("From the Particular to the Universal, and Forward") in one of Berel Lang's books.[27] It comes as something of a surprise, for otherwise he has a firm normative stance—at least against postmodernist writing of history. In fact, it is this position he intends to refute, because for him, its relativism seems clearly untenable in the light of the Holocaust. Therefore, for Lang, talking about the particularity of the Holocaust means its factual nature, that it actually happened, and that the "facts speak for themselves," while its universality carries its ethical and pedagogical implications for the future. First, Lang enumerates the well-known historical arguments in favor of uniqueness understood as specificity; he concludes that "the systematic effort at genocide . . . was historically distinctive in the deliberate and cohesive effort and organization that the Nazis brought to it. The essential part of the Nazi 'ideal,' then, was notably specific, that is, particular."[28]

Furthermore, he emphasizes contingency in the sense that the Holocaust might not have happened then and there or at all. Particularity as uniqueness only interests him insofar as it allows him to affirm that the Holocaust actually happened, "although there are two sides to many stories, for some stories there are not two sides but one. At times, in other words, the facts do speak for themselves."[29] For Lang, when we talk about the particularity of the Holocaust, this is the most important thing to mention: "We recognize that nothing intrinsic in them brought either the perpetrators or the victims to those roles. Each of the two sides could have been and acted other than they were or did."[30] He goes on to assert that it is this particularity that brings about the universality of the Holocaust. This is how he intends to follow the "universal" side of the problem: if the Holocaust was not predetermined, because, according to him, Germany's role was "underdetermined," then the acts committed by the Germans were free and human; they expressed universal human possibilities. Lang concludes that "nothing intrinsic in those groups or in the place or the time would prevent its happening elsewhere, at another time and place. Thus, there are general principles impelled by the Holocaust: evidence of what human beings are capable of willing to do to each other . . . a universal that exempts no one and no group."[31] In fact, this argument seems to be an unconscious promotion of reductive universalization.

Lang, in a similar vein to Alexander (although on different grounds), cites as an example of universalization the concept of genocide as an example of universalization. It is one of the universal implications of the Holocaust, for it is a human—that is, a universal—possibility. But what are the limits of comparison and analogy, if any? Lang never discusses this problem and does not seem to see that "human universals" are one of the means by which—for example, in some types of critical discourse—the significance of the Holocaust can be attacked and a new "Jewish problem" constituted.

This tendency is more specifically characteristic of radical leftist discourses. It seems that radical leftist social and political critics not only have recourse to the Holocaust as an archetype, metaphor, or analogy but also are equally bothered by its "Jewishness," which they interpret as monopolistic and exclusionary, while they link the existence and persistence of Israel to what they call an instrumentalized victimhood. This alleged monopoly of victimhood is often interpreted as an obstacle to social and political criticism.

A telling characterization of this obstacle and its possible solution was advanced by the philosopher Bernard Ogilvie.[32] Ogilvie asserts that, on the one hand, there is "an exclusive or exclusionary uniqueness, which makes this event a unique event in the sense that it is not comparable to any other, therefore cannot be put on the same level as any other," to which he contrasts "an encompassing or exemplary uniqueness, which, on the contrary, would look at this event as a paradigmatic scheme of understanding and explanation, not only of past, but also of present and recent events."[33] This paradox of uniqueness is similar to the one formulated by Alexander; however, it is not disguised in a neutral cultural or sociological framework but appears as something thoroughly political, and even as a political task to be achieved. Politics here means a choice between the two meanings of uniqueness, which resolves the paradox itself and establishes the preconditions of critique. The first sense of uniqueness points to the "symbolic violence" thesis: anybody stating the incomparable nature of the Holocaust is excluding all other suffering. Those who are believed to have chosen the first sense are often accused of promoting the cultural hegemony of Jews, asserting the unsurpassability of the Holocaust. (These accusations are exemplified by the discourse on the "Holocaust industry," the "Jewish lobby," and so on.) Ogilvie's second sense of uniqueness, which he takes as the only acceptable one, clearly deconstructs the notion itself by replacing it with analogical thinking, resulting in a kind of revisionist view, for he does not say what *kinds* of events could be subjected to such comparison. But this may be the price to be paid for the ability to grasp and criticize contemporary phenomena, which he is certainly willing to pay.

Universalization: Depriving the Holocaust of Its Jewishness

In addition to the combat against so-called uniqueness and alleged monopolization is still another obstacle encountered by leftist critics: the Jewishness of the Holocaust. Sometimes, when the denial of uniqueness is thought through to its logical conclusion, it necessarily leads to the "de-Judaization" of the event. The fact that it happened to the Jews is conceived as an obstacle to true politics on the left, and it should therefore be established that Nazis' designation of Jews as their victims was arbitrary and/or unimportant. Humanity was targeted through the Jews, an arbitrarily designated group. This is implied, for example, in the works of the communist writer Robert Antelme, written right after the war. Antelme disregards the fact that the camps were

mainly destined for Jews and that other prisoners (such as Antelme himself) were not treated alike.[34] He concentrates only
on what actually happened in the camps, which he interpreted
as an extreme form of exploitation. The deportee, the pauper,
and the proletarian have essentially the same lot. The camp thus
manifests a new and universalizable morality, which points to the
possible disappearance of man's exploitation by man—because
there is no genuine difference between the relations of exploit-
ative oppression in the camps and the relations of exploitation under capitalism.[35] From then on, all relations of exploitation could
be perceived through the analogy of the camp, which constitutes
the truth we could not see before.

The philosopher Alain Badiou explicitly advocates the notion
that the Nazis' designation of the Jews as their victims was an
arbitrary act. Eric Marty has written a devastating critique of
the violent pamphlet in which Badiou denounces the use of the
word *Jewish*.[36] According to Badiou, the exceptionality to which
Jews pretend and the way the Nazis thought about the Jews are
two sides of the same coin. This view implies that antisemitism
and the Holocaust are the logical outcome of the exceptionality
implied by the descriptor *Jewish*; the Nazis only pursued it to its
logical conclusion. Therefore, in the name of universality, the
word *Jewish* should be banned and the particularistic community
dispersed.

Thus, compassion for victims of the Holocaust should not be
expressed as compassion toward Jews. Badiou calls on Jews to
forget the Holocaust. The memory of the Holocaust also has to
be effaced to prevent its symbolic usage by Israel to exploit and
oppress the Palestinians. Badiou creates a symbolic inversion:
Israelis are the "new Aryans," he writes, whereas Palestinians are
the real Jews, insofar as they are designated as a particular group
to be oppressed and killed. So not only is the Jewish self-definition
as particularistic homologous to the Nazi concept of the Jew,
but also the Jewish signifier is genuinely Nazi, says Badiou, for it

establishes a right to superiority, furthered by the memory of the Holocaust.[37] In this way, Badiou creates a link between Nazism and Zionism.

It is Alain Brossat who formulated the leftist arguments against the uniqueness-universality thesis in the most clear-cut manner, which logically led him to the de-Judaization of the Holocaust.[38] His book anticipates all the arguments later advanced by Badiou.[39] Brossat is also a forerunner of Agamben in certain respects, writing on the *Muselmann* and the problem of witnessing in the camps. According to Brossat, as a result of assimilation in the era of Enlightenment (he prefers to call it the emergence of the unified demos), there ceased to be any homogeneous group that we could call Jewry. In fact, he says, this group was reinvented by the Nazis on racial grounds: "If there is a group the specificity of which can be established only by its being marked by its persecutor, it is clearly the Jews. Today, to define Jewish specificity amounts, in the first place, to the re-actualization of the Final solution: the Jews are the people who were marked by the Nazis as Jews in order to exterminate them."[40]

For Brossat, if Jews share a distinctive trait, it is their fluid character, the impossibility of attributing definite qualities to them. Therefore, if one thinks of the Holocaust as a systematic genocide against a particular people, then one reintroduces Nazi distinctions into one's analysis. Brossat thinks that the Nazis' designation of the Jews as their victims was arbitrary in the sense that the Nazis invented the notion of the Jewish people as a race. Also, Brossat continues, it is on this basis that the state of Israel was founded. Brossat is tacitly proposing to de-Judaize the Holocaust. He thinks that the assertion of its Jewish nature and the thesis of its uniqueness rid it of its universality, which should pertain to humanity as such: in the camps, "man, deprived of all human condition and quality, became visible as never before—as man, as human." The camps, as spaces of violence, brutality, and profanation, revealed "the indivisible nature of the human species."[41]

According to Brossat, we cannot talk about universality if the Holocaust is considered a Jewish affair; furthermore, Jewishness is not even a real property, an actually existing particularity of the people designated as such, but rather a Nazi construction.

Brossat contends that genocide was preceded by "democide"— the exclusion of the Jews from the demos, of which they had become part in the period of the Enlightenment. Brossat therefore suggests that now, in our epoch, talking about Jews as a people reiterates the Nazis' anti-Enlightenment gesture of democide by hypothesizing a "retribalized" people. In turn, this hypothesized "ethnos" comes to its full-fledged realization in the state of Israel, which, following this logic, was established on the same false, politically and ethically objectionable premises. Moreover, if the Holocaust is taken as a paradigm for genocide, then the ethnic perspective will always dominate our understanding of atrocities, regardless of the real nature of the conflict in question. Finally, the uniqueness thesis hinders genuine political action in the present, for all other atrocities and mass murders are downgraded in light of the Holocaust. Brossat thinks that this is also true for past conquests, killings, and wars, and especially for those contemporary with the Holocaust. According to him, building the United States Holocaust Memorial Museum in Washington, DC, was only made possible by a triple forgetting: of the extermination of the Indians, slavery, and the catastrophe of Hiroshima.

Problems with Reductive Universalization

Leftist critics such as Brossat, Ogilvie, and Badiou often present the thesis of uniqueness as a quasi-religious or metaphysical sanctification, an unhistorical view, or as something that prevents us from reflecting on the "complexity" of the Holocaust. This methodological argument is meant to underpin their ethical-political contention about exclusiveness and forgetfulness with respect to present-day genocides and other human catastrophes. However, it turns out that this accusation of sanctification is valid only for some approaches and is not currently a widespread view.[42] More-over, this accusation can easily be overturned, in that there are leftist approaches that generalize and universalize some aspects of the Holocaust in a reductive manner, thereby constructing a kind of metaphysics in which they resemble certain Christian interpretations. As we saw in Brossat, for example, this reductive universalization posits that the Holocaust simply happened to humankind, to indeterminate humans, to everybody.

In many Christian—but also leftist—interpretations of the Holocaust, the common element is that the tragic event is un-derstood only through one of its aspects—for example, human suffering. In turn, this aspect takes on an enlarged and universal meaning.[43] First, the Holocaust is deprived of its concreteness and reduced to a single aspect that is considered to be its univer-sal essence. Second, this essentialized aspect is taken to express the whole event as such, which becomes just one case among many where this essence is present. Third, there is the redemptive moment, which imparts an enhanced knowledge of the human condition as generally understood. For example, the communist writer Robert Antelme views this essentialized aspect as a gen-eral scheme of oppression, the conflict between the "rich" and the "poor," a notion accompanied by the supposition that the camps could be defined principally as completely decontextual-ized places of "dehumanization." This perspective relegates to the background the fact that only certain groups of people were de-ported to the camps.[44] In this manner, the camps can be likened to a capitalist enterprise. Both the Holocaust and exploitation are instances of this higher essence—namely, the power relation-ships between the strong and the weak. So the camps constitute a great opportunity to understand the situation of the exploited and the poor; and with exploitation and domination fully made explicit, we can start to get rid of it in all its forms.

As a consequence of such methods of interpretation, the event of the Holocaust becomes universalized, but also relativized. It is relativized because its supposedly universal essence allows it to be compared with other events in which this essence also inheres. And while the Holocaust, becoming an abstract notion, is universalized, the concrete event itself is hidden from view. The diagnosis of contemporary phenomena to be compared to the camps is already supposed to be known, and the analogy with the Holocaust is used only to reinforce its critical evaluation as a form of external criticism. Therefore, the meaning of the Holocaust is not obtained through careful analysis of the event itself; it is instead identified with other, seemingly similar events by means of arbitrary analogies. It is this purportedly universal essence, which emerges from an extremely impoverished concept of the event, that is extended or merged into other events that seem to comprise this same essence. The reduction of the Holocaust to its "universal essence" makes it possible to incorporate it into the history of human domination as a mere episode of oppression, suffering, and exploitation—thus depriving it of its concreteness, which could attest to its exceptionality (or at least to its "unprecedented" nature).

In opposition to these approaches, it is desirable to preserve the contrast between universalizing and concrete interpretations, which attribute two different types of meanings to the concept of universal. It is not about preserving the uniqueness of the event at all costs (and not even in the weak sense); there is no such general rule that could regulate all historical or philosophical accounts in the present, and especially not in the future. But political instrumentalization should still be highlighted along with its motives, and it is important to point out flawed interpretations of the concept of universal. The reason for these fallacies is to be found in the ambiguous use of this term, for it can be interpreted as part of two distinct dichotomies. In the first dichotomy, the word *universal* appears as the contrary of the particular: a universal scandal, where universality pertains to its nonparticular nature in the ethical sense. In the second dichotomy, it is the contrary of the concrete—that is, of the particular in the historical sense. When the universal is treated as the contrary of the concrete, there is no knowledge or understanding to be gained from the Holocaust; it is not treated as a paradigm for evaluating similar events but (by giving up all historical exactitude) is simply instrumentalized by being compared with other types of genocides or extreme human conditions, whether capitalist exploitation or the situations of refugees, the homeless, or detainees at Guantanamo Bay.

In fact, the approach that uses concreteness in the sense defined above does not refute the universality of the event in the ethical sense; rather, concreteness is the precondition of its universality. In turn, reductive universalization understands universality as generality in a pseudo-empirical sense, thereby shunning the concreteness of the Holocaust and reducing its significance to a hypothesized essence. Denying its nature as a universal scandal, then engaging in reductive universalization and the ensuing comparisons with other events constitute two parallel procedures in combating the significance of the Holocaust. Those who argue against these procedures run the risk of being stigmatized as having the intention to sanctify it. However, this accusation cannot be maintained as long as one maintains the distinction between the two previous dichotomies and opts for concreteness, without positively asserting the uniqueness of the event.

METAPHORIZATION

Giorgio Agamben offers a more abstract version of Robert Antelme's approach, but in a biopolitical rather than Marxist idiom. For the radical left, from Robert Antelme on, the concentration/death/extermination camp has been the fulfilment of a historical process, whereby exploitation and oppression reach their limits. It is a kind of eschatology, where the biggest catastrophe means redemption, for we have gained an enhanced consciousness and knowledge of ourselves. According to Agamben, with the Holocaust (though he refers to it only as "the camps"), and with the figure of the Muselmann in the "camps," it becomes manifest that politics has always been biopolitics fabricating "bare life." To pursue his political agenda, Agamben avoids what he takes as the usual understanding of the camps, because it is not really the camps themselves that he intends to discuss but rather the "camp" as the underlying structure of modernity and modern politics: "Instead of deducing the definition of the camp from the events that took place there, we will ask: What is a camp, what is its juridicopolitical structure, that such events could take place there? This will lead us to regard the camp not as a historical fact and an anomaly belonging to the past (even if still verifiable) but in some way as the hidden matrix and nomos of the political space in which we are still living."[45] From this starting point, he proceeds to decipher the metamorphoses of the camp in the postwar period, which constantly produce depoliticized "bare life," including refugees, detainees at Guantanamo Bay, the global poor of the third world, and many other figures. Beyond a doubt, "it is unlikely that these different phenomena are all instances of the same thing—'bare life'—and thus analyzable in terms of the same biopolitical paradigm."[46] But they relate to each other in a metaphorical way—Agamben would rather say that they have the same underlying structure or form.

Agamben's use of the concept of the camp suffers from multiple ambiguities. First, referring to the Holocaust, he asserts that "the camp is merely the place in which the most absolute *conditio inhumana* that has ever existed on earth was realized: this is what counts in the last analysis, for the victims as for those who come after."[47] However, for Agamben, this most extreme inhuman condition also constitutes an obstacle to his analysis. For this is the reason its "specific juridico-political structure" has never been examined: it "so exceeds the juridical concept of crime."[48] Thus, he proceeds to the hitherto lacking juridical-structural analysis; however, he always refers back to the Holocaust as his main example. This leads him to a double result: first, he is able to give a merely formal and juridical definition of the camp in its abstract and unhistorical sense, which makes it possible to subsume under this same heading various phenomena that he will take as its different realizations Second, he also intends to describe the allegedly historical-empirical development of the phenomenon "camp." In the first case, the camp is simply a space where the legal order has been suspended and where authorities can act as they wish: "The camp—as the pure, absolute, and impassable biopolitical space (insofar as it is founded solely on the state of exception)—will appear as the hidden paradigm of the political space of modernity, whose metamorphoses and disguises we will have to learn to recognize."[49]

Therefore, as Agamben states explicitly, the definition of the camp is independent of the actual events taking place in it, of the nature of the crimes committed, or of the type of infringement of human rights. Only the structure counts. The refugee camps for Albanians in Bari; the Vélodrome d'Hiver, where Jews were grouped together in German-occupied Paris in 1942; and the concentration camps opened during the Weimar Republic for communists and World War I refugees all constitute cases to be included under the heading of the camp. Here, Agamben seems to offer a formal definition of this concept. However, his criticism becomes effective due to the force of the content we associate with the concept of the camp—namely, in implicit comparison with the *non plus ultra* of the camps: Auschwitz. The Holocaust not only is relativized and relegated to the background but also is covertly instrumentalized to reinforce his critique of contemporary society.

However, simultaneously (as the second usage of the "camp"), Agamben also intends to keep the empirical-historical framework. He strives to demonstrate that the camps in the Nazi period were created as a consequence of the banalization of the "state of exception"—that is, the progressive introduction of special clauses and the suspension of basic human and political rights initiated by Prussian legislators and later pursued by the Weimar Republic. He interprets this phenomenon as an organic process, leading to the Nuremberg laws and finally to the camps.

As his chapter ("The Camp as the 'Nomos' of the Modern") unfolds, these two aspects are linked. In fact, the juridical form has been spread by a historical process; Agamben even states the stereotypical and false view (echoing the statements of Nazi dignitaries) that there was no political decision made about the "final solution." In Agamben's interpretation, the Holocaust came about as a result of an organic development, during which "states of exception" became more and more pronounced in European legal systems, which led to the phenomenon of the camp: "Insofar as its inhabitants were stripped of every political status and wholly reduced to bare life, the camp was also the most absolute biopolitical space ever to have been realized, in which power confronts nothing but pure life, without any mediation."[50]

Was this development predetermined? We might suspect that it was, because what we have here is political metaphysics. Agamben asserts that the state of exception has always been the fundamental characteristic of sovereign power—not merely a possibility to which it has always had recourse but its real (if hidden) basis. In this respect, the Holocaust is part of a historical continuity; it is not something fundamentally new, for its preconditions have always been there. What is new is that now we can know that this has always been the case. The Holocaust reveals the fundamental structure of sovereign power by making it explicit: "Insofar as the state of exception is 'willed,' it inaugurates a new juridico-political paradigm in which the norm becomes indistinguishable from the exception.... The sovereign no longer limits himself, as he did in the spirit of the Weimar constitution, to deciding on the exception on the basis of recognizing a given factual situation (danger to public safety): laying bare the inner structure of the ban that characterizes his power, he now de facto produces the situation as a consequence of his decision on the exception."[51] If this is the case, it is more about epistemology than history; uniqueness not only disappears, but also its contrary is positively asserted, thereby enhancing our knowledge of the human condition as it is politically understood. The potential for a Holocaust was always present, but nobody was aware of it. Furthermore, no one is aware of it even now, despite the fact that the camps are everywhere and that the period we live in is a permanent state of exception. It is the ultimate proof of the state-of-exception theory.

This diagnosis could have been arrived at only by privileging the juridical-structural analysis to which historical description is subjected. By the same token, the Holocaust is only one example of the production of bare life, even if it constitutes its apex ("Auschwitz is precisely the place where the state of exception coincides with the rule and the extreme situation becomes the paradigm of daily life"); the production of bare life in its various forms is universal.[52]

This contradictory and dubious feature of Agamben's critique can also be formulated in a different manner: the Holocaust is an individual example of the camp, the production of bare life, which is universal. However, at the same time, it constitutes the nomos of the camp because it is an individual example of the rule but also the rule itself, for this latter is interpreted in the light of this extreme case. This clearly shows how Agamben has recourse to both relativization and universalization, always choosing the one that is the most advantageous for his theory. The Holocaust is relative when other phenomena are to be interpreted with the help of the concept of the camp, and it is universal, the "nomos of modernity," when his criticism needs to be dramatized and strengthened.

Explanations from Social Science

Besides combating the uniqueness thesis and the alleged Jewish monopoly on suffering, acknowledging the suffering of other excluded groups requires another rhetorical move that is more subtle, because it is not plainly metaphorical but rather conceptual. As has been established by Danny Trom, the characteristic type of analysis that radical social critics and critical sociologists feed on is best described as "intimism," the opposite of exoticism. Exoticism, a polemical term well known from postcolonial criticism, refers to essentialist interpretations of culture and the tendency to construct them as distant and utterly different. Intimism, on the other hand, is the opposite fallacy—a kind of sociologism that intends to get rid of all cultural and especially political factors. We constantly hear this kind of explanation of contemporary Islamist terrorism, but it has always been present in Holocaust scholarship.

Intimists intend to bring the issues in question closer to the present, as if they could just as well appear even now. In Trom's interpretation, this approach can be best characterized by a "banality of evil" type of explanation, in the wake of Hannah Arendt (or rather, Arendt's reception), the social psychologist Stanley Milgram, and the historian Christopher Browning. Christopher Browning tries to explain the motives of the perpetrators of Nazi mass murder, who were, in most cases, according to him, "ordinary men." Studying the uniquely ample documentation on Reserve Police Battalion 101, he establishes that its members acted neither because of heavy constraint (it would have been possible for them to opt out, as a few of them actually did) nor due to heavy ideological indoctrination or antisemitism. Therefore, these men's actions were simply the result of interpersonal social mechanisms such as conformity (they did not want to be considered weak or cowardly by their peers) and solidarity between perpetrators (they had to take part in the "dirty work" and not leave it to their comrades).[53] The political and ethical meaning of the situation is completely obliterated to localize the source of the crimes elsewhere—namely, in the encounter between a postulated universal human nature and a specific (but not sufficiently qualified) context. Such analyses thus become purely situational, and the actors are deprived of political and moral intentions, judged as unimportant for the matter (whereas, in reality, they are not sufficiently taken into account).

These kinds of approaches, to which critical sociology often turns, suggest that anything could be possible in our epoch as well, as if politics were something exterior, just an addition to the social dynamics that influence people's behavior. The consequence drawn from this analysis is that all humans are capable of committing the worst atrocities, depending only on the context they find themselves in—by mindless law-abiding behavior, obeying authority, solidarity among peers, and so on.

These interpretations rid the actors of their historical and especially political particularities; therefore, they are instrumental in upholding the agenda of radical social criticism. To provide a universal and unbounded explanation of human suffering and evil and to make social criticism function, the Holocaust needs to be reinterpreted and depoliticized. For if Nazi violence is not exceptional, and the Nazis, generally speaking, are not fundamentally different from us, then Nazism is always potentially present in the form of the banality of evil.[54] Every situation in which domination, power, authority, and exploitation play a role should be comparable to it, just as the Jewish victims of the Holocaust should not be regarded as fundamentally different from any other victims. But this is not all. The question of Browning's book was this: How were great numbers of ordinary men induced to participate in evil? In leftist criticism of contemporary society, the mechanism of involvement is often evoked to explain how pauperization, misery, and exclusion are organized. We live in a "gray zone" where the question of responsibility cannot be posed, for everybody is at the same time perpetrator and victim: "Evil is distributed in an infinite number of insignificant actions."[55] In this frame, laying off masses of employees under neoliberalism is conceptually parallel to mass killings under Nazism. (The career of Primo Levi's gray zone in the radical left would be worth a separate study.)

There are two fundamental reasons that leftist social and political theories combat the uniqueness thesis of the Holocaust, which they encounter in the form of the "Jewish problem". First, they take the event of the Holocaust (understood as unique in the strong sense) as something that denies the suffering of other peoples or groups, past or present, and that, thereby, also weakens the possibility of criticism and political action. Second, they fear that this event reinforces "Jewish exceptionality" (and, as a corollary, legitimizes Israel's existence), which they traditionally oppose in the name of "universalism" and "universal humanity." What are the solutions adopted by these theories? The denial of the uniqueness thesis is sometimes realized by a theoretical or empirical kind of refutation, by having recourse to reductive universalization. This procedure is an essentialist enterprise, realized in the form of political metaphysics or humanistic social science. The Holocaust is reduced to its supposedly universalistic features, which can be found in other cases of oppression or suffering. It becomes just one case of the same overarching kind, where victims suffer essentially the same lot. This tendency is epitomized by the recourse to analogies and metaphors, which cannot be viewed as simply a cultural phenomenon without considering its political aspects. But just as all kinds of victims can be compared to or identified with the Jewish victims of the Holocaust, perpetrators can be universalized in the same reductive manner. In this framework, the potentiality of committing the most monstrous crimes is "ordinary"—that is, inherently human. This amounts to postulating that Nazi perpetrators are far from being unique, thereby making it possible to compare them to others in the present for the sake of criticism.

Combating the putative uniqueness of the Holocaust often also takes the form of instrumentalization. All kinds of analogies (such as the capitalist firm or factory) and metaphors (such as the "camp") can be found in the interpretation of social and political phenomena. Therefore, the purpose is not simply the denial of the significance of the Holocaust and the "rehabilitation" of other victims in human history; for in the meantime this very significance is used to reinforce the criticism of contemporary society. In other words, a double objective is reached: Jewish suffering is downgraded, while criticism is bolstered.

Another strategy of the "democratization" of the Holocaust that is encountered in critical philosophies is the denial of its Jewishness. By declaring the arbitrariness of the designation, the event will be outright extended to "all humanity." The word *Jewish* as a particularistic designator will be considered homologous to the Nazi designation, or even identical with it. The "monopolization" of suffering, which is established on such a dubious basis, becomes all the more unjust and objectionable. Therefore, the scope of the Holocaust should be understood as universal from the beginning, before any further extension to other cases of suffering, simply because it has already happened (or at least this should be assumed) to each and every one. In turn, this extension is facilitated by this universal understanding, which avoids the above-mentioned "ethnic" and particularistic viewpoint considered as genuinely Nazi. An evident consequence of this view is the theoretical, a priori Nazification of Israel; another one is the imperative of the annihilation of Jewish memory.

What should be retained from this discussion is that many times social and political criticism on the left—in a more or less mediated manner—is almost necessarily directed against the memory of the Holocaust, and thus also against its victims. Many of the critiques formulated on the radical left encounter the "Jewish problem," for it arises inside their theories due to reasons that are not only political but also theoretical. This would also entail that theory and methodology—that is, critical thought and the framework in which it is elaborated—are linked to a highly dubious and potentially dangerous issue—namely, the Jewish problem and its undertones of violence toward Jews.

If this is the case then, consequently, taking a hostile position with regard to the memory of the Holocaust and its Jewishness and—as a more indirect consequence—also to Israel is not only dependent on some deeply rooted political vision or ideological package, as one might have thought, but also an equally well-established function in theory. For this reason, this position is also the logical extension of the Jewish problem encountered on the path to criticism. If this is true, one should look for alternative critical theories in which the Holocaust does not emerge as an obstacle to interpretation and criticism and for which a formulation of the Jewish problem does not constitute a condition of possibility. Therefore, finding this type of criticism presupposes a theoretical-epistemological reflection besides the political one.

NOTES

1. Pierre-André Taguieff, *Prêcheurs de haine. Traversée de la nouvelle judéophobie planétaire* (Paris: Mille et une Nuits, 2004).

2. Jean-Claude Milner, *Les penchants criminels de l'Europe démocratique* (Paris: Verdier, 2003), 128.

3. Rusi Jaspal, *Antisemitism and Anti-Zionism: Representation, Cognition and Everyday Talk* (Farnham, UK: Ashgate, 2014), 3.

4. Taguieff, *Prêcheurs de haine*; Alain Finkielkraut, *Au nom de l'Autre* (Paris: Gallimard, 2002).

5. For Jankélévitch's explanation, see "Pardonner?," in *L'Imprescriptible* (Paris: Seuil 1986), 5–26.

6. Eric Marty, *Bref séjour à Jérusalem* (Paris: Gallimard, 2003); Eric Marty, *Une querelle avec Alain Badiou, philosophe* (Paris: Gallimard, 2007); for a selection of his articles in English, see Eric Marty, *Radical French Thought and the Return of the Jewish Question* (Bloomington: Indiana University Press, 2015); Danny Trom, *La promesse et l'obstacle: La gauche radicale et le problème juif* (Paris: Cerf, 2007); Milner, *Les penchants criminels*.

7. Trom, *La promesse et l'obstacle*.

8. Milner, *Les penchants criminels*, 9–16.

9. Jean-Paul Sartre, *Anti-Semite and Jew* (1944; repr. New York: Schocken Books, 1976).

10. Marty, *Radical French Thought and the Return of the Jewish Question*.

11. Jean-Michel Chaumont, *La concurrence des victimes: Génocide, identité, reconnaissance* (Paris: Découverte, 1997), 180.

12. Trom, *La promesse et l'obstacle*, 87.

13. Alain Brossat, *L'épreuve du désastre: Le XXème siècle et les camps* (Paris: Albin Michel, 1996).

14. Norman Finkelstein, *The Holocaust Industry* (New York: Verso, 2000).

15. See Avishai Margalit and Gabriel Motzkin, "The Uniqueness of the Holocaust," *Philosophy and Public Affairs* 25, no. 1 (1996): 65–83.

16. Yehuda Bauer, "Holocaust and Genocide Today," in *A Companion to World War II*, ed. Thomas W. Zeiler and Daniel M. DuBois, vol. 1–2 (Oxford: Blackwell, 2012), see especially page 697.

17. See Bernard Ogilvie, "Comparer l'incomparable," *Multitudes* 7 (December 2001) 130–66.; Finkelstein, *Holocaust Industry*; Brossat, *L'épreuve du désastre*.

18. Trom, *La promesse et l'obstacle*, 88–89.

19. For a study of the metaphorization of the Holocaust in the realm of popular culture, see Alvin Rosenfeld, *The End of the Holocaust* (Bloomington: Indiana University Press, 2011). For a discussion of this topic in history writing, see Wulf Kantsteiner, "The Rise and Fall of Metaphor: German Historians and the Uniqueness of the Holocaust," in *Is the Holocaust Unique? Perspectives on Comparative Genocide*, ed. Alan S. Rosenbaum (Boulder, CO: Westview, 2001). For a discussion of Holocaust metaphorization in politics, see Daniel Levy and Natal Sznajder, *Erinnerung im globalen Zeitalter: Der Holocaust* (Frankfurt: Suhrkamp, 2001).

20. For a discussion of cultural factors, see Jeffrey C. Alexander, "On the Social Construction of Moral Universals: The 'Holocaust' from War Crime to Trauma Drama," *European Journal of Social Theory* 5, no. 1 (2002): 5–85; for a discussion of narrative constraints, see James E. Young, *Writing and Rewriting the Holocaust: Narrative and the Consequences of Interpretation* (Bloomington: Indiana University Press, 1988).

21. Alexander, "On the Social Construction."

22. See Alain Badiou, *St. Paul: The Foundation of Universalism* (Palo Alto, CA: Stanford University Press, 2003); Badiou, *Portées du mot "juif"* (Paris: Lignes, 2005); Marty, *Une querelle*.

23. Giorgio Agamben, *Homo Sacer 1: Sovereign Power and Bare Life* (Palo Alto, CA: Stanford University Press, 1998); Giorgio Agamben, *Remnants of Auschwitz: The Witness and the Archive* (Cambridge: Zone Books, 1999). For more on the camp metaphor, see Dominick LaCapra, "Approaching Limit Events: Siting Agamben," in *Witnessing the Disaster*, ed. M. Bernard-Donals and Richard Glejzer (Madison: University of Wisconsin Press, 2003), 262–304.

24. Alexander, "On the Social Construction," 31.

25. Alexander, "On the Social Construction," 60.

26. Alexander, "On the Social Construction," 51.

27. Berel Lang, *Post-Holocaust: Interpretation, Misinterpretation, and the Claims of History* (Bloomington: Indiana University Press, 2005).

28. Lang, *Post-Holocaust*, 102–3; 105.

29. Lang, *Post-Holocaust*, 106.

30. Lang, *Post-Holocaust*, 107.

31. Lang, *Post-Holocaust*, 108.

32. Ogilvie, *"Comparer l'incomparable."*

33. Ogilvie, *"Comparer l'incomparable,"* 134.

34. Robert Antelme, *The Human Race* (Evanston, IL: Marlboro, 1992); Robert Antelme, "Poor Man—Proletarian—Deportee," in *On Robert Antelme's Human Race, Essays and Commentary*, ed. Daniel Dobbels (Evanston, IL: Marlboro, 2003), 17–22.

35. Trom, *La promesse et l'obstacle*, 162.

36. Marty, *Une querelle avec Alain Badiou, philosophe*. In English, see "Alain Badiou: The Future of a Denial," in *Radical French Thought and the Return of the Jewish Question*, 53–79.

37. Badiou, *Portées*.

38. Brossat, *L'épreuve du désastre*.

39. Badiou, *Portées*.

40. Brossat, *L'épreuve du désastre*, 285.

41. Brossat, *L'épreuve du désastre*, 305.

42. Terrence Des Pres, "Holocaust Laughter," in *Writing and the Holocaust*, ed. Berel Lang (New York: Holmes and Meier, 1988), 216–33.; Berel Lang, *Act and Idea in the Nazi Genocide* (Chicago: University of Chicago Press, 1990).

43. See, e.g., Anna Fruzsina Kovai, "Holokauszt és üdvtörténet— Pilinszky problematikus emlékezete" [Holocaust and the History of Salvation—The Problematic Remembrance of Pilinszky], in *Esztétika— Etika—Politika*, ed. Megyer Gyöngyösi and Kata Inzsöl (Budapest: Eötvös Collégium, Magyar Műhely, 2013), 67–78.

44. For more on Antelme's casting of the conflict between rich and poor, see Antelme, "Poor Man"; for more on decontextualized dehumanization, see Antelme, *The Human Race*.

45. Agamben, *Homo Sacer*, 166.

46. James Gordon Finlayson, "'Bare Life' and Politics in Agamben's Reading of Aristotle," *Review of Politics* 72, no. 1 (Winter 2010): 120.

47. Agamben, *Homo Sacer*, 166.

48. Agamben, *Homo Sacer*, 166.

49. Agamben, *Homo Sacer*, 123.

50. Agamben, *Homo Sacer*, 170.

51. Agamben, *Homo Sacer*, 170.

52. Agamben, *Remnants of Auschwitz*, 49.

53. Christopher Browning, *Ordinary Men: Reserve Police Battalion 101 and the Final Solution* (New York: HarperCollins, 1992).

54. For an exceptionally profound analysis of the moral aspects, see Trom, *La promesse et l'obstacle*.

55. Trom, *La promesse et l'obstacle*, 79.

BALÁZS BERKOVITS is a postdoctoral fellow at the Bucerius Institute, University of Haifa. Previously, he has been a research fellow at the Psychological Institute of the Hungarian Academy of Sciences; assistant professor in the Department of Philosophy at the University of Miskolc, Hungary; visiting scholar at Indiana University; and a postdoctoral fellow at École des Hautes Études en Sciences Sociales, Paris. He has published widely on topics related to the sociology of education, social theory, the epistemology of the social sciences, and social constructivism.

FOUR

New Challenges in Feminism

Intersectionality, Critical Theory, and Anti-Zionism

KARIN STÖGNER

IN RECENT YEARS a peculiar trend in certain strands of feminism has emerged on an international scale: the use of inter-sectionality to legitimize an anti-Zionist bias and the Boycott, Divestment, Sanctions (BDS) movement. It is noticeable, although by no means self-evident, that a growing number of feminists and scholars in women's studies are increasingly backing BDS and thus delegitimizing Israel.[1]

In part, they base such views on intersectionality, which is one of the most important analytical concepts of the new left. Inter-sectionality focuses on the multidimensionality of oppression in modern societies and analyzes the interrelationship of race/ ethnicity, gender/sexuality, and class as central categories of dis-crimination and social inequality. Thus, it is very much about the struggle to rearticulate categories that had been ideologically separate but are connected in reality.

Intersectionality, however, is more than an analytical concept that helps capture social reality in its complexity; it is also a polit-ical program. This becomes evident, for example, in the writings and activities of Angela Davis, an iconic figure of the civil rights movement and of Black feminism. She criticizes the tension between the universal and the particular and stresses that, disguised as the universal, white male supremacy triumphs over minorities that are ethnically defined and connoted as nonmale. However, Davis's notion of intersectionality strikingly excludes Jews. They are not mentioned as a minority with special interests that need to be protected and promoted; rather, they are regarded implicitly, as representatives of the very white supremacy that is under vehement critique. Thus, they are denied the right of particularity. Accordingly, Zionism is also not viewed as a national liberation movement with a particular historical background but solely as one of the last bastions of imperialism and colonialism. Thereby, a thorough delegitimization of Israel takes place. The strategies applied for this end also include the accusation of pinkwashing, meaning that the pro-gay image that Israel affirms and the legal rights for LGBTQ people in Israel are to be regarded as mere hypocrisy and cynicism—a liberal mask that aims at ideologically covering a thoroughly racist, even an apartheid-like, system.[2]

I address these issues and analyze them against the background of critical theory and ask whether intersectionality as a methodology can be rescued on behalf of a critical feminism that does not exclude the Jews and that does not contain an anti-Zionist bias. I will first discuss different traditions of intersectionality. Second, I will refer to the tension of the universal and the particular that intersectionality tackles and the problem that arises from this preoccupation—namely, that the universal interest frequently dissolves into various special interests. As a consequence, the idea of a common goal gets lost, leaving a void that is likely to be filled by the invention of a common enemy—in this case, Israel. Third, drawing on feminism, intersectionality, and critical theory, I will explicate this tendency by referring to speeches by and interviews with Angela Davis, in which she thoroughly delegitimizes Israel.

WHAT IS INTERSECTIONALITY?
DIFFERENT TRADITIONS

The concept of intersectionality is rooted theoretically and practically in black feminism and in feminism of color.[3] Of central importance is a critical permeation of categories along which modern societies are structured: ethnicity/nation, gender/sexuality, and class. These categories mirror social cleavages from which no one can escape—they are structurally predetermined by capitalism, the principle of the modern nation-state, and patriarchy.[4] These social categories ethnicity/nation, gender/sexuality, and class should be viewed as a coordinate system—an institutionalized structure of social positioning that mirrors actual relations of power and domination. Intersectionality seeks to permeate this multidimensional structure of domination and subordination by asking the "other" question. When the question is about racism, one needs to ask about the gender dimension; when it is about gender relations, one needs to ask about the role of the class dimension; and so on.[5] Intersectionality is about reconstructing and understanding the dialectical movement that takes place within society itself. Thus, it should not be seen as merely a terminological invention.

Intersectionality is meant to focus on the relationship of different social antagonisms that are not isomorphic but that reveal different accesses to social reality, that is, different forms of experiencing society. Hence, intersectionality is applied dialectics and not entirely apart from critical theory, not only because Angela Davis, a pioneer in conceptualizing intersectionality, identifies herself as a critical theorist. Yet, in contrast to her approach, critical theory does not exclude antisemitism, but in fact views antisemitism as a key to understanding society, similar to how it views gender relations or the social relationship to nature and class relations.

Intersectionality starts from heteromorphic conflicts and views them in a totality as different problem situations, none of which are outside the capitalist mode of (re)production but are intrinsic parts of it. Antisemitism, racism, sexism, nationalism, ethnocentrism, homophobia, and transphobia are thus different but connected ideologies. Max Horkheimer and Theodor W. Adorno, in *The Authoritarian Personality*, call this wider ideological framework the antidemocratic ideological syndrome. In short, this is what intersectionality, in the tradition of critical theory, may also be about. This implies a shift in perspective. Whereas intersectionality commonly directs its attention to experiences of multiple forms of exclusion and discrimination, critical theory centrally focuses on resentments and ideologies, on how they originate in society, and on how individuals and groups, in order to exclude and discriminate against others, adopt them.

The fact that antisemitism is not viewed outside these constellations illustrates clearly the specificity of intersectionality as developed particularly in the German-speaking countries beginning in the late 1980s. Intersectionality was introduced by critical feminists who questioned and challenged the idea of a monolithic notion of gender with regard to National Socialism. One strongly held myth that persisted far into the 1980s was that women as a gender group were victims of National Socialism since the regime was regarded as the epitome of patriarchy. Sometimes this view had an antisemitic dimension, for patriarchy was perceived as something the Jews had brought on humanity. In the end, this ideology was used as a device of victim-perpetrator reversal that served the function of working off guilt; by implication, the Jews themselves were viewed as culprits of National Socialism.[6]

Critical feminist historians and sociologists challenged this narrative by asking the "other" question and thus deconstructed the unitary category of woman. They asked explicitly what non-Jewish German women actually did during National Socialism, what their scope of action was, what possibilities of resistance they had, and in what various ways they not only cooperated with the Nazi regime but even achieved pivotal positions.[7] To some degree, the integration of non-Jewish German women into the Nazi regime even served as their "emancipation" from traditional female gender roles. Jewish women or Roma women were murdered because of their ethnicity and not because they were women. But their femininity was instrumentalized in Nazi propaganda. Himmler said that Jewish women in particular were to be eliminated because they were the natural source of a constant renewal of the "Jewish race."[8] Thus, antisemitism is permeated here by sexist moments.[9]

This background illustrates the existence of a tradition of intersectional thought that does not exclude Jews but rather takes the murderous history of European antisemitism and its climax, the Shoah, as a starting point of critical reflection on the category of gender.[10] Hence, the concept of intersectionality does not lead quasi-automatically to a delegitimization of Israel. To the contrary, it is also a tool for criticizing a particular instrumentalization of gender for working off guilt with regard to National Socialism.[11]

In the United States, however, intersectionality followed a different course. The concept was developed during the civil rights movement of the 1960s. Black feminists and feminists of color pointed to the fact that their members faced discrimination based on more than gender or race alone. Their experiences always included a mediation of at least both these dimensions. In reality, it was not possible to distinguish sharply between them, because one was embedded within the other. Individual identities and social positioning were viewed as a permeation and struggle of different special interests. But strikingly, in the further development of the concept, not all interests were incorporated into the realm of special interests. Jewish interests in particular were excluded, with specific consequences for the acknowledgment of global antisemitism and its genocidal history. This idea is described by Rokhl Kafrissen: "Yet, over and over, Jews and Jewish oppression get left out of that intersectional analysis. Jewishness is conflated with whiteness, with the bizarre results of seeing the Holocaust described (and dismissed) in certain circles, as 'white on white' crime."[12] And Cary Nelson notes, "The concept has begun both to evolve and to mutate. People are now calling on intersectionality to do kinds of political work it hadn't done before. Its most dramatic new incarnation has been in the component of the Black Lives Matter movement that seeks to link the African-American struggle for equality with the Israeli-Palestinian conflict and the experience of Palestinians in Gaza and the West Bank."[13]

The confused nature of intersectionality and the related distortions of the concept may be inherent in the concept itself. It was not intended to be merely an academic concept used to theorize an antagonistic society. Its very basis is a complicated relationship of theory and praxis. However, as Nelson markedly points out, "intersectionality has been transformed from a theory into a political slogan, into a rallying call."[14] It has also shifted focus from analyzing the intersection of different forms of oppression and different antagonisms within one society to the "far more speculative claim that injustices intersect even if they occur in different parts of the world in different contexts under different political systems. Then the intersection often occurs only in the mind of the beholder or in a political manifesto, and it begins to function like a conspiracy theory."[15]

This transformation of intersectionality is evident when Angela Davis writes about the "intersectionality of movements and struggles" and not of oppressions.[16] Davis offers a prominent example of the political use of intersectionality because she is a leading figure in the civil rights movement and the black women's movement as well as in academia. She is professor emerita at the University of California, Santa Cruz, who in the 1960s studied with Herbert Marcuse in San Diego and with Theodor Adorno and Max Horkheimer in Frankfurt and subsequently located her work in the tradition of critical theory. She was a leader of the

Communist Party USA with a close relationship to the Black
Panther Party. Davis is a feminist and civil rights and queer activist and campaigns against the prison industrial complex. She
developed ideas on intersectionality that she now instrumental-
izes in favor of a thorough delegitimization of Israel. Her pronounced anti-Zionism is evident in the fact that she is a member
of the notorious Russell Tribunal on Palestine, a gathering of
outspoken Israel haters who met in Cape Town in November 2011
to sit in judgment on Israel. This tribunal is not official and has
nothing in common with the Russell Tribunal on the Vietnam
War.[17] Davis has also supported BDS, both on campus and in the
broader political public, and she repeatedly confronts Israel with
the accusation of pinkwashing. She expresses these views with
reference to both intersectionality and critical theory. It is argu-
able whether she supports BDS because of or despite her theoretical background in critical theory and feminism. Answering this
question requires tackling a more basic problem: the relationship
between the universal and the particular that serves as a basis for
intersectionality as applied dialectics.

ISRAEL, INTERSECTIONALITY, AND
THE RELATIONSHIP OF THE UNIVERSAL
AND THE PARTICULAR

Critical theorists such as Max Horkheimer, Theodor Adorno,
and Herbert Marcuse (with whom Angela Davis studied in the
1960s), while being critical of right-wing and nationalist politics
of Israel, have acknowledged not only the legitimacy but also
the necessity of Israel's existence as a sovereign Jewish state as
the only apt means to prevent a repetition of the Holocaust.[18] The
state of Israel is seen as the universal that is necessary to protect
the particular—in this case, the Jews worldwide.

In autumn 2015, Angela Davis gave a talk at the University of
Vienna titled "Life between Politics and Academia," in which

she took Herbert Marcuse's views on the dialectical relationship of past and present as the starting point of her reflections on the relationship of theory and praxis.[19] The dialectical relationship between past and present—the present is always informed by past hopes and promises but also by past terror and injustice, meaning that the present continues to reenact the past—is a cornerstone of critical theory. For Davis, this relationship serves as a rationale for expanding the concept of intersectionality to an "intersectionality of struggles." This enables her to draw a line from Ferguson to Palestine.

From the perspective of the older critical theory, however, the dialectics between past and present cannot be divided from National Socialism and the Shoah. It found its pivotal expression in Adorno's formulation of a new categorical imperative in *Negative Dialectics*: "A new categorical imperative has been imposed by Hitler upon unfree mankind: to arrange their thoughts and actions so that Auschwitz will not repeat itself, so that nothing similar will happen."[20]

Framed as categorical, the imperative commands all beings endowed with reason to inspect their actions and determine whether they are in accordance with the maxim that is valid universally and at all times, as long as conditions stay unchanged—that is, as long as mankind is not free. If the world system stays unchanged and thus global antisemitism persists, then having the state of Israel as a potential refuge for all Jews reduces the risk that something similar to Nazi violence against the Jews can happen. Thus, after the Holocaust, the existence of the state of Israel as a Jewish state is unconditional and self-evident. This is what Adorno's reformulation of the categorical imperative ultimately implies. Thus, Israel is a nation-state unlike any other.

In contrast to this imperative, Davis singles out Israel in a different way and focuses on it with a particular sharpness that she does not apply to other nation-states except for the United States. It seems that, along with the United States, Israel is the representation of all that is deplorable in the idea of the nation-state. In my interpretation of Davis's text, Israel, for its inauthenticity and artificiality, stands for the abstract state in opposition to the local Arab communities, which represent authenticity and rootedness.

But referring to the characteristics of modern antisemitism, Gerhard Scheit has convincingly pointed out that the state is per se an artificial construct. Antisemites project onto Israel what they do not want to recognize as an intrinsic feature of the state: its artificial character. Its artificiality, according to Thomas Hobbes, consists in the fact that the state is meant to monopolize power and violence. The principle of sovereignty, this artificiality that is a characteristic of any nation-state, is projected onto Israel (and the United States). Just as financial capital serves as a projection screen for all that is contested in capitalism, so, too, the nation-state of Israel serves as a projection screen for all that cannot fully be integrated into the notion of community and collectivity. Moreover, antisemites want the state to be authentic, not artificial. They identify with the state and idealize it as immediate and unmediated, a primal community (of religion, ethnicity, or nation). The abstract state shall be dissolved in the immediacy of the community.[21]

In this context, it is interesting to read Davis's positive account of communities and collectivities with special interests that will become more important than the individual. In a talk that she gave in December 2012 in a panel on "Queer Visions" at the World Social Forum: Free Palestine in Porto Alegre, Brazil, she mentioned that it would be "refreshing to be out of the USA where we don't always have to challenge the constant individualization that happens especially under the impact of neoliberal ideologies. We talk about collectivities and communities."[22] These are communities with special interests based on ethnicity, religion, tradition, and culture that according to Davis, should become more important vis-à-vis the individual. Otherwise, the individuality of the bourgeois individual exists only in the bourgeois nation-state.

Her criticism of the state is connected to a thorough criticism of individualism in neoliberal society. Although it is true that neoliberalism isolates and singularizes individuals and hands them over to the relentless mechanisms of capitalist competition, collectivity is not an alternative. Collectivization, which Davis suggests in opposition to neoliberal individualization, implies identification with the group one incidentally belongs to and thus involves surrendering any individual particularity for the sake of the collective. It is exactly by collective identification that individuals become the singularized entities driven by their careers or, on the corresponding opposite, the national comrades who swear off meaningless individuality.[23] The only solution is to strengthen the individual as an autonomous subject against the collective forces and against the mechanisms of capitalist competition and its compulsive logic of exploitation. Davis's critique of the individual is led astray because she seems to dismantle it altogether in collectivity instead of strengthening and emancipating it.

However, her critique of individualism and praise of collectivities is connected to a critique of universal concepts as manifestations of existing power relations. In her Vienna talk, she referred to this entanglement as the "tyranny of the universal." It is true that universal concepts such as the state, the individual, and the human are clandestinely ethnicized and gendered. "For most of our history the very category of the human has not embraced Black people or women," she stated. In this same talk in Vienna, she subsequently establishes a link between Ferguson and Palestine.[24] What she does not mention, however, is that Jews were also excluded from these categories for most of history. Like blacks and women, Jews also were not recognized when the powers that be spoke about humanity. So if today we hear that blacks, women, and Jews are also human, this long-standing exclusion is still present. Nevertheless, it is the wrong way to discard the universal concept of the human altogether and to dissolve it into a variety of particularities—namely, special interests. Only on the ground of the universal category that demands universality are the inalienable rights that are connected to the universal enforceable by all. Only the universal category of the human makes evident the humanity of those who are actually excluded.

Thus, the universal concepts are not only tyrannical manifestations of existing power relations but, implicitly, also their denunciation. They implicitly accuse a society, which does not satisfy its own universal claim. Viewed this way, by immanent critique, the universal concepts that Davis discards are at the same time combat terms against unequal, iniquitous, and oppressing social relationships. Immanent critique—the constant confrontation of a term with its content—is able to reveal this contradiction because it emphasizes the chasm between being and ought-to-be; it neither levels out the ought-to-be nor absolutizes the being.[25] Simply denying the universal concepts will not change the subjugation of minorities within society. Special interests are to be promoted, but they need to be sublated in an idea of universal interest and of a common goal. To put it briefly, the universal fails not because it is universal but because it is not universal enough.

We might expect Davis, as a critical theorist, to propose a profound critique of the universal and a permeation of the dialectics of the universal and the particular. However, with Davis, the universal is torn apart into a number of special interests (women, Blacks, Palestinians, eventually class interest) that are set in opposition to one another.

This fallacy in theory by implication leads to a particular drift in praxis that is problematic. Davis personalizes the universal, and she does so in the common jargon with which we are already familiar from the multilayered ideology of antisemitism. She personalizes the abhorred universal in Israel, the biggest Jewish community worldwide. As one of its major features, antisemitism contains hatred against the universal, even in the shape of civil law and universal human rights.[26] A characteristic feature of modern antisemitism is its hatred against "abstract" society, which, like the "abstract" individual, is identified with the Jews.[27] On the other hand, the Völkisch-Aryan is seen to be embodied in the supposedly concrete community, which is positioned against the equally abstract individual, society, and state. The latter are seen as nonrooted, inauthentic, artificial, and "Jewish." So when Angela Davis invokes communities and collectivities against the state and the individual, and when, moreover, she associates the state and the individual, including all the negative notions that they undoubtedly imply, with Israel, then she takes the same line that antisemites do.

During the Enlightenment period, the Jewish question targeted Jewish particularity—Jews would not fit the criteria of the universal, which, by implication, was always clandestinely marked white, male, and Christian even though the Enlightenment universalism tried to overcome all particularities.[28] But the universal is also to be seen as manifestation of a specific particularity—the hegemonic one—even if it actually means something different. So the Jewish question was one about undesired particularity that should be dissolved in the universal at best or, in the case of antisemitism, be erased.

In Davis's way of thinking, this relationship seems to be reversed—she does not blame Israel for particularism but implicitly blames Israel for representing the universal and the "tyranny of the universal." Overcoming racism and antisemitism, in her view, is bound to erase the universal—the universal that the state of Israel stands for: "We cannot call for an end to racism and to antisemitism without calling for an end to the occupation of Palestine," she said in a May 2016 talk in Paris.[29] One of the major issues for establishing peace in the world is the overcoming of racism and antisemitism. This issue is connected uniquely to a free Palestine. Davis does not clarify whether it is the Palestinian territories within the borders of 1967 or the partition plan of 1948. Consequently, world peace depends on the solution of the "Israel question," which is a new variant of the old "Jewish question." Eventually, according to the Jewish question, Jews can personify whatever is wrong, be it the particular, the false universal (sometimes equated with cosmopolitanism), or even universalism itself when it is deemed tyrannical and repressive of the particular.[30]

ERASING ANTISEMITISM

How can we conclude that Davis identifies Israel with a particular notion of the universal—that is, with white male supremacy? Since she never says it explicitly, it remains an issue of interpretation. Davis has a strong background in the civil rights movement and in black feminism. In the first chapter of her book *Freedom Is a Constant Struggle*, she writes as follows:

> Black feminism emerged as a theoretical and practical effort demonstrating that race, gender, and class are inseparable in the social worlds we inhabit. At the time of its emergence, Black women were frequently asked to choose whether the Black movement or the women's movement was most important. The response was this was the wrong question. The more appropriate question was how to understand the intersections and interconnections between the two movements. We are still faced with the challenge of understanding the complex ways race, class, gender, sexuality, nation, and ability are intertwined—but also how we move beyond these categories to understand the interrelationships of ideas and processes that seem to be separate and unrelated. Insisting on the connections between struggles and racism in the US and struggles against the Israeli repression of Palestinians is a feminist process.[31]

This passage, which links the Israel-Palestinian conflict with the black movement and black feminism in the United States, is intelligible only if we perceive Israelis as white and Palestinians as black. However, Davis does not explain how she reaches this conclusion. Rather, she seems to take it for granted that Israelis are white and Palestinians are black.

Hence, since Israelis are viewed as representatives of white hegemony, it is logical that they are denied special interests. Feminists, on the other hand, are obliged to declare their solidarity with the victims of oppression, bearing in mind that the oppression of women is also never unitary and isomorphic but intersects with other forms of oppression. The oppression of Palestinians, in Davis's view, is seen in the fact that they are denied self-determination: "The important issues in the Palestinian struggle for freedom and self-determination are minimized and rendered invisible by those who try to equate Palestinian resistance to Israeli apartheid with terrorism."[32]

Evidently, Davis does not acknowledge that major actors in the Palestinian struggle fight for a greater Palestine "from the river to the Sea," which, of course, implies the destruction of Israel as a Zionist state, and thus the end of Israel as the only potential refuge for Jews in the world. This goal is also on the agenda of some BDS activists, which becomes clear when BDS groups use maps of the region depicting a single Palestinian state that extends from the Jordan River to the Mediterranean Sea, with no trace of Israel. Omar Barghouti, the founder of BDS, has publicly said, "Definitely, most definitely we oppose a Jewish state in any part of Palestine. No Palestinian, rational Palestinian, not a sell-out Palestinian, will ever accept a Jewish state in Palestine."[33] Davis does not distance herself from this kind of political thinking. So the special interest of the Jews in having their own nation-state is implicitly denied. Although she lists an endless number of special interests and lives that matter, Jewish lives are not mentioned.[34] Nowhere does Davis relate to or affirm Jewish interests as special interests. They seem to be included in the All Lives—that is, the universal that is coined white and male.

This view, of course, completely disregards Jewish history and the history of antisemitism. The universal was certainly not coined Jewish. For most of European history, Jews were not regarded as white and they were not regarded as representing hegemonic masculinity.[35] Antisemitism used to portray Jews as standing outside the norm and as threatening the well-established "natural order of things." They were regarded as not assignable to the categories of class, gender, and nation but rather as standing somewhere in between. An undefinable position, the position of the nonidentical was assigned to them.[36] They were the total Other. In this sense, Jews are even more outside the system of sameness than blacks, who are unambiguously categorized in racist terms. To some degree, this exclusion of the Jews has changed since the founding of Israel as a sovereign Jewish nation-state. Still, the history of antisemitism and its contemporary persistence and pertinence need to be taken into account in any discussion of Israel.

Instead, Davis makes the simple and binary juxtaposition of Palestinian victims on one hand and "Israeli apartheid" on the other hand, and thus equates Israel with the white racist supremacy in the former South African apartheid system. This analogy is a slap in the face for all South Africans who suffered under the apartheid system. Meanwhile, what she says about genocide and apartheid is telling. In a speech at Boğaziçi University in Istanbul in January 2015, Davis said, "Given that my historical relationships with this country have been shaped by circumstances of international solidarity, I have titled my talk 'Transnational Solidarities: Resisting Racism, Genocide, and Settler Colonialism,' for the purpose of evoking possible futures, potential circuits connecting movements in various parts of the world, and specifically, in the US, Turkey, and occupied Palestine."[37] Again, it is not clear what Davis means by "settler colonialism"—whether this is Zionism in its entirety or a particular characteristic of Zionism in the West Bank and Gaza.

This lack of clarity opens a chain of associations and directly links three issues that, in fact, are not comparable. What is achieved is an association between settler colonialism and racism, and even with genocide. Davis continues as follows: "The term *genocide* has usually been reserved for particular conditions defined in accordance with the United Nations Convention on the Prevention and Punishment of the Crime of Genocide, adopted on December 9, 1948, in the aftermath of the fascist scourge during World War II."[38] Her use of the phrase "fascist scourge" in this context is curious. Davis usually formulates her intended meanings in an explicit and outspoken way. Why, in this case, does she use a euphemistic formulation when speaking about the genocide of the Jews? Why does she not call it what it is? The phrase seems to erase the specifics not only of the Shoah but also of Nazism itself. This erasure of the Shoah makes even more sense in the light of viewing Israel as an apartheid system and Zionism as settler colonialism that is termed racist.[39]

Just as the specificity of the Shoah is consistently erased in Davis's speeches, so is antisemitism. In *Freedom Is a Constant Struggle*, she refers to antisemitism only once, in the context of equating Israel with apartheid South Africa. It is not far-fetched to interpret this as a pretext. In a speech titled "On Palestine, G4S, and the Prison-Industrial-Complex," in December 2013 at SOAS University of London, she stated, "And I evoke the spirit of the South African Constitution and its opposition to racism and anti-Semitism as well as to sexism and homophobia. This is the context within which I join with you once more to intensify campaigns against another regime of apartheid and in solidarity with the struggles of the Palestinian people. As Mandela said 'We know too well that our freedom is incomplete without the freedom of the Palestinians.'"[40]

In her talk on the occasion of the tenth anniversary of the Parti des Indigènes de la République, Davis blames Israel for global antisemitism and racism.[41] Again, she mentions antisemitism in order to denounce Israel and blame the victims.

STRANGE ALLIANCES: "THE
INTERSECTIONALITY OF STRUGGLES"

The following are some examples of how the "intersectionality muddle" (Cary Nelson's term) actually works and how Angela Davis tries to escape the fallacies implied by the dissolution of the universal into a number of special interests.

From Ferguson to Palestine: The Prison Industrial
Complex and the Militarization of the Police

Describing the repressive apparatuses of the state that violate lives, Davis points to the fact that blacks, more specifically black men, get caught disproportionately more often in the clutches of the prison industrial complex. This is just one example of the repressive character of the modern state, and it is an illustration of reification in praxis.

But interestingly, when criticizing the repressive character of the state, Davis refers not to just any state, not to Arab states, nor to the failed states of Africa, but explicitly and only to the United States and Israel. Furthermore, she draws connections between the US prison industry and the militarization of US police forces on one hand and Israel on the other. This linkage borders on conspiracy thinking: Israel is made accountable for the structural violence applied by US police forces. She acknowledges that the individual police officers—as in the case of Ferguson—need to be held liable, but that it would be wrong to leave it at that. We need to look behind the curtain to see the structural conditions that make this sort of police violence possible. And this is where Davis brings Israel into play:

> Simply by focusing on the individual as if the individual were an aberration, we inadvertently engage in the process of reproducing the very violence that we assume we are contesting.

> How do we move beyond this framework of primarily focusing on individual perpetrators? In the case of Michael Brown in

Ferguson, Missouri, we quickly learned about the militarization of the police because of the visual images of their military garb, military vehicles, and military weapons. The militarization of the police in the US, of police forces all over the country has been accomplished in part with the aid of the Israeli government, which has been sharing its training with police forces all over the country since the period in the immediate aftermath of 9/11.[42]

That is Davis's analysis of the structural conditions of state violence: blaming one single and universal culprit, Israel—an answer that is usually provided by committed anti-Zionists to any corresponding question.

This explanation is not helpful for a thorough critique of the state and its powers, because it narrows the problem to single-issue connections. There is no doubt that state criticism is necessary, but why single out Israel and focus on this one state—and with such vehemence? Just as with the individual, only immanent critique is appropriate, which takes into account that today, in the stage of unfree mankind, only the state in its Western shape can provide legal certainty, even if in reality it does not sufficiently live up to its own standards. But which other authority today will advocate for the special interests? There is no world sovereign that could take over this task.[43] The whole concept of universal and equal rights is bound up with the state or blocs of states and not with the collectivities and communities to which Davis refers so positively. They cannot guarantee legal certainty to the individual. The point of reference of these communities is not the individual but rather the surrender of the individual in an exclusive identification with the group to which the individual incidentally belongs.

The rejection of individualism and the state altogether and their dissolution in the community is an anti-imperialist stance in Davis's approach. It is an anti-Enlightenment bias that is part of an Occidentalist view, an ideologically veiled perspective that portrays the West as uniquely abusive, shallow, and materialistic.

Robert Fine and Philip Spencer observe that this is the final departure from critical theory:

> In place of the deep and careful reflections we find in critical theory on what overcoming antisemitism requires, we find ourselves having once again to emancipate ourselves from the grip of the Jewish question. All formulations of the Jewish question come back to the harm the Jews allegedly inflict on humanity at large and to what is to be done about this harm. . . . The Enlightenment credo that "we must refuse everything to the Jews as a nation and accord everything to Jews as individuals," re-emerges as a discourse opposed to racism against Jews as individuals but correspondingly open to the stigmatisation of the Jews as a nation.[44]

Pinkwashing and Queer BDS

Ultimately, Angela Davis is aware of the problematic nature of dissolving the universal into a number of particularities and special interests—namely, that the idea of a common interest (as the universal) gets lost. At the World Social Forum: Free Palestine, she said: "The more we try to complicate ideas of struggle using concepts of race, class, gender, sexuality, nation, ability etc., it seems that we move from broad categories to more restrictive ones. It seems that we are constantly narrowing our focus."[45]

Davis does acknowledge the problem that dissolving the universal also damages the idea of a common interest and of universal solidarity. But how does she make this shift? How does she manage to broaden the focus again? To what does she link the common interest, which is about to dissolve within all the competing special interests? She opens and expands the terrain of struggle via a strange construction that actually undermines the analytical strength of intersectionality. Davis calls not for an analysis of intersecting forms of oppression in one society but for the "intersectionality of struggles." The struggles that she wants to see in intersection, however, are chosen rather arbitrarily, disregarding historical, political, and social differences. As Cary

Nelson has pointed out, intersectionality becomes "the rationalizing glue that holds together a series of historically and culturally unrelated political causes and builds alliances based on them."[46]

We have encountered this already in the case of the Ferguson-Palestine connection. However, the only evidence Davis gives that there was a connection between Ferguson and Palestine is that the same tear gas canisters (produced by the US company Combined Systems) were used in both places.[47] That is not a very convincing rationale for establishing an intersectionality of struggles between Ferguson and Palestine. Intersectionality means more than just a similarity; it indicates a structural entrenchment, a deep connection between the two issues. But here this intersectionality, and thus global solidarity, is established through the construction of one common, universal enemy— again, Israel. This is the conjuring trick with which international solidarity is to be established.

Another conjuring trick is the strange construction of queer BDS and the accusation of "pinkwashing Israel." It is not evident why queer and LGBTI movements and persons should be in favor of boycotting the only state in the region that has legislation concerning the rights of queer and LGBTI people comparable to and even going beyond the laws in progressive Western societies. It is blunt anti-Zionism that connects these two movements that actually do not share a common interest. Immediately after the passage cited above on the problem of narrowing the focus through intersectionality, Davis states:

> So this is what the work around BDS that has been done by the Palestinian queers for BDS and the other organization has demonstrated to me that it is possible to engage in this work while expanding our terrain of struggle. And I think the critique of pinkwashing is really important in this respect because it has not only revealed the shallowness, and the cynical and contemptuous character of the democracy that Israel purports to represent but it broadens the terrain of struggle against the occupation and against

the Zionist policies of Israel. This is to say that queers for BDS not only directs its message at people who identify into LGBTQ communities and it's important to direct our messages in that direction. But it is *not a question of saying simply support queer individuals in Palestine* and in fact it's clear about not wanting support from those who refuse to see that cynicism and that contemptuousness behind Israel's pro-gay image, but rather it directs its message at anyone who is a potential supporter of BDS. And that provided it seems to me a different kind of literacy. It allows us to read the racism and the violence that is covered up by the putatively pro-gay stance of Israel in a different way. And ideology is very powerful. And what is Queer BDS? Queer BDS, it seems to me, can help radical forces around the world to develop new ways of engaging in ideological struggle.[48]

Davis says it clearly: Intersectionality is not primarily about supporting queer individuals in the Palestinian territories but about fighting against Zionism. As a consequence, and because this kind of intersectionality by no means attends to the interest of the individual, it is not queer individual rights that are the main focus but the establishment of an intersectionality of struggles. The connection drawn between BDS and LGBTI movements in Queer BDS eventually erases the special interests of queers and LGBTI people.

The accusation of pinkwashing is an example of absolute cynicism.[49] But this ideology is necessary to be able to overlook the gender dimension in viewing the whole issue. Only by accusing Israel of pinkwashing is it possible for a feminist to avoid focusing on how gender and sexual rights are systematically violated in the Palestinian territories, by the Palestinian National Authority, by Hamas and Islamic Jihad, and by Islamic communities and their terror of virtue. The state of restricted and oppression that queers and LGBTI people must endure in Arab and Islamic societies is consistently disregarded by those who blame Israel for pinkwashing. Though some religious and secular communities in Israel certainly do not promote individual freedom and sexual rights of queers and LGBTI people, it is the state of Israel itself that enacts these rights. This is the very Zionist state that Davis and others so vehemently attack under the pretext of promoting the rights of Palestinian queers and LGBTI people. For her, it is Zionism that stands in the way of the rights of Palestinians—and, in this case, explicitly the rights of Palestinian LGBTI people. She equates Zionism with racism, and this racism is covered by the liberal pro-gay image—a pure cynicism in her view. Davis exploits LGBTI rights to achieve a different goal, which is nothing less than the delegitimization of Israel as a Zionist state.

The accusation of pinkwashing is a vehement critique of hypocrisy, as if hypocrisy were the first crime and not actual violence against women, queers and LGBTI people under Sharia law. However, it is regarded as particularly objectionable that Israel professes the image of a liberal society concerning the rights of women, gays, lesbians, and transgender people while in reality it is not free of gender violence. But which society is? So, indeed, hypocrisy needs to be criticized, but we must keep a sense of proportion as well. Shedding the liberal mask is no solution—it is, on the contrary, a totalitarian drift, just as is the total objection to the idea of the universal and the unmediated rejection of the state and of the individual. That shift does not make minorities safer or society fairer or the individual more free.

CONCLUSION

A comprehensive answer to the complex question of why and how feminism and intersectionality are instrumentalized for anti-Zionist agitation needs to uncover the immanent contradictions that are at stake. Thus, I focused on Angela Davis's theoretical premises and deciphered their inherent inconsistencies and fallacies. This is far more important than one might think, given the entanglement of theory and praxis. The anti-Zionist praxis is not independent from the theoretical premises. By contrasting

Angela Davis's approach with theorems of critical theory, my analysis reveals that her notion of intersectionality solely focuses on the level of groups and communities affected by discrimination and social, political, and economic inequality. It is about the struggle of communities for recognition and power, whereas the individual and individual rights in and against these communities fade into the background. This identity political orientation that does not consider the multifaceted relationship between society and the individual shows a reductionist view on intersectionality that is likely to turn into exclusion itself.

Intersectionality can be a useful theoretical and methodological device to help us understand the complex intertwining of various forms of oppression on a structural level. It is a strategy to reflect on the dialectics of the universal and the particular, of society and the individual. It enables us to view different manifestations of an antagonistic society and different ways of experiencing this antagonistic society while still seeing the special interests in the framework of a totality that produces these special interests.

Thus, intersectionality describes a relationship, a totality. This means that the particular—in this case, the special interests—need to be centrally considered but not isolated. They need to be sublated in an idea of universality that is not just a manifestation of hegemonic power relations, but a common frame of humanity that has not yet become hegemonic and in which "people could be different without fear."[50] Quite often, however, intersectionality is premised on tearing apart the universal and the particular aspects of the human condition and viewing the particular as "unreified" and authentic in opposition to the universal as the "tyrannical" aspect. This, in fact, cuts the very dialectical movement that is going on in the social relationship between the universal and the particular. This is the case in Davis's approach, where the universal does not vanish altogether but is specifically identified and personalized in Israel as a nation-state.

With this identification, she fills the gap left by the loss of a mediated concept of universality.

Anti-Zionists and BDS activists who misuse the concept of
intersectionality as a means of exclusion and of delegitimizing
Israel have brought it into disrepute. But instead of discarding
intersectionality altogether, this abuse should motivate us to reclaim the concept for a critical feminism that is not driven by
anti-Zionist ideology.

NOTES

Throughout this chapter, I have used capital B "Black" to refer to the
self-designation for people of the African diaspora; the lowercase term
remains when used as a racial descriptor.

1. To mention only one example, in 2015, the National Women's
Studies Association, the largest and most influential feminist academic
organization in the United States, opted for including a recommendation
for BDS (National Women's Studies Association, November 16, 2017,
http://www.nwsa.org/statements). On academic boycott of Israel, see the
comprehensive collection Cary Nelson and Gabriel Noah Brahm, eds., *The
Case against Academic Boycotts of Israel* (Detroit: Wayne State University
Press, 2015).

2. See Angela Y. Davis, *Freedom Is a Constant Struggle: Ferguson,
Palestine, and the Foundations of a Movement* (Chicago: Haymarket
Books, 2016).

3. For a recent discussion of this concept, see Patricia Hill Collins and
Sirma Bilge, *Intersectionality* (Hoboken, NJ: Wiley, 2016).

4. See Cornelia Klinger and Gudrun-Axeli Knapp, eds.,
ÜberKreuzungen. Fremdheit, Ungleichheit, Differenz (Münster, Germany:
Westfälisches Dampfboot, 2008).

5. See Kimberlé Crenshaw, "Mapping the Margins: Intersectionality,
Identity Politics and Violence against Women of Colour," *Stanford Law
Review* 43, no. 6 (1991): 1241–99.

6. See Susannah Heschel's thorough critique in "From the Bible to
Nazism: German Feminists on the Jewish Origins of Patriarchy," in *Tel
Aviver Jahrbuch für deutsche Geschichte*, vol. 21, *Neuere Frauengeschichte*
(University of Tel Aviv, 1992), 319–33, and in "Beyond Heroism and
Victimhood: Gender and Holocaust Scholarship. Review Essay," in *Jews

and Gender: The Challenge to Hierarchy, ed. Jonathan Frankel (Oxford: Oxford University Press, 2000), 294–304; see also Charlotte Kohn-Ley and Ilse Korotin, eds., *Der feministische Sündenfall? Antisemitische Vorurteile in der Frauenbewegung* (Vienna: Picus, 1994).

7. See Birgit Rommelspacher, "Antisemitismus und Frauenbewegung in Deutschland," in *Rassismen und Feminismen. Differenzen, Machtverhältnisse und Solidarität zwischen Frauen,* ed. Brigitte Fuchs and Gabriele Habinger (Vienna: Promedia, 1996), 112–24; Johanna Gehmacher, ed., *Frauen—und Geschlechtergeschichte des Nationalsozialismus. Fragestellungen, Perspektiven, neue Forschungen* (Innsbruck, Austria: Studien, 2007); Rita Thalmann, *Frausein im Dritten Reich* (Munich: Hanser, 1984).

8. See Astrid Messerschmidt, *Bildung und Kritik der Erinnerung. Lernprozesse in Geschlechterdiskursen zum Holocaust-Gedächtnis* (Frankfurt: Brandes and Apsel, 2003), 157.

9. See Karin Stögner, *Antisemitismus und Sexismus. Historisch-gesellschaftliche Konstellationen* (Baden-Baden, Germany: Nomos, 2014).

10. See particularly Rommelspacher, "Antisemitismus und Frauenbewegung"; Gehmacher, *Frauen—und Geschlechtergeschichte.*

11. See Karin Stögner, "The 'Feminisation of Fascism' and National Identity Construction in Germany and Austria after 1945," in *The Holocaust in the Twenty-First Century: Contesting/Contested Memories,* ed. David Seymour and Mercedes Camino (London: Routledge 2016), 221–41.

12. Rokhl Kafrissen, "Zakia Belkhiri Took a Selfie of Anti-Semitism on the Left," *Haaretz,* May 25, 2016, http://www.haaretz.com/opinion/. premium-1.721439. See also David Schraub, "White Jews: An Intersectional Approach," forthcoming in *Association for Jewish Studies (AJS) Review.*

13. Cary Nelson, "The Intersectionality Muddle," *Inside Higher Ed,* February 15, 2015, https://www.insidehighered.com/views/2016/02/15 /concept-intersectionality-mutating-and-becoming-corrupted-essay.

14. Nelson, "The Intersectionality Muddle."

15. Nelson, "The Intersectionality Muddle."

16. Davis, *Freedom Is a Constant Struggle,* 16.

17. See also, e.g., Benjamin Pogrund, "Lies Told About Israel Are Beyond Belief," *Times Live,* October 30, 2011, http://www.timeslive.co.za /local/2011/10/30/Lies-told-about-Israel-are-beyond-belief; Richard J. Goldstone, "Israel and the Apartheid Slander," *New York Times,* October 31, 2011, http://www.nytimes.com/2011/11/01/opinion/israel-and-the -apartheid-slander.html?_r=0.

18. See, e.g., Max Horkheimer, *Gesammelte Schriften 6* (Frankfurt: Fischer, 1991), 243–44; Herbert Marcuse, *Nachgelassene Schriften*

4: Die Studentenbewegung und ihre Folgen (Lüneburg, Germany: Zu Klampen 2004), 147–48; Wolfgang Kraushaar, ed., *Frankfurter Schule und Studentenbewegung. Von der Flaschenpost zum Molotowcocktail. 1946 bis 1995*, vol. 2 (Munich: Rogner and Bernhard, 1998); Stephan Grigat, "Befreite Gesellschaft und Israel. Zum Verhältnis von Kritischer Theorie und Zionismus," in *Feindaufklärung und Reeducation. Kritische Theorie gegen Postnazismus und Islamismus*, ed. Stephan Grigat (Freiburg: ça ira 2006), 115–29.

19. Angela Davis, "Life between Politics and Academia" (speech, University of Vienna, October 5, 2015), https://www.youtube.com /watch?v=XTsGpUM357I. In part, this talk corresponds to a speech titled, "The Truth Telling Project: Violence in America" (Saint Louis, MO, June 27, 2015); see Davis, *Freedom Is a Constant Struggle*, 81–90.

20. Theodor W. Adorno, *Negative Dialectics*, trans. E. B. Ashton (New York: Continuum 2007), 365.

21. Gerhard Scheit, *Der Wahn vom Weltsouverän. Zur Kritik des Völkerrechts* (Freiburg: ça ira), 2009.

22. Angela Davis, "What Is Queer BDS? Pinkwashing, Intersections, Struggles, Politics," accessed July 18, 2018, https://vimeo.com/55886232.

23. See Max Horkheimer, *Nachgelassene Schriften* (Frankfurt: Fischer, 1988), 171.

24. Davis, *Freedom Is a Constant Struggle*, 87.

25. In Adorno's words, immanent critique pits a phenomenon against its own preconditions and its own claim to truth. The critique comes from within; that is, the phenomenon is not confronted with extrinsic criteria. See Theodor W. Adorno, *Einführung in die Dialektik* (Frankfurt: Suhrkamp, 2010), 51.

26. See Robert Fine, *Cosmopolitanism* (London: Routledge, 2007).

27. Max Horkheimer, *Theodor W. Adorno: Dialectic of Enlightenment, Philosophical Fragments* (Stanford: Stanford University Press 2002).

28. For a comprehensive discussion of the development of the "Jewish question" and the corresponding relationship of the universal and the particular, see Robert Fine and Philip Spencer, *Antisemitism and the Left: On the Return of the Jewish Question* (Manchester, UK: Manchester University Press, 2017).

29. Angela Davis, "Race et impérialisme, intervention lors des 10 ans de la Parti des Indigènes de la Republique (PIR)," (speech, Paris, May 8, 2016), http://indigenes-republique.fr/race-et-imperialisme-intervention -dangela-davis-race-et-imperialisme-lors-des-10-ans-du-pir/.

30. I am grateful to Robert Fine for discussions on this issue.

31. Davis, *Freedom Is a Constant Struggle*, 4.

32. Davis, *Freedom Is a Constant Struggle*, 8.

33. Omar Barghouti, "Strategies for Change," accessed July 17, 2018, https://vimeo.com/75201955.

34. "If indeed all lives mattered we would not need to emphatically proclaim that 'Black Lives Matter.' Or, as we discover on the BLM website: Black Women Matter, Black Girls Matter, Black Gay Lives Matter, Black Bi Lives Matter, Black Boys Matter, Black Queer Lives Matter, Black Men Matter, Black Lesbians Matter, Black Trans Lives Matter, Black Immigrants Matter, Black Incarcerated Lives Matter. Black Differently Abled Lives Matter. Yes, Black Lives Matter, Latino/Asian American/Native American/Muslim/Poor and Working-Class White Peoples Lives Matter. There are many more specific instances we would have to name before we can ethically and comfortably claim that All Lives Matter." Davis, *Freedom Is a Constant Struggle*, 87.

35. See Sander L. Gilman, *Freud, Race, and Gender* (Princeton, NJ: Princeton University Press, 1991); Karen Brodkin, *How Jews Became White Folks and What That Says About Race in America* (New Brunswick, NJ: Rutgers University Press, 2000).

36. See Stögner, *Antisemitismus und Sexismus*; Karen Stögner, "Nature and Anti-Nature—Constellations of Antisemitism and Sexism," in *Internal Outsiders—Imagined Orientals? Antisemitism, Colonialism and Modern Constructions of Jewish Identity*, ed. Ulrike Brunotte, Jürgen Mohn, and Christina Späti (Würzburg: Ergon Verlang, 2017), 157–70.

37. Davis, *Freedom Is a Constant Struggle*, 131.

38. Davis, *Freedom Is a Constant Struggle*, 131–32.

39. I thank David Seymour, with whom I discussed this phrase in detail.

40. Davis, *Freedom Is a Constant Struggle*, 52–53.

41. Davis, "Race et impérialisme."

42. Davis, *Freedom Is a Constant Struggle*, 138–39.

43. Scheit, *Der Wahn vom Weltsourverän*.

44. Fine and Spencer, *Antisemitism and the Left*, 107.

45. Davis, "What Is Queer BDS?"

46. Nelson, "The Intersectionality Muddle."

47. Davis, *Freedom Is a Constant Struggle*, 140.

48. Davis, "What Is Queer BDS?" (emphasis added).

49. On a profound critique of the pinkwashing accusation, see Arthur Slepian, "An Inconvenient Truth: The Myths of Pinkwashing," *Tikkun*, July 3, 2012, http://www.tikkun.org/nextgen/an-inconvenient-truth -the-myths-of-pinkwashing?print=yes.

50. Theodor W. Adorno, *Minima Moralia: Reflections from a Damaged Life* (London: Verso 2005), 103.

KARIN STÖGNER is Visiting Professor for Critical Theory at Goethe University Frankfurt and teaches social theory and topics related to gender, antisemitism, and nationalism in the Departments of Sociology and Gender Studies at the University of Vienna. In 2017–18 she was research fellow at the Center for Austrian Studies at Hebrew University of Jerusalem. She is currently chair of the research network on ethnic relations, racism, and antisemitism in the European Sociological Association. She is author of *Sexismus und Antisemitismus. Historisch-gesellschaftliche Konstellationen* and editor (with Anton Pelinka and Karin Bisch) of *Handbook of Prejudice*.

PART II

University, Legal, and Historical Frameworks

—∿—

The Role of International Legal and Justice Discourse in Promoting the New Antisemitism

GERALD M. STEINBERG AND ANNE HERZBERG

SINCE THE FOUNDING of Israel in 1948, the discourse of international law and human rights and the associated institutions have been widely used to attack the legitimacy of the Jewish state and to intimidate its Jewish citizens. In these contexts, the right of the Jewish people to self-determination, Zionism (the movement founded to realize this right), and the modern state of Israel are often characterized as threats to the post–World War II international legal order, on a par with the contemporary world's worst evils: racism, colonialism, imperialism, and apartheid. The nation-state of the Jewish people is characterized as illegitimate and illegal, and Israel is portrayed as the primary violator of international norms, based on extreme double standards and highly disproportionate focus. The Boycott, Divestment, Sanctions (BDS) campaigns and the ritual singling out of Israel for censure in the United Nations and other international frameworks all claim to be grounded on the imperative of international law.

The use of international legal rhetoric to attack Zionism and the Jewish state was pioneered by the Arab countries and the Soviet Union as a modern and more acceptable way of expressing hostility toward Jews, particularly after the Holocaust. Such rhetoric was also used to attack Israel as a US proxy as part of the Cold

War. As the Cold War drew to a close and the apartheid regime
in South Africa was disbanded, civil society frameworks, notably church groups and nongovernmental organizations (NGOs)
claiming to promote human rights and humanitarian agendas,
embraced the Arab/Soviet rhetoric and increasingly adopted this
international legal and human rights discourse.

This campaign is a direct reflection of the growth in the normative and political significance of international law and human
rights during the past century. As many analysts and historians
have noted, the Nuremberg trials following the Holocaust and
World War II marked a key turning point and established the
legitimacy of international legal frameworks in holding political
and military officials responsible for moral failures.

The newly founded United Nations adopted the Universal
Declaration of Human Rights and the accompanying Genocide
Convention in 1948. In the 1960s and 1970s, the United Nations
established various human rights mechanisms that evolved into
the current Human Rights Council, headed by a commissioner
for human rights, as well as ancillary bodies. These instruments
enshrined the prioritization of universal requirements and principles of human rights over previously inviolable national sovereignty and established the basis for external intervention on
these moral grounds. According to Samuel Moyn, in this period,
"the moral war of Westerners shifted, opening a space . . . that
coalesced in an international human rights movement that had
never existed before."[1]

In parallel, these human rights and international legal mechanisms were directed disproportionately against Zionism, Israel,
and Jewish sovereign equality, becoming the language of a new
antisemitism, with the emphasis on international law and United
Nations resolutions.

This chapter outlines the history of this process and its manifestations. The first section discusses the emergence of these processes following the creation of the state of Israel, in the context

of classical and theological antisemitism. Then we examine how this new antisemitism presented itself in campaigns to portray Israel as a threat to the post–World War II international legal order and to label Zionism as a violation of international law and human rights. We trace these campaigns in the United Nations, spearheaded by the Arab League and the Soviet Union, and their adoption by NGOs proclaiming humanitarian and human rights mandates. A further section describes and analyzes the ways in which Israel and Zionism are presented not only as illegitimate and illegal under international law but also as the primary violators of international law and human rights. This process takes place through campaigns of extreme double standards and disproportionate focus and erases the context of Arab violence.

NEW ANTISEMITISM VERSUS OLD ANTISEMITISM

Collective antisemitism, in the form of denying the right of the Jewish people to sovereign equality, has joined classic theological antisemitism, which targeted individual Jews due to their religion and culture. The new antisemitism negates Jewish collective identity as a people and a nation with national rights, and it rejects the legitimacy of any Jewish state, regardless of borders, in the land of Israel.[2]

Following the founding of political Zionism and as the restoration of Jewish sovereignty became a reality, Israel, as the nation-state of the Jews, became the central target of hatred and rejection. The flag of postcolonial ideology was used to justify fierce opposition to Jewish self-determination while campaigning for the independence of other ethnonational groups with much weaker historical claims.[3] Expanding on this theme, Alan Johnson observes that the "left hoped to dissolve Jewish peoplehood in the solvent of progressive universalism."[4] Attacking Israel as a state in which Jewish culture thrived made antisemitism acceptable on the left, as "negative feelings [would] not be expressed against all Jews but only against Jewish Israelis—under the guise that the feelings are political rather than anti-Semitic."[5] As former Swedish deputy prime minister Per Ahlmark remarked in a May 2004 address to the American Jewish Committee, while "anti-Zionists accept the right of other peoples to national feelings and a defensible state . . . they reject the right of the Jewish people to have its national consciousness expressed in the state of Israel and to make that state secure." According to Ahlmark, "anti-Semites of different centuries had always aimed at destroying the then center of Jewish existence . . . today, when the Jewish state has become a center of identity and a source of pride and protection for most Jews, Zionism is being slandered as a racist ideology."[6]

In his comprehensive research, the late historian of antisemitism Robert Wistrich documented the formulae of the anti-Zionist narrative, in which Jews were portrayed as "rapacious, bloodsucking colonialists . . . rootless, imperialist invaders who came to Palestine to conquer the land by brute force, to expel or 'cleanse' it of its natives."[7] Zionism was described as a modern crusade that "succeeded only because of a gigantic occult conspiracy in which the Zionists (i.e., the Jews) manipulated Great Britain and subsequently America."[8] The Jewish state of Israel, they said, was created in sin—a unique sin from which other nations in Europe, North America, and elsewhere were somehow exempt.

The denial of Jewish national rights, particularly among intellectuals claiming to promote universalist values, merged with and was reinforced by the human rights and legal discourse. The Holocaust had made overtly antisemitic language in the West unacceptable, particularly on the left, but to bypass this, the language of international law and human rights was used instead.

In tracing this process, former chief rabbi of the United Kingdom Jonathan Sacks discusses the process of adaptation:

> Antisemitism always needs justification by the highest source of authority in the culture at any given age. Throughout the Middle Ages the highest authority in Europe was the Church. Hence

anti-Semitism took the form of Christian anti-Judaism. In the post-enlightenment Europe of the 19th century the highest authority was no longer the Church. Instead it was science. Thus was born racial anti-Semitism, based on two disciplines regarded as science in their day: the "scientific study of race" and the Social Darwinism of Herbert Spencer and Ernst Haeckel.

Today, that role is taken by human rights. It follows that any assault on Jewish life—on Jews or Judaism or the Jewish state—must be cast in the language of human rights. Hence the by-now routine accusation that Israel has committed the five cardinal sins against human rights: racism, apartheid, ethnic cleansing, attempted genocide and crimes against humanity. This is not because the people making these accusations seriously believe them—some do, some don't. It is because this is the only form in which an assault on Jews can be stated today.[9]

Similarly, Robert Wistrich observed, "Zionism and the Jewish people have been demonized in ways that are virtually identical to the methods, arguments, and techniques of racist anti-Semitism. Even though the current banner may be 'antiracist' and the defamation is being carried out today in the name of human rights."[10]

In this paradigm or discourse, Israel is knowingly compared to Nazism because "Nazism in the postwar world has become the defining metaphor of absolute evil." Zionism is characterized "as heir to the darkest pages of Western colonial history," and Israel is accused of exploiting the Holocaust to justify its alleged crimes. Instead of relying on tactics of the old antisemitism (which still manifests in manifold ways) via images of global conspiracy, financial control, and manipulation, the new version paints Israel as the enemy of international human rights, singularly guilty of warmongering, ethnic cleansing, and occupation. In constrast to the past, when it was necessary to "watch out" for the Jew and to denigrate Judaism, there is now "a moral obligation to wage war against Israel"—the state of the Jews.[11]

Building on this formulation, international law professor and former Canadian minister of justice Irwin Cotler declared that this new antisemitism "can best be identified from an anti-discrimination, equality rights, and international law perspective. . . . The new anti-Semitism involves the discrimination against, denial of, or assault upon, the right of the Jewish people to live as an equal member of the family of nations" masked through the language of universal public values and "under the protective cover of the UN, the authority of international law, the culture of human rights, and the struggle against racism."[12]

Based on these ideological foundations, and assisted by the ongoing Arab and Islamic effort to roll back the establishment and legitimacy of Israel in 1948, the influence of this anti-Zionist discourse expanded, skillfully exploiting the rhetoric of international law and universal human rights. As will be demonstrated in the next section, the United Nations became a central arena for broadening this campaign, and during the Cold War, Soviet and Arab propaganda relied on these themes. In addition, powerful civil society groups, ostensibly created to promote human rights, provided additional support for the campaigns targeting Israel through this form of soft power.

"ZIONISM IS RACISM" AND THE EXISTENCE OF ISRAEL AS A THREAT TO THE INTERNATIONAL LEGAL ORDER

United Nations

At the beginning, the United Nations, and its predecessor, the short-lived League of Nations, played central roles in conferring legitimacy on the right of the Jewish people to self-determination and in the creation of the state of Israel. Yet the UN has also become the central platform through which the new antisemitism has been promoted.

The foundational principles of the United Nations as expressed in the preamble of its charter are the maintenance of international peace and security and the reaffirmation of "fundamental human rights." Even before the November 29, 1947, adoption by the General Assembly of the Partition Plan for Palestine, and the declaration of the establishment of the state of Israel on May 14, 1948, Zionism was often portrayed in UN meetings as an enemy of international peace and security and a violation of equality and tolerance for all peoples.[13] In other words, in these attacks, the Zionist movement and Jewish self-determination were painted as assaults on the heart of the new postwar international legal order.

Arab leaders recognized from the outset in 1945 that "the UN era would be one that would see the proliferation of international organizations and specialized agencies, and regional arrangements."[14] They embarked on a strategy to exploit these frameworks via international diplomacy that rejected the legitimacy of Zionism. This diplomacy employed highly charged rhetoric melding the themes of classical antisemitism with the developing postwar international legal discourse.[15]

Moreover, this rhetoric was an integral part of the accompanying legal strategy to isolate and exclude Israel, such as through boycotts and sanctions. As described by the Fatah movement (headed by Arafat) in 1968, the diplomatic objective was not to gain direct support for Israel's destruction (a nonnegotiable Palestinian "right") but rather to use means "which will satisfy public opinion or be acceptable to it" so that "public opinion will not castigate us with Fascism, anti-Semitism, or other inhuman epithets."[16]

After the 1967 war, this nascent "lawfare" intensified.[17] According to Robert Barnidge, "it was not a question of the Arab world being willing to accommodate a Jewish State with territorial adjustments; the Arabs remained opposed, as they always had been to a Jewish State of any kind."[18] Instead, while the objective of destruction was unchanged, the means increasingly reflected the language of the UN Charter and of international human rights mechanisms.

Cold War Politics

Initially, Arab leaders attacked Zionism as part of the Communist conspiracy, particularly as the Soviet Union had recognized

Israel. But during the height of the Cold War in the 1960s, as Israel moved closer to the United States and the West, the Soviet leadership joined with the Arab League in aggressively attacking Zionism and the legitimacy of the Jewish state. Soviet propaganda, which reserved the term *racist* for "particularly threatening nationalist tendencies," asserted that Zionism was racist "and more especially that Zionism was vitally indistinguishable from Nazism."[19] In the UN, Arab leaders echoed the Soviets as "Arab attacks on the Zionist enterprise and on Zionist theory began to make extensive use of such terms as racist and to seek resemblances between Israel and South Africa, and even more remarkably, between Zionists and Nazis."[20] Jewish self-determination was denigrated as an abomination, and the Soviet-Arab bloc sought to have Israel declared an "illegitimate state," expel it from the UN, and replace it with a Palestine Liberation Organization (PLO)–led state.[21]

In UN resolutions and documentation, Zionism was categorized as equivalent to the evils of imperialism, colonialism, racial discrimination, apartheid, and, in some cases, even equivalent to antisemitism. It was the only national liberation movement singled out in this way. Actual racist practices such as those endemic in Islamic and Arab societies (including slavery and extreme gender and religious discrimination and segregation) were ignored, creating an entirely artificial framework in which to attack Israel. To gain support for their objectives, Latin American and African countries would join in condemnation of Zionism in return for benefits from the Soviet Union and the Gulf States.[22]

In Daniel Patrick Moynihan's elegant words,

> The UN system, in thirty years, had granted legitimacy to all manner of economic, social, and political arrangements: democratic and totalitarian; capitalist and socialist; pluralist and centralist. All were equally accepted as equally legitimate. Only regimes based on racism and racial discrimination were held to be unacceptable. This is not to say that anything that might be accorded

the standing of international law held that a state determined to be racist had no right to exist, but this was very close to political reality especially at the UN. There were now but 3 states left in all of Africa or Asia still dominated by European whites: South Africa, Rhodesia, and Israel.[23]

In this process, the Non-Aligned Movement (NAM), which at the time was the largest political bloc in the UN, was co-opted by the Arab League and as early as 1955 began repeating anti-Israel rhetoric couched in the language of anticolonialism. With the support of the NAM, it was possible for the Arab states and the Soviet Union to pass virtually any resolution attacking Zionism and the Jewish people.[24] In October 1964, Egyptian president Nasser hosted the annual NAM summit conference and secured a declaration branding Jewish self-determination as a form of "racism."[25] By 1973, the NAM conference went so far as to call for the eradication of Zionism itself and a full boycott of Israel and demanded the blocking of Jewish immigration to anywhere in the territory of Mandated Palestine west of the Jordan River.[26]

With the backing of the Soviets and the NAM, meetings on human rights treaties debated whether to include Zionism as a prohibited movement. In 1965, during the drafting of the Convention of the Elimination of Racial Discrimination, the Soviets proposed an amendment in which "State Parties condemn anti-Semitism, Zionism, Nazism, neo-Nazism and all other forms of the policy and ideology of colonialism, national and race hatred and exclusiveness and shall take action as appropriate for the speedy eradication of those inhuman ideas and practices in the territories subject to their jurisdiction."[27]

A 1973 proposed International Convention of the Suppression and Punishment of Apartheid included a definition of apartheid that would encompass Zionism. In November 1974, UNESCO adopted a resolution condemning Israel for altering the historical features of Jerusalem and rejected a motion to include Israel in the Europe regional group. The UN's 1975 World Conference on Women in Mexico City again called for the elimination of Zionism and, according to Moynihan, "equated Judaism with the nastiest forms of racial and group oppression."[28]

1975 UN "Zionism Is Racism" Resolution

These intense efforts in many UN frameworks to demonize Zionism as a violation of international human rights culminated in the 1975 vote by the United Nations General Assembly (UNGA), adopting Resolution 3379, declaring Zionism as a form of racism, which, as described by Moynihan, "gave the abomination of anti-Semitism the appearance of international legal sanction."[29] To accompany Resolution 3379, the UNGA also approved the creation of a special mechanism—the Committee on the Exercise of the Inalienable Rights of the Palestinian People—which, among other activities, expanded the legal attacks on the legitimacy of Israel. (See the discussion below in the section "Israel as the Primary Violator of International Law.")

The debate surrounding the resolution included overt expressions of antisemitism integrated with international legal rhetoric. Andrei Sakharov remarked that, "if this resolution is adopted, it can only contribute to antisemitic tendencies in many countries by giving them the appearance of international legality."[30] At the UNGA session, Idi Amin, speaking on behalf of Uganda and the Organization of African Unity, declared, "America has been colonized by the Zionists who hold all the tools of development and power. They own vitally all the banking institutions.... How can we expect freedom, peace, and justice in the world when such a powerful nation as the US is in the hands of the Zionists? ... I call for the expulsion of Israel from the UN and the extinction of Israel as a state so that the territorial integrity of Palestine may be ensured and upheld." Amin's speech received a standing ovation, and Moynihan noted that the "Zionism Is Racism" resolution "made it easier to attack the concept of a secular Jewish state and thus furnished the first new philosophical framework of anti-Semitism since WWII."[31]

Although the 1975 "Zionism Is Racism" resolution was repealed in 1991 in the context of international coalition building including Israel, responding to Iraq's invasion of Kuwait, attacks on Zionism and Jewish self-determination nevertheless continued apace. Following the fall of the apartheid regime in South Africa in 1994, Israel was portrayed as the sole remaining apartheid state. Echoing the language from the Rwandan genocide and the Balkan conflict of the mid-1990s, Israel became the main embodiment of a "genocidal" regime guilty of "ethnic cleansing."

In 2001, the UN Human Rights Commission organized a massive conference in Durban, South Africa, ostensibly held to mark the fall of the South African apartheid regime, grandiosely named the World Conference against Racism, Racial Discrimination, Xenophobia and Related Intolerance. The real focus was against Israel, with numerous displays of antisemitism and the exclusion of "pro-Zionist" speakers. The NGO Forum, which was attended by five thousand delegates from fifteen hundred groups, adopted a final declaration based on drafts written at a preparatory conference in Tehran, which referred to Israel as an apartheid state guilty of war crimes, genocide, racism, and ethnic cleansing. Keynote speakers included PLO head Yasser Arafat, and NGO participants, including Amnesty International and Human Rights Watch, adopted a plan of action, based on the South African model, designed to lead to "the complete total isolation of Israel."[32]

Post-Durban, new institutions, such as the International Criminal Court (ICC), provided additional venues for demonization. Israel was an immediate target, primarily due to the Arab League push in the final phase of the negotiation of the Rome Treaty, which established the ICC. Palestinian leaders were quick to maximize the use of this platform, and they campaigned for UN recognition as a member state in order to be able to use the ICC and other bodies for legal attacks. Writing in the *New York Times* in May 2011, PLO leader Mohammed Abbas stated that, in this way, Palestinians would pursue "the internationalization of the conflict as a legal matter."[33] As Abbas made clear, obtaining statehood would allow the Palestinians to expand the use of international law and human rights to continue their attacks on the legitimacy of the Jewish state.

The Contributions of NGOs and Civil Society to the Delegitimization Campaign

In the campaign to equate Zionism with racism and to paint Israel as an illegal and illegitimate state, nongovernmental organizations became centrally involved. At first, Arab groups, such as the Arab Higher Committee, and unions and agricultural groups associated with nationalist Palestinian factions were integral in assisting state attacks on Zionism and Judaism.[34]

Later, these campaigns were joined by NGOs proclaiming a human rights or humanitarian mandate. Church organizations such as the American Friends Service Committee, Diakonia (Sweden), ICCO (Netherlands), and Trocaire (Ireland) played a prominent role in promoting the new antisemitism. These groups began intensively campaigning both directly and through funding other NGOs active on issues such as the claimed "right of return" for Palestinian refugee descendants; commemorating the 1948 Nakba ("catastrophe"); and portraying Israel as a racist and apartheid state.

As noted above, the NGO campaign expanded significantly in the aftermath of the 2001 UN Durban Conference in response to directives laid out in the Final Declaration of the NGO Forum using international legal rhetoric. Article 162 of the declaration proclaimed "Israel as a racist, apartheid state in which Israel's brand of apartheid as a crime against humanity," demanded an "immediate end to the Israeli systematic perpetration of racist crimes including war crimes, acts of genocide and ethnic cleansing," and called "upon the international community to impose a policy of complete and total isolation of Israel as an apartheid state."

Palestinian groups such as the Sabeel Ecumenical Liberation Theology Center, an Anglican NGO based in Jerusalem that merges Palestinian "liberation theology," classical antisemitism, and Palestinian nationalism, and Badil, an influential Bethlehem-based NGO funded by a number of European countries ostensibly to assist Palestinian refugees, took up the charge of Durban. These NGOs and many others adopted the legal and human rights discourse laced with antisemitic language and imagery to advance their political agendas in UN frameworks, European parliaments, and churches.[35] When confronted with the antisemitic nature of their rhetoric, these organizations dismissed such charges as a pretext to "justify the racism of Zionism and Israeli policies."[36]

Several Israeli NGOs have also been formed to campaign for a "de-Zionized Palestine," such as Zochrot and the Alternative Information Center. Like their Palestinian counterparts, these organizations advance the concept of an "occupation" that began in 1948 (not 1967), and they repeat the standard rhetoric portraying the Jewish state, regardless of borders, as inherently racist.

As can be readily demonstrated by multiple examples, the links between officials from these organizations and UN bodies as well as European institutions are extensive, and they extend to academic institutions such as human rights and international law programs. Individuals seamlessly transition from one to the other and back again, entrenching these campaigns and agendas and amplifying attacks on Jewish sovereign equality. Many NGO officials obtain positions in which they are placed in charge of decisions to allocate funding to their former employers, and they utilize them as consultants to bolster their politics and ideologies. Again, this process reinforces a dominant narrative among international bureaucratic elites that Zionism is illegitimate and the state of Israel is illegal. Activities promoted include a widely publicized South African government–funded report titled "Occupation, Colonialism, Apartheid? A Re-assessment of Israel's Practices in the Occupied Palestinian Territories under International Law," authored by former UN officials, academics, and NGO activists to "analyze" Israel's violations of the "crimes" of apartheid and colonialism and to declare that laws to protect Israel as the nation-state of the Jewish people "are not merely symbolic formulas but establish a basis in Israeli law for racial discrimination."[37] At a May 2013 conference, "Advocating for Palestinian Rights in Conformity with International Law Guidelines," held at Birzeit University in Ramallah with many former UN officials, PLO representatives, and NGOs, participants advocated using international law to "liberate Palestine," to "expose the intent of colonization," and to "weaken Israel's legitimacy and international standing."

ISRAEL AS THE PRIMARY VIOLATOR OF INTERNATIONAL LAW

In addition to using international legal and human rights discourse to undermine the legitimacy of Zionism, Israel's founding, and Jewish self-determination, the new antisemitism portrays Israel as the primary violator of international law—and, in particular, of human rights and humanitarian law.[38] Following the end of the Cold War and the collapse of the Soviet bloc, the international human rights network, including the UN bodies and the NGOs, redirected their focus to maintain impact and funding.[39] They shifted emphasis to international humanitarian law (IHL)—the law of armed conflict.[40] Concurrently, the legal discourse on Israel expanded from claims that Zionism was a form of racism to Israel's alleged violations of IHL and its "international crimes," including war crimes and crimes against humanity. UN committees, European parliaments, NGOs, and others began issuing statements and organizing conferences where speakers strategized about how Israel could be held "accountable" for its purported abuses. These frameworks constituted what academic researchers refer to as the "human rights industry," which perpetuates itself through political campaigns (particularly in the West) generating large donations and increasing annual budgets, which, in turn, lead to further public relations activities.[41] For the reasons discussed above, targeting Israel through allegations based on international law and human rights (the two are often thrown together without distinction) became a major focus of this "industry."

The campaigns of the human rights industry involve microscrutiny and obsessive attention to Israeli actions during armed conflict, where every policy and practice, regardless of the merits, is deemed illegal. The various actors use *sui generis* interpretations of international law and what can be described as aspirational approaches focusing intensely against the Jewish state.[42] Israeli policies are characterized using the terms *occupation*, *siege*, and *collective punishment*, regardless of the actual legal definitions.[43] As Wistrich noted, the use of legal rhetoric also incorporates allegations that Israel implements "monstrous biblical doctrines" and Nazi practices toward Palestinians.[44]

The BDS campaign, which often cites the problematic 2004 International Court of Justice advisory opinion on "the Wall" (Israel's security barrier), explicitly states it will remain active until Israel "complies with international law and Palestinian rights," including ending "occupation" and implementing a "right of return."[45] The invocation of legal terminology is the primary language used in resolutions, publications, and other BDS materials, and it highlights the unique focus of these campaigns to target Israel.

Double Standards and Disproportionate Focus

The promotion of severe double standards and extreme dispro-portionate focus on Israel in contrast to other conflicts or states is the central means through which Israel is portrayed as the sin-gular violator of international law. Natan Sharansky explains that such double standards become a form of antisemitism, as op-posed to legitimate criticism of Israel, when "criticism of Israel is applied selectively" and "when Israel is singled out ... for human rights abuses while the behavior of known and major abusers ... is ignored."[46] Ultimately, this from of antisemitism is based on the "master trope" of "Jewish abuse of power."[47]

UNITED NATIONS PLATFORMS

As with campaigns portraying Israel's very existence as a viola-tion of international norms, the UN has become the primary venue for promoting double standards and disproportionate at-tacks on Israel using the discourse of international law.

Numerous UN platforms demonize the Jewish state as the primary violator of human rights and humanitarian norms. The UNGA typically issues more resolutions condemning Israel for violations of international law than all other countries combined. Annual meetings and reports of the Secretary-General's office, UNESCO, and UN Women, for instance, include resolutions condemning Israel alone.[48] Despite the facade of universality and impartiality, UN Human Rights Treaty bodies, such as the Com-mittee against Torture and the Committee on the Elimination of Racial Discrimination, are far from immune.[49]

These attacks are most acute within the special mechanisms provided by the UN uniquely for the Palestinians' cause. In 1974, only ten weeks after the Ma'alot massacre when more than thirty Israelis were killed during a Palestinian terror attack on a school,[50] the PLO was granted observer status at the UN, a status not con-ferred on any other armed guerrilla movement.[51] Following the adoption of Resolution 3379 ("Zionism Is Racism"), the Division for Palestinian Rights was created to support the Committee for the Exercise of the Inalienable Rights of the Palestinian People established by Resolution 3379, the only UN division devoted to a single national group or cause. The division hosts international conferences, events, and exhibits; issues publications; and organizes the UN's annual International Day of Solidarity with the Palestinian People, aimed at advancing the Palestinian narrative, denigrating the Jewish connection to Jerusalem and the land of Israel, and promoting claims of Israeli legal violations.[52] The division also runs the UN Information System of the Question of Palestine, providing the PLO and allied NGOs a free online platform to advertise conferences and events and to distribute anti-Israel propaganda.

In addition, the United Nations Relief and Works Agency for Palestine, ostensibly established to assist refugees, is a major source of attacks against Israel based on legal and human rights claims.[53] The agency has its own public relations apparatus and officials who are active in promoting the Palestinian narrative, a "right of return," and other pseudolegal claims.

Special attention must be directed to the UN Human Rights Council (HRC). The HRC, which was established in 2006, and its predecessor, the Commission on Human Rights,[54] have exhibited entirely disproportionate and obsessive focus on Israel. Israel is the only country with its own permanent agenda item (Item 7) at the HRC; it has been the focus of more than 80 percent of the resolutions, and one-third of the special sessions have been devoted to condemnations of the Jewish state. Since 2006, the HRC has appointed at least five fact-finding committees, most notably the 2009 United Nations Fact Finding Mission on the Gaza Conflict (also known a- the "Goldstone Mission"), to investigate alleged Israeli abuses under human rights and humanitarian law—more than any other country.[55]

Israel is also one of only fourteen countries for which a special rapporteur was appointed to monitor human rights violations, and it is the only country where the rapporteur's mandate is one-sided and does not expire.[56] Many of the thematic rapporteurs addressing particular issues such as the right to food also routinely prioritize Israel as a prime violator of these rights. The special rapporteur appointed by the HRC to "investigate Israel's violations of the principles and bases of international law, international humanitarian law and the Geneva Convention relative to the Protection of Civilian Persons in Time of War, of 12 August 1949, in the Palestinian territories occupied by Israel since 1967," is generally someone with a long history of anti-Israel campaigning.[57]

Members appointed to the HRC commissions of inquiry have a similar history of prejudicial statements singling out Israel. For instance, three of the four members of the 2009 UN fact-finding mission empaneled to investigate the 2008–2009 Gaza War—Richard Goldstone, Hina Jilani, and Desmond Travers—signed a widely publicized March 2009 letter initiated by Amnesty International accusing Israel of "gross violations of the laws of war" and stating that "events in Gaza have shocked us to the core."[58] The fourth member, Christine Chinkin, signed a letter published in the Sunday Times of London on January 11, 2009, declaring Israel's actions to be a "war crime" and denying that the operation was a legal form of self-defense. To the extent staffers can be identified for these commissions (the process is hidden), many have worked for civil society organizations that produce the biased material that largely forms the basis of the resulting reports.

The proceedings of these commissions have portrayed Israelis as uniquely immoral, child killers, psychologically disturbed, and akin to Nazis. In an exchange during hearings held in June 2009 by the Goldstone Mission, for instance, Desmond Travers asked Eyed Sarraj, head of the political NGO known as the Gaza Community Mental Health Program, the following:

TRAVERS: I would like to put a question to, it may not be entirely within your field, but nevertheless it's a question that continuously comes around in my mind. We

have heard testimony of great, uh, violence, seemingly
*un-militarily, unnecessary violence inflicted particularly
on children.* There have been instances of the *shooting of children in front of their parents* As an ex-soldier I
find that kind of action to be *very, very strange and very
unique.* I would like to ask you if you have any professional insights as to *what mindset or what conditioning or
what training* could bring around a state of behavior that
would cause a soldier, a fellow human being to shoot
children in front of their parents. Do you have any professional insights into that kind of behavior? [emphasis
added]

SARRAJ: There is a psychological process, a long-term psychological process based in the situation of dehumanization of the enemy. The Palestinian in the eyes of the
Israeli soldier is not an equal human being. This leads
to what is called, uh, the, uh, arrogance of power. The
most serious matter is that this state was not dealt with
psychologically, this state of the victim and it became a
perpetual state. It is very serious is that a victim who is
not treated and then is given a dangerous weapon. There
we see the arrogance of power and he uses it without
thinking of humanity at all.[59]

A follow-up question by Richard Goldstone prompted the following response from Sarraj: "But we, the Palestinians have a
greater capacity, in my view, to deal with the Israelis as equal
human beings, as a whole human being . . . inside Israel there is
an identification with the aggressor, the Nazi."

In the case of Goldstone,[60] as in other instances, the resulting
HRC reports lead to further condemnations and meetings in
international frameworks and on university campuses and media
reports of Israel's alleged legal violations. In 2014, for instance,
the government of Switzerland convened a meeting of the High
Contracting Parties to the Geneva Conventions to examine

Israel's violations of international humanitarian law. These meetings have taken place only two other times in history, in 2001 and 2010; as in 2014, the other two conferences were similarly focused on Israel's alleged violations of the Geneva Conventions.

The double standards and disproportionate treatment of Israel in UN and other international frameworks are greatly bolstered and amplified by corresponding campaigns carried out by local Palestinian and Israeli NGOs advancing one-state agendas, international NGO superpowers such as Amnesty International and Human Rights Watch, churches, and humanitarian organizations such as Oxfam and Médecins Sans Frontières whose massive budgets rival those of multinational corporations. The next section details this dimension and the centrality of the rhetoric of international humanitarian law in these campaigns. It also highlights the merging of classical antisemitism and Holocaust inversion with this legal discourse and the prominent role played by church organizations and "dissident" Israelis.

CIVIL SOCIETY CAMPAIGNS

Accompanying the UN bodies, churches and NGOs claiming human rights and humanitarian mandates also disproportionately focus on the Jewish state through international legal discourse and double standards. The accusations of these organizations include "wanton force," "deliberately targeting civilians," "disproportionate force," "collective punishment," and "indiscriminate weaponry." Measures to prevent civilian casualties, such as the issuing of warnings in Gaza despite the loss of strategic advantage to the Israel Defense Forces (IDF)—measures that military officials from around the world note far exceed legal requirements—are condemned and cited as further evidence of Israeli immorality, malice, and war crimes. IDF attempts to counter rocket fire and other attacks on the civilian population are branded as "pretexts" to inflict death and destruction on Palestinians—and children in particular. As Robert Bernstein, who founded Human Rights

Watch and then criticized his organization, wrote in an October 19, 2009, *New York Times* op-ed, "In recent years Human Rights Watch has written far more condemnations of Israel for violations of international law than of any other country in the region. . . . Yet Israel, the repeated victim of aggression, faces the brunt of Human Rights Watch's criticism."

A number of Israeli and Palestinian NGOs claiming to promote human rights and international law are similarly active in targeting Israel through these instruments (see the discussion below). These NGOs are largely funded primarily by European governments. For example, Sweden, Switzerland, the Netherlands, and Denmark jointly fund the International Humanitarian Law and Human Rights Secretariat based at the Birzeit University Institute of Law in Ramallah. This initiative provided at least $13 million over three years (2014–16) to NGOs to document alleged Israeli violations of law.[61] These institutions and their employees issue glossy publications, produce videos, and are highlighted at the UN and in European parliaments aimed at furthering condemnations of Israel and the imposition of sanctions and other punitive measures. A central goal of this funding is to have Israelis prosecuted by the International Criminal Court. Similarly, in 2008, Oxfam Novib and the European Union, in conjunction with the NGO Palestinian Center for Human Rights, funded a conference, "Impunity and Prosecution of Israeli War Criminals." The event was held in Cairo and broadcast on Al Jazeera; participants strategized ways in which Israelis could be prosecuted under universal jurisdiction statutes and by the ICC.

The legal language and accusations of the NGOs and UN bodies provide ammunition for the Israel boycott campaigns. For example, in February 2010, a group of British academics who penned an open letter (published in *Haaretz* and elsewhere) demanding that Elton John cancel a concert in Tel Aviv, wrote, "We're struggling to understand why you're playing in Israel on

June 17. You may say you're not a political person, but does an army dropping white phosphorus on a school building full of children demand a political response? Does walling a million and a half people up in a ghetto and then pounding that ghetto to rubble require a political response from us, or a human one?"[62]

NGO Theological Antisemitism, Holocaust Inversion

Classical antisemitic themes, such as deicide, blood libel, poisoning the wells, conspiracy, cabals, manipulation, financial control, and the all-powerful Jew, as well as references to the Jewish Bible and Holocaust inversion are woven, often overtly, within these pseudolegal texts. These "civil society" campaigns frequently increase during Christian holidays.

To coincide with Christmas, the Amos Trust, a UK church-based "creative human rights organization," sells a nativity scene with Israel's "wall" cutting through it. War on Want, a powerful UK group that "fights against the root causes of poverty and human rights violation, as part of the worldwide movement for global justice," offers a set of holiday cards, one of which shows Joseph and a pregnant Mary being stopped and searched by an IDF soldier on the way into Bethlehem. Another shows the Three Wise Men "tunneling" under the "wall." The description on the back of the card reads, "Bethlehem is one of the many Palestinian towns devastated by Israel's illegal Separation Wall. . . . Despite being ruled illegal by the International Court of Justice in 2004, construction of the Wall continues."

During the 2014 Gaza War, NGOs and the media made a point of condemning Israel for launching operations during Ramadan and while Palestinians were breaking their fasts, calling them war crimes and religious freedom violations.[63] In contrast, Palestinians were not condemned for launching rockets on Israeli Muslims and Palestinians in the West Bank at the same time. Nor were rocket launches on Tisha B'Av, one of the most somber days in the Jewish calendar, condemned.

During the 2006 Lebanon War in a July 31 letter to the *New York Sun*, Ken Roth, executive director of Human Rights Watch, condemned Israel for allegedly "bombing Lebanese civilians" and targeting "fleeing villagers." He ascribed Israel's actions to motivations from the Old Testament: "An eye for an eye—or, more accurately in this case, twenty eyes for an eye—may have been the morality of some more primitive moment. But it is not the morality of international humanitarian law." In 2014, Roth promoted on his Twitter account a highly propagandistic advertisement equating "Nazi genocide" with "the massacre of Palestinians in Gaza" under the tagline "'Never again' must mean NEVER AGAIN FOR ANYONE!" Professor Deborah Lipstadt, in a 2014 interview, refers to this language as soft-core denigration of the Holocaust.[64] The head of Human Rights Watch's Middle East and North Africa Division, Sarah Leah Whitson, has likened Israeli policy to Nazis and the crime of genocide as well as promoted the tropes of Jewish particularism and Jewish cabals. In response to a tweet praising the United States Holocaust Memorial Museum for hosting an exhibit on Syria, Whitson wrote, "@ BBCKimGhattas @DRovera @HolocaustMuseum @BBCNewsUS should also show pics of death and destruction in #Gaza," implying that the Gaza War was the equivalent of genocide and the mass murder in Syria.[65] In a 2012 op-ed published in the *Huffington Post*, "A Matter of Civil Rights," Whitson claims that Israel "strictly segregate[s] Jews from Palestinians" and violates the Geneva Conventions while singling out and chastising American Jews for supporting these alleged policies. Her ascribing culpability to US Jews for Israeli policies invokes the antisemitic canards of Jewish power, dual loyalty, and immorality.[66]

In May 2016, a group of scholars called for the cancelation of a conference of the International Network of Genocide Scholars at Hebrew University ("organized by complicit institutions and taking place in a colony on occupied land") in West Jerusalem because "Israel's actions against the Palestinian people—from the Nakba to the ongoing displacement of Palestinians from their lands, and from repeated military offensives against Gaza to the ongoing blockade—are increasingly being viewed through lenses of ethnic cleansing and genocide linked to settler colonialism."[67] The letter closed with "Never again means never again for anyone."[68]

A letter authored by activist "doctors and scientists" published in the medical journal the *Lancet* in July 2014 during the Gaza War is a particularly stark example. The letter accuses Israel of a "ruthless assault of unlimited duration, extent, and intensity."[69] The authors "challenge the perversity of a propaganda that justifies the creation of an emergency to masquerade a massacre."[70] They allege that Israel "clearly direct[ed] fire to target whole families killing them within their homes" and "targeted weaponry used indiscriminately and on children."[71] They further claim that "none of these are military objectives.[72] These attacks aim to terrorise, wound the soul and the body of the people, and make their life impossible in the future."[73] They conclude that "Israel's behaviour has insulted our humanity, intelligence, and dignity as well as our professional ethics and efforts."[74]

Notably, a few weeks after the publication of this letter, two of the main authors, Dr. Swee Ang Chai and Paola Manduca, circulated a video, "CNN Goldman Sachs and the ZioMatrix," created by white supremacist and former Ku Klux Klan grand wizard David Duke.[75] Chai's cover email stated, "This is shocking video please watch. This is not about Palestine—it is about all of us!"[76] It also contained, in bold red lettering, "SEE THIS VIDEO BEFORE IT IS REMOVED FROM CIRCULATION—Please do pass on to others who you think would be interested and would pass on>>>The whole world needs to know."[77]

Church-Supported International Humanitarian Law Frameworks
Humanitarian aid organizations, primarily operated by European churches, also routinely emphasize Israel's alleged violations of

international law, in marked contrast to how they describe other conflict zones, reflecting the double standards applied to the Jewish state. For instance, Trocaire, the humanitarian arm of the Irish Catholic Church that is supported with funding from the Irish and UK governments as well as the European Union, describes its work for "OPT [Occupied Palestinian Territory—a term incorporating legal judgment] and Israel" as working "to support those affected by conflict and human rights violations, as well as helping to raise international awareness around the injustice of human rights violations."[78] The expanded description states, "For almost half a century, Israel has maintained a military occupation of the OPT (the West Bank and Gaza). Israel continues to displace Palestinian communities by force and confiscate their land, a practice which has been ongoing for over six decades. Israeli settlements, which are illegal under international law, have been established on Palestinian land. Palestinians remain without a state, and human rights violations such as house demolitions, land confiscation, forced displacement, restrictions of movement and violence against civilians occur on an almost daily basis."[79] In this telling, Israel is the sole violator and responsible party for the conflict. Palestinians are absolved of all culpability. In contrast, Trocaire describes its work in South Sudan as "primarily focused on supporting communities affected by the country's ongoing conflict."[80] Its work in the Democratic Republic of Congo focuses on "humanitarian response and building resilient communities, supporting women's empowerment, including through governance work, and sustainable livelihood activities."[81] The introduction to the Syria page says simply that "the conflict in Syria has resulted in the worst humanitarian crisis in a generation."[82] The rest of the text discusses only the numbers of refugees created by the conflict.

None of the in-depth descriptions for these countries, in sharp contrast to the case of Israel, detail human rights or humanitarian law violations, nor does Trocaire ascribe responsibility for the conflicts. Instead, Trocaire speaks in humanitarian terms, in contrast to discourse about Israel, in which the primary framework employed is international law and alleged violations by Israel alone.

Trocaire is not unique—many of the church-aid frameworks run international humanitarian law programs exclusively focusing on Israel's violations of law and promoting the narrative that these alleged violations are unique among nations. Diakonia, a humanitarian aid organization established by five Swedish churches, runs the Global International Humanitarian Law Centre (funded by the Swedish government). Despite the universal name, the program has "a mandate to address the ongoing violations of IHL that characterise the Israeli-Palestinian conflict," centering on Israel's alleged abuses. The Harvard School of Public Health also ran an "IHL in Israel and the Occupied Palestinian Territory" program in conjunction with Diakonia and funded by Sweden, Switzerland, Norway, and the UN.

CITING "DISSIDENT" ISRAELIS AND JEWS AS SOURCES OF EVIDENCE

A common theme in much NGO activity is the moral failure of the Israeli military. The Israeli NGOs active on this issue purport to expose the Israeli public to the "evils of occupation" and Israel's "violations of international law"; the NGO officials are presented as "dissidents" opposing the "bad" Jews that are trying to suppress the truth about IDF "war crimes." As noted by Anthony Julius, the "courage" of these groups "has become a posture" aimed at taking an "adversarial stance" even in "the absence of actual risk."[83]

The Israeli NGO Breaking the Silence (BtS) is a prime example. This group of "veteran combatants" claims to "expose the Israeli public to the reality of everyday life in the Occupied Territories" and to portray the "deterioration of moral standards . . . in the character of orders and the rules of engagement, and are justified in the name of Israel's security."[84] The activists (fewer than ten in number) claim that "while this reality is well-known to Israeli soldiers and commanders, Israeli society in general continues to turn a blind eye and deny what is being done in its name."[85]

BtS carries out its objectives by publishing anonymous testimonies alleging war crimes and other international legal violations and presenting them primarily to global audiences. With over $1 million to finance its activities around the world, the organization publishes books in several languages, and international media outlets readily publish articles promoting the group's claims. Recent headlines include "New Report Details How Israeli Soldiers Killed Civilians in Gaza: 'There Were No Rules,'"[86] "Soldiers Group: In Gaza War, IDF Assumed Everyone Was a Terrorist,"[87] and "Gaza: Killing Gets Easier."[88] As noted journalist Matti Friedman observed in a May 2015 article for *Mosaic* magazine, "Breaking the Silence's money is foreign, not Israeli, and the primary customers for its product are foreign, not Israeli. At its extensive English website, Jewish soldiers are presented for international consumption as a spectacle of moral failure, a spectacle paid for by Norwegians, French Catholics, and Germans."

In 2016, the IDF asked BtS to provide evidence in order to prosecute a soldier for violations that were alleged by BtS to have taken place in the Gaza conflict. BtS refused, claiming that, like journalists, the sources of the testimonies it received were protected. The issue, which is being considered by the Israeli courts, increased Israeli criticism of the organization on the grounds that, on the one hand, it claimed that the IDF would not prosecute soldiers for violations, but, on the other hand, it refused when asked to provide the evidence for such a prosecution.[89]

Israeli NGO B'Tselem is a similar organization, and from 2012–2014, it received 64.7 percent of its income from European governments and churches.[90] Until recently, the NGO claimed "to document and educate the Israeli public and policymakers about human rights violations in the Occupied Territories."[91]

Like BtS, B'Tselem also claimed to "combat the phenomenon of denial prevalent among the Israeli public, and help create a human rights culture in Israel."[92] In November 2017, the group revised its mission and explained its new credo as, "after more than half a century of occupation, ... it is clear that this reality cannot be viewed as temporary. Therefore, B'Tselem continues to document and publicize human rights violations while also exposing the injustice, violence and dispossession that lie at the very core of this regime of occupation, challenging its legitimacy in Israel and abroad and helping to expedite its end."[93] In pursuit of that goal, aside from a few token statements condemning Palestinian terror attacks, the vast majority of B'Tselem's work is focused on alleged Israeli violations. One project provides video cameras to Palestinians to catch on film IDF and settler abuses in process. No cameras are provided to document Palestinian terrorism or wrongdoing. On its "About" page, B'Tselem embraces this bias: "We are proud to represent this part of Israel to a world which is all too often unaware of it."[94]

Other B'Tselem projects portray the IDF as brutal killers who deliberately target civilians and commit war crimes. During the 2014 Gaza War, for instance, B'Tselem initiated a campaign called "Families Bombed at Home" involving emotive accounts and sophisticated interactive graphics. This campaign often erased the details of Palestinian combatant activity and branded fighters as civilians to magnify its narrative of Israeli wrongdoing. B'Tselem's graphics and themes were adopted by many other NGOs and were a central focus of the UN Human Rights Council's report on the war. The Office of the High Commissioner of Human Rights issued its own graphics, something it had done before, mirroring B'Tselem's, so that everyone could "see" Israel's alleged war crimes.

In many cases, the "good" Israeli NGOs join with their Palestinian counterparts to issue joint statements and submissions, including to UN groups, based on the language of international law and human rights. For example, the United Nations Office for the Coordination of Humanitarian Affairs casualty claims made during the 2014 Gaza conflict were provided by the NGO "protection cluster" consisting of B'Tselem (Israel), Al Mezan (Gaza), and the Palestinian Center for Human Rights (Gaza). Both Palestinian groups, along with Al Haq, are centrally involved in lawfare—and in particular, the campaign to have the ICC prosecutor open cases against Israelis. Although B'Tselem has no personnel or verification capabilities in Gaza, its presence in the cluster provides a form of Israeli credibility to these claims. (As in the past, the allegations regarding civilian deaths in Gaza were shown to be unsubstantiated.)[95]

Erasing the Context of Palestinian Violence, Denial of Self-Defense, Promotion of Terrorism

Another central feature of the above examples is that they all minimize or erase completely Palestinian agency and the context of terrorism. Israel is the sole aggressor in its conflict with the Palestinians. Israel is acting not to protect its citizens from suicide bombings, rockets, tunnels, and other attacks but rather to punish and deliberately inflict harm on Palestinians.

Amnesty International's Gaza Platform, a collaboration between Amnesty and BDS activists, epitomizes this practice. The platform is an online tool launched in July 2015—ostensibly "an interactive map of attacks by Israeli forces on Gaza" during the 2014 Gaza conflict, using satellite imagery and advanced graphics. Users can click on a location and read a narrative account of alleged Israeli wrongdoing supplied by the Palestinian NGOs Al Mezan and the Palestinian Center for Human Rights. The context of combat with Hamas, Islamic Jihad, and other Palestinian terror groups is completely erased, instead presenting a story of arbitrary and unjustified assaults by Israel. There is no mention of the more than four thousand rockets launched from Gaza against Israeli civilians.

An extension of this theme in these campaigns is not only to erase the context of Palestinian violence but also to deny Israel's right to self-defense and at the same time promote a so-called "right of resistance" (Palestinian terrorism) as a matter of law. The right to self-defense is an inherent concept in law "and is fundamental to the system of states." It is recognized and protected by Article 51 of the UN Charter. Yet many documents issued in international frameworks and by civil society deny Israel alone the right to self-defense because it is "occupying" another people.

Often these documents make a token statement that Israel has a "right to live in security" or to "defend its citizens." Yet every policy and action taken by Israel is deemed a violation of law, and no viable or realistic alternatives to end attacks on Israeli civilians are suggested. This practice, as described by Professor Kenneth Anderson in a December 14, 2009, post on the *Volokh Conspiracy* blog, is known as "functional pacifism" or "the setting of standards" by "the human rights monitoring community . . . that in principle allow [states] to engage in war, but in the important actual situations, the use of force always turns out to be wrongfully performed."

Again, NGOs affiliated with churches are prominent in advancing this discourse. Sabeel, for example, asserts, "One of the most common refrains . . . is, 'Israel has the right to defend itself.' . . . First, we should consider that there is no clear 'self' for Israel to defend. . . . In light of the fact that Israel has no defined borders and is occupying another state, it is not even possible to define the 'self' that Israel has a right to defend." Justin Kilcullen, director of Trocaire, admonishes, "Israel says it is defending itself from Palestinian aggression. But Israel is an occupying power controlling the lives of another people."[96]

In December 2003, the Arab League and the NGO community lobbied and secured from the General Assembly a referral to the International Court of Justice for an Advisory Opinion on the "legal consequences" of Israel's security barrier, or "wall" in the request's parlance.[97] On July 9, 2004, the court issued its opinion that Israel had no right to a claim of self-defense under international law because the suicide bombings and other attacks on its civilians were not "imputable to a foreign state."[98] Although not legally binding and despite procedural irregularities, the decision was then used (and continues to be) in international frameworks and by civil society as a basis to further condemn and push for sanctions against Israel.

Coupled with the attempt to have Israel's right to self-defense nullified, these same actors justify terrorism against Israelis and Jews globally. UN Secretary-General Ban Ki Moon said in 2015 that Palestinian terrorism is understandable because it is "human nature to react to occupation." The Commission on Human Rights resolution (1993/2) establishing the special rapporteur for Israel promotes a "right of resistance": "Affirms the right of the Palestinian people to resist the Israeli occupation by all means, in accordance with the relevant United Nations resolutions, consistent with the purposes and principles of the Charter of the United Nations, as has been expressed by the Palestinian people in their brave intifada since December 1987, in legitimate resistance against the Israeli military occupation."[99]

Palestinian combatants are also frequently characterized as "resistance" fighters and attacks on Israeli civilians as "resistance operations," and those advancing this rhetoric claim as a matter of law that Palestinians should have immunity to engage in such acts.

CONCLUSION AND LOOKING FORWARD

As demonstrated in this chapter, the rhetoric and institutions claiming the mantle of human rights and international law play central roles in the development and growing impact of the new antisemitism. The repeated exploitation of terms such as *racism, apartheid,* and *war crimes* in the United Nations, continuing for decades, has had an erosive impact, while the organizations claiming to promote human rights have amplified this process. The activities of global NGOs such as Amnesty International and Human Rights Watch reflect the obsessive double standards and strategy of singling out of Israel for attacks, in clear contradiction to the moral and universal principles of human rights and international law.

In parallel, the abuse of these values against Israel has done major damage to these same values and institutions. In the words of Professor Irwin Cotler, "this laundering of antisemitism under universal public values erodes the integrity of the UN, diminishes the authority of international law, corrupts the culture of human rights, and shames the real struggle against real racism."[100] Robert L. Bernstein, the founder of Human Rights Watch, as noted, denounced in the *New York Times* his own organization for its role in this campaign of bias.

Given the formidable powers and interests that are arrayed to promote this corrosive process, the efforts that are required to halt and then reverse the damage should not be underestimated. In the United Nations, the strength of the Islamic bloc (the Organization of Islamic Cooperation) and the apparent unwillingness of Europe, in particular, to oppose this process make any change extremely difficult and unlikely. For example, although the role of the UN Human Rights Council has been noted many times, there is no indication of any significant changes.

In other arenas and platforms, the prospects for improvement based on public education and "naming and shaming" the abusers of international law and the values of human rights are somewhat better. Although the language and relevant institutions are obscure and thus readily manipulated by those given the aura of "experts," this halo effect in the case of human rights NGOs can be challenged and reversed. The *New York Times* op-ed by Robert Bernstein diminished Human Rights Watch's credibility among some major journalists, including in the *New York Times*, and the references in this central media platform citing this NGO on Israel-related issues decreased visibly. Other challenges to Human Rights Watch's activities dealing with Israel have added to this process, including the exposure of the obsessive collection of Nazi paraphernalia involving its "senior military analyst," who wrote many of the publications that falsely accused Israel of war crimes.

Similarly, the criticism of the Ford Foundation's role in sponsoring the infamous NGO Forum of the 2001 Durban Conference led to fundamental changes in the funding patterns of this powerful philanthropy. In addition to a public letter pledging not to fund organizations that call for the elimination of any state (in other words, the virulently anti-Israel and antisemitic NGOs at Durban), the Ford Foundation gradually ended funding for all NGOs that exploit human rights and international law to demonize Israel and promote virulent anti-Zionism.[101]

In academic venues, the detailed criticism of NGO fact-finding in the context of human rights and international law, including, but not limited to, Israel-related issues, has also expanded in recent years.[102] In addition, critics such as Hopgood, Moyn, and others have placed the broader questions resulting from the lack of universality and the politicization of human rights and international law on the agendas of law schools and human rights programs at major universities. Orde Kittrie's book *Lawfare: Law as a Weapon of War* explicitly confronts the politicization process, moving the lofty normative image of human rights rhetoric, which has been central to modern antisemitism, down to the realist political realm.[103]

At the same time, these processes of demystifying the institutions and rhetoric of international law and human rights, which are used to single out Israel and promote antisemitism, are only beginning. Journalists, liberal religious leaders, and other molders of public opinion, particularly in the West, still largely copy and emphasize the activities and publications of the United

Nations frameworks and the NGOs claiming to promote noble agendas, particularly in the demonization of Israel. In this area, there is still a great amount of work to be done.

NOTES

1. Samuel Moyn, *The Last Utopia* (Cambridge, MA: Harvard University Press, 2010).

2. Robert Wistrich, "Anti-Zionism and Anti-Semitism," *Jewish Political Studies Review* 16 (2004): 3, http://www.jcpa.org/phas/phas-wistrich-f04.htm

3. Gerald M. Steinberg, "Postcolonial Ideology and the Arab-Israeli Conflict," in *Israel—Geschichte und Gegenwart,* ed. Brigitte Bailer (Vienna: Barumuller, 2009), 1–19.

4. Alan Johnson, "The Left and the Jews: Time for a Rethink," *Fathom Journal* (Autumn 2015), http://fathomjournal.org/the-left-and-the-jews-time-for-a-rethink/.

5. Mirko D. Garasic and Shay Keinan, "Boycotting Israeli Academia: Is Its Implementation Anti-Semitic?" *International Journal of Discrimination and the Law* 15, no. 3 (2015): 191.

6. Manfred Gerstenfeld, *The War of a Million Cuts* (Jerusalem: Jerusalem Center for Public Affairs, 2015), 31.

7. Wistrich, "Anti-Zionism and Anti-Semitism."

8. Wistrich, "Anti-Zionism and Anti-Semitism."

9. Jonathan Sacks, "Europe's New Anti-Semitism," *Huffington Post Religion,* September 10, 2012, https://www.huffingtonpost.com/chief-rabbi-lord-sacks/europe-new-anti-semitism_b_1663157.html.

10. Wistrich, "Anti-Zionism and Anti-Semitism."

11. Wistrich, "Anti-Zionism and Anti-Semitism."

12. Irwin Cotler, "Anti-Semitism, Old and New," *Algemeiner,* January 27, 2015.

13. Robert P. Barnidge Jr., *Self Determination, Statehood, and the Law of Negotiation: The Case of Palestine* (Oxford: Hart, 2016).

14. Barnidge, *Self-Determination,* 62, 65, 113.

15. Barnidge, *Self-Determination,* 62, 65, 113; Walter Laqueur, ed., *Israel-Arab Reader* (New York: Citadel Press, 1969), 121; Palestine Liberation Organization: The Original Palestine National Charter (1964), articles 17–19, *Jewish Virtual Library,* accessed July 11, 2018, http://www.jewishvirtuallibrary.org/the-original-palestine-national-charter-1964.

16. Laqueur, *Israel-Arab Reader,* 121.

17. Anne Herzberg, *NGO "Lawfare": Exploitation of Courts in the Arab-Israeli Conflict.* NGO Monitor Monograph Series, edited by Gerald Steinberg (Jerusalem: NGO Monitor, 2008); Orde F. Kittrie, *Lawfare: Law as a Weapon of War* (New York: Oxford University Press, 2016), 1.

18. Barnidge, *Self-Determination,* 69.

19. Daniel Patrick Moynihan, *A Dangerous Place* (New York: Little, Brown, 1978), 187.

20. Moynihan, *A Dangerous Place,* 189.

21. Moynihan, *A Dangerous Place,* 172.

22. Moynihan, *A Dangerous Place,* 172; Barnidge, *Self-Determination;* Ofra Friesel, "Equating Zionism with Racism: The 1965 Precedent," *American Jewish History* 97 (2013): 283–313.

23. Moynihan, *A Dangerous Place,* 187; Bernard Lewis, "At the United Nations," *Commentary Magazine,* March 1, 1979, accessed July 12, 2018, https://www.commentarymagazine.com/articles/a-dangerous-place-by-daniel-patrick-moynihan-with-suzanne-weaver/.

24. Matthieu Rey, "'Fighting Colonialism' versus 'Non-Alignment': Two Arab Points of View on the Bandung Conference," in *The Non-Aligned Movement and the Cold War: Delhi—Bandung—Belgrade,* ed. Natasa Miskovic and Harald Fischer-Tine Nada (New York: Routledge, 2014), 172; Hennie Strydom, "The Non-Aligned Movement and the Reform of International Relations," *Max Planck Yearbook of United Nations Law* 11 (2007): 1–46.

25. Barnidge, *Self-Determination,* 66.

26. Barnidge, *Self-Determination,* 78.

27. William Korey, "The Kremlin and the UN 'Zionism Equals Racism' Resolution, *Israel Yearbook on Human Rights* 17 (1987): 133-148, 135; See also Friesel, Ofra, "Equating Zionism with Racism: the 1965 Precedent," *American Jewish History* 97 (2013): 283–313 for more on the CERD debate.

28. Moynihan, *A Dangerous Place,* 172.

29. Irwin Cotler, "The Uniqueness of Antisemitism," *The Jerusalem Post,* January 27, 2015, https://www.jpost.com/Opinion/The-uniqueness-of-anti-Semitism-389175; see also Gil Troy, *Moynihan's Moment,* 27, 2015 (Oxford: Oxford University Press, 2012).

30. Moynihan, *A Dangerous Place,* 213.

31. Moynihan, *A Dangerous Place,* 169, 231–33.

32. Declaration of the NGO Forum, World Conference against Racism, Racial Discrimination Xenophobia and Related Intolerance, Durban, South Africa, August 27-Sept 1, 2001, paragraph 424, available at

http://academic.udayton.edu/race/o6hrights/WCAR2001
/NGOFORUM/Palestinans.htm.

33. Mahmoud Abbas, "The Long Overdue Palestinian State,"
New York Times, May 16, 2011, https://www.nytimes.com/2011/05/17
/opinion/17abbas.html.

34. Barnidge, *Self-Determination*; Lauro Burkart, "The Politicization of
the Oslo Water Agreement," master's thesis,
   Graduate Institute of International and Development Studies, 2012.

35. For instance, Sabeel's Naim Ateek calls the "establishment of
Israel" a "relapse to the most primitive concepts of an exclusive, tribal
God." In one Easter address, Ateek stated, "In this season of Lent, it
seems to many of us that Jesus is on the cross again with thousands of
crucified Palestinians around him" (David Parsons, "Behind the 'Christ
at the Checkpoint' Conference," March 2, 2012, accessed July 15, 2018,
https://ca.icej.org/news/press-statements/behind-christ-checkpoint
-conference). In 2007, Badil was joined by several European churches in
a "Call to Action," advocating for anti-Israel boycotts and sanctions, and
enlisted "journalists to organize a targeted campaign to expose the lies
of AIPAC [American Israel Public Affairs Committee] and the Anti-
Defamation League and to expose the Jewish and Zionist community's
double standards regarding Nakba & Occupation" (document on file
with authors). In 2010, Badil published and awarded a prize to a cartoon
of a Jewish man garbed in traditional Hasidic attire, with a hooked nose
and side locks. He stands on a blue block branded with Jewish stars and
the year 1948 crushing two children surrounded by skulls and holds a
menorah-shaped pitchfork dripping with blood (BADIL, "4th Annual
Al-Awda Award (2010)," accessed July 15, 2018, https://web.archive.org
/web/20150102072849/http://badil.org/annual-al-awda-award/item
/1416-award2010-winners). A cartoon published in 2007 shows an
octopus with a blue Jewish star on its forehead hovering over skulls
(NGO Monitor, "BADIL," June 5, 2018, accessed July 15, 2018, https://
www.ngo-monitor.org/ngos/badil/#jp-carousel-5605).

36. Nidal Azza, "Israel the Racist Ghetto," *Defining the Conflict*, BADIL
Resource Center, 2007, http://www.badil.org/en/publication/periodicals
/al-majdal/item/438-israel-the-racist-ghetto.html.

37. Human Sciences Research Council, *Occupation, Colonialism,
Apartheid? A Re-assessment of Israel's, Practices in the Occupied Palestinian
Territories under International Law*, Democracy and Governance
Programme, Middle East Project (HSRC: Cape Town, 2009), http://www
.alhaq.org/attachments/article/236/Occupation_Colonialism_Apartheid
-FullStudy.pdf.

38. As noted by Goldsmith and Posner, international law is no longer viewed as the law among nations but rather as the law of human rights. Moyn, *The Last Utopia*, 176.

39. Aryeh Neier, *The International Human Rights Movement: A History* (Princeton, NJ: Princeton University Press, 2012); Lynn Hunt, *Inventing Human Rights* (New York: W. W. Norton, 2007); Moyn, *The Last Utopia*, 176.

40. Kahn observes that since 2001, the Geneva Conventions of 1949 have "skyrocketed in prominence."
Moyn, *The Last Utopia*, 177.

41. Stephen Hopgood, *The Endtimes of Human Rights* (Ithaca, NY: Cornell University Press, 2013).

42. Hopgood, *The Endtimes of Human Rights*, 120–25.

43. For example, according to the governing 1907 Hague Convention (Art. 42) and 1949 Fourth Geneva Convention (Art. 6), occupation requires "boots on the ground" and control of government functions of a High Contracting Party by a hostile army. Despite not meeting these conditions, the human rights industry claims that Gaza is "occupied" by Israel. A similar distortion of the law regarding occupation is not found in other conflict situations.

44. Robert Wistrich, *A Lethal Obsession* (New York: Random House, 2010), 8.

45. BDS Movement, "What Is BDS?," accessed July 12, 2018, https://bdsmovement.net/what-is-bds.

46. Natan Sharansky, "3D Test on Antisemitism: Demonization, Double Standards, Delegitimization," *Jewish Political Studies Review* 16 (2004), http://www.jcpa.org/phas/phas-sharansky-f04.htm.

47. Anthony Julius, *Trials of the Diaspora: A History of Anti-Semitism in England* (Oxford: Oxford University Press, 2010), 476.

48. In 2015, UN agencies, Human Rights Watch, and other NGOs intensely lobbied the secretary general to include Israel in the list of the "Parties that Commit Grave Violations against Children"—a list that exclusively comprises terrorist organizations, armed guerrilla groups, and militias associated with failed states. Under the standards proffered by Human Rights Watch regarding Israel, every Western country should also be listed, all the more so countries such as Russia and Ukraine (to name two). However, Israel alone was targeted.

49. For example, the Committee against Torture, which reviews state compliance with the Convention against Torture, employs severe distortions of the treaty provisions when evaluating Israel. When discussing what constitutes cruel, inhuman, and degrading treatment, or CIDT, under Article 16 of the treaty, the committee has asked Israel about

"settlement policy," "the Fence/Wall," "checkpoints and roadblocks," and even "access to health care in Gaza." These topics fall outside the scope of torture and CIDT. Questions asked by the committee pertaining to Article 16 for other countries do not contain references to such out-of-scope topics. Rather, they focus on "extrajudicial executions," detention practices, use of weaponry by security officials in prison, use of isolation cells, and prison conditions—all accepted topics of discussion under Article 16.

50. More than one hundred children were held hostage during the attack.

51. UN General Assembly Resolution 3237, UN Doc. A/RES/3237 (XXIX), November 22, 1974.

52. 2014 was declared the International Year of Solidarity with the Palestinian People, providing the division with a platform for the entire year to carry out events and to use UN resources to promote the Palestinian political agenda.

53. Arlene Kushner, "The UN's Palestinian Refugee Problem," *Azure* 22 (2005): 57–77; Martha Gellhorn, "The Arabs of Palestine," *The Atlantic*, October 1961.

54. The Human Rights Council was created to ostensibly remedy the problems of politicization and selectivity that had plagued its predecessor entity, the Commission on Human Rights. In 2005, former UN Secretary-General Kofi Annan remarked that "the Commission's ability to perform its tasks has been . . . undermined by the politicization of its sessions and the selectivity of its work." Kofi Annan (speech on creating the Human Rights Council, Geneva, April 7, 2005). In testimony before the US Congress on May 17, 2016, Hillel Neuer, executive director of United Nations Watch, detailed the continuing double standards and politicization at the UN Human Rights Council; see http://www .unwatch.org/wp-content/uploads/2016/05/Hillel-Neuer-Testimony -May-17-2016-TLHRC.pdf.

55. Fact-finding missions were established for Israel (2006, 2008, 2009, 2012, 2014), Libya (2011), Syria (2011), North Korea (2013), Eritrea (2014), Sri Lanka (2014), and Burundi (2015). The resolutions establishing the commissions declared Israel a priori to be a violator of international law.

56. The other thirteen are Belarus, Cambodia, Central African Republic, Ivory Coast, Eritrea, Haiti, Iran, Mali, Myanmar, North Korea, Somalia, Sudan, and Syria and must be renewed annually.

57. Res 1993/2, E/CN.4/RES/1993/2A. In a comment on a 2014 *EJIL: Talk!* blog post (Joseph Weiler, "After Gaza 2014: Schabas," November

4–5, 2014, https://www.ejiltalk.org/after-gaza-2014-schabas/), Christina Cerna, a well-respected expert and former member of the Inter-American Commission on Human Rights who applied for the position of rapporteur but was rejected for not being sufficiently anti-Israel, remarked that when it comes to Israel, "[i]mpartiality is not a requirement sought by the Council" and that "the Organization of Islamic Cooperation and the League of Arab States both officially opposed me . . . because I had never said anything pro-Palestinian and consequently was not known to be 'partial.'" "In my view," she continues, "Impartiality is not a requirement sought by the Council for the appointment of experts when it comes to Israel."

58. Concurrent with the Gaza War were massacres involving thousands in the Democratic Republic of Congo and a civil war in Sri Lanka involving more than forty thousand civilian deaths. No letter was organized by Amnesty International for these events, nor did the Goldstone mission members publicly express being "shocked to the core" by these far more deadly conflicts.

59. United Nations Fact Finding Mission on the Gaza Conflict, "Public Hearings—Gaza City, Morning Session of 29 June 2009," June 29, 2009, accessed July 12, 2018, https://www.ohchr.org/Documents/HRBodies/HRCouncil/SpecialSession/Session9/Transcript29062009AM.doc.

60. Judge Richard Goldstone subsequently recanted many of the findings of his report; see Conal Urquhart, "Judge Goldstone Expresses Regrets about His Report into Gaza War," *The Guardian*, April 3, 2011, https://www.theguardian.com/world/2011/apr/03/goldstone-regrets-report-into-gaza-war.

61. More than half of the NGO recipients promote BDS, antinormalization, and one-state agendas. Several have also been linked to the Popular Front for the Liberation of Palestine terror group.

62. Hagit Klaiman, "British Academics Ask Elton John to read Goldstone," YNet, February 2, 2010, https://www.ynetnews.com/articles/0,7340,L-3846340,00.html.

63. See, e.g., Peter Beaumont, "Ramadan in Gaza: life under missile-fire," *The Guardian*, July 11, 2014, http://www.theguardian.com/world/2014/jul/11/ramadan-gaza-life-under-missile-fire; Amnesty International, *Families under the Rubble: Israeli Attacks on Inhabited Homes* (London: Amnesty International, 2014), https://www.amnestyusa.org/files/familiesundertherubble.pdf; Human Rights Watch, "Gaza: Airstrike Deaths Raise Concerns on Ground Offensive," https://www.hrw.org/news/2014/07/22/gaza-airstrike-deaths-raise-concerns-ground-offensive.

64. The ad, sponsored by the International Jewish Anti-Zionist Network, was placed in the names of 327 "Jewish survivors and descendants of survivors and victims of Nazi genocide" who "unequivocally condemn the massacre of Palestinians in Gaza." In the text, Israel is condemned for "colonialism, racism, and genocide" and unnamed "right-wing Israelis" are compared to Nazis, and it ends with support for BDS in the form of a "full economic, cultural, and academic boycott of Israel." See https://globalvoices.org/2014/08/23/over-300-holocaust-survivors-and-their-descendants-condemn-israels-massacre-of-palestinians-in-gaza/.

65. Sarah Leah Whitson, Twitter, @sarahleah1, January 28, 2015, https://twitter.com/sarahleah1/status/560700886805389312. In a responding tweet, columnist Jeffrey Goldberg asked Whitson, "Is it Human Rights Watch's position that what is happening in Gaza is genocide?" He added, "It certainly would be appropriate for the Holocaust Museum to feature an exhibit on genocidal Hamas theology."

66. Julius, *Trials of the Diaspora*.

67. "Open letter to INoGS from international academics," PACBI, accessed July 13, 2018, http://www.pacbi.org/etemplate.php?id=2781.

68. "Open letter to INoGS from international academics."

69. Paola Manduca, Ian Chalmers, Derek Summerfield, Mads Gilbert, Swee Ang, on behalf of 24 signatories, "An open letter for the people in Gaza," *The Lancet*, July 30, 2014, accessed July 12, 2018, https://www.thelancet.com/gaza-letter-2014.

70. "An open letter for the people in Gaza."

71. "An open letter for the people in Gaza."

72. "An open letter for the people in Gaza."

73. "An open letter for the people in Gaza."

74. "An open letter for the people in Gaza."

75. Jake Wallis Simons, "Lancet 'hijacked in anti-Israel campaign,'" *The Telegraph (UK)*, September 14, 2014, https://www.telegraph.co.uk/news/health/news/11112930/Lancet-hijacked-in-anti-Israel-campaign.html, accessed July 12, 2018.

76. Simons, "Lancet 'hijacked in anti-Israel campaign.'"

77. https://www.ngo-monitor.org/data/images/File/CNN%20Goldman%20Sachs%20&%20the%20Zio%20Matrix.pdf

78. Trocaire, "Occupied Palestinian Territory (OPT) and Israel," accessed July 12, 2018: https://www.trocaire.org/whatwedo/wherewework/opt-israel.

79. Trocaire, "Occupied Palestinian Territory (OPT) and Israel."

80. Trocaire, "Trocaire's Work in South Sudan," accessed July 12, 2018, https://www.trocaire.org/whatwedo/wherewework/south-sudan

81. Trocaire, "Trocaire's Work in DRC," accessed July 12, 2018, https://www.trocaire.org/whatwedo/wherewework/democratic-republic-congo.

82. Trocaire, "Syria," accessed July 12, 2018, https://www.trocaire.org/whatwedo/wherewework/syria.

83. Wistrich notes, "every prestigious platform has been open for decades to Jewish anti-Zionists in Western democracies who aspire to the status of heroic dissidents." Julius, *Trials of the Diaspora*, 477; Wistrich, *A Lethal Obsession*, 527.

84. Breaking the Silence, "About," accessed July 12, 2018, http://www.breakingthesilence.org.il/about/organization.

85. Breaking the Silence, "About."

86. William Booth, "New Report Details How Israeli Soldiers Killed Civilians in Gaza: 'There were no rules,'" *Washington Post*, May 4, 2015, https://www.washingtonpost.com/news/worldviews/wp/2015/05/04/israeli-soldiers-reveal-this-is-how-we-fought-in-gaza/?utm_term=.f11e71c7272c.

87. Gili Cohen, "Soldiers' Group: In Gaza War, IDF Assumed Everyone Was a Terrorist," *Haaretz*, May 4, 2015, http://www.haaretz.com/israel-news/.premium-1.654823.

88. David Shulman, "Gaza: Killing Gets Easier," *New York Review of Books*, May 29, 2015.

89. Israeli Supreme Court Docket No. 21184-01-16.

90. NGO Monitor, "B'Tselem," March 11, 2018, accessed July 15, 2018, https://www.ngo-monitor.org/ngos/b_tselem/.

91. B'tselem, "About B'tselem," accessed July 12, 2018, https://web.archive.org/web/20160304194830/https://www.btselem.org/about_btselem.

92. B'tselem, "About B'tselem."

93. B'tselem, "About B'tselem," accessed July 12, 2018, https://www.btselem.org/about_btselem.

94. B'tselem, "About B'tselem," accessed July 12, 2018, https://web.archive.org/web/20160304194830/https://www.btselem.org/about_btselem.

95. *Filling in the Blanks: Documenting the Missing Dimensions in UN and NGO Investigations of the Gaza Conflict*, eds. Gerald M. Steinberg and Anne Herzberg (Jerusalem NGO Monitor: 2015), 115-120.

96. Trocaire, "OPT: Israel's Actions Only Serve to Feed Palestinian Contempt," Trocaire, January 6, 2009, accessed July 12, 2018, https://reliefweb.int/report/occupied-palestinian-territory/opt-israels-actions-only-serve-feed-palestinian-contempt.

97. UN General Assembly Resolution, UN Doc. A/RES/ES-10/14, December 12, 2003, accessed July 12, 2018, https://unispal.un.org/DPA/DPR/unispal.nsf/357668878a81e92785256df9005c23c2/f953b744269b9b7485256e1500776dca?OpenDocument. The advisory opinion question posed to the International Court of Justice was: "What are the legal consequences arising from the construction of the wall being built by Israel, the occupying Power, in the Occupied Palestinian Territory, including in and around East Jerusalem, as described in the report of the Secretary-General, considering the rules and principles of international law, including the Fourth Geneva Convention of 1949, and relevant Security Council and General Assembly resolutions?"

98. International Court of Justice, Legal Consequences of the Constr. of a Wall in the Occupied Palestinian Territory, Advisory Opinion, 2004 I.C.J. (July 9) See the decision at 108–0. A minority opinion written by Judge Thomas Buergenthal strongly criticized the biases in the majority opinion, in particular, the court's lack of "requisite factual bases" on which it made "sweeping findings" and its failure to address the context of terrorism. Burgenthal also admonishes, "the nature of these cross-Green Line attacks and their impact on Israel and its population are never really seriously examined by the Court, and the dossier provided the Court by the United Nations on which the Court to a large extent bases its findings barely touches on that subject." Judge Higgins took the court to task for pronouncing on only "one element of a multifaceted dispute," and that its retelling of the "history" of the Arab-Israeli conflict was "neither balanced nor satisfactory."

99. "Question of the violation of human rights in the occupied Arab territories, including Palestine," Office of the High Commissioner for Human Rights, 1993, ap.ohchr.org/documents/E/CHR/resolutions/E-CN_4-RES-1993-2.doc, 2.

100. Cotler, "Anti-Semitism, Old and New."

101. William Korey, *Taking on the World's Repressive Regimes: The Ford Foundation's International Human Rights Policies and Practices* (New York: Palgrave, 2007), 249–69; Gerald M. Steinberg, 7), "Analyzing the Durban II Conference," 9, *Jerusalem Center for Public Affairs* no. 96 (March 4, 2010), http://jcpa.org/article/analyzing-the-durban-ii-conference/.

102. Gerald M. Steinberg, Anne Herzberg, and Jordan Berman, *Best Practices for Human Rights and Humanitarian NGO Fact-Finding* (Leiden, Netherlands: Nijhoff, 2012).

103. Orde Kittrie, *Lawfare: Law as a Weapon of War* (Oxford: Oxford University Press, 2015).

GERALD M. STEINBERG is Professor of Political Studies at Bar Ilan University in Israel and president of NGO Monitor, a Jerusalem-based research institute. His research areas include Middle East diplomacy and security, the politics of human rights and nongovernmental organizations, and Israeli politics and arms control. He is author (with Anne Herzberg and Jordan Berman) of *Best Practices for Human Rights and Humanitarian NGO Fact-Finding*.

ANNE HERZBERG is the legal advisor of NGO Monitor, a Jerusalem-based research institute. Her research interests include international criminal law, universal jurisdiction, international human rights and humanitarian law, the United Nations, and the role of nongovernmental organizations in international frameworks. She is author (with Gerald M. Steinberg and Jordan Berman) of *Best Practices for Human Rights and Humanitarian NGO Fact-Finding*.

SIX

Leaving the Post-Holocaust Period

The Effects of Anti-Israel Attitudes on Perceptions of the Holocaust

CATHERINE D. CHATTERLEY

THE NEW MILLENNIUM began with the publication of a book that characterized Holocaust memorialization and education as an industry designed to promote the interests of Israel and as an extortion racket used to squeeze guilt money from European governments and banks. The book's argument was all the more shocking given the fact that the author's parents were Holocaust survivors. *The Holocaust Industry: Reflections on the Exploitations of Jewish Suffering* is an angry book that expresses Norman Finkelstein's grievances against the Jewish community, its established organizations, and the state of Israel.[1] It was the first mainstream text to put these kinds of accusations, usually made by neo-Nazis, out into the general public under the cover of a dissenting Jewish voice. Five years later, Finkelstein wrote a book in a similar vein condemning the organized Jewish community in Israel and the diaspora for "misusing" antisemitism in the same way he accused them of abusing the Holocaust—all in the service of Israel.[2] Today, these kinds of cynical accusations about the Holocaust and antisemitism are commonplace.

Unlike in Western societies, the (European) Holocaust is not a prominent concern in the Arab and Muslim worlds. It is only a public concern as it pertains to Israel. Commentators in these societies are not usually concerned with historical accuracy or historiographical interpretation; nor are they interested in the moral, philosophical, theological, and cultural implications of the Holocaust.[3] The long history of antisemitism is absent from these discussions, as is European racism, and there is little to no understanding of Christianity and its fraught relationship with the Jewish people. Instead, the concern is only that this foreign disaster was imposed unjustly on the Middle East, and therefore the Holocaust becomes key to understanding the Palestinian predicament. In other words, the Holocaust is understood as the event that caused the Western powers to establish the state of Israel, and so it alone is used to explain why there is a Jewish state in the Middle East. The state is understood to be a European construct, which is both the product of Western guilt for the Holocaust and a convenient way to alleviate this burden. Gilbert Achcar explains the common Arab understanding of the establishment of Israel in his book *The Arabs and the Holocaust*, referring to Edward Said's argument that "the Jewish tragedy led directly to the Palestinian catastrophe. . . . [and adding] Of course, the Holocaust was incomparably crueler and bloodier than the Nakba. This consideration, however, in no way diminishes the tragedy of the Palestinians, particularly since they did not, as a people, bear any blame for the destruction of European Jewry."[4]

In this way of thinking, the Holocaust—a European problem and therefore a European responsibility—was transferred to the Middle East and imposed on the Palestinian Arabs. The Arab people residing in the territory called Palestine never consented to this European solution. They had no involvement in, or responsibility for, the Holocaust and yet were made to suffer for it nonetheless.[5] A deep sense of injustice arose from this perspective, and the resentment it provokes is inseparable from Arab discussions about the Holocaust.

Since the late 1940s, the Arab and Islamic worlds have presented a range of reactions to the Holocaust.[6] Holocaust denial is only one manifestation, and it is often combined with other opinions and perspectives that logically depend on the fact that the Holocaust did indeed occur. There is little consistency here. In fact, one gets the sense that there exists enormous frustration and confusion in relation to the Holocaust throughout the Middle East, and this problem is compounded by the general lack of knowledge about European history in these countries, and about the Holocaust and antisemitism in particular.

Esther Webman and Meir Litvak have studied the shifting Arab reaction to the Holocaust over these decades and have demonstrated that until the early 1950s and for a brief time during the 1990s, there was some acknowledgment of—and even sympathy for—Jewish suffering in liberal Arab circles.[7] However, the following themes are more prominent in today's Arab and Muslim discourse on the Holocaust: (1) Jewish suffering under Nazism is justified and explained as the result of German retaliation against (supposed) Jewish crimes or as a form of divine punishment (the argument of Sheikh Youssef al-Qaradawi, head of the International Union of Muslim Scholars);[8] (2) Zionism is accused of collaborating with Nazism to destroy European Jewry for the cynical purpose of establishing the Jewish state (the subject of Mahmoud Abbas's PhD dissertation);[9] (3) the idea of a so-called second Holocaust is celebrated and people promise to "finish the job"; (4) the Holocaust is minimized through relativization by comparing it with a plethora of crimes in history, especially those believed to be perpetrated by Israel; and (5) the Holocaust is denied outright as a fact of history.[10]

Perhaps the most popular approach to the Holocaust today is the attempt to equate Zionism with Nazism. This strategy allows its purveyors to convey the so-called racism and evil believed to exist at the heart of Zionist political philosophy. The false equation of Nazism and Zionism reverses the role of the Jews in history, transforming their status as victims to that of racist aggressors who now act against a new group of victims: the

Palestinians. In this inverted Holocaust fiction, the Palestinians become the *true* victims of the Holocaust. The Jews are compensated with their own state and, beginning in 1953, receive billions of dollars in reparations, while the Palestinians suffer displacement and exile for a crime they did not commit that happened on another continent.

The last approach reflects not only Arab and Muslim perceptions of their own experience; the new narrative has also been accepted by people in Western societies as well, especially by those eager to overturn support for Israel in Western public opinion. The Zionism-equals-Nazism and Israel-equals-apartheid constructions were first propagated by the Soviet Union.[11] Today, however, these false equations appeal to young people on university campuses and those in progressive political and religious circles, all of whom claim a commitment to social justice and antiracist principles.[12] These equations are designed specifically for our consumption so that Western sympathy for Jews and Israel is reduced and replaced with growing sympathy for "their Palestinian victims." If the equation succeeds, the hope is that the same outrage expressed toward Nazism in the West will be directed toward Israel. Western protection of Israel is still perceived by many to be rooted in the Holocaust experience. Those people who are convinced that Zionism is like Nazism harbor a deep disgust and contempt for Israel and its supporters because, they believe, Jews, of all people, should know better. It is interesting to note that even Norman Finkelstein calls the comparison between the Nakba and the Holocaust "a weak historical analogy," but adds that if the comparison is made by a Jew, it is "a generous moral one."[13]

Given that many people in the Arab and Muslim worlds believe Israel was set up by the Western powers as compensation for the Holocaust and that the West continues to have a sense of obligation toward Jews and the state of Israel, it follows that the Holocaust would become a central target in the campaign to delegitimize the Jewish state. If the Holocaust is thought to form the foundation of Israel's legitimacy on the world stage and one believes that Israel has no actual historical or moral legitimacy, then one must coordinate one's attack on that foundation by either denying that the event occurred or claiming that it has been exaggerated and overemphasized or that it pales in comparison to other crimes, especially those believed to be committed by Jews themselves. What we often see is a combination of these contradictory arguments, sometimes even in the same presentation.

The former president of Iran from 2005 to 2013, Mahmoud Ahmadinejad, made the Holocaust a major theme in his rhetorical assault on the state of Israel. Beginning in August 2005, Ahmadinejad stated publicly that the Holocaust was a legend fabricated by Zionists to blackmail Europe into establishing and financing a Jewish state in the Middle East; that this so-called myth was held to be more sacred than the Almighty; and that if Germany and Austria believed Jews were massacred in Europe, then a state of Israel should be established on their soil—not in Palestine.[14] His contention that Western societies hold the Holocaust to be sacred explains why he created the International Holocaust Cartoon Competition in 2006, which had nothing to do with Israel but was designed specifically to counter the offense of a Danish newspaper printing cartoons of the Prophet.[15] Tellingly, when Western journalists insult Muhammad, return fire is sometimes directed not toward European religious figures or cultural heroes but toward the Holocaust. This tactic seems strange, but it reflects the firm belief among some in the Muslim world that the Holocaust is sacred to Western societies.

Ahmadinejad regularly articulated the view that the Holocaust was a myth created by Zionist conspirators to facilitate the imposition of a Jewish state on the Arab world. This was the "lie" he tried to expose in December 2006, when he convened a government-sponsored event called the International Conference on Review of the Holocaust: Global Vision. Held in Tehran at the Institute for Political and International Studies, an arm of the Iranian foreign ministry, the conference addressed the usual questions posed by Holocaust deniers and antisemites: Did the Holocaust happen? How many Jews died during the war? Did the gas chambers exist? What is the connection between the myth of the Holocaust and the creation of Israel? Attendees were Holocaust deniers and racist antisemites whose lies have marginalized them in the West—people such as David Duke, former grand wizard of the Ku Klux Klan; Robert Faurisson, who has stood trial in France for Holocaust denial; and Frederick Töben, who was sentenced to five years in Germany for Holocaust denial. Sixty-four other participants from thirty countries attended the event.[16]

It is important to note that this toxic compound—the lie of a worldwide Jewish conspiracy and its fabrication of the Holocaust to blackmail Europe into establishing and financing a Jewish state in the Middle East—was invented by European and American antisemites beginning immediately after World War II.[17] Like so much of the antisemitism we see today in the Arab and Islamic worlds, Holocaust denial—its myths, lies, and accusations—is European in origin and is recycled and adapted for political purposes in the Middle East.

Dismissing the Holocaust as a hoax in public is seen as a brave provocation in the Middle East. It symbolizes "speaking truth to power," as it were, by standing up to Israel and the United States, which no doubt elevates one's profile among millions of Muslims. It appears, however, that denying the Holocaust was not as effective a strategy as Ahmadinejad had expected, so he adopted another approach, asking an interviewer in Germany: If it happened, then whose fault was it? Ahmadinejad continued: "The answer to that has to be found in Europe and not in Palestine. It is perfectly clear: If the Holocaust took place in Europe, one also has to find the answer to it in Europe."[18] This approach is more effective in the West, because it has the potential to activate

European guilt, colonial and otherwise, for supporting the establishment of a Jewish state in the Middle East. Today, it is increasingly possible to hear people concede, even in public, that "Israel was a mistake."[19]

Another effective approach used by Ahmadinejad was to encourage the growth of existing resentment against the Holocaust and its ongoing memorialization in Germany and Europe, asking *Der Spiegel* in 2006:

> Why should [the Germans] have feelings of guilt toward Zionists? Why should the costs of the Zionists be paid out of their pockets? If people committed crimes in the past, then they would have to have been tried 60 years ago. End of story! Why must the German people be humiliated today because a group of people committed crimes in the name of the Germans during the course of history?

> Why is such a burden heaped on the German people? The German people of today bear no guilt. Why are the German people not permitted the right to defend themselves? Why are the crimes of one group emphasized so greatly, instead of highlighting the great German cultural heritage? Why should the Germans not have the right to express their opinion freely? . . . How much longer can this go on? How much longer do you think the German people have to accept being taken hostage by the Zionists? When will that end, in 20, 50, 1,000 years?[20]

Just how many Germans share his view is difficult to ascertain, but one can imagine that it resonates with a segment of the public. The third generation of Germans, for example, was showing a new level of disinterest and expressing feelings of saturation as of 2008, according to Dr. Benedikt Haller, a member of Germany's Foreign Ministry, who headed up the German delegation to the Task Force on International Cooperation on Holocaust Education and Remembrance that year.[21] In 2015, a Forsa poll revealed that 42 percent of Germans want closure on the Nazi past.[22] As the Nazi years continue to recede, this desire will naturally increase in the German population, especially among German youth.

An attitudinal survey conducted by the Anti-Defamation League across ten European countries in 2012 found that 41 percent believed that Jews talk too much about what happened to them in the Holocaust (the percentage was highest in Hungary, where it was 63 percent).[23] And in late 2013, the European Union released a new survey on Jewish people's experiences of discrimination and hate crime in Europe, and the data revealed that 57 percent of European Jews had heard comments denying the Holocaust or stating that it was exaggerated.[24]

The word *fatigue* may not be as accurate as the word *exhaustion* in relation to Holocaust-focused education and memorialization. There is a sense that the Holocaust has been given its due for over thirty years now and that it is time for other atrocities and episodes of human suffering to be given undivided attention, and not only discussed in relation to the Holocaust.[25] Debate about the uniqueness of the Holocaust and its relationship to other genocides is one area of conflict that has generated some hostility toward Holocaust-focused public programming.[26] There is even a sometimes hostile divide between scholars of genocide (a newer discipline dating from the 1990s) and those who study the Holocaust, as Dan Michman observes:

> Colin Tatz describes the growing problem: "Foremost is the challenge of finding a space for encompassing and embracing the Holocaust with some comfort. The judeocide is an ally, not an enemy, and not on the margins!" He sees enmity among genocide scholars toward Holocaust studies, partially resulting from "competition of victimhood" among scholars that reject the Holocaust's public and scholarly centrality. They are irritated by the notion of the "uniqueness" of one case, sometimes owing to political attitudes regarding the Israeli-Palestinian conflict.[27]

To stay relevant in such a context, some Holocaust education organizations have become champions of universalism and inclusivity, even reinterpreting the Holocaust to represent all groups harassed under the Nazi regime. These organizations increasingly engage in comparative genocide education and memorialization. Today, the only way to win support for international Holocaust remembrance activities is to shift the accepted historical definition of the Holocaust from the systematic Nazi extermination of European Jewry to a new universalizing definition that includes all populations who suffered under Nazi Germany. This shift, however, determines the occlusion of any serious attention directed toward the problem of antisemitism, which of course only targets Jews. A revealing faux pas in this regard was the European Union's 2014 public statement on Holocaust Remembrance Day, which failed to even mention Jews or antisemitism:

> Today the international community remembers the victims of the Holocaust. We honor every one of those brutally murdered in the darkest period of European history. We also want to pay a special tribute to all those who acted with courage and sacrifice to protect their fellow citizens against persecution. On Holocaust Remembrance Day, we must keep alive the memory of this tragedy. It is an occasion to remind us all of the need to continue fighting prejudice and racism in our own time. We must remain vigilant against the dangers of hate speech and redouble our commitment to prevent any form of intolerance. The respect of human rights and diversity lies at the heart of what the European Union stands for.[28]

By contrast, and no doubt in response to criticism, the European Union's Holocaust Remembrance Day statement in 2015 referenced the "violent antisemitism" of the January 2015 massacre of Jews in Paris and reinserted the Jewish people back into the Holocaust, alongside many others, calling the Holocaust a crime "in which six million Jews as well as millions of other innocent victims, Roma, political prisoners, prisoners of war, disabled people, homosexuals, were murdered in Nazi death camps."[29] At best, one can say that official European Holocaust remembrance is unscholarly, heavily politicized, and therefore unstable. What the future holds for this enterprise, especially without Jewish survivors present, is unclear.

As the EU added Jews back in to their Holocaust Remembrance Day Statement of 2015, Jews were removed from the 2016 statement of Canadian prime minister Justin Trudeau[30] (and added back the following year) and removed from the 2017 White House statement by President Trump (only to be added back in 2018).[31] A 2018 survey of 1,350 American adults has demonstrated misconceptions and ignorance of the facts of the Holocaust: "Thirty-one percent of Americans, and 41 percent of millennials, believe that two million or fewer Jews were killed in the Holocaust; the actual number is around six million. Forty-one percent of Americans, and 66 percent of millennials, cannot say what Auschwitz was. And 52 percent of Americans wrongly think Hitler came to power through force."[32] The conclusion drawn from this survey, that as the Holocaust recedes from lived experience knowledge about it declines, may not be correct at all. Accurate, detailed knowledge about the Holocaust as a historical event, especially as it relates to the Jewish experience under Hitler, should not be assumed to exist in the general population of the United States, Canada, or other Western countries, especially given the now universalized and inclusive content of contemporary Holocaust educational programming.

Compounding Western fatigue is the development of Muslim resistance to studying and memorializing the Holocaust, which is perceived to be a means of justifying the establishment of Israel and therefore a means of oppressing the Palestinians. This phenomenon among young Muslims, more than any other, will likely gain traction and cultural influence in coming years. Significantly, Hamas and teachers in Jordan have refused to teach the Holocaust as legislated in the United Nations Relief and Works Agency for Palestine curriculum.[33] A 2007 British report titled *A Report from the Historical Association on the Challenges and Opportunities for Teaching Emotive and Controversial History* described the following findings:

> In particular settings, teachers of history are unwilling to challenge highly contentious or charged versions of history in which pupils are steeped at home, in their community or in a place of

worship. Some teachers also feel that the issues are best avoided in history, believing them to be taught elsewhere in the curriculum such as in citizenship or religious education. For example, *a history department in a northern city recently avoided selecting the Holocaust as a topic for GCSE coursework for fear of confronting anti-Semitic sentiment and Holocaust denial among some Muslim pupils.* In another department, teachers were strongly challenged by some Christian parents for their treatment of the Arab-Israeli conflict and the history of the state of Israel that did not accord with the teachings of their denomination. In another history department, *the Holocaust was taught despite anti-Semitic sentiment among some pupils, but the same department deliberately avoided teaching the Crusades* at Key Stage 3 because their balanced treatment of the topic would have directly challenged what was taught in some local mosques.[34]

In 2014, the organizers of Ireland's Holocaust memorial event banned any mention of Israel at the country's annual ceremony,[35] and the student union at Goldsmith's College at the University of London voted against commemorating Holocaust Memorial Day because it was deemed colonialist and Eurocentric.[36] In April 2015, members of the Jewish Brigade were banned by Palestinian activist organizers from participating in the Italian World War II Liberation Day celebrations, and in response, Holocaust survivors refused to attend.[37] In 2016, Haneen Zoabi (member of the Knesset, Joint Arab List) refused to participate in a Holocaust Remembrance Day ceremony to which she was invited because of the "'frightening similarity' between Nazi Germany's behavior and Israel's policies in the occupied territories, [and] Israel's 'cynical exploitation' of the Holocaust."[38] In 2017, "Muslim students of Arab and Turkish origin protested participation in an International Holocaust Remembrance Day event in Germany, while their high school's administration showed understanding for their criticism of Israel."[39] In 2018, German Muslim rappers Kollegah and Farid Bang won an Echo Music Award for an album including songs with lyrics such as that their bodies are "more defined than Auschwitz inmates" and "commit another

Holocaust, come with a molotov cocktail."⁴⁰ The two were in-vestigated for hate speech in 2018 but, in the end, not prosecuted as their music was protected under Germany's constitution as it relates to artistic freedom.

Today's world is an increasingly complex place, facilitating a cacophony of competing points of view and conflicting interests, all running on a twenty-four-hour global clock via the Internet. Given our new globalized reality, we are approaching a time when there will be no common culture or common conception of his-tory available to us, except perhaps in our own personal and fa-milial networks, and this will no doubt transform our collective understanding of all phenomena, including the Holocaust. The growing ethnic, religious, and linguistic diversity of Western so-cieties is changing the nature of public priorities and the content of our conversations, and these demographic shifts dramatically alter our collective perception of past and present events. The per-spectives of Arabs and Muslims are increasingly present as their numbers increase in Western societies, and this development has a direct impact on public perceptions about the conflict in the Middle East. The Western public is beginning to be exposed to the history of the Nakba and to the Palestinian historical experi-ence since 1948, which was almost nonexistent in Western con-sciousness during the latter half of the twentieth century. There is growing sympathy in many circles for the plight of Palestinian civilians, despite widespread recognition that the Palestinian Authority is corrupt and Hamas is a totalitarian terrorist organi-zation. In fact, the lack of positive democratic leadership in the territories makes the plight of Palestinian civilians all the more tragic and compelling to Western populations.

My sense is that our well-established understanding of the his-tories of the Holocaust and Israel, and of the philosophy of Zion-ism, is under significant political assault and is well on its way to being overturned. Our collective understanding of these three phenomena was, for many until recently, in accord with lived experience, and this reality gave the state of Israel its legitimacy in the eyes of the Western world. Without this stable cultural-experiential-intellectual foundation and common understanding of the past and present, one wonders what the future holds, especially given that the new fictitious narratives gaining currency today accuse Zionism of racism and Israel of systematic ethnic cleansing and genocide and remove antisemitism almost entirely as a central defining feature of the Holocaust.[41] It is, I believe, safe to say that we are no longer living in the post-Holocaust period of history, and many of the certainties we took for granted are no longer to be assumed.

NOTES

1. Norman Finkelstein, *The Holocaust Industry: Reflections on the Exploitation of Jewish Suffering* (New York: Verso, 2000).

2. See Norman Finkelstein, *Beyond Chutzpah: On the Misuse of Anti-Semitism and the Abuse of History* (Berkeley: University of California Press, 2005). For clarification on Finkelstein's support of the Boycott, Divestment, Sanctions (BDS) movement and his criticism of some of its goals, see Jordan Michael Smith, "An Unpopular Man," *New Republic*, July 7, 2015, https://newrepublic.com/article/122257/unpopular-man-norman-finkelstein-comes-out-against-bds-movement.

3. According to Esther Webman and Meir Litvak, there are only a few academic volumes published in Arabic on the subject of the Holocaust. See Meir Litvak and Esther Webman, *From Empathy to Denial: Arab Responses to the Holocaust* (New York: Columbia University Press, 2009), 6. By contrast, in the West, the scholarly literature on the Holocaust numbers over twenty thousand volumes, and the subject is one of the most well documented in history. See Saul Friedlander, "The Holocaust," in *The Oxford Handbook of Jewish Studies*, ed. Martin Goodman (New York: Oxford University Press, 2002), 412–44.

4. Gilbert Achcar, *The Arabs and the Holocaust: The Arab-Israeli War of Narratives* (London: Al Saqi, 2009), 18.

5. One significant exception to this reality was the role played by the grand mufti of Jerusalem, Haj Amin Al Husseini, in supporting the Nazi regime and its goals of Jewish annihilation. Scholars have recently focused attention on his relationship with Adolf Hitler and their mutual agreement to annihilate the Jewish communities throughout the Middle East after

Hitler achieved victory over the Allies in Europe and North Africa. See Zvi Elpeleg, *The Grand Mufti: Haj Amin Al-Hussaini, Founder of the Palestinian National Movement* (London: Frank Cass, 1993); Walter Laqueur and Barry Rubin, eds., *The Israel-Arab Reader* (New York: Penguin Books, 2001); Matthias Küntzel, *Jihad and Jew-Hatred: Islamism, Nazism and the Roots of 9/11* (New York: Telos, 2007); Jeffrey Herf, *Nazi Propaganda for the Arab World* (New Haven, CT: Yale University Press, 2009).

6. See Litvak and Webman, *From Empathy to Denial.*

7. Litvak and Webman, *From Empathy to Denial.*

8. Youssef al-Qaradawi reaches more than sixty million Muslims on a weekly basis through his television program *Shariah and Life,* so his attitudes carry great influence. See Alexander Smoltczyk, "Islam's Spiritual 'Dear Abby': The Voice of Egypt's Muslim Brotherhood," *Der Spiegel,* February 15, 2011, http://www.spiegel.de/international/world/islam-s-spiritual-dear -abby-the-voice-of-egypt-s-muslim-brotherhood-a-745526.html.

9. The title of Abbas's dissertation is "The Other Face: The Secret Connections between Nazism and the Leadership of the Zionist Movement," which was later published as a book, but only in Arabic. See Edy Cohen, "How Holocaust Denial Shaped Mahmoud Abbas' Worldview," *The Tower,* May 2016, http://www.thetower.org/article/how -holocaust-denial-shaped-mahmoud-abbas-worldview/. This accusation of Nazi-Zionist collusion gained prominence after the Eichmann trial of 1961. See Litvak and Webman, *From Empathy to Denial,* 93–130.

10. All these themes are examined in Litvak and Webman, *From Empathy to Denial,* and some are discussed in Achcar, *The Arabs and the Holocaust.*

11. See Robert Wistrich, ed., *The Left against Zion: Communism, Israel and the Middle East* (London: Valentine Mitchell, 1979); Robert Wistrich, *A Lethal Obsession: Anti-Semitism from Antiquity to the Global Jihad* (New York: Random House, 2010); Robert Wistrich, *From Ambivalence to Betrayal: The Left, the Jews, and Israel* (Lincoln: University of Nebraska Press, 2012); Jeffrey Herf, *Undeclared Wars with Israel: East Germany and the West German Far Left, 1967–1989* (Cambridge: Cambridge University Press, 2016).

12. See Catherine Chatterley, "A History of Israeli Apartheid Week," *National Post,* March 3, 2011, http://news.nationalpost.com/full-comment /catherine-chatterley-a-history-of-israeli-apartheid-week.

13. See Jamie Stern-Weiner and Norman Finkelstein, "The American Jewish Scholar behind Labour's 'Antisemitism' Scandal Breaks His Silence," *Open Democracy,* May 3, 2016, https://www.opendemocracy

.net/uk/jamie-stern-weiner-norman-finkelstein/american-jewish
-scholar-behind-labour-s-antisemitism-scanda.

14. "Iranian Leader Denies Holocaust," *BBC News*, December 14, 2005, http://news.bbc.co.uk/2/hi/middle_east/4527142.stm.

15. The Danish newspaper *Jyllands-Posten* (Jutland post) published twelve cartoons, several depicting Muhammad, on September 30, 2005. As a reaction to this, the first Iranian cartoon competition was officially sponsored by the Iranian newspaper *Hamshahri* (Fellow citizen) in 2006. The second cartoon competition was sponsored by the Iranian House of Cartoon in 2015 as a provocative response to the *Charlie Hebdo* massacre on January 7, 2015.

16. Robert Tait, "Holocaust Deniers Gather in Iran for 'Scientific' Conference," *Guardian*, December 12, 2006, https://www.theguardian.com/world/2006/dec/12/iran.israel.

17. See Deborah Lipstadt, *Denying the Holocaust: The Growing Assault on Truth and Memory* (New York: Penguin, 1993); Richard J. Evans, *Lying about Hitler: History, Holocaust, and the David Irving Trial* (New York: Basic Books, 2001).

18. "Spiegel Interview with Iran's President Ahmadinejad: 'We Are Determined,'" *Der Spiegel*, May 30, 2006, http://www.spiegel.de/international/spiegel/spiegel-interview-with-iran-s-president-ahmadinejad-we-are-determined-a-418660.html.

19. For example, the former mayor of London, Ken Livingstone, recently called the creation of Israel a "great catastrophe" and said it was "fundamentally wrong." See "Ken Livingstone: Creation of Israel Was 'a Great Catastrophe,'" *Times of Israel*, May 5, 2016, http://www.timesofisrael.com/ken-livingstone-creation-of-israel-was-a-great-catastrophe/.

20. "Spiegel Interview with Iran's President Ahmadinejad."

21. Etgar Lefkovits, "Berlin Official: German Kids Tired of Holocaust," *Jerusalem Post*, March 10, 2008, http://www.jpost.com/International/Berlin-official-German-kids-tired-of-Holocaust. It is important to note the degree to which the views and expectations of Holocaust educators are at odds with current German reality, according to this article.

22. Madeline Chambers, "Over 40 Percent of Germans Want Closure on Nazi Past, *Haaretz*, April 15, 2015, http://www.haaretz.com/jewish/news/1.651971.

23. Anti-Defamation League, *Attitudes toward Jews in Ten European Countries* (New York: First International Resources, 2012), https://www.adl.org/sites/default/files/documents/assets/pdf/israel-international/adl_anti-semitism_presentation_february_2012.pdf.

24. European Union Agency for Fundamental Rights, *Discrimination and Hate Crime against Jews in EU Member States: Experiences and Perceptions of Antisemitism* (Luxembourg: Publications Office of the European Union, 2014), http://fra.europa.eu/sites/default/files/fra-2013 -discrimination-hate-crime-against-jews-eu-member-states-0_en.pdf.

25. One powerful example of the growing resentment against the ongoing memorialization of the Holocaust was the protracted struggle to establish the Canadian Museum for Human Rights. See Catherine Chatterley, "Canada's Struggle with Holocaust Memorialization: The War Museum Controversy, Ethnic Identity Politics, and the Canadian Museum for Human Rights," *Holocaust and Genocide Studies* 29, no. 2 (2015): 189–211.

26. For a discussion of recent scholarly debates on the uniqueness of the Holocaust and the influence of politics on this discussion, see Gavriel Rosenfeld, *Hi Hitler! How the Nazi Past Is Being Normalized in Contemporary Culture* (Cambridge: Cambridge University Press, 2015), esp. chap. 2.

27. Dan Michman, "The Jewish Dimension of the Holocaust in Dire Straits?" in *Jewish Histories of the Holocaust: New Transnational Approaches*, ed. Norman Goda (New York: Berghahn Books, 2014), 17–38, 20.

28. See Elliott Abrams, "The Eu's Mrs. Ashton and the Invisible Jews," *Council on Foreign Affairs*, January 30, 2014, https://www.cfr.org/blog /eus-mrs-ashton-and-invisible-jews.

29. European Union, "Statement by High Representative/Vice-President Federica Mogherini on the International Holocaust Remembrance Day," January 27, 2015, http://www.eeas.europa.eu/statements-eeas/2015/150127 _01_en.htm.

30. See "Statement by the Prime Minister of Canada on Holocaust Remembrance Day," https://pm.gc.ca/eng/news/2016/01/27/statement -prime-minister-canada-holocaust-remembrance-day.

31. See "Statement by the President on International Holocaust Remembrance Day," https://www.whitehouse.gov/briefings-statements /statement-president-international-holocaust-remembrance-day/.

32. Maggie Astor, "Holocaust Is Fading from Memory, Survey Finds," *New York Times*, April 12, 2018, https://www.nytimes.com/2018/04/12/us /holocaust-education.html.

33. Elhanan Miller, "Jordanian Teachers in UN Schools for Palestinian Refugees Say They'll Refuse to Teach the Holocaust," *Times of Israel*, October 16, 2012, http://www.timesofisrael.com/jordanian-teachers -refuse-to-teach-the-holocaust-in-un-run-schools/.

34. The Historical Association, *A Report from the Historical Association on the Challenges and Opportunities for Teaching Emotive and Controversial History* (London: Historical Association, 2007), http://web.archive.org /web/20081007185440/http://www.dcsf.gov.uk/research/data/uploadfiles /RW100.pdf (emphasis added).

35. See "Mention of Israel Banned at Irish National Memorial," *Haaretz*, December 12, 2014, http://www.haaretz.com/jewish-world /jewish-world-news/1.63135.

36. See Justin Jalil, "London University Rejects Holocaust Commemoration," *Times of Israel*, October 19, 2014, http://www .timesofisrael.com/london-university-rejects-holocaust-commemoration/.

37. "Italian Holocaust Survivors to Skip Liberation Day Parade after Jewish Group Banned," *Haaretz*, April 6, 2015, http://www.haaretz.com /jewish-world/jewish-world-news/1.650798.

38. Jonathan Lis and Almog Ben Zikri, "Israeli Arab Lawmaker Refuses Holocaust Day Invite: Israel Today Is Like Germany in 1930s," *Haaretz*, April 20, 2016, http://www.haaretz.com/israel-news/1.715525.

39. Benjamin Weinthal, "German Muslim Students Protest Holocaust Remembrance, Attack Israel," *Jerusalem Post*, January 27, 2017, https:// www.jpost.com/Diaspora/German-Muslim-students-protest-Holocaust -remembrance-attack-Israel-479780.

40. Alexander Pearson, "German Rrappers Kollegah, Farid Bang Charged with Hate Speech," *DW*, February 5, 2018, https://www.dw .com/en/german-rappers-kollegah-farid-bang-charged-with-hate-speech /a-43629558.

41. For a discussion of the changing perception and normalization of Nazism and of World War II after the new millennium, see Rosenfeld, *Hi Hitler!*.

CATHERINE D. CHATTERLEY is Editor-in-Chief of *Antisemitism Studies* and founding director of the Canadian Institute for the Study of Antisemitism (CISA). Chatterley specializes in modern European and Jewish history, with a focus on the history of antisemitism and the dynamic relationship between Jews and non-Jews in Western history. Her first book, *Disenchantment: George Steiner and the Meaning of Western Civilization after Auschwitz*, was a Jewish Book Award finalist. Her second book, titled *The Antisemitic Imagination*, is forthcoming from Indiana University Press.

SEVEN

Antisemitism in the Guise of Anti-Nazism

Holocaust Inversion in the United Kingdom during Operation Protective Edge

ALAN JOHNSON

THIS CHAPTER IS a case study of the moral disease of Holocaust inversion—that is, "the portrayal of Israel, Israelis and Jews
as modern-day Nazis, and Palestinians as the new Holocaust-
era Jews."[1] Its focus is the presence and meaning of the inversion in the United Kingdom during Operation Protective Edge,
the fifty-one-day conflict between the state of Israel and the
military forces of Hamas and Palestinian Islamic Jihad in summer 2014.[2]

The theoretical resources—and, unavoidably, the rather specialized language—developed by Ernesto Laclau and Chantal
Mouffe are used to read the Holocaust inversion as the heart,
the "nodal point" of a distinct discourse or way of talking about
Israel;[3] I call this discourse "antisemitic anti-Zionism."[4] Inversion talk establishes a "chain of equivalence" between the terms
Nazi and *Zionist* and, in so doing, twists the meaning of Israel
and Zionism out of shape until both become fit receptacles for
the tropes, images, and ideas of classical antisemitism. In short,
the inversion means that what the demonological Jew once was
in classical antisemitism, the demonological Jewish state now
is in antisemitic anti-Zionism: evil; uniquely malevolent; vam-
piric, full of bloodlust; the all-controlling but hidden hand in

global affairs; the obstacle to a better, purer, more spiritual world; uniquely deserving of punishment.[5]

The first section of this chapter defines Holocaust inversion and explores its *ideological* sources. The second section examines the *presences* of Holocaust inversion discourse in the United Kingdom during Operation Protective Edge. Finally, I consider the *meaning* of inversion discourse—in particular whether it is merely offensive and hurtful or also antisemitic.[6]

DEFINITIONS AND SOURCES

Definitions

Lesley Klaff has defined Holocaust inversion as "an inversion of reality (the Israelis are cast as the 'new' Nazis and the Palestinians as the 'new' Jews), and an inversion of morality (the Holocaust is presented as a moral lesson for, or even a moral indictment of 'the Jews')." Klaff also points out that, in an especially cruel twist of the knife, "those who object to these inversions are told . . . that they are acting in bad faith, only being concerned to deflect criticism of Israel." In all these ways, she argues, Holocaust inversion discourse *weaponizes* the Holocaust, turning it into "a means to express animosity towards the homeland of the Jews."[7]

Manfred Gerstenfeld extrapolated from a 2011 study of seven European countries that found high levels of agreement with the statement "Israel is carrying out a war of extermination against the Palestinians" to conclude that "out of 400 million citizens of 16 years and older, 150 million embrace a demonic view of Israel." Holocaust inversion, he concluded, was a "mainstream phenomenon in the European Union."[8] In 2009, the European Institute for the Study of Contemporary Antisemitism noted the "growing normalisation" in the United Kingdom of discursive acts "involving the use of Nazi or related terms or symbols

(Nazism, Hitler, Swastikas, etc) in reference to Jews, Israel, Zionism." Meanwhile, the lawyer and writer Anthony Julius has claimed that the inversion is now "a reflex" in certain quarters in the United Kingdom.[9] Certainly, it is no longer unusual to find, in the European public square, Israel's prime minister, Benjamin Netanyahu, portrayed as a modern-day Hitler or the Israel Defense Forces (IDF) as the modern-day Schutzstaffel (SS). Israel's antiterror operation in Jenin in 2002—in which fifty-two Palestinians were killed, about half of whom were combatants, as well as twenty-three Israeli soldiers—is routinely described as being "just like the Warsaw ghetto,"[10] where approximately three hundred thousand Jews were murdered during the Holocaust.

In response, the European Monitoring Centre on Racism and Xenophobia (EUMC) decided in 2005 to include within its working definition of antisemitism those several ways in which criticism of Israel can, depending on the context, be manifested as antisemitism, including the act of "drawing comparisons of contemporary Israeli policy to that of the Nazis."[11] Versions of the working definition are now used by the European Parliament, the UK College of Policing, the US Department of State, and the International Holocaust Remembrance Alliance.[12]

Sources

Holocaust inversion discourse draws on several disparate, even contradictory, ideological sources. In each case, it is possible, to paraphrase Theodor Adorno, "to discern . . . a concealed and . . . poisonous interest."[13] The Arabism of parts of the British civil service was embodied in the figure of Sir John Glubb Pasha, a man who routinely compared Zionists to Nazis and Israel to the Third Reich in midcentury.[14] Litvak and Webman have shown how the idea of Israelis as the new Nazis has been a theme in pan-Arabist politics since the late 1940s and early 1950s.[15] However, the most important source by far has been the left. The "anti-Zionist" campaigns waged by the communist bloc during the Cold War were uncritically adopted by large parts of the Western New Left after 1967.[16] In the decade before 2014, this far-left anti-Zionism effected a political merger with Islamist antisemitism—the so-called Red-Green Alliance—creating the basis for the partial mainstreaming of Holocaust inversion discourse in the United Kingdom.

Stalinism spread over large parts of the globe after World War II. In the new context of the Cold War, the Soviet Union and its satellites organized well-funded, long-running, and large-scale anti-Zionist propaganda campaigns through which the global left became acquainted with the idea that Zionism was the new Nazism. Wistrich observed that, by the 1980s, "the Soviet Union . . . stood in the forefront of the global campaign to equate Zionism with Nazism," and Julius claims that the inversion became "the major trope in the 1960s and 1970s Soviet antisemitism."[17] In fact, almost every idea constitutive of antisemitic anti-Zionism today, including the inversion, was promoted by the Stalinists: Zionism is nothing but a pro-imperialist and antisocialist tool to advance imperialist interests in the region; Zionism is nothing but a conspiracy to covertly control the foreign policy of the United States; Zionism controls the media of every Western state and has bought the intellectuals; there is no relationship between the rise of antisemitism and the emergence of Zionism in Europe; Zionists cry antisemitism to prevent criticism of Israel; Zionists have bought the opinion formers; Arab antisemitism is a myth spread by Zionists; Zionism itself is responsible for all antisemitism; Judaism is a dirty religion based on violence and supremacism; Israel is a racist or apartheid state; and the capstone, Zionism is itself a kind of Nazism, the Zionists collaborated with the Nazis, and the Zionists pursue the same policies toward the Palestinians as Hitler did to the Jews.[18]

According to Wistrich, it was the "willingness of supposedly anti-Soviet radical leftists to swallow these made in Russia

fabrications" that ensured that a demonizing anti-Zionism became "an integral part of the cultural code of many Leftist and
some liberal circles" in the West.[19] By 2014, the inversion had
certainly been in use for at least three decades in far-left circles
in the United Kingdom, as demonstrated by numerous cartoons
published in 1982 in the hard-left *Labour Herald* newspaper and
in the Socialist Workers Party's monthly magazine, *The Socialist
Review.*[20]

The other driver of Holocaust inversion discourse in the United
Kingdom has been the antisemitism of parts of the Muslim world,
brought to the United Kingdom with postwar immigration. According to leading UK Muslim political commentator Mehdi
Hassan, "antisemitism isn't just tolerated in some sections of the
British Muslim community; it's routine and commonplace." Hassan continues, "It's our dirty little secret. You could call it the
banality of Muslim anti-Semitism."[21] And because UK Muslims,
like everyone else, live in a global media village, they absorb the
ubiquitous Holocaust inversion discourse of the wider Muslim
world. Depictions of the last four Israeli prime ministers—Ehud
Barak, Ariel Sharon, Ehud Olmert, and Benjamin Netanyahu—
in cartoons published in the Arab world, for example, have been
shown to rest on the systematic use of Holocaust inversion.[22]

These far-left and Islamist traditions came together in the
United Kingdom in a specific political conjuncture marked by
the failure of the Israeli-Palestinian peace process, the second Intifada, the notorious antisemitic Durban conference, the 9/11 attacks, widespread opposition in the United Kingdom to the "9/11
Wars" in Afghanistan and Iraq, and the decay of the New Labour
project. The Red and the Green, both prone to use Holocaust
inversion discourse, coalesced in Stop the War, a mass movement
for which the Socialist Workers Party and the Communist Party
provided the core leadership; in George Galloway's Respect coalition, an alliance between the Muslim Brotherhood-linked Muslim Association of Britain and the Trotskyist Socialist Workers

Party; and in the Palestine Solidarity Campaign, which had deep roots in trade unions, churches, and humanitarian nongovernmental organizations—themselves more influenced by the thinking of the anti-Zionist far left than at any time in their history.

PRESENCES: HOLOCAUST INVERSION IN THE UNITED KINGDOM DURING THE 2014 GAZA CONFLICT

Operation Protective Edge triggered a spike in antisemitic incidents in the United Kingdom according to the Association of Chief Police Officers, which recorded a 221 percent rise in antisemitic hate crimes in July 2014.[23] The Community Security Trust, the UK Jewish community's monitoring organization, recorded 314 antisemitic incidents that month, the highest ever recorded monthly total, and an additional 227 incidents in August. The combined total for these two months was higher than the figure recorded for the entirety of 2013, and around one-third of those incidents involved Holocaust-related language or imagery. Statistics for the year as a whole show that 239 of the 1,168 antisemitic incidents "employed discourse based on the Nazi period, including swastikas and references to the Holocaust."[24]

The Community Security Trust pointed out that "offenders will select from a range of Jewish related subjects, particularly insults related to the Holocaust or Israel, for language or imagery with which to abuse, insult or threaten their Jewish victims."[25] For example, in 2007 in *Socialist Worker*, Mike Napier, the Chair of the Scottish Palestine Solidarity Campaign, stated, "An accurate understanding of the Nazi Holocaust is essential to grasp modern Israeli savagery towards the Palestinian people."[26] The following excerpt from a July 20, 2014, blog post by a British Jew reveals powerfully where this kind of demonizing discourse leads:

> This is what I have to live with every time Israel does something bad. Out come the swastikas, out come the pictures of Hitler, and the photos, omg, *photos* of graphic images of dead Jews set side by

side with images of whatever havoc Israel has wreaked this time.
It's a deliberate, systematic attempt to make people relive an experience that left millions of Jews dead and a wound on the collective
Jewish memory that hasn't even begun to heal. . . . Hurting an
entire group of people because you're so incandescently angry
at a particular set of them is indirect discrimination. In short,
comparing Jews, any Jews, to the Nazis is antisemitic and it's
wrong. Please stop.[27]

Holocaust inversion discourse was also present in public demonstrations, social media, and elite discourse.

Public Demonstrations

The scholar Ben Gidley analyzed several mass demonstrations
organized by the Palestine Solidarity Campaign (PSC) during
Operation Protective Edge. He concluded that, although antisemitism was not a "predominant presence"—indeed, "the overwhelming majority of messages . . . were not anti-Semitic"—it
was a feature of the street protests, especially in the form of "a
continuum of expressions emphasising the Holocaust."[28] Home-
made placards and banners contained the following messages:
"Rabid evil mass murderers Hitlers clone" and "Stop the Palestinian Holocaust now—Fascist Israel will not escape justice."
One large banner read "Genocide Apartheid Holocaust 2014" and
"Baby Killers" alongside a Star of David and "Bush and Blair are
our Adolf Hitler's and Gaza is our Auschwitz."

Although these Holocaust inversion placards were not typical, the police and other protestors tolerated their presence. The
2015 All-Party Parliamentary Inquiry found that "banners and
placards equating Israel with Nazi Germany . . . were said to
have been paraded without police interruption."[29] At one Gaza
demonstration, well-spoken middle-class protestors were very
comfortable expressing the following sentiments: "I'm not condoning Hitler's actions at all, but I think it's [i.e., the conflict in
Gaza] even worse perhaps"; "Hitler probably had more mercy";

"If you look at the Warsaw Ghetto, this is identical"; and "What they're doing is no different."[30] During the July 11 demonstration in London, James Thring, a man of the far right, was an object of much positive interest because of his T-shirt, which bore the words "Auschwitz, Iraq, Dachau, Palestine," and for his placard opposing the "Holocaust of Gaza."[31]

One marcher, Daniel Randall, wrote about his experience of challenging another protestor who held aloft a placard bearing the message, "RESEARCH * The Babylonian Talmud * The Protocols of the Learned Elders of Zion" alongside a Star of David dripping with blood and the Satanic number 666. Although Randall was physically threatened, some marchers also supported him, and he was told that because the target of the placard was the Elders of Zion—that is, Zionists, not Jews—the placard could not be antisemitic. Responding online to Randall's report of this incident, "Charli" from the Stop the War coalition said, "As for objecting to slogans equating holocausts, comparing Israeli state to the Nazi one, and star of David to Swastika—it may be uncomfortable but it has a lot of truth in it."[32]

Examples of Holocaust inversion discourse during the Gaza demonstrations also included representations of the Israeli prime minister Benjamin Netanyahu as Adolf Hitler, alongside a host of antisemitic, anti-Zionist representations of Netanyahu: as the puppet-master of the United Kingdom and the United States; as a vampire drinking the blood of Palestinians but never able to "get enough." There were depictions of Gaza as the "real Holocaust" and "Our Auschwitz" and of the Star of David morphed into, or equated with, the Nazi swastika. Some placards even stated, "Hitler would have been proud."[33]

Other examples of street-level Holocaust inversion during the conflict include a letter sent to an Israeli organization in London stating, "You loathsome killers, murdering b*****ds; you perpetrators of infanticide. Hope you ISRAELI NAZI WAR CRIMINALS all go to Hell when you die, you rotten to the core modern day NAZI JEWS." Several synagogues in Birmingham, Liverpool, and London received anonymous letters containing images of swastikas inside the Star of David, which read, "Israeli-Nazis have turned Gaza into a modern Auschwitz and are now annihilating its civilians without remorse."[34]

Social Media

Social media was an important "platform for anti-Semitic rhetoric" during the conflict, according to the Association of Chief Police Officers, and Holocaust inversion was an important component of that rhetoric.[35] This was confirmed by Paul Iganski, Abe Sweiry, and Mark McGlashan, who conducted a pathbreaking analysis of antisemitic discourse on Twitter for a 2015 all-party parliamentary group inquiry. Using the methods of corpus linguistics, they gathered 22 million tweets from July and August 2014 to analyze a subsample of 38,460 that contained the words *Israel* or *Gaza* along with the words *Jew, Jews,* or *Jewish.* Their findings suggest that Holocaust inversion discourse is moving closer to the center of contemporary antisemitic discourse. "A keyword analysis ... showed that in the sub-sample analysed, the spectre of Nazism, with words such as 'Hitler,' 'Holocaust,' 'Nazi,' and 'Nazis,' was present in the top 35 keywords for the downloaded sample. 'Hitler' was mentioned 1117 times; 'Holocaust' was mentioned in 505 tweets, and 'Nazi' or 'Nazis' were mentioned in 851 tweets. The Nazi theme was also evident in hashtags analysed for the sub-sample, with the high frequency of the hashtags #hitler, #hitlerwasright, and #genocide."[36] Using collocation analysis, the researchers then examined a subsample of the Twitter data set for the presence of invective, and they provisionally concluded, "The largest category in relation to invective, again, was Nazi references."[37]

Ben Gidley has argued that contemporary antisemitic invective is being shaped by social media's tendency to promote "cross-pollination" between different ideological traditions. "Individual posts or memes under which several tweets cluster," he argues, "are easily dis-embedded from their original source and travel in unexpected directions."[38] Social media is a perfect setting not just for ideological traditions to cross-pollinate but also for different national traditions and different genres of Holocaust inversion discourse to interact and fructify one another. For example, there was a pervasive use of Holocaust inversion in the official and semiofficial organs of the Palestinian Authority and on the Facebook pages of Fatah, both of which were promoted by UK activists.[39] The headline "Netanyahu Is a Descendant of the Nazis, Worships Hitler's Ways" in the official Palestinian Authority daily, *Al-Hayat Al-Jadida*, was typical.[40] The Iranian regime's Press TV ran the headline "Gaza Massacre Israel Re-run of Nazi Genocide."[41] The snarky tweets of the US academic Steven Salaita—including one that read, "The @IDFSpokesperson receives money to justify, conceal, and glamorize genocidal violence. Goebbels much? #Gaza #GazaUnderAttack"—ensured that the Holocaust inversion went viral.[42] A much-noted Facebook post of the influential US feminist Naomi Wolf contained images of Israelis, supposedly joyful at the air strikes on Gaza, with her gloss, "The expressions of gloating and sadism exactly the same as those of Nazis cutting off the beards of Jews."[43]

Elite Discourse

Holocaust inversion began to creep into the language of some politicians. Earlier in 2014, in a debate in the House of Commons before the conflict began, the Labour member of Parliament Yasmin Qureshi said, "Israel was founded because of what happened to the millions and millions of Jews who suffered genocide. . . . It is quite strange that some of the people who are running the state of Israel seem to be quite complacent and happy to allow *the same* to happen in Gaza."[44] During the conflict, John Prescott, deputy prime minister during Tony Blair's premiership, wrote an influential column in the mass-circulation newspaper *The Daily Mirror*.

Israel, he claimed, was "acting as judge, jury and executioner in the concentration camp that is Gaza," adding, "you would think [the Holocaust] would give Israelis a unique sense of perspective and empathy with the victims of a ghetto."[45]

The inversion remained an important part of the discourse of the anti-Zionist Jewish left in the diaspora after the 2014 conflict ended. On Holocaust Memorial Day in 2015, the UK group Jews for Justice for Palestinians posted photographs of the Gaza conflict on Facebook with the hashtag #HolocaustMemorial-Day. A photograph of razed Gazan buildings and the caption "NEVER AGAIN FOR ANYONE" was badged with the group's logo and the #HolocaustMemorialDay hashtag. A second photograph showed a Gazan child crying over a corpse of another Gazan child with the same caption and hashtag.[46] At the anti-Israel website Mondoweiss, Michael Lesher compared Israel's air strikes on Gaza with the Nazi devastation of the town of Lidice and compared Hamas with the local Czech anti-Nazi partisans.[47] "Jewish elites turn the lessons of the Nazi genocide upside down," he claimed, "using the very methods the Nazis used to convert Gaza into a killing machine." "Jewish leaders were following Goering's line," he went on, concluding that the Nazis' methods had "clearly survived the fall of the Third Reich" and were used today by Israel.[48]

MEANINGS: HOLOCAUST INVERSION AS THE NODAL POINT OF THE DISCOURSE OF ANTISEMITIC ANTI-ZIONISM

The *meaning* of Holocaust inversion discourse—specifically, whether it is antisemitic—is contested. A locus of the dispute was the contrasting submissions of two academics, David Feldman and Ben Gidley, to the All-Party Parliamentary Group on Antisemitism's inquiry into antisemitism in the United Kingdom during the Gaza conflict in the summer of 2014.[49] The final report of the inquiry noted delicately that "there was some debate between those from whom we took expert testimony regarding the nuances of the definition of antisemitism when it comes to Nazi comparison."[50] In short, Gidley defined examples of Holocaust inversion as antisemitic discourse, but Feldman, director of the Pears Institute for the Study of Antisemitism at Birkbeck University, did not, arguing that "the fact that they are wrong and hurtful does not render them anti-Semitic."[51]

Feldman advanced two reasons to deny that Holocaust inversion is antisemitic discourse. First, the inversion is banal (my word, not his)—that is, it is a "much used rhetorical device," a common rhetorical trope used in many arguments about many subjects, often light-mindedly, lacking any specifically antisemitic content. Feldman cited attacks on the UK Independence Party as Nazis as one example of banality and Israel's leaders calling its enemies Nazis as another. Second, Feldman pointed out that the inversion is not motivated by an anti-Jewish subjectivity. The target, he pointed out, is Israel, not Jews; therefore, the inversion cannot be antisemitic. Only when discourse "endorse[s] Nazi persecution of Jews" (e.g., brandishing a "Hitler Was Right!" placard on the high street, as at least one protestor did in 2014) did Feldman consider it antisemitic.[52]

However, both of Feldman's arguments—(the presence of) banality and (the absence of) individual subjectivity—risk putting beyond our understanding much that is constitutive of contemporary antisemitism. His argument of banality—that is, that because everyone plays the Nazi card about everything, it is not antisemitic when used about Israel or Jews—is innocent regarding three contexts that ensure that inversion discourse works in antisemitic ways and may have antisemitic consequences: the Jewish context, the political context, and the discursive context.

The Jewish Context

First, the language Feldman uses to describe the act of treating Israeli Jews as Nazis ("grossly misleading," "hurtful") radically mischaracterizes its object. The inversion is obscene; it verges on the demonic in its cruelty as it implicitly demands, as a matter of ethical obligation no less—and this *after* the rupture in world history that was the Shoah—the destruction of the Jewish homeland as a unique evil in the world no better than the perpetrators of the Shoah. Logically, as Elhanan Yakira puts it, the discourse is "annihilationist." Ben Gidley, using a more understated English style, notes, "To single out Hitler and the Holocaust as the frame for understanding the actions of the Jewish state is not neutral."[53] Iganski, McGlashan, and Sweiry point out that "deep wounds are scratched when the Nazi-card is played . . . in discourse against Jews." The inversion is "not simply abusive," they add, but also "invokes painful collective memories for Jews and for many others" such that "by using those memories against Jews it inflicts profound hurts" and can lead to violence.[54] In a similar vein, Dave Rich of the Community Security Trust has argued that Holocaust inversion in the United Kingdom in 2014 played on Jewish sensibilities "in order to provoke a reaction," adding, "another word for that is Jew-baiting."[55] For the Community Security Trust, "incidents equating Israel to Nazi Germany would normally be recorded as antisemitic," because the inversion has a "visceral capacity to offend Jews on the basis of their Jewishness" and "carries a particular meaning for Jews because of the Holocaust."[56] Yakira is particularly unimpressed by the banality argument because it evades the "more immoral, more significant . . . more effective . . . more widespread" character of the inversion *when applied to Jews and the Jewish state.*[57] Moreover, he points out, when it is applied to Jews, the inversion actively seeks to "suppress memory" and so "can only mean eliminating identity."[58]

The Political Context

Feldman treats each example of Holocaust inversion in isolation, missing or ignoring the important fact that the inversion is an essential part of the political practice of a global social movement dedicated to the destruction of only one state in the world—the

Jewish one. To equate this knowing, relentless, state-sponsored, well-funded political project that has spanned several decades and several continents and that has often been promoted by eliminationist antisemitic forces, with the semiserious, rhetorical use of the Nazi charge in other contexts, such as the criticism of UK Independence Party, is to miss the political point quite spectacularly.

Feldman's approach brackets the brute fact that the inversion is embedded within a worldwide anti-Israel campaign; beyond the subjectivity of any individual user of the inversion, there is, as Yakira observes, "an entire eco-system," a veritable "international community" with a shared code, language, jargon, credo and sensibility.[59] This is surely why Robert Wistrich came to believe that the inversion was "in practice . . . the most potent form of contemporary anti-Semitism."[60] A person who uses the discourse of Holocaust inversion, whatever his or her intentions, "exploit[s] the reality that Nazism in the post-war world has become the defining metaphor of absolute evil" and, by associating Zionism with Nazism and Israel with the Third Reich, promotes nothing less than "a moral obligation to wage war against Israel" as a uniquely malign force in the world.[61] To deny this the status of antisemitism is a definitional trick.

The Discursive Context

The inversion renews the core motif of antisemitism, which is that the Jews are not just Other but also malign.[62] The supposed content of this Jewish malignity changes with the times and—as David Nirenberg has described in exhaustive detail in his seminal book *Anti-Judaism: The History of a Way of Thinking*—with the needs of the antisemites: the malign Jew as a God-killer; later as a rootless cosmopolitan dissolving every nation; then as the world-controlling capitalist-Bolshevik conspirator; and finally as the *Untermenschen*, the biological pollutant of all races.[63]

It was not the final form for Jews to be marked out for death. Holocaust inversion and antisemitic anti-Zionism as a whole updates this core motif of malignity in the era of the Jewish state: the Jew as Zio-Nazi. As the 2006 inquiry by the United Kingdom's All-Party Parliamentary Group against Antisemitism put it, "a discourse has developed that is in effect antisemitic because it views Zionism itself as a global force of unlimited power and malevolence throughout history." When Zionism is redefined in this way, then "traditional antisemitic notions . . . are transferred from Jews (a racial and religious group) on to Zionism (a political movement)."[64]

Holocaust inversion discourse has a real-world impact because of the effectiveness and reach of what Ernesto Laclau and Chantal Mouffe call the "articulatory practice" that takes it into the institutions of civil society.[65] The term means "any practice establishing a relation among elements [of a discourse] such that their identity is modified as a result."[66] It is *articulatory* because "elements" from old discourses are put together creatively in new ways—as "moments" of a new discourse (e.g., Zionism = Nazism). It is called a practice because this articulation is never a purely academic exercise. It happens, if it happens at all, in "the multifarious institutions" of the real world, as Laclau and Mouffe put it—for example, in universities, publishing houses, institutions of popular culture, churches, trades unions, and political parties.

Articulatory practice takes elements from old discourses and rearticulates them as moments within a new discourse. The elements—Zionism, Holocaust, Israel, Nazi, Jenin, Gaza, Israel Defense Forces, SS, ghetto, concentration camp—are reborn in this process of rearticulation, their very meanings now secured not by their original material referents but by their places in the structure of the new discursive field that has been created. Table 7.1 illustrates Laclau and Mouffe's concept of articulatory practice applied to Holocaust inversion.

TABLE 7.1. LACLAU AND MOUFFE'S CONCEPT OF ARTICULATORY
PRACTICE APPLIED TO HOLOCAUST INVERSION

Elements in an existing discourse (Nazism)	Elements in an existing discourse (Zionism)
Third Reich	Israel
Holocaust	Israel-Palestinian conflict
Untermenschen	Palestinians

Moments in the new discourse of antisemitic anti-Zionism

An articulatory practice transforms elements in an existing discourse into moments within a new discourse, transforming their meaning in the process

Zionism = Nazism

Israel = Third Reich

Israeli treatment of Palestinians = Holocaust

Israeli Leaders = Hitler

IDF = SS

Gaza = Concentration Camp

Palestinians = Nazi-era Jews, Untermenschen

In articulatory practice, the meaning of the Holocaust is rearticulated by antisemitic anti-Zionism so that it no longer comes into focus as a descriptor of the Nazi murder of six million people. Instead, it is rearticulated as a moment within the new anti-Zionist discourse. Instead, it is rearticulated as a moment within the new anti-Zionist discourse: a lesson, unheeded for the Jews; what the Zionists are doing now to the Palestinians; a card played by Zionists to prevent their incremental genocide of the Palestinians being criticized.[67]

No court can intervene and rule against these rearticulations. Articulatory practice decides whether the description of Israel's operations to stop rockets from Gaza as a *vernichtungskreig* (war of extermination) becomes accepted. It is the clash between competing articulatory practices that decides whether representations of Israel as a *Taetervolk* (a nation of criminals) bleed from the fringe to the mainstream. As the late theorist Stuart Hall put it, in the battle to construct meaning, you lose because you lose because you lose. So when the far-left writer Tariq Ali says Israelis treat Palestinians as *Untermenschen*, he is talking nonsense.[68] But he knows he is not making a truth claim. He knows he is constructing what Elhanan Yakira calls a "transhipment mechanism"— an awkward but helpful term that means a "vehicle for transferring blame and negation . . . absolute evil, limitless guilt, and suffering" from the Holocaust to Israel and Zionism.[69]

To understand how Holocaust inversion functions as a transhipment mechanism, consider Tom Paulin's poem "Killed in Crossfire," which is notorious for its equivalencing of the IDF and the SS. Here is the poem with its opening epigraph.[70]

> To me the Zionists, who want to go back to the Jewish state of 70 AD (destruction of Jerusalem by Titus), are just as offensive as the Nazis. With their nosing after blood, their ancient "cultural roots," their partly canting, partly obtuse winding back of the world, they are altogether a match for the National Socialists (Victor Klemperer, June 13, 1934).

> We're fed this inert
> this lying phrase
> like comfort food
> as another little Palestinian boy
> in trainers jeans and a white teeshirt
> is gunned down by the Zionist SS
> whose initials we should
> —but we don't—dumb goys—
> clock in that weasel word crossfire

When challenged by Jews about his use of the phrase "Zionist SS" and the Klemperer quote, Paulin doubled down, accusing his critics of "the usual cynical Goebbels stuff."[71] But there can be nothing gained by making a window into the soul of Tom Paulin and trying to answer the unproductive question: Does Tom Paulin have an antisemitic subjectivity? It is surely more productive to think about the structure and logic of the discourse Paulin is speaking, and that is speaking through him, and the relation of that discourse to previous iterations of Jew hatred. When different subject positions (in the case of the poems "Nazi SS" and "Zionist IDF") are symbolically located together (as in Paulin's line about the "Zionist SS") and placed "in opposition to another camp" (Nazis in opposition to the Jews of Klemperer's time, Israelis in oppositions to the Palestinians today), then meaning itself is "transformed by their overlapping identifications," as the social theorist Anna Marie Smith puts it, and this is so whatever the subjective intentions of the poet.[72]

The likely consequences of Paulin's identification of Zionist and Nazi can be seen most clearly when viewed in the light cast by Laclau's and Mouffe's penetrating reading of the discourse of millenarian peasant movements. These rebellions established an equivalence between the new and detested urban culture of the city and evil itself. In establishing such a logic of equivalence (city = evil), they opened up "a logic of simplification of political space."[73] This simplification is very dangerous because it produces a "maximum separation," bringing dialogue and mediation to an end. In the jargon of Laclau and Mouffe, when the point of maximum separation is reached, "no element in the system of equivalences enters into relations other than those of opposition to the elements of the other system." As they remind us, "When the millenarian rebellion takes place, the assault on the city is fierce, total and indiscriminate."[74] In plainer terms, *slaughter can now replace politics.*

Consider again the chain of equivalence established by Paulin's poem (Zionist = Nazi, IDF = SS). By rendering impossible any relation with Zionism except a relation of absolute anathema, Paulin's logic of simplification invites readers to divide political space into two antagonistic camps. Israel will now occupy the same symbolic place in the reader's head as the city did in the heads of the millenarian peasant movement: an evil to be annihilated. Paulin's discourse is preparing the way for a fierce and total assault. So we should not be surprised by what Tom Paulin said to the Egyptian paper *Al-Ahram Weekly* about Israeli settlers: "I feel nothing but hatred for them," he spat. They are "Nazis" and "should be shot dead."[75]

NOTES

1. Manfred Gerstenfeld, *Holocaust Inversion: The Portraying of Israel and Jews as Nazis* (Jerusalem: Jerusalem Center for Public Affairs, 2007).

2. Although the focus of this chapter is the United Kingdom, Holocaust inversion discourse was a global phenomenon in 2014. Examples on several continents are reported in Anti-Defamation League, *Violence and Vitriol: Anti-Semitism around the World during Israel's Operation Protective Edge—July–August 2014* (New York: ADL, 2014). For Australia, see Daryl McCann, "Hamas's Propaganda by Deed in Gaza," *Quadrant*, October 3, 2014, https://quadrant.org.au/magazine/2014/10/hamass-propaganda-deed-gaza/. For the presence of Holocaust inversion in US academia, see Martin Kramer, "Gaza=Auschwitz," *Mosaic*, August 26, 2014. The Friedrich Ebert Foundation found slightly over one in four Germans believed that Israeli treatment of Palestinians broadly equated with Nazi treatment of Jews; see "Gaza Conflict Sparked Sharp Rise in German Anti-Semitism, Survey Shows," *Reuters*, November 20, 2014. At an election rally on August 4, 2014, Turkish president Erdogan compared Israel to the Nazis: "Just like Hitler, who sought to establish a race free of all faults, Israel is chasing after the same target"; see Dasha Afanasieva and Humeyra Pamuk, "Turkey's Erdogan Lashes Out at Israel at Election Rally," *Reuters*, August 3, 2014, https://uk.reuters.com/article/uk-turkey-election/turkeys-erdogan-lashes-out-at-israel-at-election-rally-idUKKBN0G30QB20140804. In South Africa, the African National Congress's deputy secretary-general, Jessie Duarte, issued the following statement: "As we move towards the month of August and are reminded of the atrocities of Nazi Germany, surely we must ask the people of Israel has the term 'lest we forget' lost it[s] meaning"; see World Jewish Congress, "South African Jews Call ANC Official's Outburst against Israel 'Disgraceful,'" July 19, 2014, http://www.worldjewishcongress.org/en/news/south-african-jews-call-anc-official-s-outburst-against-israel-disgraceful.

3. "Nodal point" is a concept used by Laclau and Mouffe to refer to the central privileged signifier or reference point of a discourse. (By *discourse*, I mean "communicative action expressed in speech, written text, and visual symbols," following Paul Iganski and Abe Sweiry, *Understanding*

and Addressing the "Nazi Card": Intervening against Antisemitic Discourse [London: European Institute for the Study of Contemporary Antisemitism, 2009], http://www.brandeiscenter.com/images/uploads /articleuploads/nazicard.pdf, 12). If every discourse "is constituted as an attempt to dominate the field of discursivity, to arrest the flow of differences, to construct a centre," then the discourse of antisemitism arrests the flow of differences about Israel by demonizing Israel—most obviously, as a Nazi state. See Ernesto Laclau and Chantal Mouffe, *Hegemony and Socialist Strategy: Towards a Radical Democratic Politics* (Verso: London, 1985), 112. The discourse sits alongside a program to abolish Israel and a movement to exclude Israel from the economic, educational, and cultural life of humanity. Discourse, program, and movement should be considered as one.

4. Alan Johnson, "The Left and the Jews: Time for a Rethink," *Fathom*, Autumn 2015, http://fathomjournal.org/the-left-and-the-jews-time-for -a-rethink/; Alan Johnson, "Intellectual Incitement: The Anti-Zionist Ideology and the Anti-Zionist Subject," in *The Case against Academic Boycotts of Israel*, ed. Cary Nelson and Gabriel Noah Brahm (New York: MLA Members for Scholars' Rights, 2015, 259–81).

5. Robert Wistrich, *From Ambivalence to Betrayal: The Left, the Jews, and Israel* (Lincoln: University of Nebraska Press, 2012); Johnson, "The Left and the Jews"; David Hirsh, "Anti-Zionism and Antisemitism: Cosmopolitan Reflections" (working paper, Yale Initiative for the Interdisciplinary Study of Antisemitism Occasional Papers, 2007), http://research.gold.ac.uk/2061/1/Hirsh_Yale_paper.pdf.

6. It is important to register that discourse demonizing Israel has *minority* support in the United Kingdom. A report by the Institute for Jewish Policy Research noted that "Britain remains a considerably more tolerant and accepting environment for Jews than certain other parts of Europe"; D. L. Staetsky and Jonathan Boyd, *The Exceptional Case? Perceptions and Experiences of Antisemitism among Jews in the UK* (London: JPR, 2014), 5. An online poll with a sample size of 2,007 people established that public opinion is more balanced and stable than the activist noise would suggest, with 19 percent of the public feeling warm toward Israel and 20 percent feeling warm to the Palestinians; "British Attitudes Towards Israel Survey," Populus, October 16–18, 2015, https://www .populus.co.uk/wp-content/uploads/2015/12/British-Attitudes-Towards -Israel-October-2015.pdf.

7. Lesley Klaff, "Holocaust Inversion and Contemporary Antisemitism," *Fathom*, Winter 2014, http://fathomjournal.org/holocaust-inversion-and

-contemporary-antisemitism/; see also Lesley Klaff, "Political and Legal Judgment: Misuses of the Holocaust in the UK," *Journal for the Study of Antisemitism* 5, no. 1 (2013): 45–58; Anthony Julius, *Trials of the Diaspora: A History of Antisemitism in England* (Oxford: Oxford University Press, 2010), 506–16; Gerstenfeld, *Holocaust Inversion*; Manfred Gerstenfeld, "The Multiple Distortions of Holocaust Memory," Scholars for Peace in the Middle East, December 11, 2007, http://spme.org/spme-research /analysis/manfred-gerstenfeld-the-multiple-distortions-of-holocaust -memory/4298/; Manfred Gerstenfeld, *The Abuse of Holocaust Memory: Distortions and Responses* (Jerusalem: Jerusalem Center for Public Affairs, 2009), http://jcpa.org/text/holocaustabuse.pdf.

8. Manfred Gerstenfeld, "Are 150 Million Europeans Anti-Semites or Dangerous Idiots?" *Times of Israel*, July 10, 2013. See Andreas Zick, Beate Küpper, and Andreas Hövermann, *Intolerance, Prejudice and Discrimination: A European Report* (Berlin: Friedrich-Ebert-Stiftung, 2011), 8, http://library.fes.de/pdf-files/do/07908-20110311.pdf. The study was conducted by the University of Bielefeld on behalf of the Friedrich Ebert Foundation, a political foundation associated with the German Social Democratic Party.

9. Iganski and Sweiry, *Understanding and Addressing*, 4; Julius, *Trials*, 507.

10. Ami Isseroff, "Anniversaries: The Jenin Massacre Myth, the Warsaw Ghetto Revolt and the lie of Zionists as Nazis," March 18, 2007, http://zionism -israel.com/israel_news/2007/03/anniversaries-jenin-massacre-myth.html.

11. The story of the EUMC working definition and the partly successful assault on it by the global anti-Zionist movement is told by David Hirsh, "Defining Antisemitism Down," *Fathom*, Winter 2013, http:// fathomjournal.org/defining-antisemitism-down/. See "EUMC Working Definition of Antisemitism," June 6, 2018, http://www.antisem.eu/projects /eumc-working-definition-of-antisemitism/.

12. See International Holocaust Remembrance Alliance, May 26, 2016, https://www.holocaustremembrance.com/sites/default/files/press _release_document_antisemitism.pdf.

13. Theodor Adorno, *Minima Moralia: Fragments from a Damaged Life* (1951; repr., London: Verso, 2005).

14. See Gerstenfeld, *The Abuse of Holocaust Memory*, 106–7.

15. Meir Litvak and Esther Webman, *From Empathy to Denial: Arab Responses to the Holocaust* (Oxford: Oxford University Press, 2011).

16. Gerstenfeld, "The Multiple Distortions"; Stan Crooke, "The Stalinist Roots of Left 'Anti-Zionism,'" in *Two Nations, Two States, Socialists and Israel/Palestine* (pamphlet, London: Workers' Liberty, 2001).

17. Robert Wistrich, *Anti-Zionism as an Expression of Anti-Semitism in Recent Years*, Shazar Library, The Institute of Contemporary Jewry, Vidal Sassoon International Center for the Study of Antisemitism (Jerusalem: Hebrew University of Jerusalem, 1985); Julius, *Trials*, 509.

18. Crooke, "The Stalinist Roots."

19. Wistrich, "Anti-Zionism as an Expression"; see also Steve Cohen, *That's Funny, You Don't Look Anti-Semitic: An Anti-Racist Analysis of Left Anti-Semitism* (Engage, 2005), https://libcom.org/files/thats_funny.pdf.

20. See Cohen, *That's Funny*; Wistrich, *From Ambivalence*; Ben Cohen, "The Persistence of Anti-Semitism on the British Left," *Jewish Political Studies Review* 16, no. 3–4 (2004), http://www.jcpa.org/phas/phas-cohen-fo4.htm; Gerstenfeld, *Holocaust Inversion*; Gerstenfeld, "The Multiple Distortions."

21. Mehdi Hassan, "The Sorry Truth Is That the Virus of Anti-Semitism Has Infected the British Muslim Community," *New Statesman*, March 21, 2013, http://www.newstatesman.com/politics/2013/03/sorry-truth-virus-anti-semitism-has-infected-british-muslim-community.

22. Anti-Defamation League, *Personalizing the Conflict: A Decade of an Assault on Israel's Premiers in the Arab Media* (New York: ADL, 2010), http://archive.adl.org/anti_semitism/media/57360-english-cover-revised-full.pdf.

23. All-Party Parliamentary Group against Antisemitism, *Report of the All-Party Parliamentary Inquiry into Antisemitism* (London: February 2015), http://archive.jpr.org.uk/object-uk175, 40.

24. All-Party Parliamentary Group against Antisemitism, *Report* (2015), 28.

25. All-Party Parliamentary Group against Antisemitism, *Report* (2015), 28.

26. Mick Napier, "Raising the Issues over Holocaust Memorial Day," *Socialist Worker*, 27 January 2007.

27. Sarah McCulloch, "Seriously, Stop Comparing Jews to the Nazis. Please," July 20, 2014, http://www.sarahmcculloch.com/activism/2014/stop-comparing-jews-nazis/.

28. Ben Gidley, *50 Days in the Summer: Gaza, Political Protest and Antisemitism in the UK* (subreport, All-Party Parliamentary Inquiry into Antisemitism, 2014), https://files.graph.cool/cj3e6rg8y906ho104uh8bojao/cj4muda2roo15014568kz1fv5, 6–11.

29. All-Party Parliamentary Group against Antisemitism, *Report*, 60.

30. Cited in Gidley, *50 Days*, 8.

31. Gidley, *50 Days*.

32. See Daniel Randall, "Challenging Anti-Semitism on Gaza Demonstrations," Alliance for Workers' Liberty, July 28, 2014, http://www .workersliberty.org/node/23455.

33. Gidley, *50 Days*, 6–9.

34   Community Security Trust (CST), *Antisemitic Incidents Report 2014* (London: CST, 2014), https://cst.org.uk/data/file/5/5/Incidents -Report-2014.1425053165.pdf, 27, 23.

35. CST, *Antisemitic Incidents Report 2014*, 40.

36. Paul Iganski, Mark McGlashan, and Abe Sweiry, "The Spectre of Nazism Haunts Social Media," *LancsLaw*, February 12, 2015, https:// lancslaw.wordpress.com/2015/02/12/the-spectre-of-nazism-haunts -social-media/.

37. All-Party Parliamentary Group against Antisemitism, *Report*, 52.

38. Gidley, *50 Days*, 10.

39. Palestinian Media Watch, *Special Report: Holocaust Imagery and Terminology Used by the Palestinian Authority during the Gaza War* (Jerusalem, Israel: Palestinian Media Watch, 2014), http://www .palwatch.org/STORAGE/special%20reports/Holocaust%20Nazi%20 comparisons%20during%20the%20Gaza%20war.pdf.

40. Cited in Ariel Ben Solomon, "PA, Fatah Frequently Compare Israel to Nazis," *Jerusalem Post*, August 17, 2014, http://palwatch.org/main .aspx?fi=157&doc_id=12336.

41. "Gaza Massacre Israel Rerun of Nazi Genocide," Press TV, August 3, 2014, http://www.presstv.com/detail/2014/08/03/373898/israeli-gaza -war-revives-nazi-genocide/.

42. See Subir, "The Salaita Tweets: A Twitter/Outrage Concordance," *Daily Kos*, August 18, 2015, https://www.dailykos.com/stories/2015/8 /18/1412900/-The-Salaita-Tweets-A-Twitter-Outrage-concordance.

43. Naomi Wolf, "Via Shahd W. Video from today, al Aqsa mosque where Israeli forces are keeping Muslims from worshipping," Facebook, October 19, 2014, https://www.facebook.com/naomi.wolf.author /posts/10152768777719476.

44. Press Association, "Labour MP Apologises for Holocaust Remark," *Guardian*, February 7, 2014, http://www.theguardian.com/politics/2014 /feb/07/labour-mp-apologises-holocaust-remark (emphasis added).

45. John Prescott, "Israel's Bombardment of Gaza Is a War Crime— And It Must End," *Daily Mirror*, July 26, 2014, http://www.mirror.co.uk /news/world-news/john-prescott-israels-bombardment-gaza-3918413. Several members of the British Labour Party were suspended in 2016, in many cases for the use of Holocaust inversion on social media. Examples

include Vicki Kirby, a former Labour parliamentary candidate who tweeted that Hitler was a "Zionist god"; Shah Hussain, a councillor from Burnley was suspended for allegedly tweeting at Israeli footballer Yossi Benayoun, "You and your country doing the same thing that Hitler did tour [sic] race in ww2"; Miqdad Al-Nuaimi, a Newport councillor was suspended for sending a series of tweets comparing Israel to the Nazi Party and suggesting Jews have the "same arrogant mentality as the Nazis." On the Labour Party's descent into antisemitic anti-Zionism, see Alan Johnson, "Antisemitic anti-Zionism: The Root of Labour's Crisis. A Submission to the Labour Party Inquiry into Antisemitism and Other Forms of Racism," 2016, http://www.bicom.org.uk/wp-content /uploads/2016/06/Prof-Alan-Johnson-Chakrabarti-Inquiry-submission -June-2016.pdf. In July 2018 the Labour Party leadership, against the wishes of Labour members of parliament, refused to incorporate into its new definition of antisemitism certain parts of the International Holocaust Remembrance Alliance definition, including the clause relating to the Nazi analogy. This prompted all three British Jewish communal newspapers to run an unprecedented joint editorial raising the specter of the Labour party in government becoming 'an existential threat' to British Jews.

46. Richard Gold, "Jews for Justice for Palestinians: How They Remember Holocaust Memorial Day," *Engage*, January 29, 2015, https:// engageonline.wordpress.com/2015/01/29/jews-for-justice-for-palestinians -how-they-remember-holocaust-memorial-day/.

47. Michael Lesher, "Et tu, Michael Oren?" *Mondoweiss*, July 23, 2015, http://mondoweiss.net/2015/07/et-tu-michael-oren.

48. Lesher, "Et tu, Michael Oren?"

49. David Feldman, *Sub-report for the All Party Parliamentary Committee against Antisemitism* (subreport, London: All-Party Parliamentary Inquiry into Antisemitism, 2015), https://www.antisemitism.org.uk/files /cj3e6rg8y906h0104uh8b0jao/cj4muajm500ol0137qmx04jmv; Gidley, *50 Days*.

50. All-Party Parliamentary Group against Antisemitism, *Report*, 104.

51. Feldman, *Sub-report*, 7.

52. Feldman, *Sub-report*, 7–8.

53. Gidley, *50 Days*, 8.

54. Iganski, McGlashan, and Sweiry, "The Spectre of Nazism."

55. In Gidley, *50 Days*, 8.

56. Gidley, *50 Days*, 32.

57. Elhanan Yakira, *Post-Zionism, Post-Holocaust: Three Essays on Denial, Forgetting and the Delegitimisation of Israel* (Cambridge: Cambridge University Press, 2010), 121, emphasis added.

58. Yakira, *Post-Zionism, Post-Holocaust*, 121–22.

59. Yakira, *Post-Zionism, Post-Holocaust*, 61.

60. Robert Wistrich, "Anti-Zionism and Anti-Semitism," *Jewish Political Studies Review* 16, no. 3–4 (2004), http://www.jcpa.org/phas /phas-wistrich-f04.htm.

61. Wistrich, "Anti-Zionism and Anti-Semitism."

62. Manfred Gerstenfeld, *Anti-Israelism and Anti-Semitism: Common Characteristics and Motifs* (Jerusalem: Jerusalem Center for Public Affairs, 2007), http://jcpa.org/article/anti-israelism-and-anti-semitism -common-characteristics-and-motifs/.

63. David Nirenberg, *Anti-Judaism: The History of a Way of Thinking* (London: Head of Zeus, 2013).

64. All-Party Parliamentary Group against Antisemitism, *Report of the All-Party Parliamentary Inquiry into Antisemitism* (London: September 2006), http://archive.jpr.org.uk/download?id=1274, 17.

65. Laclau and Mouffe, *Hegemony and Socialist Strategy*, 109.

66. Laclau and Mouffe, *Hegemony and Socialist Strategy*, 105.

67. See Yakira, *Post-Zionism, Post-Holocaust*, 328–29.

68. Cited in Julius, *Trials*, 512.

69. Yakira, *Post-Zionism, Post-Holocaust*, 66.

70. Paulin's poem is reproduced in Julius, *Trials*, 237.

71. Julius, *Trials*, 236–40.

72. Anna Marie Smith, *Laclau and Mouffe: The Radical Democratic Imaginary* (London: Routledge, 1998), 89.

73. Laclau and Mouffe, *Hegemony and Social Strategy*, 130.

74. Laclau and Mouffe, *Hegemony and Social Strategy*, 129–30.

75. Sarah Hall, "Death to Jewish Settlers, Says Anti-Zionist Poet," *Guardian*, April 13, 2002, http://www.theguardian.com/world/2002 /apr/13/israel.booksnews.

ALAN JOHNSON is editor of *Fathom: For a Deeper Understanding of Israel and the Region,* a quarterly online journal. He is coauthor of the "Euston Manifesto," a modern statement of social democratic antitotalitarianism, and he is editor of *Global Politics after 9/11: The Democratiya Interviews.*

EIGHT

Fraser v. University and College Union

Anti-Zionism, Antisemitism, and Racializing Discourse

LESLEY KLAFF

IN AUGUST 2011, Ronnie Fraser, a lecturer in mathematics, acting through his lawyer, Anthony Julius, filed a claim in the Central London Employment Tribunal against the University and College Union (UCU), which is the United Kingdom's largest trade union for academics, lecturers, and researchers. Fraser alleged "hostile environment harassment" by the union under sections 26 and 57 of the Equality Act 2010. The Equality Act protects individuals in the public sector from unfair treatment, including harassment and other forms of direct discrimination.

Fraser claimed that the union had created a hostile environment for him as a Jewish member (Jewish is a "protected characteristic" as both a "race" and a "religion" under the act) by engaging in a course of "unwanted antisemitic conduct" that was informed by hostility to Israel and the Zionist project. Such unwanted conduct had the effect of "violating his dignity" and/or of "creating an intimidating, hostile, degrading, humiliating," and/or "offensive environment" for him.

Fraser brought the case against the UCU because, since its formation in 2007, the union had been actively pursuing an academic boycott campaign against Israel as a response to what it perceived to be Israeli human rights abuses. Fraser experienced the boycott campaign as antisemitic in effect, if not in intent, because it treated Israel and its supporters within the union, most of whom were Jews, as pariahs and unconsciously recycled antisemitic themes and tropes. Moreover, it treated those who opposed the boycott campaign within the union, mostly Jews, as apologists for apartheid, colonialism, and racism.

Specifically, Fraser's complaint alleged a course of action by the union that amounted to "institutional antisemitism" and gave the following ten grounds as examples: (1) annual boycott resolutions against only Israel; (2) the conduct of the debates at which the resolutions were discussed; (3) the moderating of the activists' list and the penalizing of antiboycott activists; (4) the failure to engage with people who raised concerns about antisemitism and the failure to address resignations citing antisemitism as the reason; (5) the dismissive response to the 2006 *Report of the All Party Parliamentary Inquiry into Anti-Semitism*; (6) the failure to meet the Organization for Security and Co-operation in Europe's special representative on antisemitism; (7) the hosting of Bongani Masuku after he had been found guilty of antisemitic hate speech by the South African Human Rights Commission; (8) the dismissive attitude toward the Equality and Human Rights Commission; (9) the repudiation of the European Monitoring Centre on Racism and Xenophobia's (EUMC) working definition of antisemitism; and (10) the response to Fraser's "letter before action." In March 2013, the Employment Tribunal unanimously dismissed all ten grounds of Fraser's complaint as unfounded and mostly time-barred.[1]

This chapter explores the contested meanings of anti-Zionism and antisemitism in the United Kingdom using, in part, the idea of racializing discourse. Its principal focus is an examination of the arguments and judgment in *Fraser v. University and College Union* in 2013.

ANTI-ZIONISM

The key concepts and terms at issue here are highly contested. The concepts of antisemitism and anti-Zionism are neither univocal, nor can they be isolated from fields of practice and conflict, as was especially evident in *Fraser v. UCU*.

Zionists rightly believe that antisemitism is implicated in contemporary anti-Zionism, because anti-Zionism is opposition to Zionism, which is the Jewish project of establishing, developing, and protecting the state of Israel as the ancestral homeland of the Jews. This opposition is frequently expressed in the language of prejudice against Israel or the Zionist project. It was this meaning of anti-Zionism that was advanced by Fraser, his thirty-four witnesses, and his legal team in his case against the UCU.[2] And it is this meaning of anti-Zionism that is found in the official 2002 definition contained in the report of the Berlin Technical University's Centre for Research on Antisemitism drafted for the EUMC.[3] The report defines anti-Zionism as "the portrayal of Israel as a state that is fundamentally negatively distinct from all others and which therefore has no right to exist."[4]

Anti-Zionists, on the other hand, evade charges of antisemitism by representing anti-Zionism as merely opposition to Zionism, and by claiming that Zionism is a political movement or ideology that is unrelated to, and independent of, a person's race or religion. This alternative version of anti-Zionism was advanced by the UCU and accepted by the tribunal, and this had a distinctly negative consequence for the outcome of Fraser's case.

The tribunal's characterization of Zionism and anti-Zionism as mere "political" ideologies was crucial to a central question before the tribunal: whether an attachment to Israel is relevant to Jewish identity. This question was central because to succeed in a claim for hostile environment harassment, there must be a relevant nexus between the unwanted conduct and the claimant's protected characteristic. In this case, the unwanted conduct was hostility to Israel and Zionism, and the protected characteristic was Fraser's Jewish religious and racial status.

Fraser argued that an affinity with the state of Israel and the Zionist project is an aspect of the identity of the majority of British Jews, who assume an obligation to support Israel and to ensure its survival as the ancestral homeland of the Jewish people. This affinity does not equate to unconditional or unstinting support for the government of Israel or its policies; rather, it amounts to a sense of connection with, or an affiliation with, Israel and a sense of its importance in the context of Jewish history and the persecution of the Jewish people. For this reason, hostility to Israel engages Jews not only in conventional political terms but also because Israel is an aspect of their identity. Indeed, the reason that the majority of British Jews are usually at the forefront of movements opposing irrational, disproportionate, and stereotyped hostility to Israel is because they have some kind of affinity with Israel. Accordingly, said Fraser, hostility to Israel engages his protected characteristic.

The UCU, on the other hand, argued that many different positions are taken on the Israel-Palestine conflict, and specifically on the academic boycott of Israel, and that these are political positions that tend to be associated with distinct groups. Jews are represented in many such groups, and it therefore follows that any disagreements between the groups are political and do not touch on any protected characteristic—that is, on any religious or racial identity under the 2010 Equality Act. In other words, a person's political positions are completely independent of and not determined by his or her race or religion. Witnesses for both the UCU and Fraser demonstrated that not all Jewish people hold Zionist beliefs and that many people who hold Zionist beliefs are Christian or of some other faith.

Fraser countered that the fact that a range of views exists within the body of Anglo-Jewry on Israel does not override the argument that his protected characteristic is engaged when Israel is demonized. The existence of a group of Jews who are hostile to Israel and Zionism is not evidence for the proposition that an attachment to Israel is not an aspect of contemporary Jewish identity. These Jews are either marginal or nonnormative, or the form their protected characteristic takes is in their hostility to Israel and Zionism.

But the tribunal rejected Fraser's claim that an attachment to Israel is an aspect of Jewish identity. It said it could find no authority for the proposition that legal protection also attaches to "a particular affinity or sentiment not inherent in the protected characteristic but said to be commonly held by members of the protected group" (para. 18). It could find no relevant authority because the case was one of first instance. The tribunal could have stipulated that an "affinity or sentiment" fell within the scope of the protected characteristic. But it preferred to accept the UCU's "range of views" argument. Referring to a pro–Boycott, Divestment, Sanctions (BDS) member of the UCU as Jewish (para. 130), the tribunal said, "The Claimant's main contention is that the conduct of which he complains was inherently discriminatory in that it consisted of acts and omissions concerning the conflict between Israel and Palestine and so related to *his* (although of course not every Jew's) Jewish identity and, as such, *his* Jewish race and/or religion or belief" (para. 49, emphasis in original). The tribunal was then able to conclude, "It seems to us that a belief in the Zionist project or an attachment to Israel . . . is not intrinsically a part of Jewishness" (para. 150).

This reasoning demonstrates how the UK anti-Zionist movement has successfully managed to separate Israel from Jews. It claims that Jews and Israelis or Zionists are two separate and distinct entities—so much so that hatred of Israel and hatred of Jews are considered to be unconnected. In this way, anti-Zionist expression and hostility to Israel has been normalized in the British trade union movement and on British campuses and is not recognized as antisemitic harassment under section 26 of the Equality Act.

Indeed, the representation of Zionism as a political movement or ideology that is unconnected to race or religion allows anti-Zionists to deny antisemitism while representing Zionism as a uniquely racist ideology that secured, and now maintains, statehood by persecutory means. In the view of the UCU anti-Zionists, Israel was established by the dispossession of the Palestinians, was enlarged by aggressive wars, and is now maintained by oppression and brutality, making Israel an illegitimate state.

This anti-Zionism, to which Anthony Julius refers as "progressive anti-Zionism" or "the new anti-Zionism" and to which Alan Johnson refers as "anti-Semitic anti-Zionism," is found predominantly among those on the far left of the UK political spectrum.[5] It is these people—members of the far left—who dominate the UCU's national executive committee, its activists' list, and its annual Congress, where the members propose anti-Israel motions and overwhelmingly vote to adopt them. *This* anti-Zionism conceives of Israel and the Zionist project in partial and distorted form and, as Johnson explains, relies on a "distorting system of concepts: 'Zionism is racism'; Israel is a 'settler-colonialist state' which 'ethnically cleansed' the 'indigenous' people' of Palestine, went on to build an 'apartheid state' and is now engaged in an 'incremental genocide' against the Palestinians."[6] *This* anti-Zionism is firmly rooted in the global BDS movement, and its political program is the removal of Israel from the world stage.

There have been various attempts to explain the left's hostility to Israel and Zionism. One explanation is that the values of the left are secular, collectivist, internationalist, and universalist and are therefore at odds with what it perceives to be Jewish values: religious, individualist, nationalist, and particularist. These left values make leftists oppose Jewish religious and national rights. Johnson explains the hostility in terms of a phenomenon known as "anti-imperialist campism," which he describes as the left's raising of anti-imperialism to an absolute value and the reframing of Israel as the key site of the imperialist system.[7] David Hirsh believes that anti-imperialist campism has emerged "as the pre-eminent principle of the progressive movement," making hostility to Israel a key marker of political belonging.[8] British historian Simon Schama explains the left's hostility to Israel and Zionism in terms of "postcolonial guilt," which "has fired up the war against its prize whipping boy, Zionism, like no other cause."[9] This explanation would suggest that the normalization of anti-Zionism within the British trade union movement is partially explicable in terms of the left's distancing itself from a legacy of colonialism.

ANTISEMITISM

The anti-Zionist separation of Israel from Jews provides the context and rationale for disagreement between Zionists and anti-Zionists about what counts as antisemitism. This disagreement was a central issue in *Fraser v. UCU*. Fraser embraced the EUMC working definition of antisemitism, and his case against the UCU was based in part on its repudiation by the UCU at its 2011 Congress. The EUMC definition provides several explicit examples of how antisemitism can be manifested, when context is taken fully into account, with respect to the state of Israel. These include denying the Jewish people a right to self-determination; applying double standards by expecting from Israel a behavior not expected of any other state; applying the images and symbols of traditional antisemitism (e.g., the blood libel) to Israel; comparing contemporary Israeli policy to that of the Nazis; and holding Jews collectively responsible for actions of the state of Israel. The definition emphasizes that criticism of Israel, similar to that leveled against any other state, does not constitute a form of antisemitism. Motion 70 had expressed the view that the EUMC definition "confused criticism of Israeli government policy and actions with 'genuine' antisemitism and was being used to silence debate about Israel and Palestine on university and college campuses" (para. 74).[10]

The argument that the EUMC definition was used by Jews in bad faith to silence criticism of Israel had even been advanced by UCU joint general secretary, Paul Mackney, in 2006, when he told the All-Party Parliamentary Committee of Inquiry into Antisemitism that "criticism of the Israeli government is not in itself antisemitic" and that "defenders of Israel had used the charge of antisemitism as a tactic to smother democratic debate and legitimate censure" (para. 85).

Mackney's statement and the contents of Motion 70 reflect David Hirsh's "Livingstone Formulation," which is a common trope of contemporary antisemitism in the United Kingdom. It was named after Ken Livingstone, the former mayor of London, who in 2006 wrote in the *Guardian*, "For far too long the accusation of antisemitism has been used against anyone who is critical of the policies of the Israeli government, as I have been."[11] The Livingstone Formulation is the allegation that those raising concerns about antisemitism are doing so in bad faith in order to silence criticism of Israel. It is a "rhetorical device which enables the user to refuse to engage with the charge made"[12] by responding with an ad hominem attack against the person or persons making that charge.[13] Fraser told the tribunal that the key mode of harassment in the UCU was the relentless accusation of bad faith whenever Jews said they were experiencing antisemitism.[14] As discussed later, the same allegation of bad faith was deployed by the tribunal in its ruling against Fraser.

The UCU considered only classical antisemitism—hatred of the individual Jew—to be "genuine" antisemitism. In 2012 it formally adopted the following definition of antisemitism formulated by the Jewish academic Dr. Brian Klug, who has long believed that antisemitism is hatred of Jews as Jews: "At the heart of antisemitism is the negative stereotype of the Jew: sinister, cunning, parasitic, money-grubbing, mysteriously powerful, and so on. Antisemitism consists in projecting this figure onto individual Jews, Jewish groups and Jewish institutions."[15]

In the event, the tribunal decided it was not required or prepared to rule on the meaning or definition of antisemitism,
including the EUMC working definition. Noting that some
members of the union did not like the EUMC definition on the
grounds that it brands attacks on Zionism as antisemitic while
others, such as Fraser himself, did like it, the tribunal concluded
that there are legitimately held differences of view on what constitutes antisemitism and on where the line should be drawn in
relation to when criticism of Israel becomes antisemitic, and that
this, moreover, is the "stuff of political debate" (para. 51).[16]

The tribunal's refusal to rule on the meaning or definition of
antisemitism constitutes a denial of antisemitism. By characterizing all criticism of Israel as free political speech, the tribunal was
able to disregard as irrelevant all of Fraser's evidence of antisemitism. This evidence included Anthony Julius's direct examination
of Fraser and his witnesses, his cross-examination of the UCU
witnesses, a further twenty-three bundles of evidence against
the UCU, and the written statements of Fraser's thirty-four witnesses; in other words, Fraser's entire case. In a pointed criticism
of Julius's emphasis on antisemitism throughout the hearing, the
tribunal said, "We had to remind ourselves frequently that despite appearances, we were not conducting a public inquiry into
anti-Semitism but considering a lawful claim for unlawful harassment" (para. 180). Of course it was a claim for unlawful harassment, but it was also a claim for unlawful *antisemitic* harassment,
and evidence of antisemitism was entirely relevant. The problem
was that the tribunal was not prepared to rule on the question of
antisemitism. As a result, the UCU's guarantees against racism
and bigotry continue to exclude any form of antisemitism that
can conceivably be characterized as criticism of Israel.[17]

Indeed, at its 2017 Congress, the UCU voted to reject the International Holocaust Remembrance Alliance's (IHRA's) working definition of antisemitism, which is substantially the same
as the EUMC definition, on the grounds that its adoption would

constitute explicit political interference in the affairs of the union and erode free speech. This rejection of the IHRA definition means that Jewish members are not protected from the antisemitism in the UCU that disguises itself as criticism of Israel. The UCU was able to reject the definition because, despite its adoption by the British government on December 12, 2016, it has no statutory underpinning and does not have the force of law. Further, the UCU was unmoved by the fact that the definition had received Jeremy Corbyn's backing and had been adopted by the National Union of Students and the Union of Jewish Students. It is noteworthy that the overwhelming vote in favor of rejecting the IHRA definition at the 2017 Congress was matched only by the overwhelming vote in favor of carrying all other antiracist motions.[18]

RACIALIZING DISCOURSE

The tribunal was further able to disregard Fraser's evidence of antisemitism as irrelevant or inauthentic by racializing Fraser and many of his witnesses. In her book *An Unfortunate Coincidence: Jews, Jewishness and English Law*, Didi Herman notes the judicial practice of racializing and orientalizing Jews and Jewish issues in a range of English cases.[19] She uses the term *orientalism* to signify a particular way of characterizing Jews to mark them out as "Eastern" and "un-English." It involves comparing Jews and Jewish practices to those of other civilizations, especially Christian civilization, which is held up as eminently superior and is equated with that which is "English." This comparison is a racializing discourse because Jews and Jewish practices are understood and represented as inferior to Christianity and Englishness.

Accordingly, the tribunal applied unattractive characteristics to Fraser and many of his witnesses. Herman notes that judicial assessments of character are often dependent on notions of race. Their unattractiveness was found in their un-English behavior, such as "playing to the gallery," "scoring points," "ventilating opinions," and behaving in a "tactical" manner (paras. 148–49).[20] In other words, Fraser and his witnesses were not playing fair. In an echo of Fraser's good Jew/bad Jew distinction, the tribunal indulged in a good witness/bad witness distinction by juxtaposing *their* behavior against that of the UCU witnesses, each of whom gave "careful and accurate" evidence and stuck to the facts (para. 149).[21] Playing fair is a Christian notion, and a sense of fair play is a deeply embedded English value. The exclusion of emotional witnesses for Fraser avoided the political coloring of their testimony, which was problematic for the tribunal.

Fraser v. UCU contains several other examples of racializing discourse. One example is the tribunal's deployment of the Livingstone Formulation. In an echo of the UCU's attitude, the tribunal characterized the case as one in which Fraser, his Jewish lawyer, and his thirty-four witnesses wanted to abrogate free political speech in the union to shield Israel from criticism. In ruling against Fraser, it said, "We greatly regret that the case was ever brought. At heart, it represents an *impermissible attempt to achieve a political end by litigious means*. It would be very unfortunate if an exercise of this sort were ever repeated" (para. 178, emphasis added). This statement is a racializing discourse because it accuses Fraser and his team of playing the "antisemitism card" to prevent criticism of Israel. The tribunal thought that "Fraser was trying to mobilize a bad-faith allegation of antisemitism in order to silence good-faith critics of Israel."[22] They accepted the UCU's case that Fraser and his witnesses who gave evidence of antisemitism in the union were really engaged in a shared plan to dishonestly silence the UCU's campaigns against Israel.[23]

The tribunal's view that Fraser and his witnesses were acting dishonestly to shield Israel from criticism involves antisemitic ways of thinking because it sees a "secret agenda"—silencing Israel's critics—behind the charge of antisemitism. As the late Robert Fine noted, "one dodgy presumption behind this argument is that Israel cannot be defended openly, so that its defenders have to resort to underhand tactics."[24] This way of thinking also invokes classic conspiracy theory because it accuses those raising concerns about antisemitism of taking part in a dishonest Jewish (or "Zionist") plot in order to silence political speech.[25]

The use of the Livingstone Formulation is antisemitic for another reason, too: it singles out Jews as the only minority racial group in the United Kingdom who are not permitted to bear witness to the existence of racism against them or to the nature of their suffering. With incidents involving anti-black racism, the contemporary practice is to follow the recommendation of the 1999 MacPherson Report, which stipulates that a racist incident should be defined by the victim.[26] The MacPherson principle does not mean that people who report an experience of racism must necessarily be considered to be right; but what it does mean is that it should be *assumed* that they are right and should be taken seriously and listened to carefully so that an informed judgment can be made as to whether they are right. The 2006 *Report of the All-Party Parliamentary Committee of Inquiry* recommended the adoption of the MacPherson principle to decide the matter of antisemitism, but it has not been adopted, and the Livingstone Formulation is a clear violation of that principle.[27] Apart from MacPherson, since antisemitism disproportionately afflicts Jews, it is reasonable to assume that they are likely to know more about it, and recognize it more easily, than non-Jews, and the Livingstone Formulation is an outright rejection of that assumption.[28]

The systematic use of the Livingstone Formulation to respond to complaints of antisemitism prevents contemporary antisemitism from being recognized, acknowledged, and resisted. It represents a recurrent pattern of a *refusal to even try* to recognize it.[29] It further keeps alive the antisemitic trope that Jews are conspiratorial, underhanded, and dishonest, especially within the UCU itself.[30]

The specter of Jewish particularism was a strong theme throughout the judgment. The tribunal thought that Jewish particularism was so strong that Fraser and his team had been willing to abuse the Employment Tribunal as well as misuse the Equality Act in their self-serving pursuit of preventing the union from criticizing Israel. It said, "The Employment Tribunals are a hard-pressed public service and it is not right that their limited resources should have been squandered as they have been in this case" (para. 178).

Specifically, the tribunal characterized the case as one of Jewish particularism versus the universal right to freedom of expression, a right enshrined in Article 10 of the European Convention of Human Rights and protected under sections 3 and 12 of the Human Rights Act 1998, and concluded that "the *narrow* interests of [Fraser] must give way to the *wider public interest* in ensuring that freedom of expression is safeguarded" (para. 156, emphasis added). This reasoning suggests that freedom of expression cases—or cases that are characterized as being about freedom of expression—will, and indeed should, work against Jewish claimants. It is worth noting that, although the tribunal characterized this as a freedom of expression case, it was not a speech harassment case at all. Fraser's primary case was that the UCU had persistently failed to do things for him contrary to its assurances that it would and was based on a series of acts and omissions.[31] To represent the case as one in which Fraser was trying to curtail the UCU members' speech was to misrepresent it. In any event, the union's relentless pursuit of an academic boycott of Israel can hardly be represented as a free speech policy, because boycotts shut speech down rather than promote it. But as Hirsh has noted, "every racist claims that anti-racists disregard their right to free speech."[32]

Jewish particularism further surfaced in the tribunal's characterization of Fraser and his team as opposed to pluralism and tolerance. The tribunal said, "We are troubled by the implications of the claim because underlying it we sense a worrying disregard for pluralism, tolerance and freedom of expression" (para. 179).

Pitting the Jew against pluralism, tolerance, and freedom of expression amounts to orientalizing the Jew, because these are universal rights and values that are associated with Western Christian Europe.[33] In this way, Jews are represented and understood as inferior to Christianity and as Eastern in the sense of un-English. Further, because human rights are associated with the Enlightenment and democracy, Jews are represented and understood as not fully enlightened and as undemocratic.[34] This is a racializing discourse that echoes the tribunal's view that Fraser was trying to interfere in the democratic processes within the union, which merely wanted to uphold the principle of free speech and provide an arena for members to engage with one another on matters of pressing political concern, such as the Israel-Palestine conflict.

The specter of Jewish particularism was also responsible for the tribunal's rejection of Fraser's claim that an attachment to Israel is relevant to his Jewish identity (para. 150). By rejecting the attachment of Jews to Israel, the tribunal rejected Jewish nationalism and Jewish particularism in favor of a "race-less" postnational post-Holocaust Europe with its guarantee of universal rights. Such a view reinforced the tribunal's denial of contemporary antisemitism because, according to Fine, in postnational, post-Holocaust Europe, antisemitism is considered to be a thing of the past, overcome by the defeat of fascism and the development of the European Union and the European Convention on Human Rights.[35] Accordingly, Fraser and his witnesses were implicitly ascribed a Jewish particularism that was incompatible with English or European identity.

The racializing of Jews may have been one of the purposes of the tribunal's three brief references to the Holocaust.[36] Herman notes that English judges frequently use the Holocaust as a "mnemonic device" to achieve certain purposes in cases involving Jews.[37] One purpose may be to reinforce particularly English understandings of Jews and Jewishness, such that, rather than being used to recall atrocity, a Holocaust reference acts as a "racializing aid" to remembering what it is that English judges find "unattractive" and alien about "the Jew."[38]

The tribunal's Holocaust references also served to reinforce its denial of contemporary antisemitism. According to Seymour, a Holocaust reference achieves this because it associates antisemitism with state-sponsored genocide in the "old" Europe, consigning it to history as the result of the defeat of fascism and the rise of the "new" postnational Europe with its emphasis on human rights.[39] Associating antisemitism with state-sponsored genocide constructs Jews as "deserving" victims of persecution in the past but not in the present. A Holocaust reference further helps to portray the judges as sympathetic, or at least as not indifferent, to Jewish persecution and suffering while denying a claim for discrimination.[40]

The tribunal's racializing discourse reflects the nature of antisemitism in the United Kingdom, which is a phenomenon about ways of thinking about Jews. As Hirsh has noted, Jews are described, imagined, and suspected in a certain way by people who consider themselves to be just and upstanding.[41]

This chapter addresses the contested meanings of anti-Zionism and antisemitism and their relationship to each other, as well as antisemitic ways of thinking, in the United Kingdom by reference to the UCU case. Unfortunately, since the election of Jeremy Corbyn as leader of the Labour Party, the UCU's understanding of anti-Zionism and antisemitism is increasingly prevalent among some members of the Labour Party, especially those who belong to the grassroots pro-Corbyn Momentum Movement, and within the academy. It appears that the tribunal's antisemitic ways of thinking are engaged in by people who believe themselves to be virtuous opponents of antisemitism and who therefore refuse to acknowledge their own antisemitism, even when it is pointed out to them. The Livingstone Formulation is systematically deployed to deny an accusation of antisemitism and to focus instead on the hidden motive for the accusation.[42] This practice assumes not only that those who raise concerns about antisemitism are part of a secret conspiratorial plan to silence criticism of Israel but also that all criticism of Israel, including its demonization and support for a boycott, is legitimate criticism.[43] Further, it is evident from the judicial discourse that dominant and problematic assumptions exist in law. Even where there are not explicit racialized assumptions, a certain orientation inevitably excludes, marginalizes, or silences the Jewish experience.

NOTES

1. *Fraser v. UCU* was decided by the Central London Employment Tribunal on March 22, 2013. The full judgment can be found at "Mr R Fraser -v- University & College Union," Courts and Tribunals Judiciary, March 25, 2013, http://www.judiciary.gov.uk/media/judgments/2013/fraser-uni-college-union. Throughout this chapter, quotations from the judgment are referred to by paragraph number.

2. Fraser's witnesses consisted of union activists, academics (including antisemitism scholars, scientists, sociologists, historians, lawyers, and philosophers), members of parliament, and members of Jewish communal organizations. These people were Jewish, Christian, Muslim, and atheist. Many of the academics had resigned from the UCU citing antisemitism as the reason.

3. Werner Bergmann and Juliane Wetzel, *Manifestations of Anti-Semitism in the European Union,* Synthesis Report, Berlin Technical University Centre for Research on Antisemitism, First Semester 2002 (Draft February 2003), www.infopartisan.net/document/antisemitismusstudie.pdf.

4. Bergmann and Wetzel, *Manifestations of Anti-Semitism,* 18

5. Anthony Julius, *Trials of the Diaspora: A History of Anti-Semitism in England* (Oxford: Oxford University Press, 2010), 584. Julius describes "progressive anti-Zionism" as "a semi-ideology, a boutique movement," which takes the form of a comprehensive political stance, complete in itself (451). Alan Johnson, "The Left and the Jews: Time for a Rethink," *Fathom,* Autumn 2015, http://fathomjournal.org/the-left-and-the-jews-time-for-a-rethink/.

6. Johnson, "The Left and the Jews."

7. Alan Johnson, "No Jeremy Corbyn Is Not Antisemitic—But the Left Should Be Wary of Who He Calls Friends," *New Statesman*, September 2, 2015, http://www.newstatesman.com/politics/staggers/2015/09/no-jeremy-corbyn-not-antisemitic-left-should-be-wary-who-he-calls-friends/.

8. David Hirsh, "The Corbyn Left: The Politics of Position and the Politics of Reason," *Fathom*, Autumn 2015, http://fathomjournal.org/the-corbyn-left-the-politics-of-position-and-the-politics-of-reason/.

9. Simon Schama, "Why the Left Hates Us," *Jewish Chronicle*, February 26, 2016, 37. According to Schama, the left believes that Jewish self-determination has inflicted a colonial and alien enterprise on the Palestinian population, who have been penalized for the sins of Europe.

10. From the beginning of the union campaign to boycott Israeli universities in 2002, similar clauses had been included in its boycott motions to shield supporters of the boycott from accusations of antisemitism. For instance, Motion 54, which was passed in 2003 by the Council of the Association of University Teachers (AUT; a predecessor union to the UCU), stated, "Council deplores the witch-hunting of colleagues, including AUT members who are participating in the academic boycott of Israel. Council recognises that anti-Zionism is not anti-Semitism, and resolves to give all possible support to members of the AUT who are *unjustly accused of anti-Semitism because of their political opposition to Israeli government policy*" (emphasis added). See David Hirsh, "How Raising the Issue of Antisemitism Puts You Outside the Community of the Progressive: The Livingstone Formulation," *Engage*, April 29, 2016, https://engageonline.files.wordpress.com/2016/04/livingstone-formulation-david-hirsh.pdf, 12.

11. David Hirsh, "Accusations of Malicious Intent in Debates about the Palestine-Israel Conflict and about Antisemitism," *Transversal* 1 (January 2010): 47–77; Hirsh, "How Raising the Issue," 6.

12. Hirsh, "How Raising the Issue," 6.

13. Jon Pike, "Antisemitism and Testimonial Injustice," *Engage*, January 31, 2008, https://engageonline.wordpress.com/2008/01/.

14. Hirsh, "How Raising the Issue," 14.

15. University and College Union, *Antisemitism* (leaflet, 2012), https://www.ucu.org.uk/media/5122/UCU---challenging-antisemitism-leaflet/pdf/ucu_challengingantisemitism_leaflet_2012/. The union also purported to take antisemitism seriously by passing Motion 7 in 2009. This instructed the National Executive Committee to organize an annual event to commemorate Holocaust Memorial Day.

16. "So to take one of many examples, Mr Whine of the Community Security Trust, . . . did not consider that comparisons between Israel and apartheid South Africa were inherently anti-Semitic, whereas the Claimant did" (para. 151). The tribunal thought that the different opinions of a large number of Fraser's witnesses made the UCU's "range of views" point (para. 149). "Without such common ground, questions put to the witnesses for the Respondents seeking to elicit a view whether such-and-such a comment 'was' or 'was not' anti-Semitic lacked any meaning" (para. 52).

17. David Hirsh, "Defining Antisemitism Down," *Fathom*, Winter 2013, http://www.fathomjournal.org/policy-politics/defining-antisemitism -down/.

18. Mira Vogel, "Jewish Issues Again at UCU Congress 2017," *Engage*, May 31, 2017, https://engageonline.wordpress.com/2017/5/31 /jewish-issues-again-at-ucu-congress-2017/.

19. Didi Herman, *An Unfortunate Coincidence: Jews, Jewishness and English Law* (Oxford: Oxford University Press, 2011).

20. Herman states, "The law is the perfect English gentleman, as compared to the feminised characteristics of 'the Jew' revealed in his impulsive, over emotional and disruptive 'Jewish' voice"; *An Unfortunate Coincidence*, 44. There is a long tradition in English cases of depicting Jews as having a weak or bad character.

21. Fraser attempted to explain to the tribunal the good Jew/bad Jew dichotomy, designating the anti-Zionist Jews in the UCU as the "good Jews" and the Zionist Jews in the UCU as the "bad Jews. The tribunal noted that the UCU witnesses were "called for the mundane purpose of telling the Tribunal about facts rather than ventilating their opinions" (para. 149).

22. Hirsh, "How Raising the Issue," 15. The UCU's lawyer, Anthony White QC, subjected Fraser to two days of cross-examination in which Fraser was relentlessly accused of crying antisemitism in order to silence criticism of Israel within the union.

23. Hirsh, "How Raising the Issue," 14.

24. Robert Fine, "On Doing the Sociology of Antisemitism," *European Sociological Association Newsletter*, no. 33 (Winter 2012): 5.

25. Hirsh, "How Raising the Issue," 6.

26. William MacPherson, *Report of the Stephen Lawrence Inquiry* (London: Home Office, 1999), http://www.archive.official-documents.co .uk/document/cm42/4262/sli-06.htm.

27. The report said with respect to defining antisemitism, "We conclude that it is the Jewish community itself that is best qualified to determine

what does and does not constitute antisemitism." All-Party Parliamentary Group against Antisemitism, *Report of the All-Party Parliamentary Inquiry into Antisemitism* (London: Stationery Office, 2006), http://archive.jpr.org.uk/download?id=1274, 1. However, it is important to note that there are many prominent non-Jewish scholars of antisemitism, including James Parkes, Gavin Longmuir, Mary Boys, Franklin Littell, the Eckhardts, Edward Flannery, and John Connelly. More recently, a parliamentary committee set up to report on antisemitism in the UK also recommended the adoption of the MacPherson principle to decide the issue of antisemitism; see House of Commons Home Affairs Committee, *Antisemitism in the UK: Tenth Report of Session 2016–17* (London: House of Commons, 2016), https://publications.parliament.uk/pa/cm201617/cmselect/cmhaff/136/136.pdf, para. 22: "The starting point for deciding the matter of antisemitism is the perception of the alleged victim." The committee also thought that an incident "perceived to be racist by the victim *or any other person*" is a strong basis for investigation.

28. "'I think, therefore I am' is replaced by 'I am, therefore I know,'" wrote Mary Lefkowitz in *History Lesson: A Race Odyssey* (New Haven, CT: Yale University Press, 2008), 122, and quoted in Julius, *Trials of the Diaspora*, 586.

29. Hirsh, "How Raising the Issue," 1.

30. Motion 729 on "Palestine" was passed at UCU's 2016 Annual Congress. It provided as follows: "Congress notes: 1. Government guidance deterring Local Authority boycotts of unethical companies; 2. 'counter-radicalisation' to prevent campus criticism of Israel, and boycott of complicit institutions; 3. orchestrated conflation of anti-Zionism with anti-Semitism; 4. the drive by Israel to access UK campuses for state propaganda via faux debates with selected critics; 5. escalating legal threats and pressure to intimidate Israel's critics: including UCU Congress votes for BDS (2010), non-conflation of anti-Zionism with anti-Semitism (2011), and against contact with Histradrut (2010). Congress believes a. BDS responds to Western governments' failure to hold Israel accountable for war crimes and international law violations; b. scholars have a duty to ensure voices of the oppressed are not silenced on campus. Congress i. reaffirms its support for BDS, and for the boycott of Israeli academic and cultural institutions; ii. requires union officers to uphold Congress decisions when acting in their UCU capacity, and to resign from such external positions as create conflicts of interest." It is clear that Motion 729 mirrors the themes of antisemitic conspiracy theory. The union ruled that the motion would not be acted on because to do so would be illegal.

31. Fraser's primary case was that the UCU persistently failed to comply with its assurances that it would (1) ensure balance in the debates and meetings that it hosted and presided over on the Israel-Palestine conflict; (2) act against antisemitism among its members, including activists' list adjudications; (3) address concerns raised by Fraser and other Jewish and non-Jewish members with respect to its own conduct (such as dealing with complaints of antisemitism against its members); (4) address resignations by Jewish and non-Jewish members who cited antisemitism as the reason for leaving the union; and (5) pursue its stated objective of "campaigning against anti-Semitism" and thereby protect its own Jewish members.

32. Hirsh, "How Raising the Issue," 15.

33. Griffin maintains that human rights are "undoubtedly" a Western product, introduced by Christians in the late Middle Ages and further developed in the modern period of the Enlightenment as part of the growth of individualism and the sense of the dignity of man; see James Griffin, *On Human Rights* (Oxford: Oxford University Press, 2008), 133. This represents the dominant view, although other scholars have stressed the contribution of the non-Western world to the development of human rights; see Upendra Baxi, *The Future of Human Rights*, 3rd ed. (Oxford: Oxford University Press, 2008), 33; Jacques Rancière, "Who Is the Subject of the Rights of Man?" *South Atlantic Quarterly* 103, no. 2–3 (Spring /Summer 2004): 297–310, doi:10.1215/00382876-103-2-3-297; Robert Fine, "The West and the Rest: The Dialectics of Universality and Particularity: Are Human Rights Western?" teaching materials for Sociology of Human Rights, University of Warwick, Department of Sociology, accessed February 12, 2016, https://warwick.ac.uk/fac/soc/sociology/staff /robertfine/home/teachingmaterial/humanrights/lecturepodcast/are _human_rights_western.pdf, 3.

34. The "impossibility thesis" links the emergence of human rights to the development of democracy and capitalism; see Baxi, *The Future of Human Rights*, 34.

35. Robert Fine, "Nationalism, Postnationalism, Antisemitism: Thoughts on the Politics of Jürgen Habermas," *Österreichische Zeitschrift fur Politikiwissenschaft* 39, no. 4 (2010), 409–20, esp. 416-417; Robert Fine, "Fighting with Phantoms: A Contribution to the Debate on Antisemitism in Europe," *Patterns of Prejudice* 43, no. 5 (2009): 459–79, 462-463;

36. At the beginning of the judgment, the tribunal introduced Fraser as "the child of Jewish refugees who fled Nazi Germany in 1939" and stated, "Members of his family died in the Holocaust" (para. 2). It later made an

oblique reference to the Holocaust with, "so long and terrible has been the persecution of the Jewish people through history" (para. 51).

37. Herman, *An Unfortunate Coincidence*, 100.

38. Herman, *An Unfortunate Coincidence*, 101.

39.   David Seymour, "Critical Theory: The Holocaust, Human Rights and Antisemitism," paper presented at the Critical Legal Theory Conference, Harvard Law School, March 2013; David Seymour, "Holocaust Memory: Between Universal and Particular," unpublished paper, June 2014, 12–13, 16–17.

40. Herman, *An Unfortunate Coincidence*, 101.

41. David Hirsh, "Jew Hate and Today's Left," *Jewish Chronicle*, March 17, 2016, http://www.thejc.com/news/uk-news/154672//jew-hate-and -today's-Left/.

42. With respect to allegations of antisemitism within the Labour Party, a variant of the Livingstone Formulation is the counteraccusation that the allegations are a deliberate ploy to smear the Labour Party.

43. Hirsh, "How Raising the Issue," 2.

LESLEY KLAFF is Senior Lecturer in Law at Sheffield Hallam University and Affiliate Professor of Law at Haifa University. She is a member of UK Lawyers for Israel, where she has responsibility for giving legal advice and assistance to victims of campus antisemitism. She publishes on campus antisemitism, Holocaust inversion, and antisemitism in the Labour Party. She is also Editor in Chief of the *Journal of Contemporary Antisemitism*.

NINE

Conspiracy Pedagogy on Campus

BDS Advocacy, Antisemitism, and Academic Freedom

CARY NELSON

A SUBSTANTIAL BODY of scholarly literature and political commentary explains why the Boycott, Divestment, Sanctions (BDS) movement is dangerous. It demonizes, antagonizes, and delegitimizes Israel and uncritically idealizes the Palestinians. That will inhibit negotiations, not promote them. Despite some naïve followers of the movement who believe otherwise, BDS misrepresents its goal, which is not to change Israeli government policy but rather to eliminate the Jewish state.[1] It offers no specific steps toward a resolution of the conflict and no detailed peace plan. Moreover, it does not seek to negotiate a Palestinian right of return to the West Bank; rather, it seeks to impose a right for all Palestinians to return to Israel within its pre-1967 borders. BDS falsely claims to imagine a nonviolent route to ending the conflict. But there is no nonviolent way to achieve its goal of eliminating the Jewish state. Indeed, BDS demands an end to all efforts to build mutual empathy and understanding between Israelis and Palestinians. This "antinormalization" campaign rejects the communication, dialogue, negotiation, and unconditional interchange necessary to achieve a peaceful resolution of the conflict.

The year 2016 became the one in which BDS-allied groups decided it was a matter of pride to block dialogue by interrupting and silencing pro-Israeli campus speakers. Finally, in addition to consistently undermining academic freedom with its boycott agenda and its effort to silence speakers, BDS offers nothing to the Palestinian people whom it claims to champion. Perhaps that is the single cruelest and most deceptive feature of the BDS movement. Its message of hate is a route to war, not peace. With these general conditions as a context, this essay reviews the most widely publicized BDS agendas on campuses and in professional associations. This chapter's special concern is the increasing anti-Israel politicization of the humanities and soft social science classroom and the degree to which this suggests that antisemitism has found a pedagogical home.

The battles over boycott proposals in academic and professional associations have become increasingly difficult since about 2012. The sheer number of BDS faculty and graduate students attending annual meetings to promote boycott resolutions has grown, and, in some cases, the detailed reports supporting the resolutions have grown in both length and the number of accusations leveled. Those BDS advocates in academic and professional associations who are still issuing casual reports that rearrange earlier resolutions and offer little evidence are likely to borrow from the more substantive efforts. It only takes a sentence to register an accusation, but it may take weeks of research and many pages to refute it definitively. The 130-page pro-BDS report issued by the American Anthropology Association in October 2015 is a prime example.[2] Nonetheless, the strategies necessary for response—beginning with good information and continuing with tactics, rhetoric, timing, outreach, arguments, and organizing—are familiar and well tested. A tremendous amount of work is involved, but at least the nature of the work is well understood, even if its success cannot be guaranteed.

On college campuses, BDS initiates divestment resolutions that have no impact on college investment policy even if they succeed. But the resultant battles do turn some students against

Israel and promote some antisemitic perspectives. Those students become tomorrow's teachers, businesspeople, professionals, religious leaders, and politicians. In addition to promoting anti-Israel sentiment that migrates to Jews in general, this presents a long-term challenge to US policy and thus a long-term security risk to Israel. BDS often takes over the public spaces on American campuses and drives pro-Israeli students to retreat to the safe spaces of their Chabad or Hillel chapters or to their work in less politicized areas such as engineering and the sciences. But the institutional impact of BDS has still been deeper and more troubling. It has helped turn some entire academic departments and disciplines against Israel and some faculty members in the humanities and soft social sciences into anti-Israel fanatics. Fanatics do not just oppose policies; they also indulge in corrupting passions and biases. Anecdotal evidence, public hate speech, and examples of representative syllabi sent to me by students and faculty demonstrate that this trend has spread to the classroom.[3] There, the task of responding is infinitely more difficult— infinitely, not only because the classroom is not a public space in the same way a professional association or a campus quad is, but also because it is a space more thoroughly protected by academic freedom.

But the main topic here—the political corruption of the classroom—must be prefaced with a warning about the fragility of academic freedom in the contemporary university. In the early 1970s, about two-thirds of higher education faculty were eligible for tenure and thus a high degree of job security. In the new millennium, that percentage has declined to one-third. Most college teachers are now at-will employees subject to nonrenewal. They lack strong, if any, academic freedom protections. In departments with a pro-Israel or anti-Israel bias, contingent or adjunct faculty can be at risk of nonrenewal if they refuse to embrace their colleagues' politics in a syllabus. Many adjunct faculty consequently realize they are safer if they avoid controversial course topics.

That is a depressing conclusion, but it nonetheless reflects reality. The links between academic freedom and job security are now widely broken. That some in the BDS movement are willing to sacrifice the university's principles and its future in the service of their political agenda does not mean that those who oppose them should do the same. Political struggles are usually fought by deploying whatever weapons are available. That has never been the best strategy in higher education. Perhaps Israel's defenders, including university administrators and Israel's nonacademic allies, should show some reticence about using what power and influence they may have in campus conflicts.

WAR BY OTHER MEANS: THE STATE
OF THE AMERICAN CAMPUS

One can recognize the problems at stake in some classroom assignments and in the level of unqualified hostility to Israel that some faculty members express in their public statements on campus and elsewhere. When faculty members say publicly that Israel is a settler-colonialist, genocidal, racist, and apartheid state, there is reason to conclude that they believe these are factual statements, not hypotheses to be debated. Some likely present these political opinions as fact in classroom lectures as well. There is little doubt that students would be better off, that the mission of higher education would be better served, and that the reality of Israeli-Palestinian and worldwide politics would be better represented if these accusations were treated as debatable, with students provided access to opposing views. But that is commonly not the case. These accusations are being debated in the public sphere and thus they should be treated as contestable claims in the classroom as well, no matter what political opinions teachers may hold. That is not because it is a universal principle that one must cover the character of debates, especially given that some positions are discredited and become irrelevant over time, but rather because attitudes toward the Israeli-Palestinian conflict are currently inseparable from the competing arguments that shape them. It should be helpful to put these issues into context, offer some examples, and reflect on what this means.

When University of California, Santa Barbara, sociology professor William Robinson sent an e-mail to his 2009 "Sociology of Globalization" course that had photos of the 2008–9 Israeli assault on Gaza set up as parallel to photos of the German occupation of the Warsaw ghetto during the Second World War, some people urged he be fired.[4] His Nazi/Israel comparisons were irresponsible history and deplorable pedagogy, but academic freedom protected his right as a tenured faculty member to say such things. Were he a job candidate, one might also have defended his right to say what he pleased, but a search committee could certainly have decided not to hire him either as an adjunct or as a tenure track faculty member had he insisted that Israel and Nazi Germany engaged in comparable practices or constituted comparable states. But you cannot fire a tenured faculty member for saying things that are commonplace in given academic disciplines. Comparisons between Israel and Nazi Germany may be despicable, but they were not categorically rogue opinion in 2009, and they are not so now. They have a history not just in the United States and Europe but also in Israel.

Similarly, like it or not, we are long past the point where claims that Israel is a settler-colonialist apartheid state are outliers. We can and should contest such claims, but punitive responses to the advocacy of such views—as opposed to careful professional evaluation—are largely unavailable. The BDS movement did not initiate these claims, but it has widely promoted them and has helped install them as self-evident truths. And that means some faculty members feel free—indeed responsible—to treat them as truths. Unfortunately, that can intimidate some students and inhibit them from presenting opposing opinions. When entire disciplines are consumed by such views, students who differ can easily be silenced, and they can certainly experience those disciplines as antisemitic.

The Robinson case concerns an explicit communication with the students in his class, but debates about the Israeli-Palestinian conflict in academic associations also point to the state of the academy more broadly and suggest how the issues will be handled in classroom settings. At the December 2014 annual meeting of the American Anthropological Association, those in attendance were confronted by hundreds of ferociously anti-Israel graduate students excitedly voting down a resolution opposing academic boycotts. They were spurred on by faculty members presenting anti-Israel papers at formal academic session scheduled by the organization. One tenured faculty member read a paper making an antisemitic claim that Jews and non-Jews, not citizens and non-citizens, are separated on arrival at Israel's Ben Gurion Airport. That slander was met with audience applause, a chilling display of mass ignorance. A year later those same faculty and graduate students voted for an academic boycott by a margin of 1,040 to 136.[5] These students did not acquire their convictions exclusively in extracurricular settings. They had to be carefully taught, to echo the most telling (and controversial) song from the 1949 Rogers and Hammerstein musical *South Pacific*. The students at the 2014 meeting had been carefully trained in their beliefs.

During a 2014 American Anthropological Association annual meeting session devoted to small group discussion, a table with nine anthropology faculty members and graduate students engaged in analyzing the pros and cons of academic boycotts. There was unanimous sentiment that anthropologists had to "do something," that inaction was unacceptable, and on that basis alone, some felt an academic boycott was justified. Someone sensibly asked what impact the adoption of a boycott resolution would have on anthropology as a discipline. I suggested that people consider what had happened to the American Studies Association after it voted to boycott Israeli universities in December 2013.

Not one other person at the table knew about the existence of the resolution, let alone what the national response was.[6] Yet they considered themselves well informed enough to proceed with their own disciplinary debate. There was a clannish conviction that only anthropologists should be heard from and that people outside the discipline had nothing relevant to say about how boycotts violate universal principles of academic freedom.

When a boycott resolution came up for debate on a California State University campus in 2015, students reported that faculty members used classroom time to advocate that students vote for the resolution. Some faculty members refused to let students voice opposing views, a clear violation of academic freedom. Most of the courses in which faculty urged support for the resolution had nothing to do with history or political science, let alone the Israeli-Palestinian conflict. This essay will take up the topic again later, but it is worth recalling here that the American Association of University Professors (AAUP) policy for more than half a century warned against bringing politically extraneous material into the classroom. In 1970, the AAUP sensibly modified its stand by introducing a standard of persistence. That suggests that a home economics or veterinary medicine faculty member could urge students to vote for or against Israel so long as he or she did not do so repeatedly. And any such faculty advocacy must also welcome alternative student views. Although most students and faculty do not realize this, failure to do so could justify disciplinary action. A first offense would produce a warning, but repeated problems could be addressed more formally after proper due process was observed. For a tenured faculty member, consequences could range from denying an annual raise to delaying a promotion decision, but not termination. Needless to say, no sanctions of any kind were applied in the California case. We need to better educate campuses about faculty responsibilities and the way they limit academic freedom—a concept that does not free faculty to intimidate students.

At the January 2016 meeting of the Modern Language Association, a number of those in attendance routinely met pro-Israeli graduate students and young faculty who were afraid even to *attend* sessions devoted to boycott discussion or debate for fear they would be seen and asked their opinion, thereby exposing their views and potentially jeopardizing their careers. At that same meeting, when an anti-BDS speaker accused the BDS movement of antisemitism, the seventy or so BDS supporters in the room broke out in spontaneous laughter. For years, accusations of antisemitism have been met with outrage, denial, and anger. Perhaps we have turned a corner where ridicule replaces anger.

Early in 2016, David Makovsky, an advisor to John Kerry's 2013–14 Middle East peace initiative, visited the University of Illinois at Urbana-Champaign as part of a national tour. The sponsors of Makovsy's visit could not find one member of the current faculty willing to attend an invitation-only seminar with him. At his public lecture that evening, not one current member of the faculty of two thousand was in attendance. Several emeritus faculty members from engineering and agriculture came, but otherwise the faculty stood in solidarity with the campus atmosphere of anti-Israel intimidation.

We need to gather the experiences of pro-Israeli grad students and young faculty who decided not to go into Israel studies for fear they would never get a job in departments or academic fields now dominated by BDS and suggestions of antisemitism. All this is supplemental to the widely reported—but also hotly debated—anti-Jewish atmosphere in public spaces reported on some campuses by undergraduates. This atmosphere helps convince students that passionate departmental attacks on Israel may be antisemitic even if they are not. Although the intimidation of graduate students and young faculty members is less widely known than the well-publicized antisemitic incidents on campuses, the increasing examples of career intimidation are deeply troubling. An undergrad can often keep his or her head down or retreat to Hillel to avoid hostile social confrontations over Jewish identity, a retreat that encourages the ghettoizing of pro-Israel sentiment on campus. And an undergrad can move on with his or her life after graduation.

A prejudicial classroom, however, is another matter. It can shape the perception of intellectual life for a long time. So, obviously, do decisions about what kind of work will be the focus of one's career. For over forty years, many faculty members have urged students to follow their hearts, to choose the specializations and research interests to which they are most deeply drawn. In some disciplines, such as Middle Eastern studies, that advice is no longer wise. A June 2016 essay in *Legal Insurrection* analyzing the close American Anthropological Association vote against a boycott of Israeli universities ends with the following statement: "The author is a graduate student who must write under a pseudonym for fear of retribution from pro-BDS faculty."[7] Another graduate student writes that his "concern is to get BDS-supporters who have power over me to just stop bothering me, and let me pursue my career in peace": "Because of the success of BDS in North American anthropology departments, doing archaeology in Israel is becoming increasingly difficult for young archaeologists. Most North Americans who do archaeology in Israel via secular universities are Jewish. In effect, BDS is holding my career hostage to the actions of the Israeli government. I am not the only young Jew in academia who is in this situation. In my case, it has gotten to the point where I am considering making Aliyah so that I can pursue my academic career more easily."[8]

Discipline-wide intimidation represents a threat to the character of the academy and to the meaningful exercise of academic freedom.

Ad hominem attacks also play a substantial role in intimidating others. BDS is not about to shut down Russell Berman, Alan Dershowitz, Todd Gitlin, Rachel Harris, Jeffrey Herf, David Hirsh, Sharon Musher, Andrew Pessin, Martin Shichtman, me, or its various other committed opponents with personal insults, but over-the-top BDS rhetorical assaults on visible faculty are very effective in silencing many who have so far remained quiet. As we saw in Donald Trump's Republican primary campaign, delivering insults instead of confronting arguments is an effective tactic. In BDS's case, it purports to replace fear with contempt.

Not in living memory have we seen a political issue that has divided people so decisively as the debate over the Israeli-Palestinian conflict. With surprising frequency, people are willing to sever personal relationships over their differences about Israel. Even during the Vietnam War one did not see such widespread personal bitterness in the academy. For some academic disciplines, disputes about Israel are not only politically but also personally decisive.

We may have reached a tipping point in the politicization of humanities and soft social science disciplines in the United States and the United Kingdom and perhaps in some European countries. It is helpful in this context to step back and remember that it has been more than thirty years since we largely completed the disciplinarization of the academy. Instead of thinking of themselves as members of the professoriate as a whole, faculty members today think of themselves as members of the engineering, computer science, anthropology, or English professions. Many disciplines present an inadequate, uninformed, or misleading knowledge base on which to judge the complex historical, political, religious, and cultural conflict between Israelis and Palestinians. And yet the ethics of disciplinarity essentially says that one is only bound to teach both sides of an issue when disciplinary consensus does not exist. A biologist does not have to give equal time to those who oppose the theory of evolution. A historian has no reason to mention Holocaust denial. A sociologist might be expected to cover debates about global warming, but a climate scientist could well choose either to give bare mention of disbelievers or to make it clear that truth resides on only one side of the debate.

This suggests that some disciplines—without having the requisite expertise—have reached a virtual consensus about the truth regarding Israel and the Israeli-Palestinian conflict. Moreover, it appears the number of disciplines and subdisciplines where the balance has been tipped and consensual anti-Israel truth reigns is increasing. A political scientist might recognize the need to acknowledge both the Israeli and Palestinian narratives and treat them each as possessing validity. This is no longer to be expected in cultural anthropology, literary studies, and ethnic studies; in much of African American studies, Native American studies, and women's studies; and, of course, throughout Middle Eastern studies. In many areas of the academy, there is substantial social and professional support for faculty who are devoted to demonizing the Jewish state. They feel justice and the truth of history reside entirely on one side of the conflict, and they consequently feel quite righteous in teaching that perspective. They may have no awareness whatsoever that they have turned their classrooms into propaganda machines. That students experience all this as antisemitic is unsurprising.

The lopsided votes in favor of academic boycotts in some disciplines are a good indication of the state of not only political but also pedagogical consensus. In some disciplines, to be sure, the balance of power is local. A given department may have jettisoned differences of opinion and a climate for debate that prevail in the discipline at large. Jewish studies is a particularly telling example of this phenomenon, because some Jewish studies programs, including at the University of Illinois at Urbana-Champaign, have become centers of anti-Israel politics and conviction.

There is good reason to argue that requiring certain individual colleagues to make an effort to portray both sides of the Israeli-Palestinian conflict fairly, to embody balance in the classroom, is pointless. The effort by some organizations to urge universities to compel political balance in individual courses is misguided. Would there be any point to asking Judith Butler, Nadia Abu El

Haj, Angela Davis, Barbara Foley, Grover Furr, Neve Gordon, Barbara Harlow, Gil Hochberg, Joy Karega, David Lloyd, Sunaina Maira, Joseph Massad, Bill Mullen, David Palumbo-Liu, Ilan Pappé, Jasbir Puar, Bruce Robbins, Malini Schueller, Steven Salaita, Gayatri Spivak, Gianni Vattimo, or Cornel West to do so? One could list dozens of names of tenured faculty with certainty that they would be unable or unwilling to rise to the challenge. Moreover, the list above amounts to a subset of BDS's intellectual elite; even lesser acolytes are surely out there.

Students might experience more clarity if such tenured faculty simply embodied their unqualified hostility in their teaching. But then the rest of us have a great need to make certain that teaching based on mutual empathy is powerfully in evidence in the curriculum as a whole. We cannot win the day by countering pro-Palestinian fanaticism with pro-Israeli fanaticism. The best that does is strengthen or instill ideological war on campus. And in many disciplines, we would lose that war; indeed, in some quarters, it is already lost. There are moral, professional, and tactical reasons to choose another way. The bottom line is this: a university has a responsibility to ensure that the curriculum as a whole, not individual courses, displays an appropriate degree of balance. Campuses need to have conversations about the character of the balance they seek.

A REPRESENTATIVE ANTI-ZIONIST COURSE

It is helpful to examine in detail a recent course in Middle Eastern studies taught by a well-known scholar at a major university.[9] The required books for a fourteen-week spring 2016 undergraduate course on "Palestinian and Israeli Politics and Societies" at Columbia University (a copy of the syllabus for which was supplied by a Columbia student) make the course's perspective perfectly clear: Edward Said, *The Question of Palestine*; Rashid Khalidi, *Palestinian Identity*; Joseph Massad, *The Persistence of the Palestinian Question*;

Theodor Herzl, *The Jewish State;* Theodor Herzl, *Altneuland;*
Shlomo Sand, *The Invention of the Jewish People;* Ghassan Kanafani, *Men in the Sun;* Kanafani, *Returning to Haifa;* Sara Roy, *The
Gaza Strip: The Political Economy of De-Development;* Neve Gor-
don, *Israel's Occupation;* Jeroen Gunning, *Hamas in Politics;* Israel
Shahak and Norton Mezvinsky, *Jewish Fundamentalism in Israel*
(2004 edition); Ali Abunimah, *The Battle for Justice in Palestine.*[10]
Herzl is there less to represent the varieties of historical Zionism than as a foil for the course goal of demonstrating how Zionism has gone wrong. The other Jewish writers here either endorse
BDS (Neve Gordon) or are fiercely hostile to Israel (Shlomo
Sand, Israel Shahak). The result is a coherent course embody-
ing overall only one point of view—a negative one that excludes
any positive commentary on Israel or any recognition of Israel's
achievements. The course is designed to show that everything
originating in historical and contemporary Zionism is fundamentally deplorable and destructive. Thus, the content in no way
fulfills the course description, which claims comprehensiveness:

> This course covers the history of Zionism in the wake of the
> Haskala in mid nineteenth century Europe and its development
> at the turn of the century through the current "peace process" and
> its ramifications between the state of Israel and the Palestinian
> national movement. The course examines the impact of Zionism
> on European Jews and on Asian and African Jews on the one hand,
> and on Palestinian Arabs on the other—in Israel, in the Occupied
> Territories, and in the diaspora. The course also examines the
> internal dynamics in Palestinian and Israeli societies, looking at
> the roles gender and religion play in the politics of Israel and the
> Palestinian national movement. The purpose of the course is to
> provide a thorough yet critical historical overview of the Zionist-
> Palestinian encounter to familiarize undergraduates with the
> background to the current situation.[11]

The course is about convincing students that the political opinions that dominate the readings are correct and in urgent need of
adoption. Many would find the assigned books to offer a curious

account of "the impact of Zionism on European Jews," let alone of "the roles gender and religion play in the politics of Israel." Since some of the readings entertain conspiracy theories about Israel or about Jewish history and culture, some students would find them to be antisemitic; whether that can be claimed of the course as a whole is impossible to say. The essays and book chapters that are added to various weeks' readings do a good deal to flesh out Palestinian self-representation and the racial and ethnic tensions in Israeli society, but they can hardly be considered a fair representation of the varieties of Israeli culture or Jewish Israeli self-understanding. The professor assigns Ella Shohat's "Sephardim in Israel: Zionism from the Standpoint of Its Jewish Victims," but this represents the view of a tiny minority. Massad's "Zionism's Internal Others: Israel and the Oriental Jews" and a chapter from Sami Chetrit's *Intra-Jewish Conflict in Israel: White Jews, Black Jews* only reinforce the course's mission to prove that Zionism's whole legacy is corrupted by colonialism and racism.[12] One would not guess from these choices, to cite a few examples, that there are Mizrahim and Druze who actually support the state or that there is a large and distinctive Russian population.

The twelve weekly topics for the course are as follows:

1. *The Haskala and Early Zionism*; the week is split between Regina Sharif's *Non-Jewish Zionism* and Michael Selzer's polemical anti-Zionist *The Aryanization of the Jewish State*.
2. *Zionist Foundations*, for which the week's reading includes both Herzl and Shlomo Sand.
3. *Zionism and European Jews*, with Herzl's novel *Altneuland* and Shlomo Sand figuring again. A nineteenth-century utopian novel can easily seem misguided to today's students.
4. *Zionism and Nazism—Zionism and Asian and African Jews*, which opens with Walter Laqueur and Hannah Arendt but moves on to Lenni Brenner's *Zionism in the Age*

of the Dictators, which purports to detail Jewish collaboration with Hitler. Brenner notably is a source for discredited former London mayor Ken Livingston's antisemitic
remarks, which led to his suspension from the Labour
Party.[13]

5. *Zionism and Asian and African Jews, and the Palestinians.*
   Readings by Khalidi, Massad, and Edward Said offer a
   range of anti-Zionist and anti-Israel views.

6. *Zionism and the Palestinians I.* Readings are limited to
   works by Khalidi and Massad.

7. *Zionism and the Palestinians II (in Israel and the Diaspora).*
   Readings include J. Schechla's "The Invisible People
   Come to Light: Israel's 'Internally Displaced' and
   'Unrecognized Villages'" and Massad's "Producing the
   Palestinian as Other: Jordan and the Palestinians."

8. *Palestinians in the Diaspora.* Selections from Said's *The
   Question of Palestine* are supplemented by a Yasser Arafat
   speech and a Massad essay.

9. *Palestine and the Palestinians.* The week is devoted to
   Ghassan Kanafani and Neve Gordon. Kanafani's novel
   Men in the Sun has been described as "an allegory of Palestinian calamity in the wake of the nakba in its description
   of the defeatist despair, passivity and political corruption
   investing the lives of Palestinians in refugee camps."

10. *Palestinians in Gaza.* Readings are limited to works by
    Sara Roy.

11. *Religion in Israel.* Gunning's *Hamas in Politics* (2007) was
    completed before the civil war in Gaza between Hamas
    and Fatah commenced. Although he occasionally recog-
    nizes Hamas's violence, Gunning tends to credit it as a
    resistance, rather than a terrorist, organization.

12. *Women in Israel and Palestine.* The twelve essays assigned
    for this week include five essays about Palestinian women
    activists.

13. *The Peace Process.* There are numerous books about the peace process, but none of them are assigned here. Instead readings are for works by Massad, Neve Gordon, Sara Roy, and Jeroen Gunning.

14. *The End of the "Peace Process"* concludes the course with BDS advocate and *Electronic Intifada* founder Ali Abunimah, who believes the Jewish state must be brought to an end.

This is not to suggest that all these reading assignments are inappropriate. Many faculty members, including myself, would want students in a course on the Israeli-Palestinian conflict to read Rashid Khalidi and Edward Said. I quote Khalidi in *Dreams Deferred: A Concise Guide to the Israeli-Palestinian Conflict and the Movement to Boycott Israel,* and I quote Palestinians in an effort to honor their Nakba narratives, though I would not assign Lenni Brenner, Shlomo Sand, Michael Selzer, or Israel Shahak, among others—unless, of course, I wanted to provide some examples that are widely regarded as irresponsible and unreliable—and I would not dedicate so much time to such work. The fundamental problem is that the course, although claiming comprehensiveness, can be seen as part of a biased anti-Israel political campaign. The social, political, and intellectual force of the assigned readings and lectures, moreover, would make it extremely difficult for a student to voice an alternative perspective and equally difficult to gain a hearing for one; there are, after all, no assigned readings on which to ground a different historical narrative.

The professor is perfectly within his rights to teach the course this way—as a pro-Palestinian and anti-Israel polemic—and a department faculty could decide that all its courses should reflect similar viewpoints, but a university needs other points of view if it is to mount a responsible curriculum.[14] Alternative points of view would then need to be represented in other departments eager to get the funding to do so. A department dominated by courses like this one has effectively chosen to be a political, rather than an academic, enterprise. One professor's academic freedom to teach the course the way he wants does not, however, protect him from other faculty members faulting the course. Just as publications are open to criticism and debate, so, too, are courses and their syllabi.[15]

Syllabi are occasionally part of departmental conversations. They are evaluated during job searches and contract renewal and promotion and tenure decisions. Faculty members routinely make suggestions to one another about potential reading assignments. Writing about her own course on the Arab-Israeli conflict, Donna Divine observes that her "task as instructor is to help students develop their analytical and critical abilities as well as make available to them the body of knowledge necessary for making their own informed judgments" about the subject. One may reasonably ask whether the Columbia course fulfills such aims. If not, does it meet other useful pedagogical goals? Challenges about such matters are appropriate components of professional life.

CONSPIRACY PEDAGOGY

Faculty are accustomed at least to some degree to helping colleagues improve their teaching. We can schedule faculty for the kinds of teaching they do best. But we have no model for how to address political fanaticism in the classroom, let alone ideological fanaticism endorsed by a community of faculty believers. The goal has always been good teaching across the institution. Now we are left with borrowing the compensatory and corrective model from scholarship: to counter bad teaching with good teaching.

That can only take place in an environment where we combine forthright condemnation of the demonization of Israel with firm criticism of Israeli government policy when it is merited.

Again, faculty can voice their political opinions in class, but they must welcome open debate from their students. If they repress, ridicule, or disparage opposing student opinion, they should risk exposure and sanction.

Persistently using a class on an entirely unrelated topic as a vehicle for promoting either pro-Israeli or anti-Israeli views, however, is unacceptable. Many faculty members with strong views on the subject teach in fields with no connection to the conflict, and it is fair to assume most of those faculty members never deal with it in class. Many faculty members keep their politics separate from their teaching and are quite capable of signing a pro-BDS or pro-Israel petition without bringing their views to class or trying to persuade students to adopt them. Signing a BDS petition may be a warning sign, but it is not proof of classroom bias. A faculty bias against sharing one's political views also still carries a good deal of weight in the academy, but anti-Israel passion is seriously eroding that tradition in some fields. If you believe Israel is the root of all evil in the world, as some on the hard left do, then that conviction can trump all the restraints on propagandizing that have sustained the profession for so long. And it can lead to vitriol that cannot readily be distinguished from actual antisemitism.

Unfortunately, as debates unfold, the evidence suggests the tide has begun to turn on the system of values and restraints that have long shaped the ethics of teaching. The prevalence of vicious anti-Israel classroom proselytizing is increasing and will continue to increase. At the anthropology meeting in 2014, attendees encountered graduate students who seemed to be basically brainwashed, and it is rather worrying that they are the next generation of teachers. But some of these teachers are already on the job.

In February 2016, Jasbir Puar, a tenured Rutgers University faculty member in women's studies, presented a talk at Vassar College pressing an antisemitic claim that Israel has a formal policy of comprehensively maiming and stunting the Palestinians in the West Bank and Gaza.[16] She added to this a claim that Israel regularly harvests the organs of dead Palestinians. She made similar assertions at Dartmouth College a few months later, in May. The Vassar lecture was recorded by audience members, transcribed, and widely distributed both privately and on electronic mailing lists.

There are conspiracy theories that obsessively find clues everywhere; the project is to interpret myriad facts through a paranoid lens that turns them into proof. And there are projects, like Puar's, that find evidence, let alone proof as ordinarily understood, irrelevant. Neither proof nor evidence was at stake in the blood libel, still alive in Arab countries, that Jews added Christian blood to matzo dough. The existence of the matzo itself was all that was needed for antisemites to imagine any ingredient and add it rhetorically to matzo's preparation. And so with women's studies professor Jasbir Puar. Some Palestinians are maimed in confrontations with the Israel Defense Forces, so by extension Puar holds that Israel wants to stunt and maim all of them, keeping them alive as conveniently disabled enemies. According to Puar, Israelis can then bewail their own victimhood without being in any actual danger from the Palestinians. From this antisemitic perspective there is no need to find documents supporting such a policy. It is necessary only to play out the logic behind the slander. The sequential reasoning apparently constitutes scholarship. One can respond in part by marshaling counterevidence; her claims about excessive birth defects and stunting in Gaza can be readily countered.[17] The statistical evidence refutes her global assertions. But her accusations will spread and be welcomed by those already conditioned to find them appealing.

For now, Jasbir Puar represents the extreme fringe of the BDS movement, but many in the audience at Vassar applauded her, and others around the country have disputed accusations about the antisemitic character of her work, as though criticism of Puar's claims amounts to an attack on academic freedom. In fact, faculty have a responsibility to condemn slander packaged as academic reasoning. We have a responsibility to counter the impact of her work on the impressionable students who applaud her talks. Otherwise her views and those of others will spread, become more widely adopted, and be normalized within some academic communities. Unfortunately, these fanatic views are welcome already throughout the BDS movement. They are increasingly at the heart of the matter. Some will endorse her theories out of political solidarity.

One may try a thought experiment. Do we suppose Puar would feel inclined, let alone professionally compelled, in teaching about Gaza and the West Bank to reframe what she presented in lectures as factually true and treat it as hypothetical or open to debate? Would she pause before the antisemitic aura of her accusations against Israelis? There is certainly no hint in her lecture or in her publications that she feels the charges of stunting and maiming are open to debate. Quite the contrary.[18]

If these claims represent the fanatic fringe of BDS thinking, what should we make of the extremist elements of BDS cited earlier that are shared by many of its loyal soldiers, including the conviction that Israel's aims are genocidal? Add to those the claim that Zionism equals racism. It was not that long ago when that motto was considered an outlier in the humanities as a whole, despite its adoption by parts of the left. Evidence that students have been affected by campus assertions like that is now common, as remarks about Israeli genocide and the inextricably racist character of Zionism are pervasive both on campuses and on the internet.

But there are even more fanatic extremes. Oberlin College assistant professor Joy Karega's online syllabus for her fall 2015 rhetoric course on "Writing for Social Justice" included a section on the Israeli-Palestinian conflict. The rationale for the course, interestingly, contained its own trigger warning: "You may not always feel comfortable in this classroom. Social justice work is not generally geared towards making people feel comfortable.

Social justice work attempts to enact social change, and that can be quite threatening and uncomfortable on many fronts. Also, polemical and agitation rhetorics are strategies that some social justice writers employ. As such, I will not discourage their usage in your own writing. We will also examine in this course several iterations of these kinds of rhetorics at work in the writings of social justice activists." [19] The readings include Rania Khalek's "How Today's Liberal Zionists Echo Apartheid South Africa's Defenders" and Bruce Dixon's "Cowardly, Hypocritical, Subservient Congressional Black Caucus Endorses Israeli Apartheid and Current War Crimes in Gaza," along with a long combined reading on intersectionality. There were no readings sympathetic to Israel listed, but then this was a training course in writing for social justice, and social justice, as the BDS movement tells us, is embodied in only one side of the conflict.

Most of the course was focused on US-based activism on racial issues, but antagonism toward Israel was integral to the course's concept of social activism and apparently to classroom discussions. It was not a course that simply studies the topic. It trained students to participate from a particular point of view. There is no evidence that the course included the far extreme topics Karega pursues on social media, even if the two are related by her core convictions. But in her public persona she certainly employed the "polemical and social agitation rhetorics" she trained her students to use. She did assign four chapters from Christian Fuchs's book *Social Media* for this course, but whether Karega pointed to her own use of social media one cannot say with any certainty, though it is easy to imagine that Karega's own uses of social media would have come up for discussion. Would students struggle with her advocacy? Not if they were self-selected in sympathy for her anti-Israel hostility. In any case, the syllabus is perfectly rational—arguably more troubling because of that, because it was a course that could easily be emulated. Just how rational her classroom discussion of Israel would be is another matter.

The contrast between the delusional and nakedly antisemitic character of Karega's Facebook posts—"ISIS is not a jihadist, Islamic terrorist organization. It's a CIA and Mossad operation" (November 17, 2015); "it seems obvious that the same people behind the massacre in Gaza are behind the shooting down [of Malaysia Airlines Flight] MA-17" (January 10, 2015)—and the rational but politically charged character of the syllabus provides a guide to how faculty who are basically unhinged opponents of Israel can make themselves academically respectable.[20]

But the antisemitic Facebook posts are still part of Karega's public persona; they are part of Oberlin's public profile and part of the gateway to her courses. The academic profession has yet to deal with the reality that faculty members can establish a public presence through social media that completely outstrips anything they could typically achieve through teaching and research. The AAUP has—in my view, unwisely—taken the position that faculty statements on social media are not part of their professional profiles, even if the arguments and subject matter clearly overlap with their teaching and research.[21] Those legislators who have reacted with hysteria to faculty members who make a couple of intemperate remarks on Facebook or Twitter are clearly out of line, but we need to think seriously about those faculty who make persistent use of social media in the same areas in which they teach or do research.[22] In such cases, faculty members should be academically responsible for what they say.

The relationship between Karega's teaching and her social media activism, however, is still deeper, because she was effectively training students to emulate her. Not all of us would consider a for-credit tutorial on how to participate in extremist activism an appropriate college course, though some departments now would. There is yet another issue that student support for Karega suggests may be embedded in her course—a call to bind identity with a perceived social justice issue. That, however, is how the academy has evolved in recent history. Its roots go back decades, having now produced consequences we hardly imagined. When Karega's public persona is integrated with the opposition to Israel that is embedded in her pedagogy, students may be led to ground their identities not only in the pursuit of social justice but also in a commitment to antisemitic conspiracy theories. It is a toxic combination.

This is a personally painful subject for me both because I do not welcome hearing Israel demonized and because I have long argued that articulate, rational, well-supported advocacy has a place in the classroom.[23] It can help model intelligent argumentation for students. It can show students what academia brings to controversy that Washington politics often does not. But I did not have in mind Palumbo-Liu's opportunistic anti-Israel sarcasm and his repeated indulgence in antisemitic tropes or Lloyd's anti-Israel harangues, let alone Puar's elaborate hate-based conspiracy theories or Karega's antisemitic demagoguery. And it does not help matters that black students at Oberlin included a demand that Karega automatically be guaranteed tenure among the December 2015 list of demands they gave the college president.[24] At least in some quarters on the American campus there are no limits to the venom that will be embraced.

BDS did not invent this problem. It reflects trends in some disciplines over decades, but BDS's influence is intensifying and advancing the problem. And unfortunately, BDS's fanatic fringe is increasingly evident in some disciplines. What still counts as unquestioned irrationality—like Karega's Facebook posts—meanwhile helps make somewhat less rabid opposition to Israel seem reasonable. One hopes Karega could not get applause from a general audience for her claim that the Mossad was behind the *Charlie Hebdo* massacre or for continuing to promote the antisemitic delusion that Israel was behind the assault on the Twin Towers of the World Trade Center, but Puar's madness was well received by some and strongly defended by others.

All one can do about Puar, who is tenured, is to employ the fundamental practice of intellectual critique. But the call to counter defective speech with better speech does not cover all our responsibilities. We do not argue that it is fine to hire or grant tenure to someone who is incompetent as long as we compensate by hiring or granting tenure to someone smart. Based on her dissertation, there were clearly reasons to question the wisdom of hiring Karega. Her reliance on interviews with her father as her primary source for a study of a local black liberation movement is a viable strategy for a personal book, but not necessarily for a doctoral research project. Karega was untenured, which meant that the adequacy of her teaching and research would be required to be reviewed on two occasions—first in her third year and then in her sixth. Serious complaints by students or faculty could also justify a special review, as they apparently did, but due process would still be required. Calls for her summary dismissal reflected a failure to understand and honor the standards for due process necessary to preserve academic freedom. Putting her on paid leave prior to the completion of a faculty review, as Oberlin did, may also have been highly problematic, unless the faculty had already reached preliminary conclusions.

If Rutgers faculty decide that Puar promotes unacceptable standards of evidence in the classroom, there is not much they can do other than to assign her courses where her convictions will not be in play or compensate with better courses taught by others. Karega, notably, taught the basic rhetoric course. That means faculty across campus had a vested interest in whether she supported or undermined generally accepted academic standards in her teaching. Faculty members could have filed a complaint separately from her formal reviews, and that could have produced a hearing at any time. Whether the outcome would have resulted in reassignment or something more serious was impossible to say prior to the decision to dismiss her. Given that her responses to public events appeared not to be rational, it is also possible that problems with her public persona were judged likely to recur. Full details of the Karega investigation and review process have not been released, though Oberlin reported that multiple faculty committees were involved. Karega was dismissed as an Oberlin faculty member in October 2016.

Because of the risks to academic freedom and the potential for unwarranted criticism, we must tread carefully in examining the pedagogical practices of individual faculty. We certainly have no comprehensive evidence of antisemitic teaching to present, or even broad access to appropriate syllabi, but we have enough evidence to know that the problem exists. Some of what is cited here is anecdotal. But developments at public meetings in academic associations, the character of several events on campuses, and the evidence of key course syllabi are sufficient to demonstrate that there is a problem that needs to be confronted. On campus, the public sphere and the classroom are only partly discontinuous spaces. At the very least, they interact and overlap. Competing accounts of the campus climate for Jews, however, remind us that students can proceed on separate tracks, with some who become involved in campus governance or devote themselves to more politicized disciplines, encountering considerable stress and antagonism, and others who concentrate on their engineering major or socialize at Chabad and find the campus mostly hospitable.

There is too much evidence of the political corruption of academic disciplines, however, to treat pedagogy as sacrosanct. To ignore the issue, moreover, will be to watch the problem rapidly get worse. How often we confront anything as simple and unidirectional as indoctrination—especially given the complex pluralism of much campus life—is very much open to question, though the Columbia syllabus is clearly an effort to persuade and perhaps to indoctrinate. But there is no question that the campus devotion to civil discussion and debate is frequently under assault and that in many local settings the campus has become inhospitable to respectful intellectual activity. The increase in BDS efforts to silence pro-Israeli speakers is especially clear evidence of that trend. Some disciplines no longer promote self-critical intellectual reflection. The time to confront these trends is now.

Perhaps our responsibility begins with broader forms of disciplinary critique. We need to take responsibility for the state of our own academic disciplines and subject them to serious scholarly evaluation. That means producing well-supported and thoughtful analyses. And it means mixing the critique of individual faculty with disciplinary contextualization. Tempting as it is, just pursuing Puar or her equivalents without interrogating the cultural and professional developments that have made her possible is inadequate. But it is equally unacceptable to cower before the BDS intimidation campaign claim that criticizing someone's work constitutes a violation of academic freedom and a suppression of free speech rights. That message disavows the core purpose of academic research and debate, eviscerating the educational mission.

For now, it is fairly certain that in many quarters the situation will get worse; there is not much evidence it will get better. It will unfortunately take real courage for people working in the more degraded disciplines to do the kind of informed analyses we need. And it is unrealistic to anticipate that some pervasively biased disciplines will reform themselves anytime soon. Instead, some departments may choose new colleagues as part of an effort to impose a single anti-Israel political perspective on what is actually a complex, unresolved issue. It would then become necessary for colleges and universities to approve hires in such a way that students are likely to be exposed to multiple perspectives. Some departments may need to be denied hiring rights until they can be reformed or problematic members retire. But that should not be a unilateral administrative decision; the faculty senate needs to be involved in a thorough program review and a resulting decision, not only to preserve academic shared governance but also because the campus as a whole will not learn anything from an administration decision that can be discounted on procedural, rather than substantive, grounds. We need a multidisciplinary critique that draws on the resources of the academy as a whole if our educational institutions are to be insulated from the political conformity that BDS-allied faculty too often seek to impose on their students.

My thanks to Sharon Musher, Kenneth Stern, and Kenneth Waltzer for comments on a draft.

NOTES

1. This is a contentious issue, since the BDS website does not make this explicit. But every major BDS spokesperson across the world has been clear in lectures and in print that this is their aim. As I write in the introduction to *Dreams Deferred: A Concise Guide to the Israeli-Palestinian Conflict and the Movement to Boycott Israel* (Bloomington: MLA Members for Scholars' Rights / Indiana University Press, 2016), 44:

> BDS founder Omar Barghouti has argued, "accepting Israel as a 'Jewish state' on our land is impossible." California State University political scientist As'ad AbuKhalil, among many other BDS leaders, echoes those sentiments: "Justice and freedom for the Palestinians are incompatible with the existence of the state of Israel." In *The Battle for Justice in Palestine* Ali Abunimah, the Chicago-based cofounder of *The Electronic Intifada*, confidently concludes that "Israel's 'right to exist as a Jewish state' is one with no proper legal or moral remedy and one whose enforcement necessitates perpetuating terrible wrongs. Therefore it is no right at all."

Bay Area BDS activist Laura Kiswani, executive director of the Arab Resource and Organizing Center, offered a still more hyperbolic plea at a November 2014 Berkeley panel: "Bringing down Israel will really benefit everyone in the world and everyone in society, particularly workers." As I detail in an extended essay on her work, Berkeley literary theorist Judith Butler aims to have Israelis abandon their commitment to a Jewish state and a homeland of their own. In 2010, Palestinian American activist and author Ahmed Moor wrote that BDS has one ultimate aim: "Ending the occupation doesn't mean anything if it doesn't mean upending the Jewish state itself." Although the rhetoric employed in each of these examples varies, the end result, as Barghouti has put it, is the same: "euthanasia" for the Jewish state.

2. See American Anthropological Association, *Report to the Executive Board: The Task Force on AAA Engagement on Israel-Palestine* (Arlington, VA: AAA 2015), http://s3.amazonaws.com/rdcms-aaa/files/production /public/FileDownloads/151001-AAA-Task-Force-Israel-Palestine.pdf.

3. In 2012, a controversy erupted after University of Pennsylvania English professor Amy Kaplan suggested that faculty might well look for opportunities to insert anti-Israel material into courses that offer a potential thematic link with the Israeli-Palestinian conflict. She used the examples of a general course on prison culture and politics that could be enhanced with a section on Israeli treatment of Palestinian prisoners or a general literature survey that could include a section on Palestinian literature. See "University of PA Responds about Amy Kaplan's Politicizing of Her Courses," *Elder of Ziyon*, February 10, 2012, http:// elderofziyon.blogspot.com/2012/02/university-of-pa-responds-about -amy.html.

4. See Scott Jaschik, "Crossing a Line," *Inside Higher Education*, April 23, 2009, https://www.insidehighered.com/news/2009/04/23/ucsb.

5. For an account of the meeting, see Elizabeth Redden, "Big Night for Boycott Movement," *Inside Higher Education*, November 23, 2015, https://www.insidehighered.com/news/2015/11/23 /anthropologists-overwhelmingly-vote-boycott-israeli-universities.

6. For a full account of the process at the American Studies Association, see Sharon Ann Musher, "The Closing of the American Studies Association's Mind," in *The Case against Academic Boycotts of Israel*, ed. Cary Nelson and Gabriel Noah Brahm (Chicago: MLA Members for Scholars' Rights, 2015), 105–18.

7. See "Anti-Israel Boycott Resolution Rails at American Anthropology Association," *Legal Insurrection*, June 7, 2016, http:// legalinsurrection.com/2016/06/anti-israel-boycott-resolution-fails-at -american-anthropology-association/?utm_source=feedburner&utm _medium=feed&utm_campaign=Feed%3A+LegalInsurrection+%28Le·g al+In·sur·rec·tion%29.

8. See "What Israel's Nightmare Trajectory May Mean on Campus," *The Third Narrative*, March 20, 2016, http://thirdnarrative.org/bds -does-not-equal-peace-articles/what-israels-nightmare-trajectory -may-mean-on-campus/.

9. The course in question was taught by Joseph Massad.

10. Edward Said, *The Question of Palestine* (New York: Routledge, 1979); Rashid Khalidi, *Palestinian Identity: The Construction of Modern National Consciousness* (New York: Columbia University Press, 1997);

Joseph Massad, *The Persistence of the Palestinian Question: Essays on Zionism and the Palestinians* (New York: Routledge, 2006); Theodor Herzl, *The Jewish State* (1896; repr., Jewish Virtual Library translation online); Theodor Herzl, *Altneuland* (1902; repr. Jewish Virtual Library translation online); Shlomo Sand, *The Invention of the Jewish People* (London: Verso, 2010); Ghassan Kanafani, *Men in the Sun and Other Palestinian Stories* (Boulder, CO: Lynne Rienner, 1998); Kanafani, *Palestine's Children: Returning to Haifa and Other Stories* (Boulder, CO: Lynne Rienner, 2000); Sara Roy, *The Gaza Strip: The Political Economy of De-Development* (Washington, DC: Institute for Palestine Studies, 1995); Neve Gordon, *Israel's Occupation* (Berkeley: University of California Press, 2008); Jeroen Gunning, *Hamas in Politics: Democracy, Religion, Violence* (New York: Columbia University Press, 2008); Israel Shahak and Norton Mezvinsky, *Jewish Fundamentalism in Israel* (London: Pluto, 2004); Ali Abunimah, *The Battle for Justice in Palestine* (Chicago: Haymarket, 2014).

11. The syllabus was sent to me by a Columbia University student. It includes the course description quoted.

12. For a recent example of Massad's views, see his "Palestinians and the Dilemmas of Solidarity, *Electronic Intifada*, May 14, 2015, https://electronicintifada.net/content/palestinians-and-dilemmas-solidarity/14518.

13. See Paul Bogdanor, "An Antisemitic Hoax: Lenni Brenner on Zionist 'Collaboration' with the Nazis," *Fathom*, June 2016, http://fathomjournal.org/an-antisemitic-hoax-lenni-brenner-on-zionist-collaboration-with-the-nazis/.

14. The Faculty Action Network's website Israel and the Academy (www.israelandtheacademy.org) includes, among its four hundred syllabi in Israel studies and Jewish studies, a significant number that aim to teach the Israeli-Palestinian conflict in a way that represents both sides fairly. Donna Divine's essay "The Arab-Israeli Conflict: How to Teach All Sides without Taking Sides" is also on the site (http://israelandtheacademy.org/wp-content/uploads/2016/06/DIVINEessay.pdf).

15. My own university requires that each department keep copies of all current course syllabi publicly available. For some campuses, especially private institutions that do not observe similar practices, absent permission to reproduce a syllabus in its entirety, our best practice is to describe a syllabus carefully.

16. For detailed comments on the Puar lecture that include extensive quotation from it, see William A. Jacobson, "Vassar Faculty-Sponsored Anti-Israel Event Erupts in Controversy," *Legal Insurrection*, February 8, 2016, http://legalinsurrection.com/2016/02/vassar-faculty

-sponsored-anti-israel-event-erupts-in-controversy/. See also Mark G. Yudof and Ken Waltzer, "Majoring in Antisemitism at Vassar," *Wall Street Journal*, February 17, 2016, https://www.wsj.com/articles/majoring-in-anti -semitism-at-vassar-1455751940; Ken Waltzer, "BDS Scholars Defend the Indefensible," *Times of Israel*, March 13, 2016, https://blogs.timesofisrael .com/bds-scholars-defend-the-indefensible/.

17. See David Stone, "Has Israel Damaged Palestinian Health? An Evidence-Based Analysis of the Nature and Impact of Israeli Public Health Policies Practices in the West Bank and Gaza," *Fathom*, Autumn 2014, http://fathomjournal.org/wp-content/uploads/2014/12/Has-Israel -damaged-Palestinian-health.pdf. Also see Elihu Richter, "Selective, Biased and Discriminatory: The American Anthropological Association Task Force Report on Israel-Palestine," Louis D. Brandeis Center for Human Rights Under Law, April 6, 2016, http://brandeiscenter.com /blog/selective-biased-and-discriminatory-the-american-anthropological -association-task-force-report-on-israel-palestine/.

18. See Jasbir K. Puar, "The 'Right' to Maim: Disablement and Inhumanist Biopolitics in Palestine," *borderlands* 14, no. 1 (2015), http:// www.borderlands.net.au/vol14no1_2015/puar_maim.pdf.

19. Joy Karega, "Writing for Social Justice" (teaching materials, Oberlin College, fall 2015), https://new.oberlin.edu/dotAsset/04cd95b3-51a0-4807 -b1b9-5e8c24f86209.pdf. These materials have since been removed from Oberlin's website, so the URL is no longer valid.

20. Screen shots of Karega's Facebook posts are reproduced in David Gerstman, "Oberlin Professor Claims Israel Was Behind 9/11, ISIS, Charlie Hebdo Attack," *Tower*, February 25, 2016, http://www.thetower .org/3012-oberlin-professor-claims-israel-was-behind-911-isis-charlie -hebdo-attack/.

21. Had the AAUP's Committee A on Academic Freedom and Tenure been responding to social media interventions about a subject other than Israel, it might have been willing to take a more serious look at the issues involved in the changed world in which we all live. By the time the issue arose, however, two opponents of Israel, both supporters of academic boycotts, had been appointed to the group. It did not help matters that one proceeds by intense ad hominem attacks and the other by way of personal sarcasm. Such conduct did not encourage free and open discussion. During the course of drafting and revising the AAUP's investigative report on the Salaita case, there was considerable staff and appointed committee member support for claiming that Jewish donors had shaped the university's decision to withdraw Salaita's offer. In conversation with

me, one senior staff member cited the Sami Al-Arion case in Florida as an example of Jewish donor intervention proving that that was always what such people do, even though there had been no significant evidence of donor influence at the University of Illinois. In the end, there was enough disagreement that the accusations against donors were removed from the report. But the AAUP refused to consider seriously the idea that a faculty member's social media interventions in areas of his or her teaching or research might be part of his or her professional profile.

22. On the relevance of social media to a faculty member's professional profile, see Don Enron, "Professor Salaita's Intramural Speech" (https://www.aaup.org/sites/default/files/Eron_0.pdf), and Cary Nelson, "Steven Salaita's Scholarly Record and the Problem of His Appointment" (https://www.aaup.org/sites/default/files/Nelson.pdf), both in *Journal of Academic Freedom* 6 (2015).

23. For my most detailed discussion of this issue, see Cary Nelson, "Advocacy Versus Indoctrination," *Journal of College and University Law* 39, no. 3 (2013): 749–68.

24. See Blake Neff, "Oberlin Students Release Gargantuan 14-Page List of Demands," *Daily Caller*, December 17, 2015, http://dailycaller.com/2015/12/17/oberlin-students-release-gargantuan-14-page-list-of-demands/.

CARY NELSON is Jubilee Professor of Liberal Arts and Sciences at the University of Illinois at Urbana-Champaign and Affiliated Faculty Member at the University of Haifa. Among his more than thirty authored or edited books are *The Case against Academic Boycotts of Israel* and *Dreams Deferred: A Concise Guide to the Israeli-Palestinian Conflict and the Movement to Boycott Israel.*

PART III

Israeli Voices

"There Was No Uncorrupt Israel"

The Role of Israelis in Delegitimizing Jewish Collective Existence

GIL RIBAK

IN EARLY 2012, a Tel Aviv gallery, the Spaceship at 70 Yarkon Street, opened an exhibit titled "Iran," which, according to its curators, was meant to express opposition to the prospect of an Israeli war against Iran. The curators—Yehoshua Simon, Roy Chicky Arad, and Ari Libsker—explained that the exhibit focused on characters "from the biblical Haman, through Hitler and Saddam Hussein, and up to Ahmadinejad," because each of these men "is an object of the Jewish People's collective paranoia disorder" and they "provide a circumstantial alibi for our paranoia." The curators criticized what they saw as the "Israeli hysteria and fear of destruction, and the never-ending quest for a new Hitler-Nasser-Saddam at all costs." Among the artworks shown in the exhibit was a miniature wax sculpture of Ehud Barak (then minister of defense) made by Ari Libsker and Anna Appel; it was titled "The Most Dangerous Man in the World."[1]

In 2007, the former speaker of the Knesset, as well as former chairman of the Jewish Agency for Israel, Avraham Burg, said in an interview that "to define the State of Israel as a Jewish state is the key to its end" and termed the Israeli Law of Return "a mirror image of Hitler." Burg argued, "Israeli is half Jewish," that

"Israeliness has just a body. It has no soul," and he predicted that a future Knesset would pass "Nuremberg Laws." Like the curators of the "Iran" exhibit, Burg criticized Israeli fears and paranoia, asking "whether every enemy means Auschwitz, whether all of Hamas is an enemy." On a more practical level, Burg called on "anyone who can" to obtain a second passport. In a later article, in 2015, Burg argued that, "in one enlightened country" between the Jordan River and the Mediterranean Sea, "everyone will have the same rights"; he foresaw that "there will be mutiny here" (against the government's policy) and claimed the Israeli left can "finish off" the Israeli right by its "refusal to serve in the military and pay taxes" and by leading a "domestic and international shaming campaign."[2]

Much has been written about the resurgence of antisemitism in the first decade of the twenty-first century, when anti-Jewish hatred has often been cloaked in antiracist and anticolonialist garb and is aimed ostensibly not at Jews per se but rather at Zionism and the existence of the state of Israel. Attacking the Jewish state as a colonial and racist project allows latter-day or "new" antisemites to present themselves as spearheading a progressive campaign to end injustice and liberate a native population from the yoke of European colonizers. The facts that *all* Middle Eastern countries (and many countries around the world) have a much worse human rights record than Israel; that a large segment of Israeli Jews actually originated from Middle Eastern countries, from which they or their ancestors were ethnically cleansed since 1948; and that the total number of fatalities (Jews and Arabs combined) caused by the Israeli-Arab conflict since the beginning of Zionist immigration (in 1881) is far less than, say, the Algerian civil war of the 1990s are of little concern to Israel's detractors. They are determined to single out the Jewish state and delegitimize its very existence. Yet, as explicitly antisemitic discourse was largely delegitimized in the West after the Holocaust, the new antisemites have replaced the word *Jew* with *Zionist*. This semantic change has enabled them freely to use antisemitic tropes such as the Zionist control of the media and politics, Zionist violence and cowardliness, and Zionist greed for money, land, and power while arguing that they are not antisemitic but rather anti-Zionist. As German Jewish writer Henryk Broder insightfully observed, anti-Zionism is "nothing more than a left-wing version of anti-Semitism."[3]

Others scholars have called attention to the role of self-styled "progressive" Jews on the left as those who now and again take part in and even lead the attacks against Zionism, the state of Israel, and the very right of Jews to national self-determination. A long procession of academics, writers, philosophers, rabbis, political activists, teachers, and journalists has portrayed Israel as a racist, apartheid state, an illegitimate entity whose establishment was a mistake and whose very existence is a distortion of Judaism. Two Jews who might agree on very little regarding Judaism—Jewish liberation theologian Marc H. Ellis and the extreme ultra-Orthodox rabbi David Weiss—still converge in their assertion that Zionists might be worse than the Nazis.[4]

The presence of Jewish radicals/progressives/doves within the anti-Zionist camp seemingly refutes any claims that equate anti-Zionism with antisemitism. If a host of well-known Jewish intellectuals and artists such as Judith Butler, Noam Chomsky, Richard Falk, Naomi Klein, Tony Kushner, and Adrienne Rich (to mention just a few) express anti-Zionist positions, who could claim that anti-Zionism is antisemitic? Yet, as some scholars have demonstrated, such Jewish figures serve today as a fig leaf or an alibi for latter-day antisemites who seek to come across exculpated from one of the most ancient hatreds in the world.[5]

This chapter focuses on what might seem to be an even more convincing and authentic fig leaf for contemporary antisemites: Israeli Jews from the far left, whose attacks against Jewish collective existence contribute and lead to delegitimization of Jewish self-determination and help fan the flames of the new antisemitism.[6] A common argument views the individuals and organizations that strongly excoriate the Jewish state abroad as opportunists who receive international recognition, awards, prizes, and financial support from anti-Israeli sympathizers. The business of maligning Israel in Europe and North America in the name of human rights might be quite lucrative, as some Israeli journalists, artists, playwrights, and nongovernmental organizations (NGOs) have discovered.[7] While such personal or opportunistic calculations are certainly motivatiors for some Israeli detractors of their country, this chapter takes harsh, anti-Zionist critique of Israel as genuine and ideological on the whole. Such calumnies are, in fact, a continuation of a tradition of Jewish radicals/progressives that existed decades before the state of Israel was established.

One of the bitterest critics of Israel is columnist Gideon Levy, whose articles are regularly translated into several European languages. In 2011, Levy participated in the Israeli Apartheid Week at Trinity College in Dublin, Ireland, where he characterized Israelis as detached from reality and in dire need of hospitalization: "Israelis aren't willing to accept other opinions than their own and are convinced that anyone who criticizes them is an antisemite." Levy also said that "the Israeli regime is morally corrupt" and compared the Israeli rule of the West Bank to the Arab dictators who were toppled during the Arab Spring, predicting a similar fate.[8] Levy went further with that analogy in 2013, when he wished that a new Palestinian uprising would come soon and claimed, "The regimes against which Arab masses revolted were mostly less cruel than the Israeli occupation. Those regimes were also less corrupt, in the broader sense of the word corruption." In a March 2016 interview with Max Blumenthal, Levy said, "The only hopeful tool right now, the only game in town, which might show some kind of hope, is BDS [the Boycott, Divestment, Sanctions movement]. It's a nonviolent tool, a very legitimate one." In July 2016, Levy argued, "the debate about the [Israeli] occupation must take place abroad. . . . Just as the debate about the fate of the Yazidis cannot take place in Iraq . . . it is incumbent upon us to move the debate outside, so people abroad would know how the occupation looks like."[9]

Levy and Burg are acting largely as individuals, each seeing himself as the voice of conscience. More than a dozen Israeli NGOs promote a similar agenda, and with an almost Pavlovian determination condemn anything that Israel does. One example is B'Tselem. Formed in 1989, its name literally means "in the image of," but its full name is the Israeli Information Center for Human Rights in the Occupied Territories. In June 2014, B'Tselem began a campaign titled "Hitching a Ride." The campaign condemned Israel's efforts to locate three teenagers who were abducted (and shortly after, murdered by Palestinian terrorists) as cynically exploiting the deep concern for the abducted teenagers in order to "implement sweeping actions which intensify harm to the human rights of Palestinians."[10]

According to B'Tselem, any military act by Israel that might harm Palestinian civilians is categorically wrong and illegitimate, *irrespective* of the Palestinian violence against Israeli civilians that triggered the Israeli act. In an interview with Sky News at the beginning of Operation Protective Edge (July 2014), B'Tselem's director, Hagai El-Ad, argued that, whereas Hamas's attacks are "as well illegal," "the difference is significant" between the warring sides. In Israel, there were no fatalities due to the Iron Dome defense system and bomb shelters, but in Gaza, "people have no shelters and the results of the attacks that we're seeing are [an] unacceptable death toll."[11] According to El-Ad's line of thought, Israel is more condemnable because it has provided its civilian population with more protective measures than Hamas. And if one continues that logic, Israel's hands must be tied in order to refrain from Palestinian civilian casualties even when Israeli civilians are targeted by Palestinian terror groups. In an August 2014 interview with Tel Aviv Radio, El-Ad refused to define

Hamas as a terror group and termed it part of "armed Palestin-ian organizations."[12]

Another NGO is Zokhrot ("remembering," in the plural femi-nine format of the verb), which was formed in 2002. Zokhrot promotes acknowledgment of and accountability for the ongoing injustices of the 1948 Nakba—the Palestinian Catastrophe—and pushes for the Palestinians' right of return, so that Israel will "renounce the colonial conception of its existence in the region and the colonial practices it entails."[13] A cofounder of the organ-ization, Eitan Bronstein, pleaded in 2010 with the Palestinians to "persist and . . . not give up your right to return," because "If you give up this right all chance for a just life in this land will be lost and I will be sentenced to the shameful life of an eternal occupier, armed from the soles of my feet to the depths of my soul and al-ways afraid, like all colonizers." When asked in a 2004 interview about the practicality of a mass Arab return to Israel, Bronstein replied, "Anyone who would want to return can return. And then if there wouldn't be a Jewish State, then there won't be."[14]

The notion that unilaterally tying Israel's hands in defending its civilians and wiping out Israel's Jewish character will solve the Israeli-Arab conflict is a crucial feature in the worldview of some radical Israelis (or former Israelis). An interesting example is Miko Peled, the son of Matti Peled. Matti Peled was an Israel Defense Forces general (and quite a hawkish one) during the Six-Day War prior to turning to radical politics, cofounding the Progressive List for Peace and serving as a Knesset member on its behalf in the 1980s.[15] Miko Peled has argued that the trigger for focusing on the Israeli-Arab conflict and starting his political activity was the 1997 murder of his thirteen-year-old niece by a Palestinian homicide bomber in Jerusalem. At that time, Peled was already living in the United States, where he would embark on promoting both the one-state solution and a quite venomous anti-Israel critique. In the summer of 2014, during Operation Protective Edge, Peled formed a Facebook group called "Jews against Genocide" (which, by July 2018, had received more than twenty-six thousand likes). The group conducted ceremonies to commemorate the Palestinians killed in that operation in front of the Knesset and the Holocaust memorial Yad Vashem, among other places. Spoofing the Ice Bucket Challenge (a campaign to raise awareness of amyotrophic lateral sclerosis, or Lou Gehrig's disease) of that same year, activists poured buckets of fake blood over themselves after reciting statements commemorating the Palestinians killed in Operation Protective Edge.[16]

In his 2012 political autobiography, *The General's Son*, which is a self-aggrandizing, coming-of-age, moral growth story, Peled argued, "We [Jews] are all settlers, and all of Israel is occupied Palestine." In a 2013 interview at the University of Toronto, Peled described the 1948 Israeli War of Independence as "an act of terrorism that lasted for twelve months . . . and then Israel was created on the ruins of Palestine." In April 2015, at a conference in Washington, DC, titled "The Israel Lobby: Is It Good for the U.S.? Is It Good for Israel?" Peled argued that Israel is an illegitimate state because "Israel was created as a result of a brutal ethnic cleansing and established itself as an apartheid regime immediately when it was formed. There was no better Israel. There was no uncorrupt Israel. There cannot be an uncorrupt Israel because it was built on a crime and has no legitimacy."[17]

Some organizations appear to have a genuine concern for human rights and refrain from calling for the de facto elimination of Israel as a Jewish state yet in practice serve an extreme anti-Israeli line. Such an organization is Yesh Din (There Is Justice), formed in 2005, which "views the occupation as a main source of the violation of the human rights of the Palestinian population and therefore seeks to end it . . . we use the accumulation of individual incidents to highlight structural violations of human rights and advocate for change."[18]

The activities of Yesh Din are overseen by a public council that includes such illustrious members as playwright Yehoshua

Sobol, former attorney general of Israel Michael Ben-Yair, historian Ze'ev Shternhal, former deputy attorney general of Israel Yehudit Karp, and, until her death in 2014, Shulamit Aloni, a lifelong human rights activist and feminist who served as the minister of education and minister of communications in the 1990s. Yesh Din has argued that it only applies the principles of international law to the Israeli legal system; yet, as journalist Matti Tuchfeld discovered in 2010, an internal memo of the organization discussed the need to introduce "the topic of war crimes into the legal discourse in Israel regarding the actions of Israeli security forces in the occupied territories." Whereas the legal concept of war crimes is necessary for any democratic society, the memo does not specify what Israeli actions in Judea and Samaria constitute war crimes, and it implies that the Israeli rule over those territories in and of itself might amount to a war crime, and therefore what actions, if any, Israel can take to defend the lives of civilians and soldiers in those areas. The memo raises serious doubts about whether the organization's core mission, which is defined as "collecting and disseminating reliable and updated information," has remained committed to reliability or whether the political agenda has trumped that mission.[19]

Parenthetically, one can learn about the milieu of Yesh Din by looking at a 2013 Facebook post of Michael Ben-Yair, in which he claimed that Israeli settlements constitute "the most evil and foolish deed since World War II." One of his friends on Facebook asked him whether Israeli settlements were worse than, say, Stalin's massacres and purges, the Khmer Rouge regime in Cambodia, or the atrocities in Darfur. Ben-Yair replied that the settlements were a political act of a state against another people, and, as such, "it's the most evil and immoral deed since the end of World War II." One should thank Ben-Yair for refraining from equating Israel with the Nazis and only claiming it was worse than any other dictatorship *after* the Holocaust. Interestingly, according to several sources, Yitzhak Rabin's government in the

1990s—in which Ben-Yair served as attorney general—continued to expand existing settlements at nearly the same rate as its Likud predecessor. In fact, a critical report of Rabin's government settlement policy, titled "Land Grab," was published in 2002 by B'Tselem, on whose public council Ben-Yair serves as a member.[20]

The legal counselor for Yesh Din is Michael Sfard, an attorney who specializes in representing Israeli conscientious objectors who do not want to serve in Gaza and the West Bank, and who has represented many human rights NGOs' lawsuits against the Israel Defense Forces. Sfard also testified as a paid expert on behalf of the Palestine Liberation Organization and the Palestinian Authority on two different cases (in 2010 and 2015). In 2008, Sfard helped file a lawsuit in Canada seeking a declaration by the court of Israel's guilt in committing war crimes and deeming the security barrier illegal. Although the case was dismissed in 2009, in February 2013, Sfard submitted a complaint to the United Nations Human Rights Committee against the government of Canada, alleging that Canada violated the International Covenant on Civil and Political Rights when its courts ruled that it did not have jurisdiction over the case. In a 2009 interview, Sfard argued that Israel was in a process that led it "to have no soul and no moral justification for its existence," stressing that "there's no justification for the existence of a country that does not have those [moral] foundational values."[21]

Breaking the Silence (BtS, *Shovrim shtika*) is an Israeli NGO that has helped fan the flames of anti-Jewish hatred. The organization was established in 2004 by a group of soldiers to "collect and publish testimonies from soldiers who, like us, have served in the West Bank, Gaza and East Jerusalem since September 2000" in order to "stimulate public debate" and "to bring an end to the occupation." Although BtS alleges that it seeks to influence public debate within Israel, most of its activities take place abroad and are primarily directed at audiences in Europe and North America.[22] In June 2016, the Israeli press released a video in which one of the cofounders of BtS and its foreign relations director, Yehuda Shaul, is documented telling (in 2014) a group of visitors near a Palestinian village in Southern Judea that "a few years ago the settlers basically poisoned all the water cisterns of the village." That unproven claim was quickly adopted and elaborated on by a Turkish news website, and more importantly by the president of the Palestinian Authority, Mohammed Abbas, in a speech before the European Union Parliament in Brussels on June 23, 2016. Abbas said, "Just a week ago, a week, a group of rabbis in Israel announced, in a clear announcement, demanding their government, to poison, to poison, the water of the Palestinians." Within a week, an unfounded claim by an Israeli activist snowballed into reviving a classic medieval anti-Jewish libel that cast Jews as water poisoners. A couple of days later, Abbas's office retracted the allegation as baseless, but the retraction could hardly take back the antisemitic attitude and imagery that the allegation exposed, nor the standing ovation Abbas received at the European Union's legislative body.[23]

Some of the organizations and individuals under review are explicitly opposed to the existence of Israel as the national home of the Jewish people. For Zokhrot and Miko Peled, the establishment of Israel is the original sin that must be corrected. A more moderate position is presented by Gideon Levy, B'Tselem, BtS, and Yesh Din, which converge around "ending the occupation"— that is, the control by Israel of territories it conquered in the Six-Day War of 1967. But their stance on issues beyond the Israeli control of Judea and Samaria is not always clear. Gideon Levy said in a 2013 interview that "a bi-national state wouldn't be necessarily" a bad solution.[24] As for B'Tselem, it has taken a positive stand toward the "right of return"—that is, the return of Palestinians, both the remaining first-generation refugees and their offspring, to Israel in its pre-June 1967 borders. The organization's research director at the time, Yael Stein, said in a 2001 interview that, although "the issue of refugees is outside our mandate," "I feel it is important to state that there is a right of return, to state that and to have it acknowledged by the people and the Israeli government." Philosophy professor and activist Anat Biletzky, who headed B'Tselem between 2001 and 2006, was a cosigner of the 2004 Olga Initiative, which called for the creation of a de facto binational state and affirmed the right of return. B'Tselem's spokeswoman, Sarit Michaeli, flatly denied in 2010 that the organization had taken any position on the right of return, and she argued that one should not attribute to B'Tselem statements made by its members.[25]

Beyond the question of the right of return, even the organizations and individuals under review that recognize—declaratively, at least—Israel's right to exist as a national home for the Jewish people oppose virtually any security measure that Israel takes. The automatic condemnation of Israel during each round in the Gaza Strip—from which Israel withdrew to the last inch—as expressed by Hagai El-Ad and Michael Sfard virtually serves as a denial of Israel's right to exist as a Jewish state and defend its citizens. According to those Israeli individuals and NGOs, even after a complete pullout from Gaza or Lebanon, or after the kidnapping of Israeli teenagers, Israel cannot defend itself proactively without violating Palestinian human rights. At the same time, they pay mere lip service to denouncing Palestinian violence.

Harsh attacks by the Israeli far left on the Jewish state and Zionism are hardly a novelty. The poet and critic Yitzhak Laor is a lifelong radical who accused Israel in 2002 of trying to destroy the Palestinians: "Gas chambers are not the only way to destroy a nation. It is enough to destroy its social tissue, to starve dozens of villages, to develop high rates of infant mortality." The facts that mortality rates in the Palestinian population of the West Bank and Gaza fell by more than two-thirds between 1970 and 1990 and that the Palestinians made huge progress in nearly every aspect of social welfare and economic development under Israeli rule had little effect on Laor. Nearly twenty years earlier (in 1983), Laor had published a poem titled "A Hymn to the Gush," which refers to Gush Emunim (Block of the Faithful), a right-wing religious movement committed to establishing Jewish settlements across Judea and Samaria, the Gaza Strip, and the Golan Heights. The poem mentions the approaching holiday of Pesach, when the settlers will celebrate "in our unleavened bread the blood of Palestinian children"—a rather nasty reference to the centuries-old canard about Jews using Gentile blood to make unleavened bread.[26]

In addition to such imagery was the increasingly common depiction in Israeli culture of Israelis as Nazis, and even an especially vicious reversal that portrayed Nazis as Zionists. Yehoshua Sobol's 1984 play *Ghetto* features the chief Nazi officer, Kittel, who turns out to be a Talmudic scholar and an avid supporter of Zionism, especially Jabotinsky's revisionist Zionism. The play was staged in more than sixty productions around the world and yielded several prestigious prizes for Sobol in Germany and Britain, among other places. In 1991, the Akko Experimental Theater Group produced *Arbeit macht frei from Toitland Europa*, a five-hour multimedia performance that presented Israeli society as both addicted to Holocaust commemoration and cynically abusing it. Breaking the barriers between actors and spectators and bombarding audience members with music and scenes that caricatured the Zionist mind-set and Jewish nationalism, *Arbeit macht frei* equated Israelis with Nazis and Palestinians with Jews. Unsurprisingly, the theater production received critical acclaim in Germany. Contemporary critics have noted that while Germany has done much to confront the Holocaust, a common parallel trend continues, casting Israelis as modern-day Nazis and Palestinians as modern-day Jewish victims. That reversal allows Germans to demonize Israel while reducing (if not exculpating altogether) Nazi Germany's atrocities. At any rate, displays of Israeli culture such as *Ghetto* and *Arbeit macht frei from Toitland Europa* led critic Edward Alexander to term them "antisemitism,

Israeli-style," and later, journalist Uzi Zilber called them the "Jew flu."[27]

Yet a significant difference exists between those older literary and theatrical examples of the 1980s and 1990s and the individuals and organizations under review here. The former were cultural expressions that did not amount to the concerted, politicized, and well-orchestrated campaign against Israel by the Israeli far left since the beginning of the twenty-first century. There is certainly evidence that the Israeli left began turning to the path of delegitimizing Israel since the first Lebanon War (1982);[28] yet since the turn of the millennium, there has manifested a growing willingness of far-left Israeli organizations and individuals to turn abroad and appeal to world public opinion—and specifically to foreign governments, the International Criminal Court in the Hague, and the United Nations Human Rights Committee (among others). Such calls are made in an attempt to circumvent the Israeli legal system and force a far-left agenda on the Israeli public, the overwhelming majority of which loathes far-left activists and views them as no better than informers and snitches. Indeed, the last decade has witnessed an escalation in right-wing rhetoric against the Israeli far left, labeling them "traitors," "human garbage," and "scum" and calling for "death to lefties." Such shouts have also become common at public demonstrations where right-wing protesters have assaulted left-wing activists.[29]

Several scholars have tried to explain the escalation of both rhetoric and action within the Israeli far left as part of a sociological shift. According to that analysis, the hegemonic group of secular, Ashkenazi, and leftist Israeli Jews, who are descendants of the group that led the Zionist movement and Israel for many years, has gradually weakened amid the rise of new groups, such as Mizrachim, the national religious Haredim, and immigrants from the former Soviet Union. That weakening has created a deep sense of frustration among the former hegemonic group, which watched with dismay the way "the country was stolen" from them. Such frustrations have led a minority of its members to radicalize their positions against Israel. As Nitzan Horowitz, a member of the Knesset from the left-wing party Meretz, admitted in 2013, "For a long time the Left has been going around with a feeling that . . . the settlers, the Haredim, and the Right-wingers snatched the country from under our noses."[30]

There are certainly some novel characteristics to the anti-Israel campaign led by some Israelis, especially against the surge of global new antisemitism, which frequently masks itself as anti-Zionism. Yet a reality in which self-styled "progressive" Israeli Jews are those who sometimes spearhead the harshest attacks against Israel should come as no surprise, because it is part of a historical pattern that was in place decades before the Jewish state was established. It was common among radical Jews to assault or deny the very existence of a Jewish collective—let alone validate its suffering or rights—in the name of various universal ideologies, such as socialism/Marxism or anarchism. After the assassination of Czar Alexander II in Russia (in March 1881) and the eruption of the worst wave of pogroms to date, young Jewish radicals in Russia were "joyful," because they believed those were the earliest signs of a revolution against the czarist regime. Lifelong socialist Pavel Axelrod recalled how "the Jewish socialist intelligentsia abandoned the Jewish masses, leaving them 'to the natural course of events.'" A young radical admitted, "We were convinced that all Jews were swindlers." Yiddish playwright Jacob Gordin, also part of that Jewish intelligentsia, in June 1881 placed the responsibility for the pogroms onto Russian Jews themselves, blaming "Our greed for money, our insatiability, cupidity, pursuit of profit, our importunacy, abrasiveness."[31]

Yet soon those radicals were attacked as "kikes" by the Russian masses and had to flee for their lives. What the Yiddish poet Avrom Lesin wrote in 1903 about radical Jews could be applied today when describing the Israeli far left and its implementation of human rights criteria: "[Radical Jews] will consider and reconsider and re-reconsider when it comes to a Jewish issue, in case it will not please those or others of their Gentile comrades . . . hoping that their Gentile comrades will keep quiet and *forget their hatred* [toward Jews]. . . . You hear quite often the voices of those Jews thunder in favor of the Poles, the Finns, the Armenians; but they remain mute when they hear the voices of their own miserable brethren."[32]

It is highly probable that the individuals and organizations under review would have strongly opposed being likened to those Russian Jewish radicals, or even being lumped together with one another. Some of them are Zionist and advocate more moderate policies. Michael Ben-Yair and Yehudit Karp are an integral part of the Israeli legal establishment; even the source of the well-poisoning canard, Yehuda Shaul of Breaking the Silence, rejected the calls to boycott Israel at a 2013 lecture on a US campus.[33] On the other hand, Miko Peled, Eitan Bronstein, and Anat Biletzky are anti-Zionists who would like to see the disappearance of Israel in its current form.

All the same, those Israeli individuals and organizations see world public opinion as an enlightened tribunal that would support them as it condemns Israel. For example, the young Israeli artists who would like to understand and represent the "Jewish People's collective paranoia disorder" regarding Adolf Hitler clearly view the Jewish psyche as parochially deformed and attempt to transcend it in the name of some larger universal truth. But it is exactly those self-styled universalists who do not (or pretend not to) fully grasp the profound differences between appealing to audiences within Israel and abroad.

If one attributes innocence and idealism to far-left, Israeli-born and bred activists, they ironically prove the success of Zionism, which sought to create New Jews, physically and mentally healthy and free from the complications of exile.[34] Born and raised among Jews in Israel, they tend to underplay the importance of antisemitism, because it is a phenomenon with which they have had little firsthand experience. Thus, they are more than happy to share their views and seek support abroad. But a strong critique of Israel that is expressed in Tel Aviv or Jerusalem has a very different impact and different ramifications than the same critique when it is lodged in Berkeley, Brussels, or London, especially at events organized by groups with an explicit anti-Israel bias. Nevertheless, one can hardly assume just innocence and idealism, because Israeli activists are also quite aware of what their European funders expect of them. In some cases, Israeli NGOs are asked by their European donors to dig up incriminating information against Israel. Even if there is no direct pressure to blackball Israel, there is the glory of international awards, publicity, and recognition in which Israeli defamers bask. And if the cost for that fame is to invoke antisemitic imagery and vocabulary, so be it.[35]

Whether far-left Israelis are opportunistic or genuinely "useful idiots" (to use an idiom commonly ascribed to Vladimir Lenin)—that is, Israelis who support the cause of forces much more repressive and brutal than anything Israel has ever done—is difficult to determine. A common explanation for the political behavior of far-left Jews has been psychological—that those individuals are "self-hating" Jews or display some other psychological disorder. According to those analyses, due to centuries of anti-Jewish hatred and oppression, self-hating Jews largely internalized the bigotry of their persecutors and sincerely believe it to be true. Another corollary equates such Jews to abused children who constantly blame themselves for everything committed against them and are convinced they can placate their oppressors by giving in to their demands. The psychological explanation has caught on and informs much of the debate about the Jewish and Israeli extreme left. Famed historian and Middle East expert Bernard Lewis has argued, "Today the phenomenon of Jewish self-hatred is found chiefly on the far left," because it offers a way "for freeing oneself from ancestral and, more immediately, parental bonds."[36]

The term *self-hatred* is quite misleading in relation to people who are usually enamored of themselves as beacons of justice, yet gladly smear other Jews. More importantly, while there are certainly deep and substantial psychological patterns to be found among many of the extreme leftists, one should not over-psychologize their behavior and reduce it to a mental disorder. Jews who slander other Jews and call on non-Jews to act against them represent a long-standing tendency in Jewish history that frequently brought on dire consequences to the attacked Jews. Arguing that their political adversaries have psychological pathologies allows them to deflect the debate from the long-term damage they have caused; it is essentially like arguing that Zionists are using the same silencing methods as the Soviet Union, which classified regime dissenters as mentally ill before subjecting them to forced hospitalization/incarceration.[37]

The main issue is that, regardless of whether due to a psychological pathology, radical ideology, opportunism, naiveté, or feelings of a deposed elite (or a mixture of any of these), far-left Israelis serve contemporary antisemites not just as a fig leaf and an alibi but also as the most authentic proof for purported Zionist evil. What could be more authentic than a former Israel Defense Forces paratrooper (Peled) or the former speaker of the Knesset (Burg) declaring his country to be a racist apartheid state that commits Nazi-style war crimes? Relatively little research has examined the effects those Israeli individuals and organizations have had on the ebb and flow of antisemitism. Amnon Goldshtof has looked at web users' responses to articles by members of Jews against Genocide and Breaking the Silence during Operation Protective Edge and discovered tens of thousands of shares on various social media platforms. The responses ranged from "What Hitler did to them, they're doing now to the Palestinians" to "As long as Israel exists there'll never be peace" to "Allah, crush those vampires."[38]

That is just the tip of the iceberg, and much more research is needed to understand the role of Israelis in delegitimizing their country in general and the Jewish right to self-determination and to being an independent nation-state in particular. Ultimately, anti-Zionists within the Israeli far left are not so different from the Jewish revolutionaries of more than a century ago. An important difference, however, is that, while for socialist, anarchist, and communist movements the universal component was significant (at least at face value), today anti-Zionists have aligned themselves with a cause and a host of movements (such as BDS) that represent either radical Islam or exclusionary Palestinian nationalism (or both). Those movements have cynically used a Western human rights discourse to lambast Israel, yet they have not shown even a semblance of interest in human rights anywhere else on the planet. In their ongoing campaign to vilify Israel, they have lost even the facade of true universalism. Unfortunately, such attacks are always in high demand because the defamers are Israelis, and their voices carry more credence outside Israel.

The Israeli far left has utterly failed to convince other Israelis, and in the process it has become increasingly detached from Israeli society. Representing a tiny faction, radical leftists have failed to convince the Israeli public and Israeli courts of their way, so they have turned to world public opinion, foreign governments, United Nations agencies, and whoever is willing to listen to (and fund) them in an attempt to impose their political agenda on Israel. As they are continually rejected within Israel, far leftists have become even more intransigent, serving as informers and as a fig leaf to antisemites as they deny Jews the same national rights they demand for the Palestinians.

NOTES

1. "Exhibition Iran," Roy Chicky Arad, March 13, 2012, https://chickyoo.wordpress.com/2012/03/13/iran/; Daniel Rauchwerger, "From Haman to Ahmadinejad" [in Hebrew], *Haaretz*, March 16, 2012, http://www.haaretz.co.il/news/education/1.1665147; Galya Yahav, "Iran: Substandard Is Indeed Substandard" [in Hebrew], *Haaretz*, March 23, 2012, http://www.haaretz.co.il/gallery/art/1.1668409; Shai Harlev, "From

Avigdor Liberman to Auschwitz: The Exhibit 'Iran' Criticizes the Israeli
Panic" [in Hebrew], *Achbar Ha-'eer*, March 14, 2012, http://www.mouse
.co.il/CM.articles_item,610,209,66899,.aspx.

2. Ari Shavit, "Avraham Burg: Canceling the Definition of Israel
as a Jewish State" [in Hebrew], *Marker*, June 7, 2007, http://www
.themarker.com/misc/1.446433; Avraham Berg, "I'm a Leftist. Stand
Up" [in Hebrew], *Saloona*, December 12, 2015, http://saloona.co
.il/?p=295718?ref=saloona_tags.

3. One can mention only a fraction of the literature on that topic:
Robert S. Wistrich, "Converging Pathologies: From Anti-Zionism to
Neo-Antisemitism," *Antisemitism International* 3–4 (2006): 6–17; Bernard
Harrison, "Anti-Zionism, Antisemitism, and the Rhetorical Manipulation
of Reality," in *Resurgent Antisemitism: Global Perspectives*, ed. Alvin H.
Rosenfeld (Bloomington: Indiana University Press, 2013), 8–41; T. J.
Caplan, "The Z Word," *Notes from a Mad Planet*, October 24, 2014, https://
notesfromamadplanet.wordpress.com/2014/10/24/the-z-word-by-tj
-caplan/; Natan Sharansky, "3D Test of Antisemitism: Demonization,
Double Standards, Delegitimization," *Jewish Political Studies Review* 16,
no. 3–4 (Fall 2004), http://www.jcpa.org/phas/phas-sharansky-fo4.htm;
Irwin Cotler, "Anti-Semitism, Old and New," *Times of Israel*, January
26, 2015, http://blogs.timesofisrael.com/anti-semitism-old-and-new/.
Broder is quoted in Kenneth L. Marcus, *The Definition of Anti-Semitism*
(New York: Oxford University Press, 2015), 146. See also Shira Sorko
-Ram, "The UN and Human Rights: A Kangaroo Court," *Maoz Israel
Report*, May 2014, http://www.maozisrael.org/site/News2?id=10232.
On the Algerian civil war, see Fouad Ajami, "The Furrows of Algeria,"
New Republic, January 26, 2010, https://newrepublic.com/article/72807
/the-furrows-algeria.

4. Alvin H. Rosenfeld, *"Progressive" Jewish Thought and the New
Anti-Semitism* (New York: American Jewish Committee, 2006), 20–21;
Alan Mittleman, "Marc Ellis: The Torah as a Suicide Pact," in *The Jewish
Divide over Israel: Accusers and Defenders*, ed. Edward Alexander and Paul
Bogdanor (New Brunswick, NJ: Transaction, 2006), 177–94. An array of
such American Jewish progressives has appeared in Tony Kushner and
Alisa Solomon, eds., *Wrestling with Zion: Progressive Jewish-American
Responses to the Israeli-Palestinian Conflict* (New York: Grove, 2003). A
more recent example is an article by a young supporter of Senator Bernie
Sanders, Jesse Alexander Myerson, "The Heresy and Evangelism of Bernie
Sanders," *Village Voice*, March 29, 2016, http://www.villagevoice.com
/news/the-heresy-and-evangelism-of-bernie-sanders-8450444. This article

focuses on far-left Israelis and not on anti-Zionist ultra-Orthodox such as Neturei Karta (to which David Weiss belongs). The participation of the latter in a Holocaust denial conference in Tehran in 2006 caused even the anti-Zionist Satmar Hasidim to attack them. See Mark I. Dunaevsky, "Traditional Judaism in the Twenty-First Century," in *The Wiley-Blackwell History of Jews and Judaism*, ed. Alan T. Levenson (Malden, MA: Wiley-Blackwell, 2012), 524; Neta Sela, "Satmar Court Slams Neturei Karta," *Ynetnews*, December 15, 2006, http://www.ynetnews.com /articles/0,7340,L-3340592,00.html.

5. Emanuele Ottolenghi, "Present-Day Antisemitism and the Centrality of the Jewish Alibi," in Rosenfeld, *Resurgent Antisemitism*, 424–66; Uzi Zilber, "The Jew Flu: The Strange Illness of Jewish Anti Semitism," *Haaretz*, January 1, 2009, http://www.haaretz.com/beta/the-jew-flu-the -strange-illness-of-jewish-anti-semitism-1.267172. See also Judith Butler, *Parting Ways: Jewishness and the Critique of Zionism* (New York: Columbia University Press, 2012); Cary Nelson, "The Problem with Judith Butler: The Philosophy of the Movement to Boycott Israel," in *The Case against Academic Boycotts of Israel*, ed. Cary Nelson and Gabriel Noah Brahm (Chicago: MLA Members for Scholars' Rights, 2015), 164–201.

6. A recent study of that phenomenon, especially in the Israeli cinema, is by Ilan Avisar, "The Israeli Scene: Political Criticism and the Politics of Anti-Zionism," in Rosenfeld, *Resurgent Antisemitism*, 362–81. See also Arieh Stav, "Israeli Anti-Semitism," in *Israel and the Post-Zionists: A Nation at Risk*, ed. Shlomo Sharan (Tel Aviv: Ariel Center for Policy Research, 2003), 163–87.

7. Steve Apfel, "One Industry That Will Never Boycott Israel," *American Thinker*, October 21, 2012, http://www.americanthinker.com /articles/2012/10/one_industry_that_will_never_boycott_israel.html; Amnon Rubinstein, "The Counterfeit Human Rights Industry," *Haaretz*, March 21, 2004, http://www.haaretz.com/the-counterfeit-human-rights -industry-1.117409; Gerald M. Steinberg, "False Witness? EU-Funded NGOs and Policymaking in the Arab-Israeli Conflict," *Israel Journal of Foreign Affairs* 7 (2013): 59–73; Anne Herzberg, "NGOs and the New Antisemitism," in *Global Antisemitism: A Crisis of Modernity*, ed. Charles Asher Small (Leiden, Netherlands: Martinus Nijhoff, 2013), 171–86. Ben -Dror Yemini, *Ta'asiyat ha-shkarim* (Tel Aviv: Yediot Achronot, 2014).

8. Yossi Nissan, "Gideon Levy: 'Settlements Are a Crime,' Israel Is Cut Off from Reality" [in Hebrew], *Globes*, March 15, 2011, http://www.globes .co.il/news/article.aspx?did=1000630341. See also Joshu Muravchik, "Trashing Israel Daily," *Commentary* 135 (June 2013): 28–34.

9. Gideon Levy, "Waiting for a Palestinian Uprising" [in Hebrew], *Haaretz*, July 4, 2013, http://www.haaretz.co.il/.premium-1.2062396; "Gideon Levy: Americans 'Are Supporting the First Signs of Fascism in Israel,'" *Real News Network*, March 22, 2016, http://therealnews.com /t2/index.php?option=com_content&task=view&id=31&Itemid=74& jumival=15951. His last quote is in Gideon Levy, "Yes, to Book Abroad" [in Hebrew], *Haaretz*, July 10, 2016, http://www.haaretz.co.il/opinions /.premium-1.3001436. Ben-Dror Yemini has termed Levy "the Baron" of the propaganda industry against Israel; see a 2010 article dedicated to Levy, Ben-Dror Yemini, "Haaretz, Gideon Levy, and the Israel Apartheid Canard," October 26, 2012, https://blogs.timesofisrael.com /haaretz-gideon-levy-and-the-israel-apartheid-canard.

10. B'Tselem, "Hitchhike on the Kidnap" [in Hebrew], June 24, 2014, http://www.btselem.org/hebrew/campaignlist/201406; "B'Tselem's Expanding Credibility Gap," *NGO Monitor*, July 16, 2014, http://www.ngo -monitor.org/reports/b_tselem_s_expanding_credibility_gap/.

11. El-Ad's interview is available on YouTube, at "Israel Is Illegally Bombing Homes of Hamas Commanders in Gaza: Sky News Interview with Hagai El-Ad," July 10, 2014, https://www.youtube.com/watch?v=0 EUmnG42JgE&feature=youtu.be (from minute 3:30 on). See also Eric Greenstein, "B'Tselem as a Hamas Mouthpiece" [in Hebrew], *Mida*, August 19, 2014, http://mida.org.il/2014/08/19/btselem-hamas-mouthpiece/.

12. A link to the radio interview is available at "B'Tselem's Director General Refused to Define Hamas as a Terrorist Organization" [in Hebrew], *nrg News*, August 12, 2014, http://www.nrg.co.il/online/1 /ART2/607/207.html.

13. "Our Vision," Zochrot, http://zochrot.org/en/content/17.

14. Eitan Bronstein, "An Israeli on Nakba Day: 'Our Humanity Is Bound Up with Your Right to Return,'" April 30, 2010, http://zochrot.org/en /press/50958; Aviv Lavi, "Seen the Light" [in Hebrew], *Haaretz*, August 3, 2004, http://www.haaretz.co.il/1.988725.

15. Joseph Finklestone, "Obituary: General Matti Peled," *Independent*, March 15, 1995, http://www.independent.co.uk/news/people/obituary -general-matti-peled-1611418.html; Eitan Haber and Israel Lior, *Ha-yom tifrots milḥamah: zikhronotav shel tat-aluf Yiśra'el Li'or, ha-mazkir ha-tseva'i shel rashe ha-memshalah Levi Eshkol ve-Goldha Me'ir* (Tel Aviv: 'Idanim, 1987), 211–12.

16. Miko Peled, *The General's Son: Journey of an Israeli in Palestine*, 2nd ed. (Charlottesville, VA: Just World Books, 2016), 17–20, 103–4; Jews against Genocide, Facebook, https://www.facebook.com

/pages/Jews-Against-Genocide/694634937278932. The blood bucket statements and ceremonies can be seen at "Never Again—Jews against Genocide," *YouTube*, September 27, 2014, https://www.youtube.com /watch?v=RloIwxlMo2o.

17. Peled, *The General's Son*, 233. His 2013 interview is at "Miko Peled—Myths of 1967," *YouTube*, February 28, 2013, https://www.youtube.com /watch?reload=9&v=ZsvIT4xXglk. Peled's conference speech is quoted in http://blog.adl.org/tags/miko-peled.

18. Yesh Din, "About Us," http://www.yesh-din.org/en /about-us/. See also "Yesh Din—Volunteers for Human Rights," *NGO Monitor*, May 28, 2018, http://www.ngo-monitor.org/ngos /yesh_din_volunteers_for_human_rights/.

19. *Israel ha-yom*, December 24, 2010, http://www.israelhayom.co.il /site/newsletter_article.php?id=9380. The quote from the organization's mission is at "About Us," Yesh Din, http://www.yesh-din.org /en/about-us/.

20. The Facebook quotes are in *Yediot acharonot* [in Hebrew], April 22, 2013, copied in http://www.kr8.co.il/BRPortal/br/P102. jsp?arc=577811. B'Tselem's report [in Hebrew] (2002) is at www.btselem .org/download/200205_land_grab_heb.doc, 12–13. See also Geoffrey Aronson, *Settlements and the Israel-Palestinian Negotiations* (Washington, DC: Institute of Palestinian Studies, 1996), 11, 48–51; and the report by Clyde Haberman, "Besieged Settlements: Are They Worth Keeping?" *New York Times*, April 10, 1995, http://www.nytimes.com/1995/04/10/world /besieged-settlements-are-they-worth-keeping.html.

21. Sfard appeared on Rino Tsror's show "Cross Israel—Reno Tzror in an Interview with Attorney Michael Sfard" [in Hebrew], *YouTube*, April 25, 2012https://www.youtube.com/watch?v=lo_VuiEjBZw (around minutes 2:10, 4:40); "Michael Sfard, NGOs, and Government Funding," *NGO Monitor*, February 9, 2015, http://www.ngo-monitor.org/reports /michael_sfard_ngos_and_government_funding/.

22. "Organization," Breaking the Silence, http://www .breakingthesilence.org.il/about/organization; see also "Breaking the Silence," *NGO Monitor*, November 27, 2017, http://www.ngo-monitor.org /ngos/breaking_the_silence_shovirm_shtika_/.

23. The video with Shaul's voice and other details is at "Abu Mazen: Rabbis Asked to Poison Palestinians" [in Hebrew], *NRG*, June 23, 2016, http://www.nrg.co.il/online/1/ART2/791/552.html. On Abbas's speech and his allegations, see Diaa Hadid, "Mahmoud Abbas Claims Rabbis Urged Israel to Poison Palestinians' Water," *New York Times*, June 23, 2016,

http://www.nytimes.com/2016/06/24/world/middleeast/mahmoud
-abbas-claims-rabbis-urged-israel-to-poison-palestinians-water.html?
_r=0; "Abbas Walks Back Claim Rabbis Sought to 'Poison' Palestinian
Wells," *Times of Israel*, June 25, 2016, http://www.timesofisrael.com/abbas
-walks-back-claim-rabbis-sought-to-poison-palestinian-wells/. On the
well-poisoning allegations and their bloody consequences to Jewish
communities across medieval Europe, see James Carroll, *Constantine's
Sword: The Church and the Jews—A History* (New York: Houghton Mifflin,
2001), 277, 301, 306–7, 338–39, 403; and Walter Laqueur, *The Changing Face
of Antisemitism: From Ancient Times to the Present Day* (New York: Oxford
University Press, 2006), 60–62.

24. "Gideon Levy Surfers: I Prefer My Truth" [in Hebrew], *Haaretz*,
July 22, 2013, http://www.haaretz.co.il/1.2075497.

25. Stein's interview is at "BADIL Interview: With Yail Stein," al
majdal, no. 10 (Summer 2001), http://www.badil.org/en/component
/k2/item/1131-badil-interviewwith-yael-stein.html. See also Jonathan D.
Halevi, "B'Tselem ba'ad zechut hashiva'" [in Hebrew], *News 1*, June 7, 2008,
http://www.news1.co.il/Archive/003-D-30033-00.html (Biletzky and the
Olga Initiative are quoted in Halevi). B'Tselem's former executive director,
Jessica Montell, is also quoted in Halevi as supporting a binational state
with a Palestinian majority. Michaeli's response appears in Sarit Michaeli,
"The Right to Return and the Right to Think" [in Hebrew], Gadi Taub,
May 21, 2010, http://www.gaditaub.com/hblog/?p=610.

26. Yitzhak Laor, "After Jenin," *London Review of Books*, May 9,
2002, http://www.lrb.co.uk/v24/n09/yitzhak-laor/after-jenin. Data on
Palestinian mortality rate is in Efraim Karsh, *Arafat's War: The Man and
His Battle for Israeli Conquest* (New York: Grove, 2003), 43–45. Laor's
1983 poem [in Hebrew] is at http://www.newlibrary.co.il/page_1571. On
the history of blood libels against Jews, see Raphael Israeli, *Blood Libel
and Its Derivatives: The Scourge of Anti-Semitism* (New Brunswick, NJ:
Transaction, 2012).

27. On Sobol and *Ghetto*, see Steven Dedalus Burch, "Joshua Sobol,"
http://sburch.people.ua.edu/uploads/2/9/7/9/29797403/sobol-routledge
.pdf. On *Arbeit*, see Regine Mihal Friedman, "The Double Legacy
of 'Arbeit Macht Frei,'" *Prooftexts* 22 (2002): 200–20. Friedman also
discusses the penetrating documentary film by Asher Tlalim, *Al tig'u li
ba-shoah* [Don't touch my holocaust] (1994), which follows the troupe to
its performances in Germany. See also Sarit Fuchs's review [in Hebrew]
of *Arbeit*, September 6, 1991, at http://www.saritfuchs.co.il/?p=200.
Edward Alexander, *The Jewish Wars: Reflections by One of the Belligerents*

(Carbondale: Southern Illinois University Press, 1996), 26–45; Zilber, "Jew Flu."

28. See, e.g., Steven Plaut, "Lebanon 1982: The War That Drove Israel's Left Insane," *The Jewish Express*, May 30, 2003, at http://www.jewishpress.com/indepth/front-page /lebanon-1982-the-war-that-drove-israels-left-insane/2003/05/30/0/?print.

29. Liel Leibovitz, "Can the Israeli Left Save Itself?" *Tablet*, January 14, 2016, http://www.tabletmag.com/jewish-news-and-politics/196585/can -israeli-left-save-itself. The number of instances in which members of the Israeli left are termed "traitors" due to their turn to foreign governments and organization is staggering—a recent example was in March 2016, when then defense minister Moshe Ya'alon referred to some of Breaking the Silence's activities as "treason," though he later qualified his statement; Jonathan Lis and Noa Spiegel, "Ya'alon: Breaking the Silence Collects Operational Secrets—It's a Betrayal," *Haaretz*, March 21, 2016, http:// www.haaretz.co.il/news/politics/.premium-1.2889501. In 1995, the late right-wing politician and retired military general Rehavam Ze'evi accused the members of the Israeli left of being "snitches"; see https://www .youtube.com/watch?v=MPNHpyKvrK8. For more vehement rhetoric and sometimes violent attacks against left-wing activists, see Gilad Morag, "Left-Wing Demonstrators Were Attacked" [in Hebrew], *Ynetnews*, July 13, 2014, http://www.ynet.co.il/articles/0,7340,L-4542748,00.html; "The Hateful Remarks of Professor Gadi Algazi of Tel Aviv University at the Sakhnin Day Assembly" [in Hebrew], *Rotter*, October 13, 2015, http://rotter.net/forum/scoops1/255531.shtml; and the online responses (talkbacks) to Ben-Dror Yemini's article, "Mihu 'semolani," *nrg*, February 6, 2010, http://www.nrg.co.il/online/1/ART2/050/546.html.

30. Baruch Kimmerling, *Kets shilton ha'achusalim* (Jerusalem: Keter, 2001). See also Uri Ram, "Why Secularism Fails? Secular Nationalism and Religious Revivalism in Israel," *International Journal of Politics, Culture, and Society* 21 (2008): 57–63. Horowitz was interviewed by Uri Orbach, "Nitzan Horowitz: The Left Feels That They Stole Our Country" [in Hebrew] *nrg*, March 31, 2013, http://www.nrg.co.il/online/1 /ART2/455/245.html.

31. Pavel B. Axelrod, "Socialist Jews Confront the Pogroms," in *The Golden Tradition: Jewish Life and Thought in Eastern Europe*, ed. Lucy S. Dawidowicz (Boston: Beacon, 1967), 408. The young radical is quoted in Axelrod, "Socialist Jews Confront the Pogroms," 408. Gordin is quoted in Barbara Henry, *Rewriting Russia: Jacob Gordin's Yiddish Drama* (Seattle:

University of Washington Press, 2011), 56–57. See also Jonathan Frankel, *Prophecy and Politics: Socialism, Nationalism, and the Russian Jews 1862–1917* (New York: Cambridge University Press, 1981), 52.

32. Lesin wrote in *Forverts*, May 20, 1903, 4 (italics added, my translation). On Lesin's unique blend of socialism and Jewish nationalism, see Gil Ribak, *Gentile New York: The Images of Non-Jews among Jewish Immigrants* (New Brunswick, NJ: Rutgers University Press, 2012), 108, 163, 166, 169; Yoysef Mlotek, "Avrom Lesin—der dichter fun doyresdiker yidishkayt," *Tsukunft* 97 (1992): 33–38. Lesin's scathing indictment parallels another socialist, labor Zionist leader Berl Katznelson, who, in 1936, lambasted Jews who identify with their enemies—quoted in Alexander, *Jewish Wars*, 26.

33. The anecdote about Shaul is mentioned in Nancy Koppelman, "'When You Want to *Do* Something, Join Us!' The Limits of the Social Justice Mandate in American Higher Education," in Nelson and Brahm, *The Case against Academic Boycotts of Israel*, 493n128.

34. On Zionism and the aspiration to create a New Jew, see Anita Shapira, *Yehudim chadashim, yehudim yeshanim* (Tel Aviv: Am oved, 1997); Oz Almog, *The Sabra: The Creation of the New Jew*, trans. Haim Watzman (Berkeley: University of California Press, 2000); David Biale, *Power and Powerlessness in Jewish History* (New York: Schocken, 1986).

35. On the NGOs, see Steinberg, "False Witness?" 59–73; Herzberg, "NGOs and the New Antisemitism," 171–86; and "Europe to Breaking the Silence: Bring Us as Many Incriminating Testimonies as Possible," NGO Monitor, May 4, 2015, http://www.ngo-monitor.org/reports /europe_to_breaking_the_silence_bring_us_as_many_incriminating _testimonies_as_possible/. On Israeli filmmakers and their thirst for international recognition at the price of recycling antisemitic discourse, see Avisar, "The Israeli Scene," 377–78.

36. Bernard Lewis, *Semites and Anti-Semites: An Inquiry into Conflict and Prejudice* (New York: W. W. Norton, 1986), 255–56. A study that is often quoted is Sander L. Gilman, *Jewish Self-Hatred: Anti-Semitism and the Hidden Language of the Jews* (Baltimore: Johns Hopkins University Press, 1986). The Index of Articles on Jewish Studies points to nearly two hundred items about "self-hate." One can mention just a fraction of the vast literature on the subject: Kenneth Levin has elaborated on the abused children analogy in *The Oslo Syndrome: Delusions of a People under Siege* (Hanover, NH: Smith and Kraus, 2005). See also Evyatar Friesel, "On the Complexities of Modern Jewish Identity: Contemporary Jews against

Israel," *Israel Affairs* 17 (2011): 504–19; Antony Lerman, "Jewish Self-Hatred: Myth or Reality?" *Jewish Quarterly* 210 (2008): 46–51; Ottolenghi, "Present-Day Antisemitism," 427–30. See also Philologos (Hillel Halkin), "At the Heart of Self-Hatred," *Forward*, August 10, 2011, http://forward.com/culture/141206/at-the-heart-of-self-hatred/.

37. A deflection attempt can be seen in Mike Marqusee, *If I Am Not for Myself: Journey of an Anti-Zionist Jew* (London: Verso, 2008), ix. See also Mairav Zonszein, "How Israel Silences Dissent," *New York Times*, September 26, 2014, http://www.nytimes.com/2014/09/27/opinion/how-israel-silences-dissent.html.

38. Amnon Goldstof, "Breaking the Silence and Understanding Hitler" [in Hebrew], *Mida*, August 25, 2014, http://mida.org.il/20 14/08/25/%D7%A9%D7%95%D7%91%D7%A8%D7%99%D7%9D -%D7%A9%D7%AA%D7%99%D7%A7%D7%94-%D7%95%D7%9E%D7% 91%D7%99%D7%A0%D7%99/.

GIL RIBAK is Assistant Professor of Judaic Studies at the University of Arizona. He is author of *Gentile New York: The Images of Non-Jews among Jewish Immigrants*.

The Appropriation of the Israeli "New Historians" Work by Anti-Zionists

ILAN GREILSAMMER

ON JUNE 10, 1994, Aharon Megged, one of the most famous Israeli writers belonging to the Zionist left and the Israeli peace camp, wrote in the daily *Haaretz*, "Now they rewrite the history of Zionism in the spirit of our enemies! There is a suicidal instinct in Israel, and it appears clearly among the intellectuals. The top of the Israeli society, writers and men of spirit, are now preaching that justice is not on our side. Not only since the Six Day War, since the 'conquest' of the territories, and not only since the creation of the State, but since the very beginnings of the Zionist settlement in the 19th century." At the end of his impassioned article, the writer implored Israelis to stop this crazy movement, which "slowly spreads the virus throughout the body of the Nation."[1]

A huge intellectual and public controversy about collective memory and Israel's history took place in Israel in the latter half of the 1980s and during the 1990s. During that period, over more than a decade, well-known Israeli historians and sociologists published many books and articles that generated heated debates in Israeli- and English-language media. In Israel, the debates were called *Mahloket HaHistorionim*, the Controversy of the Historians.[2] These books, to mention only a few, included *The Birth of the Palestinian Refugee Problem, 1947–1949* by Benny Morris, *The Birth of Israel: Myths and Realities* by Simha Flapan,

Collusion across the Jordan: King Abdullah, the Zionist Movement and the Partition of Palestine by Avi Shlaim, and *The Seventh Million: The Israelis and the Holocaust* by Tom Segev.[3] All challenged entrenched Israeli beliefs and teachings regarding the history of the Jewish people, the Zionist movement, the Jewish settlement in Palestine, the attitude of the Yishuv during World War II, and especially the Israeli war of independence (1948–49) and the Palestinian exodus.

It is essential to remember the political context of that epoch. The late 1980s in Israel were years of deep intellectual reappraisal and moral crisis. It was the time of the national unity government formed by the Labor Party and the Likud, under Shimon Peres and Yitzhak Shamir alternately, and harsh questions were raised about Israel's 1982 war in Lebanon (the "Peace in the Galilee" military campaign against the Palestine Liberation Organization), a prolonged military conflict during which many young Israeli soldiers died every day. It was also the time of the first Intifada, the "stone-throwing uprising" that broke out in 1987, twenty years after the Six-Day War. The Peace Now movement called forth demonstrations in major cities and denounced the "hypocrisy" of the political leadership. Professor Yeshayahu Leibowitz described the occupation of the West Bank and Gaza as a catastrophic situation leading to a moral disaster, and he coined the term "Judeo-Nazi" to describe the attitude of Tsahal. Minister of Defense Yitzhak Rabin, confronting the intifada riots, ordered the soldiers of Tsahal to "break the bones" of the Palestinians.

In Israel's five universities (Hebrew, Tel Aviv, Bar-Ilan, Ben-Gurion, and Haifa), a new school of young historians—some defining themselves as Zionists, others as post-Zionists—expounded views that were influenced by postmodernism and by the writings of Michel Foucault, Eric Hobsbawm, Benedict Anderson, and Andrew White. They used a new terminology, with expressions such as "meta-history," "historical relativism," and "deconstruction of myths." These Israeli scholars all questioned the basic assumptions of official Zionist history as taught over the years in Israeli schools and universities.

In an important article published in *Tikkun* in 1988, Benny Morris—who had been born at kibbutz Ein Hahoresh to parents of English origin, later became a journalist at the *Jerusalem Post*, held a PhD from Cambridge University, and was then forty years old—called this group to which he belonged the New Historians of Israel, in opposition to the "old historians."[4] The name was an explicit reference to the French *Nouvelle histoire des mentalités*, founded by Marc Bloch and Lucien Febvre and centered on the Paris École des Hautes Études en Sciences Sociales, which had carried out a radical reappraisal of traditional methods of writing about history. These young Israeli scholars said that the major Hebrew University historians of the state's first generation, among them Gershom Scholem, Yitzhak Baer, and Ben-Zion Dinur, had presented an ideological history of the Jewish people and of Israel that was mobilized in support of Zionism and the nation-building process, and more specifically of the dominant Zionist Socialist movement, Mapai. They asserted that these great historians, supported by the state (particularly by David Ben-Gurion), had always sought to prove that a Jewish nation had existed long before Zionism and that a Jewish aspiration to return to statehood had truly existed since ancient times. From this perspective, these older historians portrayed the Jews as a unified people who, throughout the diaspora, had maintained a cohesiveness across time and space and were continually focused on a Jewish return to the ancient homeland, Eretz Israel. In other words, consciously or unconsciously, they viewed nineteenth-century political Zionism as the perfect and logical continuation of Jewish history as a whole. The new historians also said that Israel's official history had presented the 1948 war as a black-and-white story of Jewish supreme heroism, a tale of good and idealistic Jewish soldiers fighting bad and cruel Arab terrorists.

This "official Zionist history" was enshrined in popular books such as *Sefer Toledot Hahaganah* (History of the Haganah) and *Sefer HaPalmach* (History of the Elite Battalions of the Palmach), in publications of the Defense Ministry, and in memoirs written by Tsahal fighters. The reality of that war, claimed the younger historians, had been extremely different.[5]

According to the new historians, the ideas and books of the eminent historians of the first generation had been immediately adopted and disseminated by other scholars, universities, researchers, schoolteachers, journalists, education officials, youth movement leaders, writers, and poets. In short, they had a huge impact and became a kind of consensus among various categories of the population.

The controversy ignited by the new historians in the 1980s spread quickly to all the social sciences in Israel, which at the time were strongly influenced by American sociology. The old Israeli sociology, mainly represented by the Shmuel Noah Eisenstadt school of thinking at the Hebrew University, was fiercely accused by young academics—including Yonatan Shapiro, Sammi Smooha, and Baruch Kimmerling—of placing itself at the service of the Ashkenazic establishment and, by stressing the "tremendous success" of the so-called melting pot, trying to hide the exploitation of oppressed minorities, especially Israeli Arabs, Oriental Jews, and women at the Hebrew University.[6] Baruch Kimmerling, a major sociologist, criticized the fact that Israeli historians used certain terms as if they were objective and neutral: for example, *Eretz Israel* (the land of Israel, for Palestine), *aliyah* (ascending, for immigration to Israel), *milchemet hashich'hour* (the war of liberation, for the war of 1948), *geulat hakarka* (the redemption of the land, for buying the land), and *kibbush Hahavoda* (the conquest of employment, for reserving any work for Jewish settlers). Kimmerling also criticized the fact that Zionist historiography counted five *aliyot*, or waves of immigration before the creation of the state, while declining to count the *aliyot* (mostly of Jews from Arab countries) of 1948 and after; Kimmerling considered this to be clear ethnic discrimination.[7]

After these social scientists, literary critics such as Yitzhak Laor and Yerah Gover began to say that important Israeli writers, including Amos Oz and A. B. Yehoshua, had "forgotten" certain categories of the population, such as Israeli Arabs or Sephardic Jews.[8]

The main question I wish to ask is this: What role have the writings of the new Israeli historians on Zionist history and sociologists on discrimination in Israeli society played in fostering the wave of anti-Zionism and delegitimization of the state of Israel that is now increasingly in vogue? In what ways have these works been used as a tool to delegitimize not only Israeli policies but also the state of Israel itself? In short, where should the line be drawn between criticism, however scathing, and delegitimization?

To answer this question in each of the four fields of research engaged in by the new historians, it is helpful to recognize that a semantic shift, or semantic change, has been anti-Zionism's essential tool in the transition from criticism to delegitimization. The semantic shift can be defined as the conscious twisting of the qualifications of certain events, to the point that new qualifications result in a falsification that entails an immediate delegitimization. In the specific case of Israel, this semantic shift to "ethnic cleansing," "transfer," "apartheid," "fascism," "genocide," and even "Nazism" occurs through widening, metaphorical transformation, or generalizing.[9]

THE HISTORY OF THE JEWISH PEOPLE IN
RELATION TO MODERN ZIONISM

The first field of study examined by the new historians was the history of the Jewish people in relation to modern Zionism. What they questioned above all was the teleological vision of the old

Hebrew University historians, who gave past events a determinist meaning, linking them to an inevitable national destiny that was to be accomplished by Zionism and the state. They criticized the traditional historians for their deliberate emphasis on the persecutions of Jews in the diaspora and on the texts of ancient Jewish writers longing for a return to the land of Israel while making no mention of the periods of Jewish assimilation and full integration into their host societies. This official metahistory, in the traditional historians' view, drew its strength from its roots in the sacred biblical story of a people exiled for disobeying God who repents and then returns, as a matter of course, to their homeland.

Another bedrock of this traditional history was Jewish exceptionalism. The survival of the Jewish people had been systematically presented as a unique case in human history. This emphasis on uniqueness led to a methodological opposition to any comparison of Israel, and of Jews in general, with other peoples. It was (and remains) absolutely politically incorrect in Israel, for example, to compare the church inquisition against the Jews with other historical forms or events of religious intolerance, or to compare the expulsions of Jews with the expulsions of other persecuted communities. In Israel, it is considered the height of political incorrectness to compare the Shoah to other genocides or even to suggest a comparison between them. When, in 1995, the Education Ministry, under Professor Amnon Rubinstein, proposed to teach the history of the genocide of the Gypsies or of the Armenians alongside the Shoah, nearly all Israeli historians opposed the proposal, and the idea was abandoned.[10] Some historians, such as Professor Yair Oron (Open University), an expert on the Armenian genocide, tried unsuccessfully to revive it. More recently, the vice commander in chief of Tsahal, Yair Golan, caused a huge scandal when he told an audience including Shoah survivors the following: "If there is anything that frightens me in the remembrance of the Shoah, it is discerning nauseating trends that took place in Europe in general, and in Germany specifically back then, 70, 80 and 90 years ago, *and seeing evidence of them here among us in the year 2016.*"[11] In other words, Golan said that he found elements of fascism in present Israeli society. His remarks immediately provoked outrage, particularly his reference to an Israeli soldier who shot dead a wounded Palestinian terrorist in Hebron since the terrorist had ceased to pose a threat.[12] In short, such comparisons are forbidden.

Another point of criticism bears on the constant search for Jewish roots in Eretz Israel by historians who set out to prove that the Jews had once formed the majority of the indigenous population, had lived in the land continuously, and therefore had a historical right to possess it. According to the new historians, the Jerusalem school of history had presented Jewish history as a single, coherent, uninterrupted story that transcended place and time and was focused entirely on one territory, Eretz Israel. In so doing, that school had broken with the works of previous leading Jewish historians of the nineteenth century such as Isaac Marcus Jost (1793–1860), Heinrich Graetz (1817–1891), Abraham Geiger (1810–1874), and Simon Dubnow (1860–1941), who, though using very different approaches, all rejected the historical unity of the Jewish diaspora and insisted on its cultural, not its national, identity. The scholar most strongly criticized by the new historians was Ben-Zion Dinur, a distinguished professor of Jewish medieval history at the University of Jerusalem from 1930 to 1959 and a prominent member of Ben-Gurion's Mapai. He was a member of the Knesset, minister of education from 1951 to 1955, author of the Education State Law (1953), and founder and subsequently president of Yad Vashem (1956–1959). In his books, such as *Israel on Its Land*, *Israel in Exile*, and *History of Hovevei Zion*, and especially in his major article "The Historical Consciousness of the People and the Problems of Studying It," he constantly stressed the unity of the Jewish people and their historical continuity.[13] To this end, he placed the start of the diaspora and the exile at a very late date, in the seventh century, coinciding with the Muslim conquest. He located the start of Jewish modernity, heralding political Zionism, as early as the seventeenth century with Shabtai Zvi and the *aliyah* movement of Rabbi Yehuda Hahassid. In this way he could substantially condense Jewish history and, by neglecting the period of exile, reduce the weight of the diaspora phenomenon. This move was in the spirit of Ben-Gurion himself, who often referred to the Bible, the Jewish people's deed of ownership to its land, but never to the Talmud, the literature of diaspora and exile.

The new historians also criticized the state's exploitation of the great myths of Jewish history once they had been nationalized and secularized: the exodus from Egypt, Hanukkah and the revolt of the Maccabees, the story of the siege of Masada (stripped of its disturbing final episode of collective suicide), and the great Bar-Kokhba revolt, presented as the first Zionist national revolution.[14] For example, Ruth Firer has shown that, since the 1930s, Zionist historiography constantly insisted on the continuity between biblical stories and modern Zionism.[15] Events of the past that had a bad or unfortunate conclusion (such as the siege of Masada or the Bar-Kochba revolt) were systematically transformed into tales of heroism and victory. This has been criticized most of all by Yehoshafat Harkaby, professor of international relations at the Hebrew University and former head of the Mossad, for whom the Bar-Kochba disaster has been unduly transformed into a nationalistic tale.[16]

The new historians sincerely believed that the official history taught in Israeli schools had a pernicious effect. Silence about the exile experience and Jewish integration in host countries encouraged a rejection of the diaspora instead of accepting it as a positive and creative phenomenon. Conceiving of the history of the Jewish people as unique, denying any comparison with it, and ignoring the exile experience, they said, contributed to Israeli ethnocentrism and prevented Israelis from empathizing with other exiles and refugees throughout the world and from showing greater openness to other social groups, such as African refugees, Oriental Jews, or Palestinian Arabs.

Last, the new historians criticized the traditional view that, throughout its history, the Jewish people had always systematically sought peace and compromise. For example, Israel Bartal of the Hebrew University stressed that episodes of violence, in some cases extreme violence, were very frequent in Jewish communities. Elimelekh Horowitz, from Bar-Ilan, highlighted episodes of community brutality, violence, and exclusion. And Doron Mendels, from Jerusalem, stated that in ancient times, pagans did not hate the Jews; on the contrary, it was the Jews who provoked the pagans by their disdainful attitudes.[17]

What connects the new historians to the delegitimization of Israel? In my view, this legitimate process of reconsideration, reevaluation, and correction of so many important aspects and events of Jewish history, together with the repeated charges of exploitation and conscious distortion that the new historians leveled against the Zionist establishment and official history, has gradually led to a global and total reappraisal that calls into question the whole history of the Jewish people and, in fact, its very existence. Of course, this dramatic development was not what the Israeli new historians had intended, but it presents an excellent example of semantic shift by widening.

The new historians had confined their criticism to the erroneous instrumentalization of specific episodes in the history of the Jewish people, because they thought that a country, forty years after its birth, could look seriously into its past and eliminate unnecessary distortions based on ideological bias. They thought that such a reconsideration would be helpful and would not endanger the state of Israel. Obviously, a serious scholar like Morris did not intend to call into question the whole of Jewish history and the existence of the Jewish people!

But then some intellectuals, writers, journalists, and academics began to appropriate the views of the new historians and take them in extreme directions.[18] They started to use the term *invention* to describe the Jewish people. In their view, not only had

Jewish history been altered and distorted, but all of Jewish history was a fabrication, even to the extent that the Jewish people do not exist. If such charges were credible, the Zionist narrative and the arguments for Israel's right to exist would collapse like a house of cards. Yet there is a certain resemblance between the intellectually honest work of the new historians and Tel Aviv professor Shlomo Sand's best-selling trilogy, *The Invention of the Jewish People*, *The Invention of the Land of Israel*, and *How I Stopped Being a Jew*—certainly a turning point in what can be called intellectual anti-Zionism.[19] Sand's books, especially the first one, on the invention of the Jewish people by modern Jewish nationalists and Zionists, became best-sellers, especially in Europe (and particularly in France), among leading academics who are now on the side of delegitimization and the Boycott, Divestment, Sanctions movement. Sand received a major French literary prize in 2009, the Prix Aujourd'hui. For many of these European intellectuals, the theory that the Jewish people is a pure invention is quite comforting, because if the Jewish people do not exist, then antisemitism must not exist. Can there be hatred and persecution of a people that does not exist? These extreme revisionist views have taken hold particularly in France, where many people would like to forget the shameful period of the Vichy regime.[20]

THE HISTORY OF ZIONISM

A similar contention was raised about the history of Zionism, as the new historians contested the Zionist central figure of the "male Ashkenazi socialist pioneer." For instance, they reevaluated the hidden role of women in the pioneer movement and exploded the myth of equality between male and female pioneers in what had been an essentially "macho" movement.[21] The same reappraisal was made of the hidden role of Oriental Jews in the history of the country and the cruel discrimination in the kibbutzim against Yemeni Jews, for example.[22] And what of the pioneer himself? Was he really a socialist, a manual worker, a simple, austere man who hated violence and took up arms only in self-defense against Arab terrorist gangs? In the writings of the Israeli new historians and sociologists, there is evidence leading to the conclusion that the pioneer movement had nationalist or militarist features and that the fathers of socialist Zionism, as Professor Zeev Sternhell of the Hebrew University asserts, were in fact nationalist and not at all socialist.[23] Or, as Uri ben Eliezer of the University of Tel Aviv states, far from being immune from militarism, the Jews in prestate Palestine, particularly the sabras, were fascinated by military force and weapons, and their community ethos typically was not a defensive but an offensive one.[24]

Here again, on the basis of the new historians' claims, and by a process of semantic widening, Zionism as a whole came to be defined as a militaristic, racist, and colonialist ideology that warrants total delegitimization.

THE YISHUV DURING THE SHOAH

The third field of inquiry that interested the new historians concerned the attitude of the Yishuv, the Jewish community living in Palestine, during the Shoah. The debate centered mainly on *The Seventh Million*, a book published in 1991 by the *Haaretz* journalist Tom Segev. In Segev's view, Zionists in the Yishuv, who had remained passive and noncommitted during the Shoah, are "the seventh million." The book presented an unflattering image of future Israeli leaders, especially of David Ben-Gurion. The author contended that they did little to help Europe's Jews during the Shoah and mostly tried to use the tragedy to further state interests; after the war, they behaved badly toward the survivors, contrary to what should have been their moral and political duty, and they exploited the memory of the Shoah for the benefit of the state. According to Segev, many more Jews could have been saved if Zionist leaders had been more militant—for instance, if the Yishuv political press had given greater coverage to the catastrophe. He asserts that the pogrom of November 1938 was the moment when emotions and solidarity in the Yishuv reached their highest pitch, but that after 1938 the matter was given less and less space in the Yishuv media and public life (see, for example, the famous photographs of the crowds enjoying Tel Aviv beaches in 1942). Worse, he says, some Zionist leaders saw Nazism as useful to Zionism because it could be a catalyst for massive Jewish emigration to Palestine. That is how the author interprets the so-called transfer agreements. Segev was severely critical of the inadequacy of rescue efforts, the poor welcome given to survivors after the war, and the exploitation of the Shoah not only to obtain more war reparations from Germany but also to demonize the Arabs as being "the new Nazis."[25]

All leading Shoah historians—from Yehuda Bauer to Dina Porat, from Dan Michman to Tuvia Friling, from Anita Shapira to Shlomo Aronson, and many others—condemned Segev's book for having significantly distorted the historical reality. An excellent article by Tuvia Frilling, in particular, dismantled Segev's arguments and accused him of substantially contributing to dehumanizing and delegitimizing Zionism.[26] Although Segev defines himself as a staunch Zionist, there is an obvious thread running from *The Seventh Million* to Norman Finkelstein's *The Holocaust Industry,* and perhaps even beyond that, to Shoah deniers, such as the famous French Shoah denier Roger Garaudy, a former Communist Party leader who, in the annex to his negationist book *The Founding Myths of Modern Israel,* quotes verbatim passages from Moshe Zimmerman, a professor of Germanic studies at the Hebrew University and a highly controversial critical historian.[27]

CHANGING PERCEPTIONS OF THE
1948 WAR OF INDEPENDENCE

Most important, the Israeli new historians contributed to changing the perception of the 1948 war of independence, which was unanimously regarded in Israel as a just, clean, and heroic war. They revealed that the massive exodus of Palestinian Arabs during the war had in fact been caused mainly by Jewish violence and Israeli military brutality. Benny Morris, but also Uri Milstein, Uri Bar-Yosef, Avi Shlaim, and others, denied the official history of the Palestinian drama.[28] They accused writers whom they called "mobilized" historians, such as Netanel Lorch, Elhanan Oren, and Meir Pa'il, of having willingly imposed self-censorship in addressing uncomfortable questions raised by the war. They accused them of being biased historians, concerned only with justifying Israel's actions. For example, a crucial point is the rejection by Morris and others of the Israeli claim that the Palestinian Arabs had voluntarily left their homes in 1948 after a radio appeal by their leaders, who asked them to leave the country and then return after all the Jews had been massacred. This radio appeal had been widely accepted as the official Israeli explanation of the Palestinian exodus, claiming that the Israelis had not instigated their departure and therefore bore no responsibility for it. Morris's most important contribution in his book *The Birth of the Palestinian Refugee Problem* was to prove—on the basis of archives—that the story of the Palestinians' voluntary departure was largely false. There had been no radio appeal, and the Palestinian Arabs had left for various reasons, among them acts of brutality designed to spread panic. Far from being clean, Morris said, the 1948 war had been a dirty war on both sides, during which numerous acts of atrocity were committed.

These books were deeply shocking for people of the Palmach generation, those who had fought in the war of independence, because they replaced accounts of the sufferings of the Jews with those of Palestinian Arabs. They replaced a story of Jewish heroism with charges of Jewish brutality that could, metaphorically, and for people with bad intentions, evoke Nazi atrocities. The views of the new historians on a subject as sensitive as the Palestinian exodus were not readily accepted in Israel, and leading Israeli historians contested their assertions. Mordechai Gazit, Shabtai Teveth, Efraim Karsh, Mordechai Bar-On, and Meir Pa'il all vigorously challenged the new historians' narrative of the expulsion of the Arabs. Yet this narrative of forced evacuation is today the main argument used by those who assert that a state that deliberately expelled the indigenous population in order to take its place lacks legitimacy. A great number of Palmach veterans have testified that no one was expelled intentionally and that they saw no Arabs being forced to flee. Shabtai Teveth, Ben-Gurion's biographer, had a ferocious polemic with Benny Morris, as did Elhanan Oren, who said that the order to evacuate the Arabs from Lod and Ramle was given only in response to extreme Arab violence, while Efraim Karsh simply accused the new historians of falsifying the archives.[29]

For the new historians, the Zionist account of the 1948 war was a fabrication, as was the account of the Six-Day War and the occupation of the territories after 1967. One can see how the writings of the new historians, though they cannot be held responsible, were used by anti-Zionists to delegitimize Israel. When Plantu, the cartoonist of *Le Monde*, the major French daily, published a front-page drawing of a Nazi soldier with a swastika pointing a weapon at the back of a Jew who is pointing a weapon at the back of an Arab, he was promoting the view that both soldiers represent exactly the same kind of violence. The semantic shift, by means of widening and metaphorizing, from acts of violence to ethnic cleansing and then to Nazism, was thus completed. The anti-Zionist Ilan Pappé wrote the following about the education of his children: "They will do all they can to prevent the Nazi venom from slipping through the veins of its own and ultimate victims, who came and colonized Palestine, uprooted its population and occupied and brutalized many of them."[30] Anti-Zionist writers such as Pappé, Nureldeen Masalha, and Rosemary Esber promoted the use of the term *ethnic cleansing* to describe these events.[31] This semantic shift means three things. First, that these acts of brutality were not sporadic acts, but a total cleaning, a full-blown expulsion. Second, that these acts were part of a pre-meditated Jewish plan to rid Palestine of its inhabitants and take their place. Last, it suggests that it was a racist plan targeting a whole ethnic group.

Another example of this kind of metaphorical semantic shift can be found when criticism—which is perfectly legitimate—of the steps taken to separate Israelis from Palestinians in the oc-cupied territories (bypass roads, the security fence, roadblocks, etc.) uses the term *apartheid* to describe these measures. This qualification and the reference to racial segregation in South Africa under white minority rule lead to an immediate and total delegitimization of Israel.[32]

While the Israeli new historians opened a door through which the anti-Zionists rushed, the importance of their contribution to improving Israeli consciousness should not be forgotten. First, they made people understand that some important voices in Is-raeli history and the history of Zionism had been deliberately si-lenced (in particular, the reevaluation of the role of women in the history of Zionism, and of the diaspora's significant contribution in the face of Zionist early contempt for the *galutic* Jew). Further, they have contributed to a degree of accountability on the part of present-day Israelis with regard to the Palestinian tragedy of 1948, and they have made Israeli citizens aware of the inescap-able need to create a Palestinian state alongside Israel. Also, the most staunchly Zionist among the new historians, such as Benny Morris, have not hesitated to condemn publicly the harmful and biased use that anti-Zionists such as Finkelstein, Masalha, Pappé, or others have made of their writings.

Semantic shift, or semantic change, occurs when disturbing events in a nation's history—and there are disturbing events in every nation's history—are included under a general heading that automatically generates delegitimization, such as the words *eth-nic cleansing, colonialism, apartheid, genocide, racism, Nazism,* and *fascism*. Why? Such terms suggest the following: (1) these acts were part of a systematic policy; (2) they were part of a premeditated plan from the outset; (3) this plan was based on an ideology; and (4) these disturbing events in the nation's history are, as Plantu's cartoon illustrates, similar to perverse acts committed elsewhere in the world. As such, they need to be condemned in exactly the same way as apartheid in South Africa, Rwandan-style genocide, French- or British-style colonialism in Africa, and Nazism. In short, it is precisely such a semantic shift that distinguishes the current discourse of the Israeli Zionist left, the Zionist peace camp, from the discourse of the anti-Zionists and other promoters of the Boycott, Divestment, Sanctions movement.

Although this was not their intention, the Israeli new historians framed a way of thinking that led anti-Zionists to question the very existence of the Jewish people and of Israel. In this sense, it might be said that anti-Zionists performed a semantic shift, appropriating the work of the new historians as the historical and intellectual ground for delegitimization.

NOTES

1. Aharon Megged, "The Suicidal Instinct of Israel" [in Hebrew], *Haaretz*, June 10, 1994.

2. See Megged, "Suicidal Instinct of Israel"; Anita Shapira, "Politics and Collective Memory: The Debate over the New Historians in Israel," *History and Memory* 7, no. 1 (Spring–Summer 1995): 9–40; Dan Michman, "Those Who Destroy Zionism" [in Hebrew], *Meimad* 5 (August–September 1995): 9–40; Rochelle Furstenberg, "Post-Zionism, A New Era on the End of Israel as a Jewish State," presentation at Argov Institute, Bar-Ilan University, Ramat-Gan; Shlomo Simonsohn, "On Historical Research at a Time of Post-History" [in Hebrew], *Gesher* 133 (Summer 1992): 38–42; Mordechai Bar-On, "The Story Which Never Happened: Supplementary Comments on the New History" [in Hebrew], *Yaadut Zmanenu* 10 (1996): 3–40; Mordechai Bar-On, "The Negation of a Negation" [in Hebrew], *Kivunim* 13 (1981): 169–76. The main texts

of the historians controversy were published in Yechiam Weitz, ed., *From Vision to Revision: One Hundred Years of Zionist Historiography* [in Hebrew] (Jerusalem: Zalman Shazar Center, 1997); and in "Zionism: A Controversy of Our Time" [in Hebrew], *Iyunim Betkumat Israel* 6 (special issue).

3. Benny Morris, *The Birth of the Palestinian Refugee Problem 1947–1949* (Cambridge: Cambridge University Press, 1987); Avi Shlaim, *Collusion across the Jordan: King Abdullah, the Zionist Movement and the Partition of Palestine* (Oxford: Oxford University Press, 1988); Simha Flapan, *The Birth of Israel: Myths and Realities* (London: Croom Helm, 1987); Tom Segev, *The Seventh Million: The Israelis and the Holocaust* (New York: Hill and Wang, 1993).

4. Benny Morris, "The New Historiography: Israel Confronts Its Past," *Tikkun* 3, no. 6 (November–December 1988): 19–23; and his answer to Shabtai Teveth: "The Eel and History, A Reply to Shabtai Teveth," *Tikkun* 5, no. 1 (January–February 1990): 19–22.

5. Ben-Zion Dinur, ed., *Sefer Toledot Hahagana* [The book of Harana's history] (Tel Aviv: Defense Ministry, 1955); Zerubavel Gilad, *Sefer HaPalmach* [The Book of Palmach] (Tel Aviv: HaKibbutz Hamehuhad, 1953).

6. Shmuel Noah Eisenstadt was one of the greatest sociologists in modern times, the founder of sociology studies in Israel, and a major figure in Israeli social sciences. His first book on the Jewish state, *Israeli Society* (New York: Basic Books, 1967), described the country as a "heroic, modern, immigrant society," where immigrants were eager to be integrated in the "melting pot." He was accused of emphasizing the Ashkenazic socialist element of Israeli society and showing "despise" toward immigrants from Arab countries, women, and Arabs.

7. For example, see Baruch Kimmerling, "Between the Primordial and the Civil Definitions of the Collective Identity: The State of Israel or Eretz Israel," in *Comparative Social Dynamics: Essays in Honour of Shmuel Eisenstadt*, ed. Erik Cohen, Moshe Lissak, and Uri Almagor (Boulder, CO: Westview Press, 1984), 262–83; Baruch Kimmerling and Joel Migdal, *Palestinians: The Making of a People* (New York: Free Press, 1984); Baruch Kimmerling, "Patterns of Militarism in Israel," *European Journal of Sociology* 2 (1993): 1–28.

8. Itshak Laor, *Narratives with No Natives: Essays in Israeli Literature* [in Hebrew] (Tel Aviv: HaKibbutz Hamehuhad, 1995); Yerah Gover, *Zionism: The Limits of Moral Discourse in Israeli Hebrew Fiction* (Minneapolis:

University of Minnesota Press, 1994); Dan Orian, *The Representation of the Arab in Israeli Theater* [in Hebrew] (Tel Aviv: Or-Am, 1996).

9. On theoretical aspects of semantic shift, or semantic change, see Andreas Blank, "Why Do New Meanings Occur? A Cognitive Typology of the Motivations for Lexical Semantic Change," in *Historical Semantics and Cognition,* ed. Andreas Blank and Peter Koch (Berlin: Mouton de Gruyter, 1999), 61–90.

10. Israeli governments regularly refused to include in schoolbooks the stories of other genocides, probably for fear that it would minimize the centrality of the Shoah and to preserve good relations with Turkey. In November 1993, a major initiative was launched by Professor Yair Oron (Open University) to teach the genocide of the Armenians. But in January 1995, the Education Ministry canceled any attempt to include in schoolbooks teachings on genocides in the twentieth century. Since then, the idea of teaching other genocides in Israeli schools has regularly been thwarted.

11. Gili Cohen, "IDF Deputy Chief Yair Golan Has History of Outspokenness, Bold Action," *Haaretz,* May 5, 2016.

12. Cohen, "IDF Deputy Chief Yair Golan."

13. For a critical view on Ben-Zion Dinur's work, see Uri Ram, "Zionist Historiography and the Invention of Modern Jewish Nationhood: The Case of Ben Zion Dinur," *History and Memory* 7, no. 1 (Spring–Summer 1995): 91–124. On Dinur, see also Jacob Katz, *Jewish Nationalism: Essays and Studies* [in Hebrew] (Jerusalem: Zionist Library, 1979), 230–38; David N. Myers, "History as Ideology: The Case of Ben Zion Dinur, Zionist Historian 'Par Excellence,'" *Modern Judaism* 8, no. 2 (May 1988): 167–93; Efraim Shmueli, "The Jerusalem School of History (A Critical Evaluation)," *Proceedings of the American Academy for Jewish Research* 53 (1986): 147–78.

14. On that subject, see David N. Myers, *Reinventing the Jewish Past: European Jewish Return to History* (New York: Oxford University Press, 1995).

15. Ruth Firer, *The Agents of Zionist Education* [in Hebrew] (Haifa: Haifa University-Oranim, 1985).

16. Yehoshafat Harkaby, "Jeremiah and Bar-Kochba: Reality and Policy," *Jerusalem Quarterly* 24 (Summer 1982): 64–76.

17. Elimelekh Horowitz, *Haaretz,* December 6, 1996; Doron Mendels, *Haaretz,* February 12, 1997.

18. The ways in which writers can be held responsible for the use of their works by people with ulterior motives is an important and eternal question that has no definitive answer. Was Karl Marx responsible for the

use Lenin and Stalin made of his works? In Israel, was Rabbi Avraham Kook, one of the most important Jewish thinkers of the twentieth century who died in 1935, responsible for the subsequent use of his works by the present settlers in the territories? Personally, I think that the writer who dies a long time before the use of his or her works bears no responsibility for how they may come to be used. Some people disagree. On this topic, the French philosopher André Glucksmann has written an excellent book, *The Master Thinkers* (New York: Harper and Row, 1980), in which he maintains that European philosophy, and in particular German idealism, spawned the modern totalitarian state and that the corruption of philosophy has led to the debasement of the intellectual.

19. Shlomo Sand, *The Invention of the Jewish People* (London: Verso, 2009); Shlomo Sand, *The Invention of the Land of Israel* (London: Verso, 2012); Schlomo Sand, *How I Stopped Being a Jew* (London: Verso, 2014).

20. The controversy that took place in France around Sand's first book is well analyzed in Pierre Assouline, "*Comment le livre de Shlomo Sand fut accueilli*" [How Sand's book was received], *Le Monde, Le Monde des Livres*, February 11, 2010; and "Autour de comment le peuple juif fut inventé de Shlomo Sand," *Le débat*, no. 158 (January–February 2010): 146–92.

21. See Hana Herzog, "Women's Organizations: A Forgotten Chapter of the Historiography of the Yichuv" [in Hebrew], *Cathedra* 69 (January 1994), 111–33; Margalit Shilo, "The Transformation of the Role of Women in the First Aliyah," *Jewish Social Studies* 2, no. 2 (Winter 1996): 64–86.

22. Yehoudah Nini, *Did It Happen, or Was It a Dream? The Yemenites of Kinneret, Their Settling and Their Departure, 1912–1930* [in Hebrew] (Tel Aviv: Am Oved, 1996).

23. Zeev Sternhell, *The Founding Myths of Israel: Nationalism, Socialism, and the Making of the Jewish State* (Princeton, NJ: Princeton University Press, 1999); and the harsh criticism of Sternhell's book by Anita Shapira, "The Complaint of Sternhell" [in Hebrew], *Iyunim Betkumat Israel* 6 (1996): 553–67.

24. Uri Ben Eliezer, *The Making of Israeli Militarism* (Bloomington: Indiana University Press, 1998).

25. Segev serves anti-Zionist propaganda when he asserts that the Zionist establishment, instead of assisting the Jewish people in times of dire need, behaves according to its own interests. The main thesis of Segev's book is that, far from doing everything it might have done to save the Jewish people during the Shoah, the Zionist establishment was generally indifferent and only interested in the promotion of *aliyah* and other Zionist aims. This argument has been fiercely criticized.

26. Tuvia Frilling, "Tom Segev's Seventh Million, Madness and Naughtiness of the Zionist Movement" [in Hebrew], *Iyunim Betkumat Israel* 2 (1992): 317–67.

27. Roger Garaudy, *Les mythes fondateurs de la politique israélienne* [The founding myths of Israel politics] (Paris: La Vieille Taupe, 1995). Garaudy was condemned by a French court in 1998 for "incitation to racial hate." Professor Moshe Zimmerman, extensively quoted by Garaudy, is the foremost Israeli expert in German modern history at the Hebrew University and a very critical opponent of Israeli policies in the Palestinian territories.

28. For an encompassing study of the controversy concerning the war of 1948, see Yossi ben Artsi, "On the Historiography of the War of Independence" [in Hebrew], *Cathedra* 65 (September 1992): 159–67; and the point of view of leading new historian Avi Shlaim, "The Debate about 1948," *International Journal of Middle East Studies* 27 (August 1995): 287–304. For the opposite perspective, read Mordechai Bar-On, "A Second Look Back: Revisionism in the Historiography of the 1948 War and the Beginnings of the State" [in Hebrew], *Yaadut Zmanenu* 6 (1990): 67–117.

29. Against the theses of the new historians, see Abraham Sela, "Transjordan, Israel and the 1948 War: Myth, Historiography, and Reality," *Middle Eastern Studies* 28, no. 4 (1992): 623–58; Efraim Karsch, *Fabricating Israeli History: The New Historians* (London: Frank Cass, 1997); Shabtai Teveth, "Charging Israel with Original Sin," *Commentary* 88, no. 3 (September 1989): 24–33.

30. Response to the article of Benny Morris, "Politics by Other Means," which had been published on March 3, 2004, in the *New Republic*. This article by Morris was a review of Pappé's book *History of Modern Palestine: One Land, Two Peoples* (Cambridge: Cambridge University Press, 2003). Pappé sent his response to the *New Republic*, which refused to publish it, so it appears on the web page *The Electronic Intifada*, March 30, 2004.

31. Ilan Pappé, *The Ethnic Cleansing of Palestine* (London: Oneworld, 2006); Nureldeen Masalha, *Expulsion of the Palestinians: The Concept of Transfer in Zionist Political Thought 1882–1948* (London: I. B. Tauris, 1994); Rosemary Esber, *Under the Cover of War: The Expulsion of the Palestinians* (Alexandria, VA: Arabicus Books and Media, 2008).

32. The use of the word *apartheid* has become a major instrument of anti-Zionism. It probably began in 1961, when the South African prime minister and architect of South Africa's apartheid policies, Hendrik Verwoerd, dismissed an Israeli vote against South African apartheid at the United Nations, saying, "Israel is not consistent in its new anti-apartheid

attitude . . . they took Israel away from the Arabs after the Arabs lived there for a thousand years. Israel, like South Africa, is an apartheid state." Since then, several sources have increasingly used the apartheid analogy. In 1967, after the Six-Day War, Ben-Gurion himself stated that, "unless Israel managed to 'rid itself of the territories as soon as possible,' it would become an apartheid state." In the early 1970s, Palestinian terrorist organizations began to compare the Israeli proposals for a Palestinian autonomy to the Bantustans of South Africa. In 1979, the Palestinian sociologist Elia Zureik argued that, while not de jure an apartheid state, Israeli society was characterized by a "latent form of apartheid." The analogy emerged with increasing frequency in academic writings in the 1980s and 1990s, when some Israeli left-wing intellectuals and new historians began to use this word to describe Israel's treatment of the Palestinians. In the 1990s, the analogy gained prominence after Israel, as a result of the Oslo Accords, granted the Palestinians limited self-government and established a system of permits and checkpoints. The analogy has gained additional strength in anti-Israeli and anti-Zionist circles following Israel's construction of the West Bank fence, and it is now a central theme of the campaign against Israel.

ILAN GREILSAMMER is Professor of Political Science at Bar-Ilan University, Israel. His main fields of research and teaching are European politics and the Israeli party system. He has published extensively on French politics, including a biography of Prime Minister Leon Blum, and on Israeli political parties. He is author of *La nouvelle histoire d'Israël: Essai sur une identité nationale*.

—w—

Christian BDS

An Act of Love?

GIOVANNI MATTEO QUER

THE CALL TO boycott, divest from, and sanction Israel has increasingly been heard in the Christian world among both Protestants and Catholics. A growing number of Christian churches and organizations are adopting initiatives of the Boycott, Divestment, Sanctions (BDS) movement, which include divestment from specific corporations that are active in the post-1967 territories. BDS's annual conferences debate the definition of Israel as an apartheid state and engage in theological disquisitions on the legitimacy of Zionism. These initiatives are usually advanced by groups of activists who promote a peculiar theological-political vision of the Arab-Israeli conflict rooted in what is known as Palestinian Liberation Theology (PLT).

Developed in the late 1990s, PLT has contextualized liberation theologies in the Arab-Israeli conflict to provide theological support for the Palestinian cause. In presenting theological interpretations of the conflict, PLT builds on liberation theologies' main concepts of power, oppression, justice, and struggle by fostering novel interpretations of the Bible "through Palestinian eyes."[1] Specifically, PLT has developed its own theological-political manifesto, the Kairos Document, adopted in 2009, which defines BDS as a form of nonviolent struggle against the Zionist occupation. The Kairos Document has been adopted by several

Christian organizations and is promoted by advocacy groups in many churches. As part of the political agenda outlined in the document, BDS initiatives aim to represent a genuine Christian response to what is seen as the injustice of Israeli occupation and continuous oppression of the Palestinians. Theologically, the BDS movement is defined as an "act of love": Christians are called to confront injustice by respecting the commandment to "love thy enemy," thereby refusing violence in the struggle for liberation. Rooted in PLT, the Christian BDS movement sanctions a specific theological-political interpretation of the conflict that promotes the delegitimization of Israel and perpetuates anti-Judaic visions that have long been part of the Christian world.

By facing the reality of a Jewish state grounded in Jewish history and biblical references, PLT endeavors to resignify the Bible in Palestinian terms. In this respect, PLT revives Christian replacement theology, which for centuries has considered Judaism an obsolete religion superseded by the new Covenant between God and the Christians. In a similar fashion, PLT replaces Jews with Palestinians, stripping the Bible of its Jewish meanings. In the attempt to read the Bible through Palestinian eyes, PLT authors criticize Zionism by elaborating theological arguments that sometimes seem to reproduce ancient Christian anti-Judaic principles.

This essay analyzes the theological support for BDS in the Christian world to assess the extent to which this conceptualization of Israel, Zionism, and the Israeli-Palestinian conflict contributes to the delegitimization of Israel.

LIBERATION THEOLOGY

Liberation theologies developed in the 1960s as a Christian response to the rapidly growing importance of civil rights, equality, and social justice in the political consciousness of Western countries. Such ideas were not foreign to Christian tradition and found sound expression in the Catholic social movement of the late nineteenth century and the Protestant social gospel of the early twentieth century. Yet a thorough theological exegesis came only some years later when, in an effort to interpret the scriptures in line with new philosophical ideas, Christian theologians began developing a Christian discourse on human rights and equality.

A first elaboration of themes that are central to liberation theologies evolved in the work of Protestant theologians Karl Barth and Reinhold Niebuhr, who were among those who conceptualized the idea of God standing with the poor and the oppressed. In his monumental work *Church Dogmatics*, the Swiss theologian Karl Barth theorizes the nature of God as intrinsically connected to the idea of justice, which means that God "stands" with the powerless and the poor.[2] Reinhold Niebuhr, an American pastor involved in several social battles, also theorized a divine "bias in favor of the poor."[3] It is, however, only after the papal encyclical *Nostra Aetate* that liberation theology surfaced as a new, widespread drift in Christian thought.

By opening up to modern ideas of pluralism and equality, the Catholic Church paved the way for the groundbreaking work of South American theologians Gustavo Gutierrez and Leonardo Boff. In his *Theology of Liberation*, Gutierrez theorizes God's "preferential love for the poor," explaining that inherent in Christian teaching is the utmost concern for the poor, defined as victims of economic, political, and social structures of injustice.[4] Furthermore, Gutierrez explains the need to historicize theological thought in order to empower the poor for changing those structures that victimize them. In a similar fashion, the Brazilian theologian Leonardo Boff has elaborated a liberation theology centered on the figure of Christ, who becomes the liberator of the poor and the leader of mass struggle against injustice.[5]

Liberation theologians show a positive inclination toward Marxism and combine some of the basic Marxist tenets with Christian thought, such as structural analysis of oppression and poverty, which leads to often-apodictic criticism of power structures and ruling elites, and convergence of analysis with praxis, which leads to the urge for revolution. These Marxist tendencies, including the ideological assumptions such as class struggle and structures as well as the ability to mobilize masses to fight the oppressing elite, and even to stir people's hearts against the hierarchy of the church, have been the object of harsh criticism.

Joseph Ratzinger, at the time prefect of the Congregation for the Doctrine of the Faith, expressed his concerns in the "Instruction on Certain Aspects of the 'Theology of Liberation'" on August 6, 1984.[6] In this document, Ratzinger points out that one cannot "localize evil principally or uniquely in bad social, political, or economic 'structures' as though all other evils came from them so that the creation of the 'new man' would depend on the establishment of different economic and socio-political structures."[7] Furthermore, the document criticizes the integration of the Marxist notion of class struggle as a necessary law of history, which subordinates the individual to the communal. Specifically, Ratzinger denounces the "disastrous confusion between the 'poor' of the Scripture and the 'proletariat' of Marx," whereby liberation theologians "pervert the Christian meaning of the poor, and they transform the fight for the rights of the poor into a class fight within the ideological perspective of the class struggle," because "for them the 'Church of the poor' signifies the Church of the class which has become aware of the requirements of the revolutionary struggle as a step toward liberation and which celebrates this liberation in its liturgy."[8]

Yet liberation theologies have thrived in both the Catholic and Protestant worlds, differently identifying in the "poor" the modern "marginalized," the object of social, economic, political, racial, and cultural oppression. Theologians such as James Hal Cone, Allan Boesak, and Robert Beckford have developed a theological interpretation of racial struggle for black liberation in America, South Africa, and the United Kingdom, respectively. Similarly, Arvind P. Nirmal has developed a Dalit theology dedicated to the liberation of the outcasts in India.[9] As part of this trend, Palestinian theologians have developed a contextualized theology committed to the Palestinian cause.

The political message of liberation theologies first found expression in the South African Kairos Document, a political-theological manifesto that historicizes the theological message of God's love for the oppressed and sets forth an agenda for the mobilization of the Christian masses. This document defines certain principles that are instrumental to organized Christian social action and have subsequently been used by Palestinian Christian movements. Such principles include the denunciation of both "state theology" and "church theology," opposition to injustice as a Christian duty to resist evil, and the role of violence and nonviolence in resistance struggles. The document denounces state theology as the political use of the Bible by ruling elites to justify oppression (point 2.4) as well as the apathy of the church in developing an empowering theology for the oppressed masses (chapter 3). According to the document, there is a Christian duty to oppose injustice (point 3.1) and to participate in struggles for liberation, including boycotts (point 5.1). Finally, the document differentiates between violence used as an instrument for oppressing the masses, which is condemned by the Bible, and violence used as a means for resistance against an oppressor, which is permitted as long as the oppressed has no other choice (point 3.3). In this sense, the document also challenges the theological stance on nonviolence as an absolute principle, because it would disempower the oppressed in the battle for liberation.

PALESTINIAN LIBERATION THEOLOGY:
LAND AND JUSTICE

Palestinian Liberation Theology has evolved as a result of the theological application of these principles to the Arab-Israeli conflict. In the first comprehensive work that laid the foundations of

PLT, *Justice and Only Justice—A Palestinian Theology of Liberation*, Naim Stifan Ateek formulates a political agenda for the church in Palestine that aims to give Christians theological instruments for political activism against the Zionist project. Pointing to the absence of the church in Palestinian political struggles in the aftermath of the establishment of the Jewish state, the author intends to address the quest of young Christians for an identity-based agenda.[10]

His primary concern is the support of the Christian world for Israel, encapsulated in two positions that he seeks to confute: the continuity between biblical Israel and the modern state of Israel, and the validity of an explicitly Jewish narrative in the Bible. Denouncing Christian Zionism as naive and fundamentalist, Ateek criticizes Christian support for Israel as a misreading of the Bible and history. The author draws a distinction between biblical Israel and the modern state of Israel, whose population is made up of mostly "strangers," and he suggests that Christian support for Zionism may sanction the idea of a tribal God, on which nationalist readings of the Bible rely.[11]

A Christian political agenda for the Palestinian cause faces one primary obstacle: a Jewish Bible and a Jewish reality on the ground. Although Zionism was conceived as a secular movement, it is rooted in Jewish history, which is intrinsically connected to the Jewish Bible. The reality on the ground also confirms the Jewish biblical narrative, increasingly important after the 1967 Six-Day War and the evolution of religious Zionism as a social and political force in Israeli society. In an attempt to offer a Palestinian alternative to the Jewish narrative, Palestinian Liberation Theology construes Zionism as the result of a narrow, sectarian vision of God in opposition to the universalist message of Christianity.

By addressing questions that are central to the Palestinian cause, such as the claim to the land and the plea for justice, PLT seeks to void the biblical narrative of its Jewish significance in order to debunk Israeli claims. In this respect, the question of the land acquires a central meaning in the theological-political discussion of the conflict, not only because it lies at the heart of Israel's foundation and of the dispute between Israelis and Palestinians but also because it becomes the first step to a theological reflection on the conflict, which defines Christian perspectives on Israel and Zionism.[12] For instance, the recent disputes on the Jewish character of Jerusalem and Hebron, denied by UNESCO decisions that refer to these cities as primarily Arab-Muslim, have resounded in certain PLT activists' declarations.[13] The Jerusalem-based Sabeel Center, a PLT Christian advocacy institution, in two issues of its weekly political-liturgical publication *Wave of Prayer*, praised both resolutions. The May 11, 2017, issue affirms the first Christian, then Muslim, and last Jewish identity of Jerusalem and recalls that international actions such as UNESCO's will "bring to an end the evil military occupation."[14] The July 13, 2017, issue condemns Israel's opposition to the UNESCO Hebron decision and reasserts a general importance for "all Abrahamic religions" of the holy sites—the statement prefers using the Islamic formulation Al-Ibrahimi Mosque first and Cave of the Patriarchs in a second position.[15]

Following the recent clashes in the Temple Mount due to terrorist attacks and the subsequent decision to install security devices to control worshipers accessing the site, PLT activists have expressed solidarity with the Palestinian predicament and struggle. The controversies over the Temple Mount also involve widespread propaganda against Israel and security forces blamed for desecrating the holy site, plotting to destroy the al-Aqsa Mosque, and changing the status quo that recognizes Muslim-Jordanian rule over the site.[16] The "Sabeel Wave of Prayer" of July 27, 2017, denies Palestinian violence and accuses Israel of enacting policies of injustice.[17] Christian leaders of the National Coalition of Christian Organizations in Palestine, led by Sabeel and Kairos Palestine (both PLT organizations), manifested in July 27, 2017, in solidarity with the al-Aqsa struggle. PLT Lutheran activist Mitri Raheb defined this manifestation as an expression of "Christian-Muslim unity as a tool of creative resistance."[18] As an expression of the PLT political agenda, these political statements endorse the Palestinian national narrative on the land and its sites in the attempt to incorporate a Christian religious perspective.

The Zionist narrative and Western support for Israel have encouraged Jewish claims to the land based also on biblical references that justify Jewish statehood and the historical mission of a Jewish national state. This political, historical, and ideological vision would jeopardize the notion of divinity and the meaning of the scripture; in Ateek's words: "God's character is at stake. God's integrity has been questioned."[19]

By sanctioning Jewish claims to the land based on a biblical narrative that considers the land of Israel the Jewish homeland, Zionists and their Christian champions are guilty of perpetuating "the old, more pervasive idea of God's exclusiveness, which involved a special and unique relationship to Israel."[20] This notion has been superseded by an inclusive, universalist God of the New Testament in line with the prophetic tradition of the Bible.[21] Therefore, Zionism represents "a retrogression of the Jewish community into the history of its very distant past, with its most elementary and primitive forms of the concept of God," which lays the foundation of Jewish nationalism.[22]

The theological dispute over the land is pivotal to the second issue that constitutes the core of Palestinian Liberation Theology: the question of justice.[23] The creation of Israel and the consolidation of the Zionist project are considered to be at the heart of the continuing injustice suffered by the Palestinian people. Israel's internal policies, oriented to affirming the Jewish nature of the state, and its external policies, dictated by security concerns or by its military presence in the West Bank, are regarded as the incarnation of oppression that liberation theologians decry and against which they fight.

The idea of justice is intrinsically associated with the prophetic notion of righteousness, explained as the universalist tradition of the biblical message that transcends the boundaries of Jewish religious identity. Hence, righteousness requires theological opposition to Jewish national identity, embodied in Zionism, and Israel and its policies, which are worldly manifestations of a political project that per se contradicts essential Jewish values. Indeed, "ethical Judaism, with its universalist look, has been swamped by the resurgence of a racially exclusive concept of a people and their god."[24]

Accusations of the obsolescence of Judaism are an underlying element of religious and political forms of anti-Judaism and antisemitism. Since the times of early Christianity, the advent of Jesus as the Messiah has led to theological abolition of Judaism as a no-longer-valid religion, which did not recognize the Messiah in Christ and kept the ancient law. Hence, supersessionist theology has developed, spreading the belief that the Christian community has replaced Israel and its covenant with God. Furthermore, this view of Jews as an antiquated religious group stubbornly clinging to outmoded laws and traditions manifested itself in modern political antisemitism, which considered Jews unfit for modern life. The Hegelian thinker Bruno Bauer clearly stated that what made Jews incapable of integrating into German society was their sterile law, whose anachronistic views aimed to separate Jews from the rest of the German people and perpetuate traditions that rendered the Jewish people unfit for living in a modern society.[25] While analyzing Jewish "primitive traits," Bauer underlines that sectarianism is also an aspect that Christianity has modified by liberating people from a narrow form of tribal belonging and reconnecting man to his natural, familiar, national circles through an inclusive sense of belonging. In this sense, Jewish "tribalism" is considered a primitive religious stage that Christianity has modified and overcome.[26]

While not taking a stance on Judaism in general, Naim Ateek and other PLT authors consistently refer to Zionism by developing a theology that denies Jewish nationhood and, consequently, Jewish national claims. Yet this theological interpretation of the Arab-Israeli conflict seems to resuscitate the traditional view of Judaism as an obsolete religion epitomized by replacement theological thought and a Jewish proclivity to apartness entrenched in unprogressive conceptions of God. Zionism would then be reduced to a nationalist movement that draws on benighted religious beliefs that are not only superannuated by the universalist Christian message but also bear the primary responsibility of Palestinian suffering and of the whole Arab-Israeli conflict. Thus, Zionism enacts a matrix of oppression that is justified religiously by its adherents and supported by Christians through mistaken and ungodly interpretations of the scriptures. Therefore, only a nationless Judaism is theologically acceptable and politically admissible. As Robert Wistrich has stated, "This is especially true for those Christians whose vision of Zion has remained purely spiritual, ethereal, and disembodied. For them, Israel betrayed its mission from the moment it abandoned its role as a model victim or exemplary sacrifice. Only a poor, powerless, disinherited 'nation' such as the Palestinian Arabs could be permitted to collectively represent the vision of the Christian savior." Zionist betrayal of the scriptures and regression to a primitive, nationalist God in opposition to the prophets' inclusive animating principles "revive the anti-Semitism of traditional Christian replacement theology, negating the legitimacy of an independent Jewish political existence in Zion."[27]

In this political-theological frame, the Zionist project is the source of injustice, constituted by the establishment of the state of Israel and the occupation, which persistently batters Palestinian freedom in the name of twisted religious beliefs. As a consequence, Christians are called on to face injustice and stand up against oppression in ways that respect the tradition of nonviolence set out in the New Testament.[28] In the beginning, the political action of Christian activists was oriented to the de-Zionization of the Bible, opposing Christian support for Zionism, condemning the settlements, and encouraging Christian-Muslim dialogue. In 2009, Palestinian Christians began organized political action as defined in the Kairos Document.[29]

KAIROS PALESTINE: BDS AS AN ACT OF LOVE

The Kairos Document was drafted in 2009 by an interdenominational group of Christian Palestinians who condensed the main tenets of PLT and called for the boycott of Israel as a form of Christian struggle against the occupation. This political-theological manifesto builds on liberation theology's main concepts and draws on the political action formulated in the 1985 South Africa Kairos Document. In the years following the launch of the document, Kairos Palestine has created a worldwide movement that reunites groups of oppressed people who have formulated a political agenda based on Christian theological principles.

The Kairos Document is the result of previous efforts to mobilize international Christian organizations to champion the Palestinian cause. It was preceded by the 2007 Amman Call and the 2008 Bern Perspective documents. Adopted in 2007 during the world conference "Churches Together for Peace and Justice in the Middle East," which was organized by the interdenominational Christian organization World Council of Churches, the Amman Call embraces many political stances later incorporated into the Kairos Document that define the theological-political views of the Arab-Israeli conflict.[30] By using a language typical of liberation theologies, including an emphasis on the dispossessed and the refugee, who exemplify the theological "oppressed," the Amman Call urges people to "pray and work" to put an end to the occupation.

The following year, on the occasion of a conference co-organized by the Palestine-Israel Ecumenical Forum and the World Council of Churches, the Bern Perspective was adopted. This document focuses on the theological implications of the conflict and, specifically, on the role played by the Bible. It appeals to the faithful to "acknowledge the context of our interpretations and to recognize distinctions between biblical history and biblical story as well as distinctions between the Israel of the Bible and the modern State of Israel. In these distinctions, we are challenged to comprehend the philosophical underpinnings of our interpretations and their ethical implications."[31] Refusing to acknowledge modern Jews as the descendants of biblical Israel equates to denying Jewish historical continuity as a national, cultural, and religious group through the centuries. Depicting diaspora Jews as a religious group that has no connection to the national group described in Bible is an intellectual operation that aims to negate modern Jewish national consciousness, its national aspirations, and claims to Jewish statehood. This point, repeated by the Kairos Document and by the Christian organizations that adopted it, is central to the political action against Israel, since it refutes Zionism as the political project of a national people.

The denial of Jewish statehood is theologically elaborated by rejecting the historical continuity of Jewish national consciousness to show that Zionism is "stuck in the Bible," and, therefore, its claims to the land have no legitimacy. This theological-political stance has several ramifications, including the call to resist the occupation, and the definition of Zionist oppression as a sin.

Israel's policies in the post-1967 territories are considered the result of distorted biblical interpretation and, therefore, a sin. As the Kairos Document states, "the military occupation of our land is a sin against God and humanity because it deprives the Palestinians of their basic human rights, bestowed by God. It distorts the image of God in the Israeli who has become an occupier just as it distorts this image in the Palestinian living under occupation."[32] In this view, the Zionist sin is represented by Israel's military and civilian presence in the post-1967 territories, which constitutes an "evil and a sin that must be resisted and removed."[33] Resistance to evil is formulated as "a right and a duty" for all

Christians, which must, however, respect the commandment to love thy enemy, involving the respect for the other's humanity and refusal of violence in order to "correct the evil and stop the aggression."[34]

Consequently, "resistance to the evil of occupation is integrated, then, within this Christian love that refuses evil and corrects it. It resists evil in all its forms with methods that enter into the logic of love and draw on all energies to make peace. We can resist through civil disobedience."[35] As a form of "peaceful resistance," the document calls for the boycott of "everything produced by the occupation," since boycott and divestment are "tools of nonviolence for justice, peace and security for all," "a system of economic sanctions," which the international community is urged to apply against Israel.[36]

Hence, BDS becomes an act of love, a form of Christian resistance against the evil, which fulfills Christian duty and mission to correct injustice and witness the message of God. Christians are invested with a prophetic mission to resist injustice and act for the restoration of justice. The BDS movement would be a means for fulfilling this prophetic goal through "purification" of political regimes that enact injustice, and through support of the oppressed and resistance against the oppressor.[37]

The BDS call has evolved in theological reflections and agendas for political action further elaborated in the context of the Global Kairos Network, an international Christian movement that promotes the Kairos agenda. Global Kairos has grown as a result of the 2010 Kairos Palestine Conference, which gathered delegates of several Christian churches and organizations to further the boycott agenda.

BDS AS CREATIVE RESISTANCE AGAINST THE EMPIRE

The Christian discourse on BDS has evolved theological-political reflections on land, justice, and resistance in the context of the

Arab-Israeli conflict. The argument of false claims to the land developed by a misconstrued conception of God and distorted reading of the scriptures entails a novel reading of the Bible that justifies and encourages opposition to Zionism.

Besides the Christian duty to resist evil, Christian BDS discourse defines Zionism as a form of empire that Jesus commanded people to oppose. Jesus becomes a source of inspiration for resistance against foreign occupation and ruling elites, a leader of the oppressed whose message conforms to the prophetic tradition of justice and who will lead Palestinians to liberation. The definition of Zionism as a form of empire builds on theological arguments that associate the Jewish state with colonialism, neoimperialism, and racism, which are Western manifestations of oppressive power relying on false interpretations of the Bible.

In the attempt to redefine the theological duty to resist, Jesus is portrayed as a leader of the oppressed whose message incites the faithful to resist power in order to establish justice. The call to resist is entrenched in biblical references, and its contextualization in the contemporary Middle East leads to a modernized version of theological replacement.[38]

Portrayed as a resistant, Jesus becomes a Palestinian who fights against the occupation and Zionist ideology, just as he opposed Roman rule and Pharisee elites. While modern Israel becomes the Roman Empire and biblical Israel becomes the Palestinian people, the theological elaboration of BDS attacks the core of Israel's existence as a misfortune of history, for which Western powers are to be blamed. It is all a result of the perversion of the scriptures entrenched in Zionism's primitive conception of God.

In this sense, the delegitimization of Israel's existence and the theological replacement of Jews with Palestinians intertwine in the Christian BDS discourse, which aims to mobilize Christian masses by developing an eschatological vision of Palestinian liberation. The liberation of Palestine represents not just the goal of the struggle against Israel's oppressive policies but also the liberation of the Bible from what is considered a perverted theology that lies at the core of the Zionist project.

Defined as any form of power that oppresses people, "empire" acquires different shapes, such as the Roman domination in the Middle East, European colonization, America's international policies, and Israel.[39] The situation in Palestine becomes, therefore, the act of an empire that "casts its deathly shadow on every nook and cranny of this planet" through "the empire's cooptation of religious language; its forming a theological language for conquest and occupation; and its ability to build a religious consensus for silence if not outright support for a crusader religious discourse. For many decades now, the occupation has thrived on the perverted militancy and neo-crusader ethos of right-wing Christianity, and on the macabre silence of many of the world's religions."[40] PLT theologians and activists alternatively portray Israel as the last remnant of Western imperialism, a puppet of the United States, or even the scheming maneuver of the United States. The Palestinians then become victims "of the hegemonic grip of the American Empire with Israel constituting an integral and essential strategic partner and extension of it," which through the occupation aims to "get rid of the Palestinian people, both Christians and Muslims and to take their land."[41] Driven by colonial appetite, Israel becomes the worst of the imperialist systems because it created "walls around occupied peoples" and "open air prisons."[42] It can get away with its violations of international law because it is protected by the same US power that it influences through a pro-Israeli lobby.[43] The belief in the existence of a powerful pro-Israeli lobby is sometimes comparable to traditional conceptions of Jews as scheming people who control America to enact their military plans in the region.[44]

Historical references to the Roman Empire are also commonly used to describe the imperialist nature of Israel, which combines the colonialist accusation against the Zionist project with the novel replacement doctrine developed by Palestinian Liberation

Theology. Mitri Raheb, a Lutheran pastor and PLT theologian, has elaborated a political reading of the Middle East through liberationist eyes that portrays Israel as the last of a long chain of empires that for centuries have fought for the domination of Palestine.

Raheb considers the "Israeli- Palestinian conflict" as "an inseparable aspect of European colonial history," identifying a historical pattern of domination of Palestine from the Assyrians to the Romans, from the Crusaders to Israel.[45] According to the author, the numerous foreign dominations affected the identity of the native peoples who never left the land and cultivated a strong connection to it. Raheb means the "native inhabitants throughout history," who changed language, national affiliation, and religion.[46] In his view, Palestinians, "Christians, Muslims, and Palestinian Jews" alike "stand in historical continuity with biblical Israel."[47]

Yet he subsequently denies Jewish nationhood, arguing that European Jews developed an ideal bond to the land of Israel, which was only exploited by the Zionist agenda in order to establish a state with a biblical name in "historical Palestine."[48] This view connects to the underlying assumption that Zionist claims to the land ensue from an exclusivist god of the Old Testament in opposition to the inclusive message of the New Testament, which is clearly defined by Ateek as "an exclusive biblical tribal god who commands the expulsion and destruction of the indigenous people of the land."[49] In this novel interpretation of Palestine as a metahistorical nation and Palestinians as the native people of the land, Jews and Israel find little place in the region as a legitimate political entity despite being backed by the Western Christian world through the "myth of Judeo-Christian tradition," which is "unequivocally part of imperial theology that sees and believes itself as supreme."[50]

In the logic of empires and the oppressed, Raheb exhorts, "We have to connect the Israel of the Bible with the Palestinians because they are our forefathers and we must connect the modern state of Israel with the Empire."[51] The militarist, occupant state of Israel is associated with the Romans of the time of Jesus and with Herod's rule, while the oppressed Jewish people become the Palestinian people.[52] Of special importance is that "Jesus was a Palestinian under imperial rule."[53]

The replacement of Jews with Palestinians in the biblical narrative also implies a new reading of the contemporary Middle East as well as of the figure of Jesus, which ultimately encompasses novel notions of justice and resistance. This new historical-theological frame is well explained by Raheb, who describes Israel as an imperialist regime that controls resources, oppresses people, dispossesses the indigenous population, and forces them into exile just as the Romans and Herod destroyed villages, built infrastructure, subjugated local people, and forced them into exile.[54] The association of the ancient Jewish people forced into exile by the Babylonians with the Palestinians of today exiled by the Israelis epitomizes this pattern of replacing biblical history with the Palestinian narrative.[55]

In an effort to redefine biblical history, PLT theologians elaborate on the figure of Jesus as a model for resistance against imperial oppression. Ched Myers describes the Roman Empire as a regime that strangled local economics and particularly affected fishermen's communities. In his view, Jesus "offered an alternative social vision" by "building his movement among these marginalized workers," like Gandhi and Martin Luther King.[56] The figure of Jesus as leader of the oppressed, typical of liberation theologies, is further developed into the epitome of a revolutionary who stands against hegemonic power and "seeks to transgress social and political borders in the interests of bringing liberation."[57]

The embodiment of resistance in Jesus's message and practice is central to the Christian BDS discourse as part of the replacement narrative. The biblical narrative and Jesus's teachings are interpreted as a liberating message calling to resistance and opposition to power and injustice.[58] In this sense, "the belief in Jesus as the yearned-for Messiah replaced the idea of divine intervention with direct intervention of the faithful. It was now those who believed in Christ who had to step into this world to engage and to bring change to the empire."[59] Resistance is therefore an imperative of Christian action, for "it is not an optional extra for Christians, but is, in fact, the core of our faith and our relationship with God."[60] The ultimate purpose is to restore justice in the name of Christian love, which entails the liberation of both the oppressed and the oppressor.[61] In the context of the Israeli-Palestinian conflict, it acquires the form of opposition to Zionism, discredited as "theology that feasts on death," and to Christian support for Israel, decried as "gospels that feast on death."[62] Jesus's opposition to imperial rule and its collaborators was based on his ability to mobilize the marginalized masses through a message of hope that entailed nonviolent defiance of the ruling elites. "Jesus'[s] agenda of the renewal of the people and his opposition to the rulers" is associated with current forms of Palestinian popular confrontation with Israeli authorities.[63] Such opposition is considered a Christian social response to the injustice of the occupation in line with Jesus's and the prophetic tradition of liberation from oppression. "Resistance becomes an act of faith."[64]

In this logic of replacement, Israel is the Roman usurper that subdued the poor masses of Jews just as the Zionist occupier exploits Palestinians, but "we have been trained to naively connect Israel today with the Israel of the Bible, instead of connecting it to the . . . chain of occupying empires. If we focus on the latter, Jesus' words make perfect sense."[65]

If the duty to resist is in itself Christian, so also are the commandment of love and the refusal of violence, which is a well-established principle in Christian social thought and Christian theology of peace. Hence, the boycott movement is considered a natural response to the Palestinian struggle in that it is portrayed as a form of nonviolent resistance that then responds to the necessary Christian principles of confrontation of evil and love. As the Kairos Document elucidates, "boycott and divestments" are "tools of nonviolence for justice, peace and security for all," which respond to a Christian concept of justice in that they "integrate the logic of peaceful resistance." BDS would then be inherently Christian, because its "object is not revenge but rather to put an end to the existing evil, liberating both the perpetrators and the victims of injustice."[66]

The conceptualization of BDS as a call for Christian action in which hope, faith, and love meet is presented as a form of "loving resistance," or "creative resistance, whose sole goal is the pursuit of justice and the empowerment of the oppressed masses."[67]

The emphasis on love and nonviolence does not exclude, however, ambiguous stances on terrorism and Palestinian armed resistance. The Kairos Document repeatedly affirms the necessity of nonviolent struggle but simultaneously condones armed struggle as a form of resistance that ensues from the occupation; "if there were no occupation, there would be no resistance."[68] On the same issue, the drafters of the document state, "We respect and have high esteem for all those who have given their life for our nation. And we affirm that every citizen must be ready to defend his or her life, freedom and land."[69]

The unclear position on terrorism and Palestinian violence is connected to the figure of Jesus, whose acts of resistance involving physical opposition and words referring to violent struggle are interpreted as a justification for "symbolic violence" in the way to liberation.[70] Similarly, the target of the boycott is also unclear. While the major emphasis is on the occupation as the source of Palestinian suffering, some authors expressly support a total boycott of Israel, since "the occupation . . . is a complete matrix of control. Boycotting Israel, then, signifies boycotting this entire range of injustice."[71]

The use of concepts such as justice, love, hope, and faith in the BDS discourse is integrated in the constant call for churches to actively participate in the endeavor of "creative resistance" to fulfill their prophetic mission.[72] The 2011 international conference titled "Kairos for Global Justice" adopted the Bethlehem Call, which asks churches to adopt BDS to show their support for justice and the Palestinian cause.[73]

CHRISTIAN CHURCHES AND BDS

The boycott of Israel as a means of political action on behalf of justice has spread among Christian organizations as a form of commitment to human rights. The analysis of BDS initiatives in Christian organizations shows a pattern of action that involves activists' engagement in the promotion of PLT principles and BDS. Activists usually operate in solidarity groups within congregations by advancing the Kairos Document, often in connection with interdenominational organizations active in the Arab-Israeli conflict such as the World Council of Churches, the Ecumenical Accompaniment Programme in Palestine and Israel (EAPPI), and the Palestine-Israel Ecumenical Forum (PIEF).

A fundamental difference characterizes the respective attitudes of the Catholic and Protestant worlds toward PLT in general and BDS in particular. Whereas the Catholic Church is hierarchical and no official position has yet been consolidated on theological interpretations of the Arab-Israeli conflict, Protestant churches are independent organizations that consolidate theological stances in congregational policies. This does not mean that the Catholic world is immune to BDS. On the contrary, some Catholic organizations have endorsed the appeal to boycott Israel, such as the Catholic pacifist organization Pax Christi and the Italian Associazione Papa Giovanni XXIII.

Pax Christi International is cofounder of the EAPPI, sponsored by the international interdenominational World Council of Churches, an ecumenical Christian organization engaged in social projects, which organizes tours and volunteer work in Israel

322 ANTI-ZIONISM AND ANTISEMITISM

and in the Palestinian Territories.[74] Pax Christi International also supports the PIEF, an advocacy initiative that promotes the Kairos Document and PLT visions of the Arab-Israeli conflict.[75] By promoting the Kairos Document, these groups also endorse the call to BDS and its theological perspective. Moreover, certain national chapters actively promote boycott initiatives. For example, in Germany, Pax Christi works with the interchurch network Kairos Europa, which is an initiative of Christian denominations in Germany that has an ecumenical aspiration and anti-imperialist ideological basis.[76] Another example is the Associazione Papa Giovanni XXIII, a Catholic organization that is active in the Arab-Israeli conflict and has endorsed the Italian call for BDS together with the initiative Operazione Colomba, a peacemaking program operating in the Arab-Israeli conflict.[77]

In Protestant churches, BDS initiatives and stances are included in congregational policies. Although it is not the purpose of this section to give a complete account of the evolution of PLT principles in Protestant denominations, it is important to note the principal churches that have adopted BDS initiatives as part of theological policies. BDS initiatives are incorporated into discussions on human rights and justice, in which fundamental PLT principles, such as the distinction between biblical Israel and the modern state of Israel and the theological narrative on oppression, play an important role.

The Presbyterian Church of the United States is among the most active denominations in advocating for human rights and world justice. The discussions about divestment from Israel date back to 2003, when the 215th General Assembly adopted the "Resolution on Israel and Palestine: End the Occupation Now." It was at this assembly that the first initiative on divestment and theological backing of the Palestinian narrative were introduced.[78] The resolution marks the beginning of the endorsement of PLT theological perspectives by encouraging participation in pilgrimages and EAPPI visits and "challenging . . . discussion of theological interpretations that confuse biblical prophesies [*sic*] and affirmations of covenant, promise, and land" (section E). While recognizing the continuity of the covenant, including the promise of the land, the resolution confirms the theological arguments of the 1987 document "Toward a Theological Understanding of the Relationship between Christians and Jews," which includes the distinction between biblical Israel and the modern state of Israel that is at the basis of PLT claims. Among the suggested actions, the resolution urges the United States to revise the allocation of the Middle East budget, condemning US aid to Israel that supports the "illegal occupation" (preamble).

In 2004, divestment became an official policy of the Presbyterian Church, while PLT principles made their way into congregational discussions. The 216th General Assembly of the Presbyterian Church adopted a series of resolutions that were precursory to the Christian BDS movement founded by Kairos Palestine. At the same venue, the assembly adopted the "General Assembly Action Resolution on Israel and Palestine: Initiating Divestment and Ending Occupation," which was meant to "support the Geneva Accord."[79] The document mandates that the Committee on Mission Responsibility through Investment should elaborate guidelines for the implementation of "Phased, Selective Divestment Related to Israel and Palestine." According to these guidelines, the mission will engage in dialogue with the selected companies and mobilize shareholders to pressure companies toward a certain policy.[80] The *MRTI Report to 2012 General Assembly: Engagement with Corporations on Israeli-Palestine Issues from 2004 to 2011* was pivotal in identifying companies operating in the post-1967 territories to be divested. It also shows a growing interdenominational network of organizations and churches engaged in advancing divestment initiatives and a connection to the Kairos movement.[81] In subsequent occasions, the General Assembly discussed divestment initiatives advanced by local congregations, as well as political issues, such as the definition of Israel as an apartheid state, with language that reiterates the terms of the Kairos Document.[82] Certain local congregations, such as the Presbytery of Chicago, played a major role in advancing the Christian BDS narrative as well as the Israel-Palestine Mission Network established in 2004.[83]

The US United Methodist Church is also active in BDS initiatives, mainly promoted by the United Methodist Kairos Response, an advocacy group founded in 2010. The divestment policy of the church dates back to 2004, with the adoption of the church's "Opposition to Israeli Settlements in Palestinian Land." The resolution echoes the Presbyterian call of 2004 to end military support of Israel and to divest from companies that benefit from the "occupation."[84] While refraining from addressing theological issues directly, the 2012 publication "Addressing Human Rights—Israel and the Palestinian Territories," the result of a visit to Israel and the Palestinian Territories by a delegation of the Methodist Church and drafted by the investment board of the church, considers divestment *tout court* counterproductive and instead adopts a case-by-case approach considering human rights standards and equal employment opportunities of companies operating in the conflict.[85] However, the activities of the United Methodist Kairos Response show the connection with the Kairos movement, the endorsement of its language, and advocacy for BDS.[86]

The United Church of Canada also backs BDS initiatives endorsing PLT language and supporting the Kairos movement. In 2012, the Working Group on Israel/Palestine Policy published its report, which was adopted by the 41st General Council in the same year. The theological vision of the report is centered on the notion of human dignity, whereby "in the neighbour, through the stranger at our door, by the weakest and most vulnerable among us, we see the face of God," which echoes certain principles of liberation theology.[87] While preferring to focus on international law rather than on theological arguments, the report condemns Israel's policies and praises activities of engagement in the conflict that include BDS. What is interesting is that the Kairos Palestine language has become part of the liturgy, with prayers for ending the occupation.[88]

The United Church of Christ also shows a consistent involvement in the Arab-Israeli conflict. Already in 1999, the church synod adopted a resolution calling on the US government to stop financial aid that would support the settlements.[89] In 2003, the synod adopted a similar resolution, condemning Israel's defense policies. Later, in 2013, the synod adopted a resolution that endorsed PLT language, associating the Roman Empire with the current Israeli presence in the post-1967 territories, and called for a review of US aid to Israel and divestment initiatives.[90] This resolution also encouraged the endorsement of the Kairos Document. Subsequently in 2015, the synod confirmed BDS policies and expressed concerns about Israel becoming an apartheid state.[91]

These examples show how the Kairos call to Christian BDS has permeated the theology of various churches and denominations through a global network that promotes the boycott of Israel as a Christian response to injustice.

CHRISTIAN BDS: WHAT IS AT STAKE?

The discussion around BDS often focuses on its efficacy and capability of jeopardizing Israel's economic interests. In addition to the economic weight of the BDS, its narrative is pivotal in terms of political and ideological views on Israel, Zionism, and Judaism. In particular, Christian BDS encompasses far-reaching consequences that may affect Jewish-Christian relations.

Christian BDS is rooted in Palestinian Liberation Theology and, as such, is an expression of theological arguments that aim to delegitimize Israel's existence and deny Jewish statehood. The legitimacy of the discussion of the historical developments that brought about the establishment of the state of Israel or of the political movements that initiated the Zionist enterprise are not in question. The BDS controversy raises concerns with respect to its political and, in the case of Christian BDS, theological-political narrative.

Politically, the BDS movement uses arguments based on justice and human rights to portray the establishment of the state of Israel and its policies as a continuous crime that has no precedent in post–World War II history. The attack on Israel's legitimacy is rooted in arguments against nation-states, yet exhibits a contradiction that denies Jewish statehood and, at the same time, supports the Palestinian quest for a state. This view is increasingly accompanied by the denial of Jewish nationhood, for which Judaism would find its ethical dimension in the diaspora only. The resort to a state, which inevitably involves national interests and military power, represents for several detractors of Zionism a betrayal of Jewish ethical principles. On this point, Christian proponents of BDS find a solid basis for developing theological arguments of far-reaching importance.

The establishment of the state of Israel and the Zionist project put an end to the Jewish diaspora as a symbol of ethical disempowerment and found expression in liberationist theological thought as a rupture of Jews' historical role as eternal victims, as the symbol of the oppressed and the repository of God's preferential love. Israel, with its politics and army, has inverted the role of Jews from an oppressed people to the oppressors on the basis of a political movement, Zionism, which is considered imperialist and brutal. The political thrust of Palestinian Liberation Theology is to realign the scripture with current history by equating biblical Israel with the Palestinians, who are now vested with Jews' traditional role of victims. The association of Israel with the Roman Empire and biblical Israel with the Palestinian people feeds a narrative of replacement that implies, first, the extraneousness of Israelis to the region, which supports the argument that Israel is a colonial state, and, second, the role of Palestinians as the indigenous and ultimate victims of imperialist oppression. If Israel represents foreign usurpation, Zionism represents the result of a theological regression of Judaism to a tribal conception of divinity that legitimizes national claims, in opposition to the universalist message of the Prophets and the New Testament.

The emphasis on nonviolent struggle against the occupation as the ultimate injustice is centered on theological arguments that promote the vision of Zionism as a perversion of the Bible. Therefore, the Palestinian cause acquires an eschatological meaning. The Palestinian struggle not only responds to the Christian duty of opposing injustice in order to liberate Palestinians under the Zionist yoke but also pursues the liberation of the scripture from what is perceived as a Zionist misappropriation of the biblical narrative. The liberation of Palestine becomes the liberation of the Bible from a narrow-minded, primitive reading that Zionism offers to justify its oppression of the Palestinians.

These views alarmingly repeat the historical accusations of Jewish particularism and obsoleteness, which have nurtured antisemitic and anti-Judaic sentiment in the Christian world. Therefore, the Christian BDS, presented as a Christian response to injustice, seriously jeopardizes the progress made by interfaith dialogue in revising traditional anti-Judaic conceptions. The same Jewish-Christian dialogue and its accomplishments are considered a result of Zionist influences. As such, the understanding of a common Judeo-Christian tradition is blamed as a Western imperialist theological assault on the Palestinian cause.

Palestinian liberation theology claims to be the sole repository of the true meaning of the Bible, which demands the opposition to injustice and oppression, overall represented by the Pharaoh, the Romans, and Herod. Once the state of Israel becomes the modern Roman Empire or Herod oppressing the modern biblical Israel—that is, the Palestinians—there is little room for discussion of the conflict or of Israeli policies, since Israel has no right to exist as a Jewish state. Indeed, the very notion of Jewish nationhood becomes a myth. Jewish national identity as entrenched in the biblical narrative is denied as the historical continuity of the Jewish nation.

The Christian BDS narrative is increasingly discussed among organizations active in the Arab-Israeli conflict of diverse denominations, and even when officially rejected as a general policy, BDS case-to-case initiatives are endorsed and become part of congregational policies. Under the cover of human rights actions and the struggle for justice, BDS initiatives consolidate Palestinian Liberation Theology's reckoning with Zionism and Israel, imbued with arguments that continue traditional anti-Judaic themes and jeopardize the strenuous efforts of Jewish-Christian dialogue over many years to come to mutual understanding and respect.

Therefore, Christian BDS has profound implications: by integrating Israel's delegitimization with a renewed emphasis on replacement theology in the approach to the Bible, the boycott movement in the Christian world promotes a view of Zionism and Judaism that is overwhelmingly negative and may have protracted harmful consequences on Jewish-Christian relations.

NOTES

1. This expression is often used by Mitri Raheb, a PLT theologian.
2. Karl Barth, *Church Dogmatics*, vol. 2, part 1 (Edinburgh: T and T Clark, 1956), 386.
3. Reinhold Niebuhr, *Pious and Secular America* (New York: Scribners, 1958), 92.
4. Gustavo Gutierrez, *Teología de la Liberación: Perspectivas* (Lima, Peru: CEP, 1971).
5. Leonardo Boff, *Jesus Cristo libertador. Ensaio de cristologia crítica para o nosso tempo* (Petrópolis, Brazil: Vozes, 1972).
6. Joseph Cardinal Ratzinger, "Instruction on Certain Aspects of the 'Theology of Liberation,'" Congregation for the Doctrine of the Faith, August 6, 1984, http://www.vatican.va/roman_curia/congregations/cfaith /documents/rc_con_cfaith_doc_19840806_theology-liberation_en.html.

7. Ratzinger, "Instruction on Certain Aspects," part IV, "Biblical Foundations," point 15.

8. See Ratzinger, "Instruction on Certain Aspects," part IX, "The Theological Application of This Core," point 10.

9. As happens in the case of social postmodern theories, which draw inspiration from neo-Marxist thought and apply it to other notions of oppression, liberation theologies also inspired feminist and queer theologies, developed in the studies of theologians such as Rosemary Radford Ruether and Marcella Althus-Reid.

10. Naim Stifan Ateek, *Justice and Only Justice—A Palestinian Theology of Liberation* (Maryknoll, NY: Orbis, 1989), 57–61.

11. Ateek, *Justice and Only Justice*, 105, 64.

12. Manuel Hassassian, "The Issue of the Land in the Post Peace Process," *Al-liqa Journal* 9/10 (December 1997): 98–104; Munib A. Younan, "The Land: A Christian Perspective," *Al-liqa Journal* 9/10 (December 1997): 85–88.

13. In July 2017, the UNESCO World Heritage Committee adopted a resolution that inscribes Hebron old city in the list of world heritage endangered cites, denying its Jewish history. Earlier in May, UNESCO had adopted a controversial resolution that used Arab-Muslim formulations of Jewish sites (al-Buraq plaza instead of Western Wall Plaza) and accused Israel of altering the Arab identity of the city, consequently denying its Jewish character.

14. See "Sabeel Wave of Prayer," Friends of Sabeel UK, May 11, 2017, http://www.friendsofsabeel.org.uk/wave-of-prayer /sabeel-wave-of-prayer-thursday-11th-may-2017/.

15. See "Sabeel Wave of Prayer," Friends of Sabeel UK, July 13, 2017, http://sabeel.org/wp-content/uploads/2017/07/12-7-2017.pdf.

16. See Nadav Shragai, *The "Al-Aksa Is in Danger" Libel: The History of a Lie* (Jerusalem: Jerusalem Center for Public Affairs, 2012), http:// jcpa.org/text/downloads/the-al-aksa-is-in-danger-libel-the-history -of-a-lie.pdf.

17. See "Sabeel Wave of Prayer," Friends of Sabeel UK, July 27, 2017, http://www.friendsofsabeel.org.uk/wave-of-prayer /sabeel-wave-of-prayer-thursday-27th-july-2017/.

18. See "Muslim and Christians Pray Together for a Just Peace in Al Aqsa Mosque," World Council of Churches, July 28, 2017, https://www.oikoumene.org/en/press-centre/news /muslim-and-christians-pray-together-for-just-peace-in-al-aqsa-mosque.

19. Ateek, *Justice and Only Justice*, 78.

20. Ateek, *Justice and Only Justice*, 93.

21. Ateek, *Justice and Only Justice*, 97.

22. Ateek, *Justice and Only Justice*, 101.

23. Rafiq Khoury, "Palestinian Contextual Theology: Its March and Its Message," *Al-liqa Journal* 14–15 (December 2000): 39–88.

24. Ateek, *Justice and Only Justice*, 102.

25. Bruno Bauer, *Die Judenfrage* (Brunswick, Germany: Druck und Verlag von Friedrich Otto, 1843), 39–43.

26. Ateek, *Justice and Only Justice*, 47–48.

27. Robert Wistrich, *A Lethal Obsession: Anti-Semitism from Antiquity to the Global Jihad* (New York: Random House, 2010), 502.

28. Ateek, *Justice and Only Justice*, 136–38.

29. For more information on de-Zionization of the Bible, see Ateek, *Justice and Only Justice*, 159. For more on opposing Christian support for Zionism, see Maroun Lahham, "The Palestinian Church vis-à-vis Christian Zionism," *Al-liqa Journal* 23 (December 2004): 50–64. For more on condemnation of settlements, see Rafiq Khoury, "Palestinian Theology and Israeli Colonial Settlements," *Al-liqa Journal* 23 (December 2004): 65–71.

30. "The Amman Call," World Council of Churches, June 20, 2007, http://www.oikoumene.org/en/resources/documents/wcc-programmes /public-witness-addressing-power-affirming-peace/middle-east-peace /the-amman-call. In particular, see points 5.4, 5.6, 5.8, and 11. Such views include the statement about Jerusalem as an international city, the general condemnation of violence, the return of the Palestinian refugees, and the condemnation of settlements and the occupation.

31. See "Bern Perspective," World Council of Churches, September 13, 2008, http://www.oikoumene.org/en/resources/documents/wcc -programmes/public-witness-addressing-power-affirming-peace /middle-east-peace/bern-perspective.

32. Kairos Palestine, *A Moment of Truth: A Word of Faith, Hope, and Love from the Heart of Palestinian Suffering* (Jerusalem, Israel: Kairos Palestine, 2009), point 2.5. The English text of the document is available at http://www.kairospalestine.ps/sites/default/files/English.pdf.

33. Kairos Palestine, *A Moment of Truth*, point 4.2.1 (para. 2).

34. Kairos Palestine, *A Moment of Truth*, point 4.2.3; point 4.2.1 (para. 1).

35. Kairos Palestine, *A Moment of Truth*, point 4.2.5.

36. Kairos Palestine, *A Moment of Truth*, point 4.2.6; point 4.2.6; point 6.3; point 7.

37. Kairos Palestine, *A Moment of Truth*, point 3.4.3.

38. The figure of Jesus as a revolutionary is an interpretation of his figure as a renovator and specifically drawn from episodes narrated in the Gospels. The expulsion of the merchants from the Temple (Matthew 21:12–17; Mark 11:15–19, and Luke 19:45–48) certainly represents a major source of inspiration for active revolution. Second, Jesus's reference to the sword he brought into the world (Luke 10:34–36) is a disruptive message that associates with revolution. Finally, in his dialogue with the Roman ruler Pontius Pilate, Jesus uses the expression "my kingdom" and refers to a fight to be led by his servants—these formulations are interpreted as directly defying Roman rule and its complacent local elites (John 18:36) as part of Jesus's overall ministry imbued with a message of justice, equality, and liberation. Jesus's figure as a revolutionary has also been historically analyzed in light of social and political groups active at the time, including the militant zealots who opposed Roman rule and the ruling Pharisees. See Marcus Borg, *Jesus: Uncovering the Life, Teachings and Relevance of a Religious Revolutionary* (New York: HarperCollins, 2008). For a more specific analysis of Jesus's figure in political perspective, see Phil Gasper, "Jesus the Revolutionary?" *Socialist Worker*, December 14, 2011, https://socialistworker.org/2011/12/14/jesus-the-revolutionary. This position has been criticized by John Paul II on the occasion of his visits to Central America in 1979. Addressing the third general conference of the Latin American Episcopate, he claimed, "By confusing the insidious pretexts of Jesus's accusers with the—very different—attitude of Jesus himself, some people adduce as the cause of his death the outcome of a political conflict, and nothing is said of the Lord's will to deliver himself and of his consciousness of his redemptive mission." See "Address of His Holiness John Paul II," Third General Conference of the Latin American Episcopate, Puebla, Mexico, January 28, 1979, http://w2.vatican.va /content/john-paul-ii/en/speeches/1979/january/documents/hf_jp-ii _spe_19790128_messico-puebla-episc-latam.html.

39. At the 2011 Kairos for Global Justice conference, Ferdinando Anno defined the "empire" as "the combined economic, military, political, and cultural domination by a powerful state, assisted by satellite states and aided by local elites of dominated countries, to advance its own interests on a global scale. United States military dominance, conjointly with transnational corporate power, makes up the heart of today's empire." See Ferdinand Anno, "Reclaiming the Good News of the Holy Land and the Imperative of Interfaith Solidarity to Resist Empire: A Philippine

Theological Response to Kairos Palestine," in *Kairos for Global Justice*, ed. Robin Meyers (Bethlehem: Kairos Palestine, 2011), http://www.kairospalestine.ps/sites/default/files/Kairos%20for%20Global%20Justice.pdf, 47.

40. Anno, "Reclaiming the Good News," 47.

41. Hind Khoury, "An Introduction to Challenging Empire: God, Faithfulness and Resistance," in *Challenging Empire—God, Faithfulness, and Resistance*, ed. Naim Ateek, Cedar Duaybis, and Maurine Tobin (Jerusalem: Sabeel Ecumenical Liberation Theology Center, 2012), 21.

42. Mazin Qumsiyeh, "Mapping Empire Today in Palestine and Israel," in Ateek, Duaybis, and Tobin, *Challenging Empire*, 28.

43. Qumsiyeh, "Mapping Empire Today," 35–36. According to the author, the pro-Israeli lobby would be responsible for the Iraq War and for influencing the naturalization process of its dependents.

44. As Afif Safiyeh stated, "as far as the Middle East is concerned, Israel is Rome and has used America as its regional belligerent Sparta from the two Gulf Wars to today's discussion about a possible attack on Iran." Afif Safiyeh, "Current Political Realities," in Ateek, Duaybis, and Tobin, *Challenging Empire*, 44.

45. Mitri Raheb, *Faith in the Face of Empire: The Bible through Palestinian Eyes* (New York: Orbis, 2014), 11, 10.

46. In the brief description of the changing features of identity of the "native people of the land," Raheb interestingly forgets to mention Hebrew as a language of the land, while he states that "they changed their language from Aramaic to Greek to Arabic"; Raheb, *Faith in the Face of Empire* 12.

47. Raheb, *Faith in the Face of Empire*, 13.

48. Raheb, *Faith in the Face of Empire*, 14–19.

49. Raheb, *Faith in the Face of Empire*, 71–73; Naim Ateek, "Theology as a Tool of Empire," in Ateek, Duaybis, and Tobin, *Challenging Empire*, 95.

50. Raheb, *Faith in the Face of Empire*, 65. The author goes so far as to denounce that such a myth "is utilized theologically and implicitly against the Palestinian people and within the context of the clash of civilization against Islam."

51. Mitri Raheb, "Blessed Are the Meek," in Ateek, Duaybis, and Tobin, *Challenging Empire*, 54.

52. Raheb, "Blessed Are the Meek," 55.

53. Richard Horsley, "Jesus Confronting Empire," in Ateek, Duaybis, and Tobin, *Challenging Empire*, 56, 65 ("Yeshua bat Yousuf was a Palestinian living under imperial rule").

54. Raheb, *Faith in the Face of Empire*, 55–62. As he states, "Herod utilized Roman technology and the cheap labor provided by the native peoples to create long aqueduct lines to collect the water. . . . The control of water under Israeli occupation is a continuation of this imperial natural resource strategy" (58). In an attempt to describe the imperialist nature of the Zionist project, the author asserts that "the Greeks, Romans, Byzantines, Crusaders, and Ottomans each had extensive settlement projects. Yet the State of Israel has exceeded all of them, when it comes to settlements activities" (59). With the word *settlements*, the author refers to all Jewish establishments, even those predating the birth of the state of Israel. As he affirms, "the building frenzy began in the late nineteenth century with small, mainly agricultural, settlements, and continued after 1948 and after 1967, becoming a powerful and prime tool to control the whole of historic Palestine . . . Israeli settlements follow the same imperial pattern" (59).

55. Raheb, *Faith in the Face of Empire*, 61–62.

56. Ched Myers, "Sea-Changes Part I—Jesus' Call to Discipleship as Resistance to Colonizing Economics," in Ateek, Duaybis, and Tobin, *Challenging Empire*, 112.

57. Ched Myers, "Sea-Changes Part II—Re-Imagining Exodus Liberation as an 'Exorcism' of Imperial Militarism," in Ateek, Duaybis, and Tobin, *Challenging Empire*, 119.

58. Raheb, *Faith in the Face of Empire*, 86.

59. Raheb, *Faith in the Face of Empire*, 96.

60. Christopher Ferguson, "The Church and Empire," in Ateek, Duaybis, and Tobin, *Challenging Empire*, 87.

61. Michel Sabbah, "Spiritual Encouragement for Pursuing Justice," in Ateek, Duaybis, and Tobin, *Challenging Empire*, 162–68.

62. Anno, "Reclaiming the Good News," 49.

63. Horsley, "Jesus Confronting Empire," 68, 64.

64. Raheb, *Faith in the Face of Empire*, 100.

65. Raheb, *Faith in the Face of Empire*, 99.

66. Kairos Palestine, *A Moment of Truth*, points 6.3, 4.2.6.

67. Rifat Odeh Kassis, *Kairos for Palestine* (Ramallah: Badayl, 2011), 108–9; Raheb, *Faith in the Face of Empire*, 120–21.

68. Kairos Palestine, *A Moment of Truth*, point 1.4.

69. Kairos Palestine, *A Moment of Truth*," point 4.2.5.

70. Raj Bharath Patta, "Towards an Emmaus Experience: An Indian Response to Kairos Palestine Document," in Kairos Palestine, *Kairos for Global Justice*, 43.

71. Kassis, *Kairos for Palestine*, 108.

72. Kassis, *Kairos for Palestine*, 135.

73. "The Bethlehem Call: Here We Stand—Stand with Us," in Kairos Palestine, *Kairos for Global Justice*, 114.

74. Pax Christi International, "Middle East: Ecumenical Accompaniment Programme in Palestine and Israel," http://www .paxchristi.pairsite.com/our-work/regions/middle-east#.

75. See Palestine Israel Ecumenical Forum, accessed January 2016, https://pief.oikoumene.org/en.

76. See the letter by the Pax Christi German Chapter to the authors of Kairos Palestine document, September 10, 2011, http://kairoseuropa .de/wp-content/uploads/2015/10/pax_christi_antwort_an_Kairos .pdf; "Wirtschaft im Dienst des Lebens," internet page of the group Kairos Europa explaining the theological views about economy, http:// kairoseuropa.de/wir-ueber-uns/fuer-eine-wirtschaft-im-dienst-des -lebens-2/. The group promotes a theological-political narrative that aspires to offer alternatives to neoliberalism and globalization.

77. BDS Italia, accessed February 2016, http://www.bdsitalia.org /index.php/la-campagna-bds/campagna-bds.

78. Presbyterian Church USA, 215th General Assembly, *Resolution on Israel and Palestine: End the Occupation Now* (2003), accessed in January 2016, http://oga.pcusa.org/media/uploads/oga/pdf/endoccupation03.pdf.

79. The document portrays a supposed Palestinian total despair, of which Israel solely should be held responsible and leaves the door open to action against injustice: "God has not given us a spirit of timidity, nor have we been called to surrender hope to an attitude of despair" (point 2), Presbyterian Church USA, http://index.pcusa.org/nxt/gateway .dll?f=templates$fn=default.htm. See also Presbyterian Church USA, *Minutes, 216th General Assembly*, part 1 (Office of the General Assembly: Louisville, KY, 2004), accessed in January 2016, http://oga.pcusa.org /media/uploads/oga/pdf/journal2004.pdf, 853.

80. See guidelines at Presbyterian Church USA, *Guidelines for the Implementation of Phased, Selective, Divestment Related to Israel and Palestine* (Office of the General Assembly: Louisville, KY, 2006), http://www.pcusa.org/site_media/media/uploads/mrti /pdfs/20guidelinesdivestment.pdf. The criteria for divestment are involvement of a corporation in relations with the Israeli military and support or maintenance of the occupation; involvement of a corporation in services or acts related to settlement establishment, maintenance,

or expansion; involvement in policies or services that contribute to Palestinian or Israeli violence against civilians; and finally, involvement in construction or maintenance of the separation barrier. By adopting this resolution, the Presbyterian Church endorses the divestment narrative based not on ethical principles against violence but on a clear, one-sided political vision, whereby Israel is responsible for the conflict through the occupation and Israeli presence in the post-1967 territories; this is per se a violation of international law and the root of the conflict.

81. See Committee on Mission Responsibility through Investment (MRTI), *MRTI Report to 2012 General Assembly: Engagement with Corporations on Israeli-Palestine Issues from 2004 to 2011* (2011), http://www.pcusa.org/site_media/media/uploads/mrti/pdfs/2012-mrti-report-9-9-11.pdf.

82. Agenda item 15-02 of the 2012 220th General Assembly (advanced by the Presbytery of San Francisco) calls for the boycott of products coming from post-1967 territories and for encouraging organizations that endorse this boycott (naming AHAVA, Israel Date Growers Cooperative). Agenda item 15-01 discusses the definition of Israeli policies as apartheid, quoting NGOs such as B'Tselem and the Abraham Fund. The proposal was eventually disapproved on the rationale that the use of the word *apartheid* is detrimental to the general discussion on the conflict, while it is preferable to focus on the several restrictions of rights and liberties of the Palestinians. At the 221st General Assembly in 2014, another proposed resolution (item 04-03) tried to advance the definition of Israel's policies as apartheid; it was, however, quashed. Agenda items 15-10 and 15-11 call for "creative action," an expression used in the Kairos Document, with respect to the conflict, which also includes the divestment from corporations implicated in the "occupation."

83. The Ecumenical and Interreligious Work Group of the Presbytery of Chicago elaborated the document "Perspectives on Presbyterian Church (USA) Support for a Just and Peaceful Compromise of the Israeli-Palestinian Conflict," which encourages partnerships with groups that endorse the boycott of settlements' products (2). While officially recognizing Jewish statehood, the paper defines Palestinians as the "indigenous population" (7) and repeatedly focuses on the "occupation" and the nation-state ruled by ethnic rationales as main causes of the conflict (8–9). The Middle-East Task Force of the Chicago Presbytery states in the document that BDS is a form of nonviolent resistance while accusing Israeli governments of enacting policies harmful to both Jews and Palestinians (24). See Ecumenical and Interreligious Work Group

of the Presbytery of Chicago, *Perspectives on Presbyterian Church (USA) Support for a Just and Peaceful Compromise of the Israeli-Palestinian Conflict* (2008), http://www.chicagopresbytery.org/wp-content/uploads/2008/07 /perspectives-on-pcusa-support-for-just-and-peaceful-compromise.pdf.

84. See "Book of Resolutions: Opposition to Israeli Settlements in Palestinian Land," United Methodist Church, 2016, http://www.umc.org /what-we-believe/opposition-to-israeli-settlements-in-palestinian-land. Particularly, the position of the resolution resounds the apparently neutral condemnation of violence, which equates Palestinian suicide bombings and attacks on civilians to Israel's military operations, and profusely condemns Israel for systematically violating human rights, stealing water resources, confiscating lands, dehumanizing Palestinians, illegally building settlements and expanding, and so on. This language is reflected in the writings of several PLT advocates.

85. See the 2016 publication "Addressing Human Rights—Israel and the Palestinian Territories," January 2016, Wespath Investment Management, agency of the United Methodist Church, https://www .wespath.org/assets/1/7/4787.pdf.

86. The UMKR was initiated in October 2010 by a group within the UMC as a response to Kairos Palestine's call. "About UMKR," United Methodists for Kairos Response, https://www.kairosresponse .org/about_umkr.html. On the same website, the main argument relied on is the necessity as Christians to respond to the continuous eviction and expulsion of Christians (considered indigenous) by Israelis and policies of occupation. Stated goals of the group include advocacy for divestment, boycott initiatives (in UMC General Conferences and outside the church), responsible tourism (in line with the activities of Alternative Tourism Group promoted by Kairos), and education regarding the history of Palestine. The *Why Boycott the Israeli Settlements?* brochure repeats that the boycott is a nonviolent measure to oppose occupation, which is the main cause of suffering for Christians and Muslims, therefore repeating the rhetoric of the Zionist empire against Muslims and Christians. See the brochure at https://www.kairosresponse.org/why_boycott_broch _may2015.html. Advocating for BDS in the UMC, the UMKR argues that Christians are victims of systematic destruction of properties and that the occupation is the major threat to Christian presence in the Holy Land. "Resources | General Conference 2016: Briefing for General Conference 2016 Delegates," UMKR, accessed in March 2016, https:// www.kairosresponse.org/briefing_gc2016.html.

87. See "Report of the Working Group on Israel/Palestine Policy,"
Working Group on Israel/Palestine Policy of the United Church of
Canada, presented at the Forty-First General Council, August 11–18,
2012, available at https://commons.united-church.ca/Documents
/Governance/General%20Council/41st%20General%20Council%20
(2012)/Background%20Material/Report%20of%20the%20workgroup%20
on%20Israel-Palestine.pdf, 1–2.

88. See "Prayer for Peace with Justice in Israel/Palestine,"
United Church of Canada, http://www.united-church.ca/prayers
/prayer-peace-justice-israel/palestine.

89. See "UCC General Resolutions on Israel/Palestine,"
Global Ministries, http://www.globalministries.org/
israel_palestine_resolutions.

90. See United Church of Christ, *Report to the Executive Council of
the United Church of Christ on Implementation of General Synod 25 (2005)
Resolution "Concerning the Use of Economic Leverage to Promote Peace in the
Middle East"* (2013), http://uccfiles.com/pdf/EC-13-06-06b-Collegium
-Report.pdf.

91. The United Church Fund restates the goal of divesting from
corporations that profit from the occupation: United Church Funds,
"United Church Funds Adopts Exclusionary Guideline Addressing
Human Rights Abuses in the Occupied Palestinian Territories" (press
statement), https://d3n8a8pro7vhmx.cloudfront.net/globalministries
/pages/10712/attachments/original/1448419652/SKMBT
_C654e15070711511.pdf?1448419652; as does the UCC Pension Board,
United Church of Christ, "The Pension Boards United Church of Christ"
(press statement, June 30, 2015), https://d3n8a8pro7vhmx.cloudfront.
net/globalministries/pages/10712/attachments/original/1448419656
/SKMBT_C654e15070711520.pdf?1448419656. For more on the synod's
concern about Israel becoming an apartheid state, see United Church of
Christ, "The Rev. James Moos—Executive Minister of United Church
of Christ Wider Church Ministries" (press statement, June 30, 2015),
https://d3n8a8pro7vhmx.cloudfront.net/globalministries/pages/10712
/attachments/original/1448419648/SKMBT_C654e15070711510.
pdf?1448419648. Mitri Raheb also spoke at the general synod about the
peoples of Palestine under occupation, equating Jews under Babylonian
and Roman occupation, and Jesus under Roman occupation, with
Palestinians under Israeli occupation ("Jesus lived under Roman
occupation and I live under Israeli occupation"). Talking about hope,

he says that God operates in unexpected places, such as through church divestment initiatives. See "Rev. Dr. Mitri Raheb Sermon," YouTube.com, June 29, 2015, https://www.youtube.com/watch?v=URLofIIyiLI.

GIOVANNI MATTEO QUER is a researcher at the Kantor Center for the Study of Contemporary European Jewry. (At the time of writing, he was a fellow with the Komper Center for the Study of Antisemitism and Racism, University of Haifa.) He has also worked for nongovernmental organizations and international organizations. His interests include diversity management, human rights, and Israel studies.

PART IV

National Contexts

THIRTEEN

—ᴍ—

Configurations of Antisemitism

The Anti-Zionist Campaign in Poland 1968

SIMON GANSINGER

TRAVELERS AT DWORZEC Gdański, the train station in the north of Warsaw, may notice a plaque reading, "Here they left behind more than they possessed." In 1998, the small Jewish community in Poland chose this quote by the author Henryk Grynberg to commemorate the involuntary departure of their family members, friends, and colleagues who, thirty years earlier, were forced to leave the country. Even in 1968, when the campaign that precipitated their exodus unfolded, it was evident that they had to leave for no other reason than the fact that they were Jewish. Only back then, the nomenclature was different: in the eyes of the public, these people who boarded the train toward Vienna, presumably to go to Israel, were Zionists. And Zionists, the fable said, constituted the vanguard of the conspiracy against the Polish nation. Nowadays, the antisemitic campaign against so-called Zionists, which reached its climax in March 1968, seems of merely historical interest. After the fall of the socialist regimes in Eastern Europe, nothing similar would happen again in a Europe that has learned to take antisemitism seriously. This verdict, however, may be premature. The antisemitic campaign in Poland in 1968 illustrates that antisemitism itself can adapt to historical developments. By studying its ideological structure, we can enhance our understanding of the transformation of antisemitism into anti-Zionism. Anti-Zionism, I argue later in this chapter, is not merely antisemitism in disguise but an inflection of antisemitism with distinct ideological features. The historical outline in the first part of the chapter substantiates my claim that in anti-Zionism, the hated object—that is, Zionists and Zionism—is mainly located in the political sphere.

CHRONOLOGY OF A WITCH HUNT

Israel's victory in the Six-Day War was met with hostility among the leaders of the Warsaw Pact. After all, the Arab armies had suffered a humiliating defeat against the Israeli forces despite the support of the Soviet Union. With the exception of Romania, all member states cut diplomatic ties with Israel following a summit of East European leaders in Moscow.[1] In the days during and after the Six-Day War, a smear campaign against Israel pervaded the Polish media. The Israeli ambassador to Poland was ordered out of the country on June 12, 1967, only one day after the cease-fire between Israel and the belligerent Arab countries had been signed. When the Israeli legation left the country shortly thereafter, its members experienced the effects of the anti-Israel incitement firsthand: an enraged and agitated crowd bade them a frightening farewell at the airport, shouting slurs at the ambassador and even assaulting embassy personnel.[2]

The party leadership was probably not displeased with this reaction. Already at the summit in Moscow, Władysław Gomułka, the first secretary of the Polish United Workers' Party (Polska Zjednoczona Partia Robotnicza, or PZPR), voiced the idea of launching a propaganda war against domestic Zionists. Leonid Brezhnev rejected the idea on the grounds that it could stir racial hatred.[3] Gomułka, however, was not deterred from taking on the Zionist enemy within Poland. In a nationally broadcast speech on June 19, he addressed the issue of clandestine Zionists in Poland for the first time in public.[4] Some Polish Jews, Gomułka divined, celebrated the victory of the "Israeli aggressors," thereby displaying a lack of loyalty to the Polish nation. Not only could they not be trusted, but they also constituted a potential "fifth column" in the country, which had to be eradicated before it could gain strength. Every Polish citizen must have only one fatherland, Gomułka declared; solidarity with the Jewish state was incompatible with one's allegiance to the Polish patria.[5]

The significance of Gomułka's fifth column comment was not missed by his contemporaries. Political logic would dictate that the existence of an internal enemy necessitates urgent and drastic measures, but such measures were unrealistic in light of the loosely organized, largely apolitical Jewish community of Poland, which in 1967 counted no more than thirty thousand members.[6] Several politburo members, among them Edward Ochab and Eugeniusz Szyr, immediately protested against the unfounded and, in their eyes, dangerous claim that there was a Zionist conspiracy under way among Poland's Jews and demanded that the published speech be corrected—a "quite unprecedented" occurrence in People's Poland.[7] Although Gomułka insisted that he had good reason to address the problem of a fifth column, the relevant passage was deleted from the print version and two sentences were added to emphasize that "the overwhelming majority of Polish citizens of Jewish nationality . . . faithfully serve our country."[8]

The damage, however, was already done. The basic elements of what would develop into an antisemitic campaign in March of the following year were already in place in June 1967. Gomułka's speech introduced the image of a vicious Zionist specter that could easily be conjured up again. In the confrontation between several politburo members, the internal tensions among powerful party members were already visible. Ochab's and Szyr's opposition to Gomułka's hate mongering foreshadowed the political complexity of the events to come. Both their careers would end abruptly in spring 1968. Szyr, who was Jewish, and Ochab, who could not reconcile the party's condoning of antisemitism with his internationalism, would soon be fundamentally at odds with the dominant bigotry within the PZPR.[9]

At first, the campaign against the imagined Zionist danger seemed to be averted by opposition within the party. But even though the public did not concern itself with the enemy in its midst, some groups in the state apparatus did so ever more eagerly. Even before June 1967, high-ranking officials in the Ministry of the Interior (Ministerstwo Spraw Wewnętrznych, or MSW) took a special interest in the activities of Jewish institutions in Warsaw.[10] Minister Mieczysław Moczar, whose fervently antisemitic views were no secret to his comrades, harbored the belief that the Jewish community was courted by "the Israeli embassy or international Zionist circles and home nationalist groups."[11] As a direct reaction to the Six-Day War, the MSW stepped up the surveillance of the Jewish community in what it conceived as a fight against Zionism.[12] Under Moczar's lead, MSW officials worked tirelessly to gather information on individual Jews and expose or fabricate their ties to Israel.[13] Although the intelligence was not immediately put to use, it would prove useful to the regime—and devastating to many Jews—some months later.

The anti-Zionist fury did not take as long to materialize in the military. Jewish military officials had also faced antisemitism in previous years.[14] The concentrated campaign against pro-Israel or revisionist elements in the armed forces that started in summer 1967, however, was unprecedented in its intensity.[15] Accredited speakers toured the garrisons and, while ostensibly lecturing on the situation in the Middle East, disseminated antisemitic propaganda, which contributed to displays of open defiance to Jewish superiors. In the end, the campaign, which was conducted under the auspices of the PZPR, resulted in the dismissal of one hundred fifty out of no more than two hundred Jewish officers.[16] The purge of Jewish officers even threatened to become too efficient. Rumors caught on that Minister of Defense Marian Spychalski was Jewish—or at least that his wife was Jewish—and therefore, as a likely traitor to the country, he had to be ousted.[17] Unlike many others who were suspected to be Zionists by blood or by conviction, Spychalski survived the purge unharmed and eventually was promoted to the chairman of the Council of State.

With the files on Zionist fifth columnists piling up in the MSW and with hastily created commissions stripping Jewish officers of their ranks, the full-blown assault on the Jewish community in Poland was already in the offing. And yet, when on January 30, 1968, three hundred students took to the streets of Warsaw to protest the ban of Dziady, a play by the Polish poet Adam Mickiewicz with anti-Russian undertones, they certainly could not have guessed that their courageous acts would usher in the anti-Zionist frenzy of March 1968.[18] The MSW officials were quick to realize that some of the arrested protesters were Jewish and did not hesitate to act according to their antisemitic motivations. During their confinement, Jews were subjected to particularly harsh treatment.[19] As a punishment for their involvement in the Dziady protests, two students, Henryk Szlajfer and Adam Michnik, who happened to be Jewish, were expelled from the University of Warsaw. On March 8, a Friday, their colleagues responded with a large demonstration at the university, which was brutally dissolved by security forces.[20] The demand for freedom of speech and civil rights, however, was soon heard at campuses all over the country, and before the weekend was over, tens of thousands of students and sympathizers rallied for this cause.[21]

The regime became nervous. The protests had grown too large in too short an amount of time to be quietly suppressed. Now it was imperative to limit their influence and stop their expansion beyond the borders of academia. If the voices of the workers entered into the chorus of free speech, free education, and—horribile dictu—free elections, the student unrest could quickly evolve into a full-fledged rebellion. The Hungarian and, though still developing, Czech examples loomed large. In the MSW headquarters, everything was prepared to defang the movement in its early stage. Moczar's men, utilizing their recently acquired knowledge, compiled lists of the alleged leading instigators, the vast majority of whom were Jewish.[22] After Gomułka and other high-ranking party members approved the document, it was handed to the press with the intention of neutralizing the protests by kindling a campaign against alien provocateurs.[23] The working masses, the reasoning seemed to be, would hardly join ranks with a Jewish elite.[24]

The publication of the list alone would have sufficed to brand the official propaganda against the student unrest as an antisemitic stunt. In their comment on the events of the previous weekend on March 11, the official party organ, *Trybuna Ludu*, contented itself with this type of indirect incitement against Jews. Apart from naming eight chief instigators, the article contained a diatribe against "bankrupt politicians" who controlled the protests and manipulated the students behind the scenes. Notably, *Trybuna Ludu* did not point to Zionist conspirers in its propaganda piece.[25]

This was left to *Słowo Powszechne*, the newspaper of the Catholic splinter group PAX.[26] An article titled "To the Students of the University of Warsaw," which was published on the same day, did not simply present readers with a list of exclusively Jewish culprits; it also tied the list back to Gomułka's infamous Zionist fifth column.[27] Although the article was similar and in parts even identical to the one in *Trybuna Ludu*, its emphasis on a distinctly Zionist conspiracy was unique. The author pointed to the "alliance between the State of Israel and the Federal Republic of Germany"—a common theme in subsequent weeks. Not only would Israel try to cleanse Germany from its Nazi past and make the Polish people responsible for the Holocaust, but it aimed "to undermine the authority of the political leadership of People's Poland." The "Zionists in Poland" have only contempt for "world peace and the interests of Poland," which had come to light during the Six-Day War, and they encourage intellectuals and the youth to dismiss their patriotic responsibilities.

Fortunately, the author reveals, "antisemitic sentiments are alien to [the Polish youth]," and so the question "Who are these people" who undermine the body politic may be answered with unabashed honesty. A list follows of ten students who are described as the main organizers of the demonstration at the University of Warsaw. In case one couldn't tell from the names alone that "these people" were natural-born Zionists, the author added that some of them "held meetings at the 'Babel' club at the Social and Cultural Association of Jews," a popular youth club at the time mainly known for its discussion events and dance nights.[28] "Serving foreign interests," the protesters "wanted to cut the patriotic bond between society and people's power."

While *Trybuna Ludu* furnished the claim of a Jewish conspiracy with legitimacy, *Słowo Powszechne*, a newspaper of secondary political importance, set the campaign's tone. From then on, the media abounded with condemnations, denunciations, and exposures of Zionist traitors. Within the following ten days, 250 articles were published, a good portion of which endorsed the anti-Zionist conspiracy theory.[29] Under the headline "Instigators," the *Kurier Polski*, nominally the paper of an opposition party, declared on March 12 that "the time has come to reveal the sources of evil, show the facts, and call the instigators of the incidents by name." In case the instigators' names were not sufficiently incriminating, the article, as *Słowo Powszechne* had done, identified them as members of the Babel Club and as Israeli propagandists.[30] On March 14, *Trybuna Ludu* acknowledged the anti-Zionist thrust of the campaign and confirmed that "among the instigators of recent events an essential role was played by young people with Zionist connections."[31] These articles were the rule rather than the exception. During the first weeks of the campaign, "Poland was literally showered with millions, and in time tens of millions, of *anti-Zionist* messages."[32]

But the campaign was not restricted to hateful columns in magazines or outraged talking heads on television.[33] In thousands of public meetings in factories, party offices, and even sports clubs all over Poland, anti-Zionist resolutions were passed in which people condemned the Zionist attacks on the Polish nation. Overall, more than one hundred thousand meetings were held.[34] One representative resolution from the beginning of April reads, "[We demand] a complete removal of Zionist elements and other enemies of our socialist reality from the political, state administrative, educational, and cultural apparatus and also from social organizations.... Those who in their nihilism and cosmopolitanism poison the spirit and heart of the youth should lose their influence on it."[35] In Łódź, the "antisemitic campaign took the most vicious form."[36] The city's journalist club banned Jewish journalists, and in the local eye clinic, the administration demanded baptism certificates from the physicians. A mass emigration of the Jews of Łódź quickly ensued. Paul Lendvai, referring to the Nazi term for areas "cleansed from Jews," poignantly summarizes the developments: "Within two months Łódź becomes practically 'judenrein.'"[37]

Some authors noted the conspicuous absence of physical violence during the spring of 1968.[38] Dariusz Stola invoked the concept of "symbolic aggression" and interpreted the March events as a "verbal rather than physical pogrom."[39] However, one should not overemphasize the lack of physical violence in the wake of the anti-Zionist propaganda. One prominent victim was journalist Stefan Kisielewski, who was beaten up on the streets of Warsaw the same day he was called a "lackey of anti-Polish policies" in *Słowo Powszechne*.[40] Several people—Paul Lendvai speaks of "forty known cases"—committed suicide after they found themselves publicly vilified and socially isolated.[41]

It took Gomułka an unusually long time to respond to the anti-Zionist campaign in public. On March 19, he addressed a large crowd of party activists. Toward the end of this televised speech,

Gomułka elaborated on the topic of Zionism. There are, he emphasized repeatedly, "Jewish nationalists who believe in Zionist ideology." According to Gomułka, the Jewish population of Poland was divided into three groups: first, "Polish citizens who are emotionally and in their thoughts not connected to Poland but to the State of Israel"—these people will "sooner or later leave our country"; second, Jewish citizens who identify "neither as Poles nor as Jews"—and these cosmopolitans may, under certain conditions, stay; and third, "the largest group of our citizens with Jewish origins, . . . for whom Poland is their only fatherland."[42] By making this division, Gomułka downplayed the importance of a Zionist conspiracy while acknowledging its existence. Some members of the audience expected a clearer stance and "began encouraging the speaker with shouts of 'Bolder, bolder,' 'Go further, Wiesław, give names.'" When he referred to emigration, they responded with cries of "Now, today."[43] Heckling the first secretary of the PZPR, the audience attested to the rapid acceleration of the antisemitic witch hunt, which had ceased to be a contained campaign controlled by the party.

Over the next few weeks, while Poland was gripped by anti-Zionist fever, the Jewish community could only hold its breath and wait for the frenzy to die away. In fact, the Zionist threat did not preoccupy the public for very long. In June 1968, the Central Committee decided to discontinue the campaign, which it deemed a success.[44] At the Fifth Party Congress in November, Zionism was no longer on the agenda. When asked by a comrade whether the protests in March were linked to a Zionist conspiracy, the attorney general replied, "No, we have no proof whatsoever for this supposition."[45] Nine months after the full-blown assault on the Zionist fifth column was ordered, the regime acknowledged that it had been chasing ghosts.[46]

The consequences, though, were no less disastrous for Polish Jewry. The fear of being unveiled as a treacherous Zionist was connected to the very real threat of losing one's job, apartment, and social standing. Within a year, "the Party had expelled from its ranks approximately 8,300 members, nearly all of them Jews," among them dozens of high-ranking PZPR officials.[47] As a result of the campaign, nine thousand people, most of them Jewish, lost their jobs, and hundreds were thrown out of their apartments, which were gladly taken over by their former neighbors.[48] The regime allowed Jewish citizens to leave the country under two conditions: they had to revoke their citizenship, and they had to declare Israel as the country of their destination. The regime thus legitimized the purge of Zionist elements after the fact in a most cynical fashion: Why would these people choose Israel as their destination if they hadn't been Zionists all along?

Many Jews seized the opportunity. Whereas in April 1967 only 29 people applied for exit visas to Israel, the number rose to 168 one year later and reached 631 in October 1968.[49] Estimates for how many Jews left Poland between 1968 and 1971 vary. The most conservative estimate holds the number at twelve thousand;[50] earlier estimates believed that more than twenty thousand were forced out of the country.[51] The correct figure might lie somewhere in between, around fifteen thousand.[52] Only about 30 percent ended up in Israel, with the rest going to countries such as Sweden, France, and the United States.[53]

Material losses and public humiliation were not the only reasons for the exodus. The anti-Zionist campaign also served as a reminder of the destructive potential of antisemitism. Jerzy Jedlicki, who participated in the student protests, identified alienation and fear as the driving motivations behind emigration: "Many decided to leave, for in the atmosphere of persecution and slander they stopped feeling at home, and feared for their children's future."[54] Małgorzata Melchior believes that March 1968 may have been the "most dramatic period in the post-war biographies of the Polish Jews who survived the Holocaust."[55] With the majority of Poland's Jews, many of whom were survivors of the Holocaust, forced into exile; most Jewish institutions destroyed; and the few thousands who decided to stay demoralized and intimidated, March 1968 signifies a catastrophe from which Poland and Polish Jews have not yet fully recovered.[56]

WHO'S A ZIONIST?

If the campaign had not had such tragic consequences, one could even find comedic episodes in it. In its early phase, a participant in the congress of Warsaw journalists made the telling comment, "One cannot exclude the possibility that as a result of unsatisfactory information the people do not know what Zionism means and exactly whom one should remove."[57] This was only half true. They might not have known what Zionism was but they certainly knew who the Zionists were and what they did. For those who frantically hunted for Zionists, for the devoted anti-Zionists of March 1968, the term did have a distinct meaning—that is, one distinct from what is conventionally understood by Zionism. Just as the antisemite attaches to the word or the concept *Jew* a certain meaning that has no material relation to what Jews are or to what Jews do, the anti-Zionist attributes numerous features to the Zionists, none of which are necessarily derived from actual Zionism.[58]

This is not to say that the image of Zionists that dominated the public discourse during the antisemitic campaign was a purely arbitrary fabrication. Although the Zionists who populated the pages of *Słowo Powszechne* had nothing to do with real Zionists—after all, there were hardly any Zionists in Poland in 1968—their imaginary qualities might still be grounded in reality.[59] These qualities did not correspond to the qualities of the objects to which they referred, and this reality was not to be found in the objective world. Instead, the analysis of the ideology of anti-Zionism ought to be primarily concerned with the subjective reality of the anti-Zionists. But even if the image of Zionists was imaginary, it still had a meaning. What, then, was the meaning of the anti-Zionist demagogy?

At first, the question seems straightforward. What appeared as anti-Zionism in 1968 was simply antisemitism cloaked in socially acceptable language. Most of the authors who deal with the ideological formations of the campaign seem to believe that anti-Zionism simply stood for antisemitism. Dariusz Stola, for example, suggests that *Zionism* and *Zionists* "were substitutes for 'Jew' and 'Jewish,' including cases where the person referred to as a Zionist was neither Jewish nor pro-Israeli at all," and Daniel Blatman writes, "Traditional anti-Semitic equations were now replaced [by] a new slogan: 'Jews = Zionism = Reactionism.'"[60] Since outright attacks on Jews could not have been defended in light of the official doctrine of internationalism and would have harmed Poland's reputation, Zionists were cast into the role of the Jews. When certain groups in the PZPR felt the need to launch a scapegoat campaign to discredit the student protests, it seemed convenient to present the public with a Zionist conspiracy. By directing the outrage against Zionists, the opposition to antisemitism could be maintained while antisemitic energies could still be unleashed. This "identity thesis" holds that anti-Zionism is a surface phenomenon that can be reduced to classical antisemitism. The anti-Zionist's obsession with Zionists and Israel merely distracts from the ideological core. The meaning of anti-Zionism, then, consists in its being a direct translation of antisemitism into a socially permissible code. Consequently, Zionists refer to Jews not unlike euphemisms that refer to the tabooed term: you say the first, but you mean the latter.

The plausibility of the identity thesis can hardly be denied. The reference object of the anti-Zionist and the antisemite seems to be the same. During the anti-Zionist campaign, being Jewish was the one criterion that sufficed to brand someone as a likely enemy of the Polish nation. Even though non-Jews occasionally became the victims of the anti-Zionist campaign, the party purges specifically affected Jews. Of the 8,300 people who were expelled from the party in the year after March 1968, almost all were Jewish.

Obviously, other groups also suffered under the regime's crack-down on dissidents and students, as well as under the internal struggle for power in the PZPR. In the first three weeks after the first demonstration at the University of Warsaw, 2,591 people were arrested, among them 597 students, only a tiny minority of whom were Jewish.[61] But the anti-Zionist campaign, even when it was intertwined with the cleansing of alleged revisionists and Stalinists from the ranks of the party, was chiefly a campaign against Jews.[62] Non-Jews who came under fire from anti-Zionists, such as the minister of defense, Marian Spychalski, tended to be identified as Jews.[63] The infamous dictum of the mayor of Vienna, Karl Lueger, also applies to the 1968 campaign: the anti-Zionists decided who is a Zionist—that is to say, a Jew.

Lueger's precept, though often quoted, is liable to suggest a defective notion of antisemitism. The antisemite does not de-cide who is a Jew and who is not by deliberating on the mer-its of his or her decision. The decision is not subject to critical reflection. Horkheimer and Adorno characterize antisemitism as the "exclusion of reflection from [projective] behavior." The antisemitic subject irrationally projects its repressed desires and lustful wishes onto the world: "Instead of the voice of conscience, it hears voices; instead of inwardly examining itself in order to draw up a protocol of its own lust for power, it attributes to oth-ers the Protocol of the Elders of Zion."[64] Antisemitism, then, would be misconstrued if it were to be understood as a means to a given end that the antisemite willfully employs. Antisemitism, as the violent disruption of reflection, transcends—or maybe subverts—instrumental reasoning. It is for this fundamental lack of rationality that the persecution of the Jew does not simply stand for something else—for example, one's economic blight or one's dissatisfaction with the regime. For the antisemite, an-tisemitism is an end in itself. "The anti-Semite," Sartre famously wrote, "is a man who wishes to be a pitiless stone, a furious tor-rent, a devastating thunderbolt—anything except a man."[65] To him, the decision about who is a Jew is as much his own as it is a force of nature. The antisemites find their targets before they concoct the justification for their fury: "The obscure impulse which was always more congenial to them than reason takes them over completely."[66] The theories they cook up to explain their own behavior are not the foundation but the offspring of their hatred. The obscure impulse remains untouched by enlightenment.

The substitution of *Zionist* for *Jew*, as it occurred during March 1968, is often thought of as a tactical measure, if not a deliberate deceit. Several authors interpret the anti-Zionist witch hunt as a scapegoat campaign, which supports the assumption that its essence can be found in the distraction from material problems in People's Poland and in the pacification of the student unrest.[67] If we can't offer the people civil rights and prosperity, we might imagine that Gomułka and his comrades argue in the party headquarters, let's at least offer them a good villain. The scapegoat explanation is certainly not to be dismissed offhandedly. One should be wary, however, of the trivialization of antisemitism by analyzing it as an ideological tool that can be turned on and off at the pleasure of the ruling class. Whereas some factions in the party seemed to have an interest in stirring and maintaining the campaign without having ideologically invested in it, its self-sustaining dynamic, language, and internal logic must remain incomprehensible from the point of view of scapegoat theory.[68] Since scapegoat theories revolve around pure instrumental reasoning on the part of the initiators of the campaign, all those aspects that stand in no premeditated relation to political costs and benefits lie outside of their scope. It is even unclear whether the scapegoat theory of antisemitism is a theory of antisemitism and not just the explication of a certain aspect of any political hate campaign. When "furious torrents" surge through the town, shrewd citizens will seek dry shelter while diverting the water to wash away the hated neighbor's house. Maneuvering the mob by presenting them with a scapegoat is certainly a valuable skill in the political arena. But the mob cannot be conjured up at whim and cannot be freely navigated. The same is true for the anti-Zionist campaign in March 1968: its instrumental value to the regime did not determine its ideological content. The decision about who and what Zionists are preceded the decision to capitalize on their fate.

Clearly, antisemitic movements that display hostility toward the political order are less likely to have as great an effect as movements aligned with the ruling power. By no means do I want to deny this correlation between political efficacy and ideological motivations. The success, as it were, of an antisemitic campaign may well be chiefly dependent on its usefulness for the regime. Horkheimer and Adorno reflect on this factor when they write, "[Antisemitism] serves as a distraction, a cheap means of corruption, a terrorist warning. The respectable rackets condone it, the disreputable ones carry it out."[69] But it would be wrong to say that the disreputable elements of society go after the Jews *because* the dominant groups approve of it. Likewise, the meaning of the anti-Zionist campaign is not exhausted by proving its usefulness for certain figures in the PZPR. Stola thus rightly identifies the "pursuit of rationally defined interests and . . . irrational impulses" as the driving forces of the campaign.[70] The crucial point, though, is that this kind of rationality is conditional on a fundamental irrationality that characterizes the antisemitic mind.

This issue has direct consequences for the identity thesis. It undercuts the idea that an anti-Zionist is merely an antisemite in disguise. If the anti-Zionist campaign was truly an antisemitic campaign—and we have no reason to doubt this—its agents did not reflect on the irrationality of their behavior. The identity thesis, however, seems to imply some sort of deliberative process at the end of which the antisemitic subject discovers that it is convenient to target Jews as Zionists and not simply as Jews, because, for instance, outright Jew hatred is socially impermissible. If the identification of Jews with Zionists is a conscious and therefore deceitful act, this comes into conflict with the insight into the fundamental irrationality of antisemitism. If the substitution of *Jews* with *Zionists* occurs unconsciously, then it is not entirely clear which kind of identity we are dealing with here.

There is a lot to be said in favor of the second interpretation. Most notably, one major element of the campaign was the explicit rejection of its being an antisemitic spectacle. In fact, in many articles and resolutions, the authors apparently took great pleasure in expounding on the hazards and origins of antisemitism. If the purpose of selecting Zionists as the scapegoat was to cover up the antisemitic character of the campaign, it would seem odd that the antisemitic mob felt an urgent need to address the problem of antisemitism. The author of an article in *Trybuna Ludu* on March 15, 1968, asserted that "Zionist activity provides grist for the mill of antisemitism," evidently in an attempt to shift the blame for the antisemitic hysteria onto the Jews themselves.[71] An article in *Głos Pracy*, published on March 18, makes the same point: "Antisemitic excesses are . . . favorable to the Zionists, and on the other hand, provide them with arguments."[72] Similar rhetoric could be observed outside the party-controlled media. A popular sign at demonstrations read, "Antisemitism—No! Anti-Zionism—Yes!"[73] Warsaw factory workers declared in a resolution, "We will not permit revisionist and Zionist rioters to accuse us of antisemitism."[74] There is no reason to doubt that the authors of these texts genuinely dreaded the thought of being called antisemites—even though they most likely were antisemites. Their false defenses should not be understood as blunt lies but rather as reaction formations: the repression of a thought "by intensifying an opposite."[75] Just as the repressed thought can structure the conscious mind without ever entering it, the hatred of Jews can guide the actions of the antisemitic subject without ever being recognized by it. And just as the repressed deflects and modifies the contents of consciousness, antisemitism is affected by the mode in which it is realized. Likewise, the displacement of Jews through Zionists transforms the ideological structure of antisemitism. The object that is hated—that is, the ideological symptom—resonates with the "obscure impulse" that drives the antisemite.

ANTI-ZIONISM AS AN INFLECTION OF ANTISEMITISM

The Zionists who had to be purged from the party, universities, and factories did not simply and directly stand for Jews. Rather than a codified version, the anti-Zionism of March 1968 is an inflection of antisemitism. In linguistics, the term *inflection* refers to the "rules for computing the different forms of lexemes" in accordance with the syntactical context and the meaning the speaker wishes to express.[76] Lexemes can be thought of as words in an abstract sense; they unify the various forms of the same word. For example, the word forms *go* and *went* belong to the same lexeme go even though *went* looks nothing like its grammatical parent. The reason for the difference in appearance is merely historical. If two words are sufficiently similar in meaning, it may occur that certain forms of the one are absorbed into the other.[77] I suggest that an analogous dynamic is at play in classical forms of antisemitism and the more modern anti-Zionist form; they are instances of the same antisemitic paradigm. And just as the grammatical context governs the inflection of words, different historical conditions activate different forms of antisemitism.

Of course, many of the classical elements of antisemitism also characterize the campaign of March 1968: the conspiracy theories, paranoia, anti-intellectualism, and anticosmopolitanism have been a part and parcel of the ideological repertoire of Jew hatred since the nineteenth century. By identifying Jews with the Zionist fifth column, they "emerged not as a population or ethnic group but as an organization" whose aim it was—and always has been—to demolish the Polish nation by sowing discord and by weakening the bond between the elite and the people.[78] The absurdity of this idea was prosaically captured by local farmers in Włoszczowa, who were reported to have said in public: "Up to now, we've heard that the peasants and workers ruled Poland, while in reality the Jews do."[79] One could easily sympathize with the farmer of Włoszczowa. A very bizarre idea was superseded by an even more bizarre idea. The campaign was not only hideous but also could be confusing.

A typical case of antisemitic projection can be seen in the denigration of Jewish students as "banana youth" who lived lavish lives in mansions at the beach.[80] In this slur, bananas figure as a symbol of wealth. The attack on the banana-eating students reflects the rampant anti-intellectualism of the campaign. The association of studying with signs of luxury invokes the absence of toil and the free rein of leisure. The association with bananas, however, simultaneously cancels the positive evaluation; these students are apelike, primitive, and alien. Again, we are reminded of the ambivalence of antisemitism. "The banker and the intellectual, money and mind, the exponents of circulation," Horkheimer and Adorno write, "are the disowned wishful image of those mutilated by power."[81] Behind the resentment against the banana youth lies the repressed—and in consequence detested—aspiration to become like them. In a similar vein, while Moczar's paranoid warnings about a Zionist coup in Poland had no foundation in political reality, they do attest to Moczar's own ambitions of seizing power in the PZPR.[82] The delusional character of the anti-Zionist conspiracy is probably most succinctly expressed in the article that initiated the campaign. On March 11, *Słowo Powszechne* stated, "Abusing our youth's devotion to the tradition of national culture and democracy, [the Zionists] wanted to cut the patriotic bond between society and people's power."[83] In this regard, the image of the Zionist and the image of the Jew are congruent. Both are a threat to the nation's integrity, to the unity of people and state, not because of their overt and overwhelming superiority but because of their invisible, uncanny, hidden power. "It is this mixture of a weak enemy, if you're on your guard, and a possible ruler, if you don't watch out, that turns the other into an ambivalent object of envy and desire," Detlev Claussen writes about the paradoxical psychology of antisemitism.[84] The description is equally applicable to the anti-Zionist variant of antisemitism: the Zionist conspiracy appears as an immensely powerful fifth column within Poland, which then appears to be absolutely helpless against its demolition within a few weeks.

The anti-Zionist campaign shares all these features with classical antisemitism. After all, it was an *antisemitic* campaign. Nevertheless, as I suggested earlier, it would be premature to stop at this judgment. The anti-Zionist campaign displayed a distinctly anti-Zionist character in its ideological structure. The persecution of Zionists left an imprint on the delusional formation itself: in anti-Zionist antisemitism, the idea of a strictly political conspiracy gains salience.

ANTISEMITISM'S CONQUEST OF THE POLITICAL SPHERE

The political conspiracy has always been a quintessential element of modern antisemitism, just as the Jewish dominance of the economy has been an antisemitic stock-in-trade. In the economic as well as in the political sphere, the idea of a Jewish conspiracy stems from the obsessive desire to concretize abstract social relations. The antisemite declines to accept the fundamentally apersonal character of society. To him or her, the incessant transformation of labor into capital, which manifests itself in money, and the opaque monopoly of power on which state sovereignty is founded are only comprehensible as functions of personal domination. The antisemite abhors the thought that society is controlled by *something* and replaces it with the idea that *we* are controlled by *someone*.[85] Instead of conceiving the world in abstract terms, she or he imagines it in concrete images.

The Jewish conspiracy is not a generic concept; it has a proper name, sometimes in a quite literal sense: the "East Coast," "the

Rothschilds," or, more recently, "Tel Aviv." This is connected to the antisemitic desire to identify, locate, and, if possible, eliminate the culprit; the crime itself is secondary. The concretization of the abstract is not a purely theoretical enterprise; the antisemite strives to see his or her delusion realized in the world. In National Socialism, Moishe Postone contends, the Jews "became the *personifications* of the intangible, destructive, immensely powerful, and international domination of capital as a social form."[86] But the personification of the intangible is not confined to the categories of value production. The campaign in Poland illustrates that the integration of Israel, or rather the anti-Zionist image of Israel, into antisemitic ideology facilitates this ideological process of obsessive concretization in the political sphere. The political conspiracy is made tangible in Zionism. And consequently, the political conspiracy can be attacked in Israel's alleged lackeys, the Zionists.

Dariusz Stola highlights this feature of the campaign: "The word 'political' and its derivatives were the most frequently used that March to depict the enemy: political instigators, political rabble-rousers, political imposters, political bankrupts, political delinquents, political degenerates, political provocateurs, political saboteurs, shrewd political players, and pseudopoliticians."[87] On the other hand, descriptions of Zionists as wealthy, greedy, ruthless exploiters of the hardworking masses, which are typical of classical antisemitism, were conspicuously absent. In 1968, the imaginary Jew occupied the political, not the economic, sphere. Depicting the Jew as agents of Zionism, the antisemites linked their object to state sovereignty, which gave their delusional account of the political greater cohesion.

One of the most prominent slogans of March 1968 was the fight against "international Zionism."[88] This oxymoron—how could a nation-state be international?—expressed the ideological function of the Jewish conspiracy in its most condensed form. The conspiracy had an address and a name, but it was also unbound and pervasive. On March 15, *Trybuna Ludu* revealed how international Zionism maintained its paradoxical character: "[The Zionist leaders] oblige the rest of the Jewish community, scattered all over the world—instigating among it feelings of nationalism and religious fanaticism—to lend an all-round support to Israel. . . . The assistance for which the Zionist leaders call is therefore an assistance for Israeli expansionism, behind which stand the forces of imperialism, particularly West German and American imperialism."[89] The connection of Zionism to West Germany was a popular theme throughout the campaign, although the pamphleteers could not quite agree on who secretly manipulated whom. In any case, both conspired against the Polish nation.

On March 14, Edward Gierek, the powerful head of the Silesian branch of the PZPR, spoke to an audience of one hundred thousand about the nature of the Zionist conspiracy: "Whom do these people serve? What kind of people are they? These Zambrowskis, Staszewskis, Słonimskis and company, men like Kisielewski, Jasienica and others have irrefutably proved that they are serving foreign interests."[90] Gierek's use of the plural is noteworthy. The cited Jews were not to be judged according to their individual actions; they must be judged as members of a secret society. They were guilty by association. Gierek spelled out the political dimension of the antisemitic delusion. In classical antisemitism, which was chiefly concerned with Jewish economic dominance, the Zambrowskis, Staszewskis, and so on served Mammon. In anti-Zionism, political serfdom is emphasized. The fusion of both aspects, the economic conspiracy and the political conspiracy, can be seen in a March 18 article in *Głos Pracy*: "[Zionism] hobnobbed with French and British capital and even was born under the influence of that capital. Recently it stakes on American and West German imperialism."[91]

In the anti-Zionist campaign, a twofold identification was at play: first, the equation of abstract political order and Israel; and second, the equation of Israel and imagined Zionists. This was the underlying dynamic of the campaign in Poland 1968. But this dynamic was not restricted to the Polish case.[92] Rather, the campaign in Poland illustrates how productive the anti-Zionist ideology can be within the tradition of antisemitism. Anti-Zionism localizes a hitherto politically indeterminate conspiracy.

It took less than a week to mobilize hundreds of thousands of Poles against the fifth column in the nation. The chimera of Israel—a concrete political object—contributed to the efficacy of the campaign. The hateful vigor of the antisemites often correlates to the cohesion of their delusion. Antisemites want their objects to be easily identifiable and ready at hand. In this regard, the Zionist bogey is identified with Jewish world dominance in the political sphere. Here lies the historic relevance of the campaign, which transcends the political conditions of Poland in 1968.

NOTES

1. Cezar Stanciu, "Romania and the Six Day War," *Middle Eastern Studies* 50, no. 5 (2014): 775–95; Dariusz Stola, "Anti-Zionism as a Multipurpose Policy Instrument: The Anti-Zionist Campaign in Poland, 1967–1968," *Journal of Israeli History* 25, no. 1 (March 2006): 181.

2. Bożena Szaynok. "'Israel' in the Events of March 1968," in *Polin: Studies in Polish Jewry*, ed. Leszek W. Głuchowski and Antony Polonsky, vol. 21, *1968: Forty Years After* (Oxford: Littman Library of Jewish Civilization, 2009), 150–51.

3. Włodzimierz Rozenbaum, "The March Events: Targeting the Jews," in Głuchowski and Polonsky, *Polin*, 69.

4. Joanna B. Michlic, *Poland's Threatening Other: The Image of the Jew from 1880 to the Present* (Lincoln: University of Nebraska Press, 2006), 247.

5. Rozenbaum, "The March Events," 70.

6. Dariusz Stola, "The Hate Campaign of March 1968: How Did It Become Anti-Jewish?" in Głuchowski and Polonsky, *Polin*, 18. Daniel Blatman estimates the number of Jews between eighteen thousand and twenty-three thousand for 1967. Depending on whether Poles with Jewish origins are included, the number could be significantly higher. Daniel Blatman, "Polish Jewry, the Six Day War, and the Crisis of 1968," in *The Six-Day War and World Jewry*, ed. Eli Lederhendler (Bethesda: University Press of Maryland, 2000), 294–96.

7. Stola, "Anti-Zionism as a Multipurpose Policy Instrument," 184–185.

8. Stola, "Anti-Zionism as a Multipurpose Policy Instrument," 185; Rozenbaum, "The March Events," 70.

9. Stola, "Anti-Zionism as a Multipurpose Policy Instrument," 184, 194.

10. Jerzy Eisler, "1968: Jews, Antisemitism, Emigration," in Głuchowski and Polonsky, *Polin*, 42.

11. Arthur J. Wolak, *Forced Out: The Fate of Polish Jewry in Communist Poland* (Tucson, AZ: Fenestra Books, 2004), 76–83; quote cited in Rozenbaum, "The March Events," 67.

12. Stola, "The Hate Campaign," 24.

13. Eisler, "1968: Jews, Antisemitism, Emigration," 43–46.

14. Tadeusz Pióro, "Purges in the Polish Army, 1967–1968," in Głuchowski and Polonsky, *Polin*, 291.

15. Pióro, "Purges in the Polish Army," 304–5.

16. Stola, "Anti-Zionism as a Multipurpose Policy Instrument," 188.

17. Paul Lendvai, *Anti-Semitism without Jews* (New York: Doubleday, 1971), 147–48.

18. Mikołaj Kunicki, "The Red and the Brown: Bolesław Piasecki, the Polish Communists, and the Anti-Zionist Campaign in Poland, 1967–68," *East European Politics and Societies* 19 (2005): 210.

19. Eisler, "1968: Jews, Antisemitism, Emigration," 50.

20. Lendvai, *Anti-Semitism without Jews*, 96.

21. Wolak, *Forced Out*, 62.

22. Stola, "The Hate Campaign," 21–23.

23. Stola, "The Hate Campaign," 26.

24. Stola, "Anti-Zionism as a Multipurpose Policy Instrument," 193–94.

25. Stola, "The Hate Campaign," 20–21.

26. PAX was led by Bolesław Piasecki, a truly bizarre figure. After gaining prominence as a Catholic fascist leader in prewar Poland, he narrowly escaped being executed by the Red Army during the war and eventually became the favorite Catholic among Gomułka and his allies. Piasecki's antisemitism was almost proverbial. Kunicki, "The Red and the Brown," 185–225.

27. "Do studentów Uniwersytetu Warszawskiego," *Słowo Powszechne*, March 11, 1968.

28. Joanna Wiszniewicz, "Jewish Children and Youth in Downtown Warsaw Schools of the 1960s," in Głuchowski and Polonsky, *Polin*, 227–28.

29. Dariusz Stola, "Fighting against the Shadows. The *Anti-Zionist* Campaign of 1968," in *Antisemitism and Its Opponents in Modern Poland*, ed. Robert Blobaum (Ithaca, NY: Cornell University Press, 2005), 295.

30. Lendvai, *Anti-Semitism without Jews,* 114; March 12 declaration cited in Stola, "The Hate Campaign," 27.

31. Cited in Lendvai, *Anti-Semitism without Jews,* 115.

32. Stola, "The Hate Campaign," 28 [original emphasis].

33. Paul Lendvai mentions the case of Kazimierz Kakol, a close ally of Moczar, who "initiated a new TV program—'Questions and Answers'—in which he enlightened the viewers about the sinister forces behind the domestic 'Zionists.'" Whatever the question may have been, one answer was: "Zionism counted on our fundamental Marxist attitude which restrains us from disclosing certain facts, if only in order not to give rise to anti-Semitic attitudes. They were quite right. It was finally the disturbances inspired and organized by Zionists that forced us to put our cards on the table." Lendvai, *Anti-Semitism without Jews,* 119–20.

34. Stola, "The Hate Campaign," 29.

35. Cited in Lendvai, *Anti-Semitism without Jews,* 115.

36. Eisler, "1968: Jews, Antisemitism, Emigration," 51–52.

37. Lendvai, *Anti-Semitism without Jews,* 160.

38. Paul Lendvai writes: "In view of this incessant whipping-up of racial hatred, it is both a wonder and a tribute to the Poles that no reported cases of physical violence [against Jews] occurred." Lendvai, *Anti-Semitism without Jews,* 169. And Eisler, while pointing to occasional attacks on individuals, notes: "The antisemitic hysteria in spring 1968 did not result in anti-Jewish pogroms." Eisler, "1968: Jews, Antisemitism, Emigration," 51.

39. Stola, "Fighting against the Shadows," 288.

40. "Do studentów Uniwersytetu Warszawskiego"; Eisler, "1968: Jews, Antisemitism, Emigration," 51.

41. Quote found in Lendvai, *Anti-Semitism without Jews,* 94; Eisler, "1968: Jews, Antisemitism, Emigration," 56–57.

42. Władysław Gomułka, "Przemówienie na spotkaniu z aktywem warszawskim," in *Gomułka i inni: dokumenty z archiwum KC 1948–1982* (London: Aneks, 1987), 74–75.

43. Stola, "The Hate Campaign," 32. After Gomułka mentions the "academic youth of either Jewish origin or of Jewish nationality," the transcript of the speech notes "Shouting for about two minutes." Institute of Jewish Affairs, *The Student Unrest in Poland and the anti-Jewish and Anti-Zionist Campagin* [sic] (background paper no. 9, Institute of Jewish Affairs in association with the World Jewish Congress, 1968), 20.

44. Rozenbaum, "The March Events," 90–91.

45. Cited in Lendvai, *Anti-Semitism without Jews,* 182.

46. Even though the campaign was officially disbanded, it did not stop completely. Especially the MSW continued to entertain a vivid interest in domestic Zionists. In 1970, it published a series of brochures titled "Short Biographies of Some Emigrants to Israel" that exposed three hundred supporters of Zionism, imperialism, and revisionism; Szaynok, "'Israel' in the Events of March 1968," 157.

47. Quote found in Blatman, "Polish Jewry," 308; Jan B. de Weydenthal, *The Communists of Poland: An Historical Outline*, rev. ed. (Stanford, CA: Hoover Institution Press, 1986), 128.

48. Wolak, *Forced Out*, 73; Eisler, "1968: Jews, Antisemitism, Emigration," 58.

49. Szaynok, "'Israel' in the Events of March 1968," 156.

50. Blatman, "Polish Jewry," 307.

51. Eisler, "1968: Jews, Antisemitism, Emigration," 56.

52. Eisler, "1968: Jews, Antisemitism, Emigration," 56. According to the MSW, whose numbers are most likely too low, 13,333 people left Poland between 1967 and 1971. See Rozenbaum, "The March Events," 92.

53. Wolak, *Forced Out*, 116.

54. Anna Jarmusiewicz, "Domestic Shame: A Conversation with Professor Jerzy Jedlicki," in Głuchowski and Polonsky, *Polin*, 267.

55. Małgorzata Melchior, "Facing Antisemitism in Poland during the Second World War and in March 1968," in Głuchowski and Polonsky, *Polin*, 197.

56. Rozenbaum, "The March Events," 91. It took thirty years until the woeful fate of those who were forced to give up their Polish citizenship was officially recognized. In 1998, then president Aleksander Kwaśniewski "apologized on behalf of the state to all individuals who had been forced to leave the country in . . . the anti-Zionist purge of 1968–69, announcing that they had the right to reclaim their Polish citizenship." See Michlic, *Poland's Threatening Other*, 232.

57. Lendvai, *Anti-Semitism without Jews*, 117.

58. Consequently, any defensible theory of antisemitism is based on the study of antisemites and not on the study of Jews. This is because, as Horkheimer and Adorno propound, antisemitism distorts its objects; it is "based on false projection. It is the reverse of genuine mimesis and has deep affinities to the repressed; . . . If mimesis makes itself resemble its surroundings, false projection makes its surroundings resemble itself. If, for the former, the outward becomes the model to which the inward clings, so that the alien becomes the intimately known, the latter displaces the

volatile inward into the outer world, branding the intimate friend as foe. Impulses which are not acknowledged by the subject and yet are his, are attributed to the object: the prospective victim." Max Horkheimer and Theodor W. Adorno, *Dialectic of Enlightenment: Philosophical Fragments* (Stanford, CA: Stanford University Press, 2002), 154.

59. The vast majority of Zionists had emigrated by the late 1950s. See Blatman, "Polish Jewry," 293.

60. Stola, "The Hate Campaign," 16; Blatman, "Polish Jewry," 306.

61. Stola, "The Hate Campaign," 17; Blatman, "Polish Jewry," 305.

62. To some extent, the terms *Zionist, revisionist, Stalinist, imperialist*, and so on were coextensive. The semantic overlap can be explained with reference to the antisemitic notion of a *żydokomuna*, or "Judeo-Communism," which was popular in interwar Poland. According to this belief, the Jews had imported communism to Poland; the communist rule was in fact a Jewish rule. For obvious reasons, the classical concept of a *żydokomuna* could not be publicly affirmed in People's Poland, but it could be modified. If one replaces *communists* with *Stalinists*, etc. and identifies those people, "the dark side of communism" (see Stola, "Fighting against the Shadows," 293), with Jews, then *żydokomuna* is alive and well again. See also Jan T. Gross, *Fear: Anti-Semitism in Poland after Auschwitz* (Princeton, NJ: Princeton University Press, 2006), 192–243.

63. Eisler, "1968: Jews, Antisemitism, Emigration," 50.

64. Horkheimer and Adorno, *Dialectic of Enlightenment*, 156.

65. Jean-Paul Sartre, *Anti-Semite and Jew: An Exploration of the Etiology of Hate* (New York: Schocken, 1976).

66. Horkheimer and Adorno, *Dialectic of Enlightenment*, 140.

67. "Evidently, Jewish Communists were for the party the best scapegoat available." Stola, "Anti-Zionism as a Multipurpose Policy Instrument," 192. "The official anti-Semitism involved an effort to use the Jews as scapegoats for the particularly odious aspects of the communist past." de Weydenthal, *The Communists of Poland*, 130. Lendvai quotes Zygmunt Bauman, who was one of most prominent victims of the campaign, to make this point: "Thus the final settling of accounts with the remnants of Polish Jewry is to give vent to the frustration of that new middle class, as well as to provide it with a target for its disappointed hopes and ambitions, and a semblance of fulfillment for its problems and anxieties." Lendvai, *Anti-Semitism without Jews*, 169.

68. Arthur J. Wolak supposes that Gomułka might have been such a case. Wolak, *Forced Out*, 83–88. Paul Lendvai is even more explicit: "It is

certain that Gomułka has never been consciously or 'subconsciously' an anti-Semite." Lendvai, *Anti-Semitism without Jews*, 225.

Hannah Arendt remarks that, in its pure form, the scapegoat theory of antisemitism "implies that the scapegoat could have been anyone else as well." Why the antisemite is so obsessed with Jews stays a mystery. Hannah Arendt, *The Origins of Totalitarianism* (Cleveland, OH: Meridian Books, 1958), 5. We see the necessary consequence of this mistaken view in Wolak's book: "While it must be always remembered that in 1967–68 Polish Jews served as the scapegoat of a failing Communist regime, the significance of this fact must never be forgotten. In a future market by similar or different circumstances, this unfortunate role could be filled by anyone." Wolak, *Forced Out*, 165.

69. Horkheimer and Adorno, *Dialectic of Enlightenment*, 139. In contrast to antisemitism, however, anti-Zionism finds vocal support not just among the disreputable. In the words of Jean Améry, anti-Zionism has become a form of "respectable antisemitism." Jean Amery, "Antisemitism on the Left," in *Radical Humanism. Selected Essays*, ed. and trans. Sidney Rosenfeld and Stella P. Rosenfeld (Bloomington: Indiana University Press, 1984), 47.

70. Stola, "Fighting against the Shadows," 300.

71. Institute of Jewish Affairs, *Student Unrest in Poland*, 16.

72. Institute of Jewish Affairs, *Student Unrest in Poland*, 17.

73. Cited in Stola, "The Hate Campaign," 29.

74. Cited in Stola, "The Hate Campaign," 29.

75. Sigmund Freud, "Repression," in *The Standard Edition of the Complete Works of Sigmund Freud*, vol. 14 (London: Hogarth, 1915), 157.

76. Geert Booij, *The Grammar of Words: An Introduction to Linguistic Morphology* (Oxford: Oxford University Press, 2005), 4. For a more extensive discussion of inflection, see Booij, *The Grammar of Words*, 99–122.

77. For a discussion of this process, which linguists call suppletion, see Joan L. Bybee, *Morphology: A Study of the Relation between Meaning and Form* (Amsterdam: John Benjamins, 1985), 91–95.

78. Quote found in Stola, "Fighting against the Shadows," 292.

79. Cited in Eisler, "1968: Jews, Antisemitism, Emigration," 54.

80. Quote found in Michlic, *Poland's Threatening Other*, 250.

81. Horkheimer and Adorno, *Dialectic of Enlightenment*, 141.

82. Stola, "Anti-Zionism as a Multipurpose Policy Instrument," 185. On Moczar's desire for power, see Lendvai, *Anti-Semitism without Jews*, 232.

83. "Do studentów Uniwersytetu Warszawskiego."

84. Detlev Claussen, *Grenzen der Aufklärung. Die gesellschaftliche Genese des modernen Antisemitismus* (Frankfurt: Fischer, 2005), 160.

85. The idea that anything bad in the world can be traced to the actions of particular people entails the idea that the world as a whole is the willful product of someone's mind. On the basis of Horkheimer and Adorno's theory of false projection, we could conjecture that the antisemite's hate against these clandestine powers in fact expresses his or her wish for omnipotence.

86. Moishe Postone, "Anti-Semitism and National Socialism: Notes on the German Reaction to 'Holocaust,'" *New German Critique* 19, no. 1 (Winter 1980): 112 (emphasis in original).

87. Stola, "Fighting against the Shadows," 290.

88. See, for example, the March 13 resolution of the Union of Fighters for Freedom and Democracy, a staunchly Moczarite organization, which was printed in *Trybuna Ludu*: "The constant development of our country and the achievements of Poland in the world have caused an increased ideological-political campaign conducted by the imperialist and revanchist centers of the USA and the FGR [that is] levelled against us. In this slanderous campaign against People's Poland and socialism, a particularly active role is being played by international Zionism and its agencies." Institute of Jewish Affairs, *Student Unrest in Poland*, 12.

89. Institute of Jewish Affairs, *Student Unrest in Poland*, 16.

90. Institute of Jewish Affairs, *Student Unrest in Poland*, 15.

91. Institute of Jewish Affairs, *Student Unrest in Poland*, 17.

92. That is not to say that the political and social conditions in People's Poland were irrelevant for the course and the terrible efficacy of the campaign. Intraparty rivalries, censorship of the press, lack of freedom of speech, and a strong presence of Christian and racial antisemitism surely contributed to the anti-Zionist torrent. But like antisemitism, anti-Zionism does not depend on these factors. The basic function, the delusional and destructive concretization of the political, has never been confined to socialist regimes.

SIMON GANSINGER is a postgraduate student in the Philosophy Department at the University of Warwick.

FOURTEEN

—⟋w⟋—

Germany's Changing Discourse on Jews and Israel

MARC GRIMM

IN THE SUMMER of 2016, a series of terror attacks shook Germany. On July 18, a seventeen-year-old Afghan, inspired by the Islamic State, attacked passengers with an ax and a knife on a train to Wuerzburg. Four days later, an eighteen-year-old German Iranian Aryan supremacist, proud to be born the same day as Adolf Hitler, killed nine people outside a Munich shopping mall. Two days later, a twenty-seven-year-old Syrian detonated a bomb at the entrance to a music festival in Ansbach, killing himself and wounding fifteen others. The attacks have fueled a radicalization of German society. The anti-immigration and anti-Islam party Alternative für Deutschland is on the rise, and acts of politically motivated violence against immigrants have reached a new peak.[1]

On the one hand, refugees are under fire from a growing radical right. At the same time, those refugees, many of whom come from countries where antisemitism is a social norm, have put Germany's Jewish population in a trying situation. The Central Council of Jews in Germany has been at the forefront of those arguing for opening the borders to refugees. But many Jews are also worried about the mind-set of the refugees and fear that Germany might import the problems France faces with radical Muslims. The number of Jews leaving France because of antisemitism and the tense security situation there has been growing for years.[2]

The current state of affairs challenges not only Germany's and Europe's security agencies but their politics as well. German interior minister Thomas de Maizière insists, "Everyone who comes here must know what we stand for: This country has a special commitment to the Jews and to the state of Israel. This country has a very good reason to protect Jewish life and encourage its free expression. This country is a place where Jews should never again have to live in fear of persecution."[3] De Maizière's need to proclaim what should be self-evident—that Germany protects all its citizens, including Jews—indicates that Jews are in an especially vulnerable situation. To confront the problem and danger of antisemitism, proclamations on all political levels that denounce antisemitism are helpful. Yet in most cases, the media filters and comments on political rhetoric. With this function comes power and responsibility. The media does not simply collect and present information and opinion; it shapes opinion, offers perspectives, and sets the boundaries of what can and cannot legitimately be said about certain issues. This reality gives the media discourse on Jewish issues and antisemitism special relevance.

In the current political climate, strong condemnation of all forms of antisemitism is and will remain essential. It is therefore troubling that the norms of what can be said about Jews and Israel in the mainstream media have shifted since German reunification, and antisemitic resentment and imagery that seemed to have disappeared have found their way back into the discourse. This chapter illustrates this shift by examining the controversy between the influential publicist Jakob Augstein and the Simon Wiesenthal Center (SWC) over Augstein's political stance on Israel and Jews. Jakob Augstein is not just any publicist; he is heir to Rudolf Augstein, the founder and editor of *Der Spiegel*. *Spiegel* magazine was founded in January 1947 and became *the* leading medium for the German newspaper market. Jakob Augstein's columns in question were published in *Spiegel Online*, which is among the most successful German news portals, with about 17 million unique users per month.[4]

The controversy involving Jakob Augstein and the SWC took place in late 2012 and early 2013. Now, after some years, it is possible to conclude that it marks a milestone in Germany's slowly changing public discourse on Jews and Israel. To illustrate the shift that the Augstein debate represents, I will first discuss how the discourse on Jews and Israel in Germany developed following World War II. I will then examine the Augstein-SWC controversy, which soon developed into a broad public debate, and identify the main arguments used to defend Augstein and, further, the arguments that are becoming commonplace in German anti-Israel discourse. Finally, I will outline some of the problems evolving from the shift in discourse and their impact on future attempts to challenge German antisemitism.

A LONG-RANGE PROBLEM

It comes as no surprise that the end of World War II did not mark the end of antisemitism in Germany. Early opinion research conducted by the US Office of Military Government in occupied Germany perceived antisemitism as "a long-range problem."[5] The Americans especially made the treatment of Jews a litmus test for German democracy. Torn between stabilizing Germany on the one hand and de-Nazifying and reeducating Germans on the other, the Americans chose stability as tensions between the Soviet Union and the United States increased. No longer an enemy nation but an allied one at the front line of the Cold War, Germany dropped reeducation programs and reintegrated the vast majority of its citizens who had lost their jobs due to the denazification efforts of the US military government.[6] Fears and misgivings that the integration of former elites would prompt the return of National Socialism proved wrong. Yet, as Germans abandoned reeducation efforts, authoritarian, nationalist, and antisemitic attitudes were left unchallenged.

Studies show that antisemitism in early postwar Germany did not vanish but rather morphed.[7] Among the elite, antisemitism first became taboo, then positive references to Jews became standard. This postwar philosemitism was useful on both the individual and political levels. Positive reference to Jewish issues allowed people to distance themselves from National Socialism and to demonstrate their democratic catharsis. For the German state, symbolic politics toward the Jewish community and Israel were likewise instrumental. They provided evidence for the democratic character of the newly founded German state.[8] These philosemitic attitudes coexisted with antisemitism, which until the 1950s was still openly proclaimed and adapted to a specific postwar context. When public debate erupted over the alleged privileged treatment of displaced persons, the image of the greedy, selfish Jew was ascribed to (the mainly Jewish) displaced persons who had survived the war in Germany.[9] Similar images surfaced in the context of public discussions about reparation payments to Israel that started in 1952.[10] Although antisemitism emerged during those debates, hence illustrating the preservation of antisemitic imagery, opinion research shows a steady decline in antisemitic attitudes. When asked in 1952 if they thought it would be better if there were no Jews in Germany, 37 percent of Germans responded positively. The number dropped to 26 percent in 1956 and to 18 percent in 1963.[11] In the same time period, the number of those indifferent to the question varied between 50 percent in 1956 and 42 percent in 1963. This might indicate indifference to Jews, but it may also be interpreted as insecurity or a certain unease in commenting on any Jewish issue.[12]

In late 1959, the synagogue in Cologne was reopened, only to be vandalized soon afterward with antisemitic graffiti. In the following four weeks, 470 antisemitic incidents were reported throughout Germany.[13] The spontaneous and widespread outbreaks that

ensued surprised the political authorities. The government reacted by intensifying its efforts to educate its citizens, especially
the young generation, politically. The Adolf Eichmann trials in
Jerusalem in 1961 and the Auschwitz trials in Frankfurt starting
in 1963 strengthened the will of a growing number of Germans to
come to terms with the National Socialist past and antisemitism.
However, neither the trials nor the public discourse about the
Nazi past of the political elites translated into the political will to
prosecute Nazi perpetrators. In the mid-1960s, more than half of
adult Germans spoke out for ending the legal persecution of Nazi
perpetrators. The idea of a *Schlussstrich*, of leaving the past behind, gained ground and intertwined with nationalist discourse
and antisemitic imagery. Auschwitz and the Jews were obstacles
for those Germans who wanted to identify positively with the
German nation. It was a stubborn political task to integrate Auschwitz into the national narrative. Until the end of the 1990s, all
German governments emphasized the view that German history
cannot be reduced to twelve dark years. The Holocaust thus became externalized as an alien element in German history.

The wish to put an end to the commemoration of the troubled
past put the German Jews in a precarious situation. On the one
hand, they were forced into the role of democracy's guardians and
experts on antidemocratic thought. On the other hand, they were
living reminders of German guilt and shame, and as such they
disturbed the desired normalization. This secondary form of antisemitism (*Sekundärer Antisemitismus*) minimizes, relativizes, or
trivializes the Holocaust and German guilt, with the purpose of allowing a positive identification with the German nation.[14] It is also
referred to as antisemitism *because of*, not *despite*, the Holocaust.

It was not until the US television miniseries *Holocaust* was
broadcast on German television in 1979 that National Socialism became a constant political topic.[15] The impact of the series
on interest in the Holocaust can hardly be overestimated. It offered Germans the possibility to identify with Jewish victims

and brought "the mass murder of the European Jews" (as it was called before the series popularized the term *Holocaust*) into German living rooms. That year, the number of those wanting an end to the legal prosecution of Nazi crimes dropped by 20 percent to 47 percent.[16] Yet the general trend was still a desire for normalization.

Two controversies in the 1980s, the Bitburg affair and the Historikerstreit, erupted over a dispute about national pride and the widespread wish to let the past be past and to discard the rhetoric of shame and guilt.[17] After German reunification, the government of Gerhard Schröder took a new approach to solving the riddle of how to be proud to be German in light of Auschwitz. The new perspective it offered focused on German efforts to come to terms with the past. The Germans, so the new narrative goes, can be proud not *despite* Auschwitz but *because* they have come to terms with it. "The remembrance of National Socialism has become part of our identity," Schröder said in 2005 at the sixtieth anniversary of the German defeat.[18] The same year that Schröder came to power, a major debate about the German nation and the commemoration of the Shoah was triggered by Martin Walser's speech in Frankfurt's Paulskirche. Walser, a prominent novelist who received the widely recognized *Friedenspreis des Deutschen Buchhandels* in Frankfurt, concluded that, due to the ritualization of the commemoration of Auschwitz, commemoration should be limited to the private realm. "Auschwitz," he said, "is not suited to be a tool of intimidation, a flexible and constant menace or a moral cudgel or even just a compulsory exercise."[19] Walser also spoke out against the Holocaust memorial in Berlin, which he described as "a nightmare the size of a soccer field."[20] Ignatz Bubis, head of the Central Council of Jews in Germany and one of Walser's few critics, denounced Walser's speech as "intellectual arson."[21]

Among the political, social, and media elite, though, Walser's speech was well received. It fed the growing desire for normalization and created an opportunity to talk about the interrelation of commemoration and national pride. Rudolf Augstein later argued that Auschwitz was indeed instrumentalized "as we just recently witnessed, by New York lawyers."[22] He was referring to the then-ongoing demands for financial reparation for Jewish victims of Nazi forced labor. For Augstein, the demands themselves were scandalous, not the fact that the victims received no funds for decades. His reference to New York lawyers can be deciphered as a code for Jewish lawyers. Like Walser, Augstein spoke out against the planned Holocaust memorial, which he believed would spark antisemitism if it were forced on the Germans.[23] Augstein was vague about who was forcing the Germans to build a memorial, but readers were expected to understand. His comment combines images of classic and secondary antisemitism. What he basically says is that New York Jews are instrumentalizing the Holocaust for financial gain, and to be able to keep doing so, Jews need the Germans to remain an unpatriotic, guilt-ridden people. With reference to the Holocaust memorial, it was only logical that Augstein asked whether it was legitimate "to commit our descendants to prolonging our personal shame."[24] As discussed below, it is evident that Rudolf Augstein's son, Jakob Augstein, had a clear answer to that question.

Summing up post–World War II German-Jewish relations, antisemitism declined over the decades, and open antisemitism became taboo in the 1960s. Yet the decline of classic antisemitism went hand in hand with the rise of new forms of so-called secondary antisemitism, which perceives Jews as living reminders of German guilt, making it impossible for Germans to be proud of Germany again. Antisemitism has morphed into another form that has been gaining ground: Israel-related anti-semitism, which I will refer to as anti-Zionism. In contrast to outdated classic antisemitism, anti-Zionism presents itself as a postcolonial, postnational, highly moral critique of an ethnically defined Jewish state.[25] Because Augstein focuses especially on German-Israeli relations, I will elaborate on the political relations between Germany and Israel, the media reporting about Israel in Germany, and the attitudes of Germans toward Israel.

On a political level, German-Israeli relations have been predominantly positive since they were officially established in 1965. Both countries have benefited from such good relations. Germany is a reliable ally, especially when it comes to votes in the United Nations and other international organizations. In turn, the positive relations with Israel show the international community that the Germans have come to terms with their past. However, in contrast to the popular cliché, Germany was never self-sacrificing in its relations with Israel but has pursued its own interests, if necessary, in opposition to Israel.[26] It does so by maintaining good relations with Palestinian organizations and parties to this day and by drawing nearer to the Arab States once again after the establishment of German diplomatic relations with Israel had put a halt to them.

Germany's role in the struggle over the Iranian nuclear program may be a perfect example of how Germany is shifting between declaring Israel's safety an element of Germany's raison d'état while working to reopen the Iranian market for German companies, thereby politically and economically strengthening Iran.[27] Except on the pragmatic and interest-driven political level, the dominant images of Israel in German media and society were and are overloaded with projections. Against the background of the Holocaust, Jewish issues were generally highly sensitive and political. To avoid political traps, media coverage of Israel was positive, and German journalists "portrayed the young Jewish state and its society in the same philosemitic manner as . . . their Israeli colleagues, and turned a blind eye to the more unpleasant aspects of Israeli life."[28]

The Six-Day War in 1967 fueled the German media's enthusiasm for Israel.[29] Israel was admired for its military capabilities and strategy and for the bravery, nationalism, and readiness of its citizens to make sacrifices. The reporting was positive, but it idealized what had become taboo in Germany: an efficient military, backed by a toughened, patriotic society.[30] This idealization and romanticization of Israel, argues Amos Oz, contained the seeds of disillusionment.[31] These idealized images still exist, but since 1967 the image of Israelis and Israel has deteriorated. Media studies show that Israel is no longer perceived as the little David that defends itself against powerful Arab States, but that it has become Goliath, an aggressive state that suppresses the Palestinians.[32]

Also, with Germany's shift in memorial politics, the roles for Jews and Israelis have changed, and so have the keywords in the discourse. The Holocaust is no longer a matter of *shame* or *guilt* but of *responsibility*. Responsibility is not only less scathing than guilt, but it also appears that the term as understood in Germany comes with no obligations. A 2015 survey found that 61 percent of Germans believe that Germany has a special responsibility because of World War II—while it remains unclear how they define responsibility. However, only 40 percent agree that Germany has a special responsibility for the Jewish people.[33] How strong, then, is anti-Zionism in Germany?

In his cutting-edge definition of the difference between a critique of Israel and anti-Zionism, Natan Sharansky names three criteria: double standards, delegitimization, and demonization.[34] In addition, we may speak of anti-Zionism if Jews are identified with and held responsible for Israel's politics, and if Israel *alone* is held responsible for the situation in the Middle East.[35] Anti-Zionism is embedded in a specific German context where secondary antisemitism is strong and intertwines with a so-called critique of Israel that demonizes the Jewish state. This critique, which equates Israel's policy toward the Palestinians with Nazi crimes, offers psychological relief. If Israelis are identified as the perpetrators of a second Holocaust, then the Germans are relieved of the burden of having committed a singular crime. And once the Jews have become perpetrators, they no longer disturb the desired normalization of the German self-image. It is here that secondary antisemitism and anti-Zionism intersect. A major German study from 2004 found that 68.3 percent of Germans agree fully or somewhat with the statement: "Israel is pursuing a war of annihilation against the Palestinians."[36] In addition, 51.2 percent agree fully or somewhat that "What the state of Israel does with the Palestinians today is in principle no different from what the Nazis did with the Jews in the Third Reich."[37] Follow-up studies show a decline to 30 percent in 2007 and a rise to 41 percent in 2013.[38] The high numbers support what a 2003 European Union report concluded: 65 percent of Germans perceive Israel—together with North Korea—as the biggest threat to world peace.[39]

It could be argued that these perceptions do not indicate a demonization but rather a rational evaluation of Israel's politics. However, this argument has been proven wrong. A 2011 survey by the independent expert panel on antisemitism (Expertenkreis Antisemitismus) established by the German Bundestag concluded that "the facets of antisemitism significantly relate to each other: . . . Those who criticize Israel in a way that also contains antisemitic stereotypes and connotations rather tend to hold traditional or secondary antisemitic views."[40] Based on the analysis of the relation between different forms of antisemitism, the authors declared that a non-antisemitic critique of Israel was possible but that it rarely occurred.[41]

For our purposes, it seems especially pertinent to relativize the interrelationship of secondary antisemitism and a wish for a national normalization. Whereas in secondary antisemitism the Holocaust is downplayed along with German guilt, secondary antisemitism that is directed against Israel demonizes Israel as the new Nazi regime and thereby relativizes and questions German guilt and Germany's responsibility for Israel.

TOWARD NORMALIZATION?

On December 29, 2012, the Simon Wiesenthal Center, a nongovernmental organization devoted to combating antisemitism, published a list titled *2012 Top Ten Anti-Semitic/Anti-Israel Slurs*.[42]

As in previous years, it listed political regimes (Iranian regime), political parties (e.g., far-right Hungarian Jobbik party), individuals (e.g., Louis Farrakhan), and events (e.g., Israel slandered by Brazilian cartoonist). The list's categories and format suggest that it aims to draw attention to the wide geographical spread of antisemitism and to the diverse forms that antisemitism takes. In ninth place is Jakob Augstein under a headline that makes reference to his columns: "Influential German Media Personality's Bigotry."[43] The publication of the list caused an outcry in German media because of Augstein's prominence in the media community. He is a liberal, eloquent, and well-respected figure in the media business and a regular guest on German talk shows—and he is heir to one of the most influential people in the postwar media business. Although his legal father is Rudolf Augstein, founder of the weekly magazine *Der Spiegel*, in 2009 Jakob Augstein announced that his biological father is Martin Walser, one of Germany's most prominent intellectuals and writers, perhaps best known for his infamous speech in Frankfurt in 1998. Jakob Augstein is part owner of the Spiegel publishing house, editor and publisher of the weekly newspaper *Der Freitag*, and a columnist for the web and print edition of *Der Spiegel*. His weekly column, titled "Im Zweifel Links," roughly translates as "In case of doubt, I stand on the left."

The public discussion that followed the publication of the SWC list made clear the antisemitic character of Augstein's columns. More than the list itself, the discussion illustrates that when it comes to Jews and Israel, the post-Holocaust period in which Israel was "handled rather cautiously in the German media," is over.[44]

GERMANY—LED ON A LEASH

A closer look at excerpts from Augstein's columns substantiates the SWC's contention; for example: "With backing from the US, where the president must secure the support of Jewish lobby groups, and in Germany, where coping with history, in the meantime, has a military component, the Netanyahu government keeps the world on a leash with an ever-swelling war chant."[45] In general, short excerpts are hard to interpret accurately because they lack the wider context, which may shed light on the political situation, the political culture of the country or countries in question, and their respective speech codes. All of these factors need to be known in order to decipher the antisemitism that may inhere in them. In the case of the Augstein quote, the task is straightforward because it combines several core antisemitic elements. Augstein stresses the charge of Jewish world domination and Jewish influence; the most powerful man in the world must secure the support of Jewish lobby groups. Certainly, the US president needs to secure the support of sundry groups, including Jewish lobby groups. But the picture Augstein presents is that, together with its branch office in the United States, the Jewish lobby, Israel, is holding the United States, Germany, indeed the entire world *on its leash*; that is, Israel allows others scant freedom to act independently. This is a traditional antisemitic trope. The United States, after all, is a superpower and Germany has become *the* European hegemonic power. Claiming that these powers are controlled—led on a leash—by Israel is highly irrational. But the claim is understood and accepted by Augstein's readers because the image of Jewish power informs their cultural knowledge.

The second aspect I will focus on is Augstein's cryptic reference to Germany's having come to terms with its past ("Germany, where coping with history, in the meantime, has a military component"). He is referring to Chancellor Merkel's speech in the Knesset in 2008, in which she stated that Germany's responsibility for Israel's security has become part of Germany's raison d'état. When Germany delivered submarines to Israel that were partly tax-funded and obviously part of a political deal, Augstein called this policy a betrayal of German interests. "When Israel is concerned," he writes, "there are no more rules: politics, law, or economy—whenever Jerusalem calls, Berlin bows to its will."[46] The image he paints is that the Germans have a bad conscience about the Holocaust, so now they do whatever pleases Israel. Israel, on the other hand, exploits the Germans' bad conscience, asks for whatever it needs, and gets it. These are images that stem from secondary antisemitism, except it is not the Jews that profit from the Holocaust, but Israel. The Jewish state, Augstein argues, uses the Holocaust to pressure Germany.

Similar images can be found in the second Augstein quotation on the SWC's list. Augstein here refers to a poem that Günter Grass published in *Süddeutsche Zeitung* in 2012. "'Israel's nuclear power is a danger to the already fragile peace of the world.' This statement has triggered an outcry. Because it's true. And because it was made by a German, Günter Grass, author and Nobel Prize winner. That is the key point. One must, therefore, thank him for taking it upon himself to speak for us all."[47] As in Grass's poem, the threat to peace is neither Iran's nuclear program nor the Iranian leadership's insistence that it will wipe Israel off the map; it is Israel itself. According to Augstein, without Israel's nuclear capability, world peace would not be in danger. To which world peace is Augstein referring? There was a time when it was basic to left-wing identity, for good reason, to point out the countless and nameless victims of capitalism worldwide and to denounce foreign policies that ignored human rights issues. But Augstein disregards the countless victims of conflict and war—for example, in Africa—because only by ignoring ongoing conflicts and the victims they create can Israel be identified as the major threat to world peace. Therefore, it is no surprise that Augstein did not devote a single column to such major conflicts as those between Pakistan and India or North Korea and South Korea. He writes about Israel not because he is concerned with the conflicts in the region, nor does he care about Israel. A lack of basic knowledge about Israel, which he has never visited, and the region characterizes his columns. As

Matthias Küntzel rightly points out, Augstein focuses on Israel because as a German he wants to free himself from the norms that prevent him from saying what he feels it is necessary to say about the Jewish state.[48]

Augstein writes, "Grass's statement triggered an outcry. Because it is true."[49] This makes sense only if we consider that what Grass wrote is taboo. And what exactly is taboo? The truth, Augstein says. And who is preventing us from speaking the truth? We are left in the dark here, but we can read between the lines, because we have already learned who leads the world on a leash. Grass, however, caused an outcry not just for telling the truth but also for telling it even though he is German. And as a German—and that is the subtext here—he cannot freely speak his mind about Israel. Again, the wish to normalize the German self-image translates into a reversal of perpetrators and victims and a demonization of Israel. Augstein and Grass alike present the image of Germans who dare to speak the truth about Israel and are censored and silenced for it. That image is false. German media and academic research are both highly critical of Israel. What is taboo, however gingerly, in the media and the public is antisemitism. It is this distinction that Augstein obscures by making the most irrational and demonizing attitudes toward Israel acceptable.

A WHOLESALE MEDIA DEFENSE OF AUGSTEIN

When the SWC's list was published, Augstein defended himself by stating that the SWC was defaming critical journalism.[50] Every major newspaper commented on the case and supported Augstein's claim. Yet, as the philologist Lukas Betzler and political scientist Manuel Glittenberg rightly put it, the commentators rarely touched on the quotations, but rather focused on the question of whether a left-winger or a well-known journalist could possibly be an antisemite.[51] The comments indicate two major lines of argumentation: First, the SWC was accused of defaming Augstein as an antisemite without grounds. Second, Augstein's supporters accused the SWC of devaluating the term *antisemitism* by falsely applying it to people like Augstein, who are not antisemites at all.

Jan Fleischhauer, also a columnist at *Spiegel Online*, paradigmatically argued that the whole story was absurd and that the SWC was just fishing for attention. He asked, "Should I really take this whole case seriously? Should I assume that Augstein believes that the Jews are evil? ... And the next time I'm at Augstein's place for dinner, will I have to check his bookshelf for copies of the Protocols of the Elders of Zion or a copy of Mein Kampf?"[52]

Fleischhauer unwittingly explains the failure to see the problem with Augstein's slurs. Antisemites, he suggests, are people who demonize Jews and venerate Hitler. By this definition, left-wingers cannot be antisemites, nor can anti-Israel statements— that is, statements that demonize or delegitimize Israel or that apply double standards—be antisemitic.

Other major columnists supported this limited understanding of antisemitism. Frank Drieschner of the liberal *Die Zeit* asked, "So, which crime is Augstein charged with? It is hard to believe, but what he wrote are nothing more than trivial conclusions."[53] Furthermore, Christian Bommarius argued in the liberal-left *Frankfurter Rundschau*, "Augstein ... neither insulted the Jewish people nor the state of Israel. He neither advocated annihilation nor expulsion; his articles don't contain hate or resentment."[54] Fleischhauer, Drieschner, and Bommarius advocate an understanding of antisemitism that is limited to classic antisemitism, which makes it impossible to detect antisemitic codes or look into the sociopsychological motivation of people who put so much of their energy into depicting Israel as a rogue state.

In the second line of argumentation, the SWC was accused of devaluing the term *antisemitism* by falsely applying it to someone who in truth is not an antisemite. This claim seems to have become a more general trend, because it presents itself as morally acceptable. The argument does not deny the problem of antisemitism but redefines it. It claims that those who expose coded forms of antisemitism are the real problem because they harm the fight against antisemitism.

Stefan Reinecke of the left-wing *taz—die tageszeitung* writes that "the inflation [of the use of the term antisemitism—M.G.] is dangerous because the accusation of antisemitism will in the long run become a blunt sword. If everybody who condemns Israel's occupation policy is considered an antisemite—then welcome to the club."[55] The headline of Reinecke's article is "We Antisemites," and the gist of his argument is that, by the standards of the SWC, he himself must be considered an antisemite as well. Reinecke is not rejecting the accusation or arguing against it, he is ironizing it. His conclusion is that the case of Augstein shows that many accusations of antisemitism are groundless and that they damage the fight against real antisemitism. Despite the facts that empirical research proves the high level of antisemitism in German society and that Augstein's columns contain several key elements of classic, secondary, and Israel-related antisemitism, Reinecke claims that false accusations of antisemitism are the major problem.[56]

Drieschner of *Die Zeit* follows a similar line of argumentation: "Everywhere in the world people are criticizing nuclear arms. But when you voice concern against the only power in the region in the possession of nuclear arms, then you must be an antisemite!"[57] However, Augstein is on the SWC's list not for protesting against nuclear arms but for applying double standards and irrationally declaring Israel a threat to world peace.[58] Drieschner's argument in defense of Augstein is off the point, but we can see that the problem is not so much the inflationary use of the term *antisemitism* but the inflationary accusation of the misuse of the term *antisemitism*. Additionally, this line of argumentation confines antisemitism to classic antisemitism, which has been in retreat for a longer time now, while tending to ignore secondary and Israel-related

antisemitism altogether. The assertion of an increase of false accusations of antisemitism smoothly connects with a strategy of
(self-)victimization, in which Augstein becomes the victim of a
powerful Jewish lobby that allegedly tries to censor him.[59] This
assertion once again connects with the claim that the accusation
of antisemitism is used as a political weapon. Reinecke argues
that, "instead of participating in a rational debate, the Wiesenthal
Center is using the weapon of denunciation."[60] Against whom are
they using it? Reinecke argues, "Those who criticize Israel are being shot at with the antisemitism pump gun." The image is vivid:
the Jewish lobby shoots down whoever criticizes Israel.

The different lines of argumentation with which Augstein was
defended mark different levels of radicalization. In reality, these
arguments blend and form a self-perpetuating discourse. It is
a short distance between the assertion that antisemitism is applied to people who are not antisemitic—which is one that can
be discussed—to the image of a powerful, vengeful Jewish lobby
that uses the accusation of antisemitism as a political weapon to
silence critics of Israel. What is most troubling about the Augstein case is how, in immediate reaction to the publication of the
SWC's list, he was defended in all the leading newspapers. The
arguments brought forward in his defense indicate that images
that seemed to have vanished are vital among journalists: images
of a powerful Jewish lobby that silences critics, and a Jewish state
that has the power to keep the United States and Germany from
pursuing their own interests. However, the very fact that every
major newspaper defended Augstein triggered a series of comments that evaluated the columns in question and the arguments
of those defending Augstein.[61]

IN DEFENSE OF ISRAEL

The most prominent critique was penned by Josef Joffe, editor of
the weekly *Die Zeit*. In strong contrast to Drieschner's comments

in the same newspaper, Joffe stated, "These days it is worse to call someone an antisemite, than to be one."[62] In Augstein's columns, Joffe argues, "we find classic antisemitic topoi. However, they are not applied to Jews but to the Jewish state: omnipotence, conspiracy, ultimate evil. That is not critique, but demonization."[63] Augstein's obsession with Israel, Joffe argues, is fueled by the wish for salvation; the proof that the Israelis are worse than the Nazis brings the Germans moral relief.[64]

It is hard to evaluate the impact of Joffe's commentary, but we can conclude that the softening of tone in the debate is a result of Joffe having put his foot down. After the appearance of his article, no one called the accusations against Augstein groundless. Only Augstein remained unswayed. *Der Spiegel* set up a debate between Dieter Graumann, head of the Central Council of Jews in Germany, and Augstein.[65] Augstein repeated that he was not applying double standards to Israel and that he felt he was being silenced for speaking his mind. When asked why he had never been to Israel, he answered that he had also never been to South Africa, thereby equating the South African apartheid regime with Israel. This time, however, surprisingly few articles about the debate appeared in the German media.[66] Küntzel concluded that this might be because Augstein's comments proved that the SWC had rightly included him on its list. It seemed that some realized the accusations were not as absurd as they had claimed in their immediate defense of Augstein.[67] At the end of January 2013, the Augstein case concluded with a press conference to which the Mideast Freedom Forum Berlin invited Rabbi Abraham Cooper, the head of the SWC. In contrast to the debate between Graumann and Augstein, the press conference received broad media coverage. Peculiarly, the vast majority of articles refrained from taking a position. Cooper's critical examination of Augstein's positions toward Jews and Israel was reported but not commented on. Not even Cooper's assessment that Augstein's comments in the debate with Graumann proved that he indeed is an antisemite pro-voked a reaction or discussion.[68]

CONCLUSION

The fact that Augstein could publish his columns without dis-sent from other commentators illustrates how the discourse on Israel has changed over time.[69] Media events that focus on issues connected to Jewish life or Israel create an opportunity for the expression of antisemitism. The news reporting about the Gaza Flotilla in 2010, the debate about Günter Grass in 2012, and the debate about banning circumcision the same year were all ac-companied by public eruptions of antisemitism, especially on the internet. They came as no surprise. What is most troubling, however, is that the problematic idealized reporting about Israel in early postwar Germany has given way to an even more prob-lematic biased reporting that supports the steady shift in attitudes that Germans hold toward Israel.[70] While a growing majority of Israelis (in 2007, 57 percent; in 2015, 68 percent) have a positive image of Germany, Germans are split in their judgment of Israel: 46 percent have a very or rather positive opinion about Israel, and 44 percent have a very or rather poor opinion.[71] The support for Germany's pro-Israel policy among Germans is declining, espe-cially with respect to topics that are vital to Israel—for example, the delivery of arms, the political support of Israel's policies of deterrence, and ultimately the support for military action.[72] The Augstein case must be understood and judged in this wider con-text. Augstein is shifting the borders and injecting phrases into public dialogue that had seemed to have vanished—images of powerful and conspiring Jews that pressure the Germans.

But Augstein offers more than just phrases. He is a role model as a likable left-winger who wants to leave the guilt-ridden rela-tion with Israel behind and who speaks out for human rights and disarmament. Augstein is an indicator of a far bigger change. He is giving a voice to the growing number of people who question the close political relations between Israel and Germany, especially regarding issues of military action.[73] It is at this crucial point where the consequences that the two peoples have drawn from Auschwitz collide. Israelis rely on a strong military to guarantee the very existence of the Jewish state, while Germans lack the ability for empathy when it comes to the military threats that Israel faces, because they tend to be critical of military action per se. In the debate about Augstein, Josef Joffe's intervention made a difference and shows that, in Germany, elites play a special role in the discourse. Thus, one can conclude that campaigns against an "influential media personality's bigotry" can reap results.[74] In this case, Augstein's slurs actually became a topic of public debate, and broader segments of German society were confronted with articles that convincingly deciphered Augstein's antisemitic imagery.

At the same time, the course of the debate allows us to predict that the next discussion will come soon, because what underlies it was left untouched: an understanding of Israel's security situation and a discussion about the basis for German-Israeli relations in the twenty-first century and, most of all, a discussion about biased reporting on Israel in German media and the use of antisemitic stereotypes in media discourse.

NOTES

1. Lizzie Dearden, "Refugee Crisis Sparks Record Year for Political Violence in Germany as Right and Left Wing Clash," *Independent*, May 24, 2016, http://www.independent.co.uk/news/world/europe /refugee-crisis-sparks-record-year-for-political-violence-in-germany-as -right-and-left-wing-clash-a7044521.html.

2. Michael Brenner, "Bringen die Flüchtlinge mehr Antisemitismus nach Deutschland?" *Süddeutsche Zeitung*, September 20, 2015, http:// www.sueddeutsche.de/kultur/debatte-bringen-die-flüchtlinge-mehr -antisemitismus-nach-deutschland-1.2655933. For more on Jews leaving France, see Oren Liebermann, "Au Revoir and Shalom: Jews Leave

France in Record Numbers," CNN, January 25, 2016, http://edition.cnn
.com/2016/01/22/middleeast/france-israel-jews-immigration/.

3. Thomas de Maizière, "What Will Never Change," Federal Ministry
of the Interior, November 5, 2015, http://www.bmi.bund.de/SharedDocs
/Kurzmeldungen/EN/2015/11/what-will-never-change.html.

4. Average number of visitors per month between March and May
2016. See "Spiegel Online," Spiegel Media, accessed March 20, 2018, http://
www.spiegel-qc.de/medien/online/spiegel-online.

5. US Office of Military Government Report No. 49, in Frank Stern, Im
Anfang war Auschwitz (Gerlingen: Bleicher, 1991), 126.

6. Stern, Im Anfang war Auschwitz, 142.

7. See Werner Bergmann and Rainer Erb, "Privates Vorurteil und
öffentliche Konflikte. Der Antisemitismus in Westdeutschland nach
1945," in Jahrbuch für Antisemitismusforschung, Band 1, ed. Wolfgang Benz
(Frankfurt a.M.: Campus, 1992), 15.

8. See Stern, Im Anfang war Auschwitz, 467.

9. See Julia Schulze-Wessel, "Die neue Gestalt des Antisemitismus
in der deutschen Nachkriegsgesellschaft. Eine Analyse deutscher
Polizeiakten der Jahre 1945–1948," in Jahrbuch für Antisemitismusforschung
8, ed. Wolfgang Benz (Frankfurt a.M.: Campus, 1999), 183.

10. Bergmann and Erb, "Privates Vorurteil," 16, 19.

11. Bergmann and Erb, "Privates Vorurteil," 16.

12. Bergmann and Erb, "Privates Vorurteil," 23.

13. German Federal Government, Die antisemitischen und nazistischen
Vorfälle. Weißbuch und Erklärung der Bundesregierung (Bonn: n.p.,
1960), 45.

14. The term was phrased by a member of the Frankfurt School: Peter
Schönbach, Reaktionen auf die antisemitische Schmierwelle im Winter
1959/60 (Frankfurt a.M.: Europäische Verlagsanstalt, 1961).

15. Lars Rensmann, Demokratie und Judenbild. Antisemitismus in
der politischen Kultur der Bundesrepublik Deutschland (Wiesbaden: VS,
2004), 221.

16. Bergmann and Erb, "Privates Vorurteil," 16.

17. Rudolf Augstein, ed., "Historikerstreit": Die Dokumentation
der Kontroverse um die Einzigartigkeit der nationalsozialistischen
Judenvernichtung (Munich: Piper, 1987). For the Bitburg controversy,
see Torben Fischer and Matthias N. Lorenz, eds., Lexikon der
"Vergangenheitsbewältigung" (Bielefeld, Germany: Transcript, 2009); Kurt
Lenk, "Neokonservative Positionen im 'Historikerstreit' oder wie Täter

zu Opfer werden," in *Rechts, wo die Mitte ist* (Baden-Baden, Germany: Nomos, 1994), 271–79.

18. Gerhard Schröder, "Die Erinnerung an die Zeit des Nationalsozialismus ist Teil unserer Identität geworden, Gedenken an den 8. Mai 1945," *Süddeutsche Zeitung*, May 6, 2005, 7, own translation.

19. Original, "Auschwitz eignet sich nicht dafür, Drohroutine zu werden, jederzeit einsetzbares Einschüchterungsmittel oder Moralkeule oder auch nur Pflichtübung," in Martin Walser, *Dankesrede von Martin Walser zur Verleihung des Friedenspreises des deutschen Buchhandels*, accessed March 20, 2018, https://hdms.bsz-bw.de/files/440/walserRede .pdf, own translation.

20. Original, "Die Betonierung des Zentrums der Hauptstadt mit einem fußballfeldgroßen Alptraum," in Walser, *Verleihung des Friedenspreises*, own translation.

21. "Geistige Brandstiftung," quoted in Tobias Jaecker, "Die Walser -Bubis-Debatte: Erinnern oder Vergessen?" *haGalil*, October 24, 2003, accessed March 20, 2018, http://www.hagalil.com/antisemitismus /deutschland/walser-1.htm, own translation.

22. Rudolf Augstein, "Was Walser im Oktober sagte, mag er bei falscher Gelegenheit gesagt haben, es bleibt trotzdem richtig. Es bestätigt sich, was wir erst jüngst von einigen New Yorker Anwälten erlebten und was selbst Bubis, wenngleich in anderer Form, kritisierte: Auschwitz wird instrumentalisiert," *Der Spiegel*, November 30, 1998, accessed March 20, 2018, http://www.spiegel.de/spiegel/print/d-7085973.html, own translation.

23. Rudolf Augstein, "Man würde untauglichen Boden mit Antisemitismus düngen, wenn den Deutschen ein steinernes Brandmal aufgezwungen wird," *Der Spiegel*, November 30, 1998, http://www .spiegel.de/spiegel/print/d-7085973.html, own translation.

24. Rudolf Augstein, "Aber können wir unsere Nachkommen darauf verpflichten, unsere persönliche Scham weiterzutragen?" November 30, 1998, http://www.spiegel.de/spiegel/print/d-7085973.html, own translation.

25. For a critical analysis, see Julia Edthofer, "Israel as Neo-colonial Signifier: Challenging De-colonial Anti-Zionism," *Journal of the Study of Antisemitism* 7, no. 2 (2015), https://www.academia.edu/20500949 /Israel_as_neo-colonial_Signifier_Challenging_de-colonial_Anti -Zionis.

26. Shlomo Shafir, "Helmut Schmidt. Seine Beziehungen zu Israel und den Juden," in *Jahrbuch für Antisemitismusforschung 17*, ed. Wolfgang Benz (Berlin: Metropol, 2008), 297–321.

27. Stephan Grigat, Die Einsamkeit Israels: Zionismus, die israelische Linke und die iranische Bedrohung(Hamburg: KVV konkret, 2014). Also see Stephan Grigat, "Delegitimizing Israel in Germany and Austria: Past Politics, the Iranian Threat, and Post-national Anti-Zionism," in *Deciphering the New Antisemitism*, ed. Alvin H. Rosenfeld (Bloomington: Indiana University Press, 2015), 454–81

28. Gilad Margalit, "Israel through the Eyes of the West German Press 1947–1967," in *Jahrbuch für Antisemitismusforschung 11*, ed. Wolfgang Benz (Berlin: Metropol, 2002), 242.

29. From the Six-Day War on, the left started identifying Israel as a colonial state. For the left, the Jews were destined for the role as victims. When the Israeli Jews violated this role and fought and won a war, the left turned away and found a new victim: the Palestinians.

30. Jean Améry, "Der ehrbare Antisemitismus," in *Widersprüche* (Stuttgart: Klett-Cotta, 1971), 243–45; Hans-Joachim Bieber, "Zur bürgerlichen Geschichtsschreibung und Publizistik über Antisemitismus, Zionismus und den Staat Israel," *Das Argument*, no. 75 (1972), 231–74.

31. Amos Oz, *Israel und Deutschland. Vierzig Jahre nach Aufnahme diplomatischer Beziehungen* (Berlin: Suhrkamp, 2005), 42.

32. Rolf Behrens, "Raketen gegen Steinewerfer," Das Bild Israels im "Spiegel," (Berlin: Lit, 2003), 8–10.

33. Steffen Hagemann and Roby Nathanson, *Deutschland und Israel heute. Verbindende Vergangenheit—trennende Gegenwart* (Gütersloh, Germany: Bertelsmann Stiftung, 2015), accessed March 20, 2018, https://www.bertelsmann-stiftung.de/fileadmin/files/BSt/Publikationen/GrauePublikationen/Studie_LW_Deutschland_und_Israel_heute_2015.pdf.

34. Natan Sharansky, "3D Test of Anti-Semitism: Demonization, Double Standards, Delegitimization," *Jewish Political Studies Review* 16, no. 3–4 (Fall 2004), http://www.jcpa.org/phas/phas-sharansky-f04.htm.

35. Aribert Heyder, Julia Iser, and Peter Schmidt, "Israelkritik oder Antisemitismus? Meinungsbildung zwischen Öffentlichkeit, *Medien und Tabus*," in *Deutsche Zustände*, Band 3, ed. Wilhelm Heitmeyer (Frankfurt a.M.: Suhrkamp, 2004), accessed March 20, 2018, https://www.researchgate.net/publication/282672083_Heyder_A_Iser_J_P_Schmidt_2005_Israelkritik_oder_Antisemitismus_Meinungsbildung_zwischen_Offentlichkeit_Medien_und_Tabus_S_144-165_In_W_Heitmeyer_Hrg_Deutsche_Zustande_Folge_III_FrankfurtMain_Suhrkamp.

36. "Israel führt einen Vernichtungskrieg gegen die Palästinenser." See Heyder, Iser, and Schmidt, "Israelkritik oder Antisemitismus?" 151, own translation.

37. "Was der Staat Israel heute mit den Palästinensern macht, ist im Prinzip auch nichts anderes als das, was die Nazis im Dritten Reich mit den Juden gemacht haben." See Heyder, Iser, and Schmidt, "Israelkritik oder Antisemitismus?" 151, own translation.

38. Hagemann and Nathanson, *Deutschland und Israel heute*, 39–40.

39. European Commission, *Flash Eurobarometer 151—Iraq and Peace in the World* (Wavre, Belgium: EOS Gallup Europe, 2003), http://ec.europa .eu/public_opinion/flash/fl151_iraq_full_report.pdf, 81, 85.

40. Andreas Zick and Beate Küpper, *Antisemitische Mentalitäten. Bericht über Ergebnisse des Forschungsprojektes Gruppenbezogene Menschenfeindlichkeit in Deutschland und Europa* (Berlin: Expertise für den Expertenkreis Antisemitismus, 2011), accessed March 20, 2018, http:// www.bagkr.de/wp-content/uploads/kuepper_zick_antisemitismus_2011 .pdf, 29, own translation.

41. Zick and Küpper, *Antisemitische Mentalitäten*, 32.

42. Simon Wiesenthal Center, *2012 Top Ten Anti-Semitic/Anti-Israel Slurs* (Los Angeles: Simon Wiesenthal Center, 2012), accessed March 20, 2018, http://www.wiesenthal.com/atf/cf/%7B54d385e6-f1b9-4e9f-8e94 -890c3e6dd277%7D/TT_2012_3.PDF.

43. Simon Wiesenthal Center, *2012 Top Ten Anti-Semitic/Anti-Israel Slurs*, 4.

44. Margalit, "Israel through the Eyes," 235.

45. Simon Wiesenthal Center, *2012 Top Ten Anti-Semitic/Anti-Israel Slurs*, 4. In the original piece, in the sentence following this quote, Augstein refers to an article that he believes does prove his point. The cited article is by *Haaretz*'s Gideon Levy. Augstein's implicit argument is that if even a Jewish Israeli supports his view, then it must be correct. The argument ignores the wide range of attitudes toward all fields of Israeli society and politics.

46. "Denn wenn es um Israel geht, gilt keine Regel mehr: Politik, Recht, Ökonomie—wenn Jerusalem anruft, beugt sich Berlin dessen Willen." Jakob Augstein, "Die deutsche Atom-Lüge," *Spiegel Online*, June 4, 2012, accessed March 20, 2018, http://www.spiegel.de/politik/ausland/u-boote -fuer-israel-wie-deutschland-die-sicherheit-in-nahost-gefaehrdet-a-836816 .html, own translation.

47. Simon Wiesenthal Center, *2012 Top Ten Anti-Semitic/Anti-Israel Slurs*, 4. Original: "Es musste gesagt werden," *Spiegel Online*, April 6,

2012, http://www.spiegel.de/politik/deutschland/jakob-augstein-ueber
-guenter-grass-israel-gedicht-a-826163.html.

48. Matthias Küntzel, "Die Augstein-Debatte: eine verpasste Chance,"
in *Gebildeter Antisemitismus*, ed. Monika Schwarz-Friesel (Baden-Baden,
Germany: Nomos, 2015), 55.

49. Simon Wiesenthal Center, *2012 Top Ten Anti-Semitic/Anti-Israel
Slurs*, 4.

50. See Lukas Betzler and Manuel Glittenberg, *Antisemitismus im
deutschen Mediendiskurs. Eine Analyse des Falls Jakob Augstein* (Baden-
Baden, Germany: Nomos, 2015), 14.

51. Betzler and Glittenberg, *Antisemitismus im deutschen Mediendiskurs*, 14.

52. Jan Fleischhauer, "Der Fall Augstein," *Spiegel Online*, January
6, 2013, accessed March 20, 2018, http://www.spiegel.de/politik
/deutschland/antisemitismus-debatte-der-fall-augstein-a-875976.html,
own translation.

53. "Was also hat Augstein verbrochen? Es ist kaum zu glauben:
Was ihm vorgehalten wird, geht über triviale Feststellungen kaum
hinaus." Frank Drieschner, "Wer hasst da wen? Das Simon Wiesenthal
Center diffamiert einen Israel-Kritik," *Zeit Online*, January 3, 2013,
http://www.zeit.de/2012/02/augstein-antisemitismus-vorwurf, own
translation.

54. "Augstein hat weder in seinen Artikeln im Freitag noch als
Kolumnist von Spiegel online Juden beleidigt oder den Staat Israel. Er
hat für keine Vernichtung plädiert und für keine Vertreibung, aus seinen
Texten spricht kein Hass und kein Ressentiment." Christian Bommarius,
"Broder diffamiert Augstein," *Berliner Freitung*, January 2, 2013, http://
www.berliner-zeitung.de/kultur/antisemitismus-broder-diffamiert
-augstein-3790446, own translation.

55. Stefan Reinicke, "Gefährlich ist diese Inflationierung, weil der
Vorwurf des Antisemitismus damit langfristig zum stumpfen Schwert
wird. Wenn jeder, der die Besatzungspolitik für fatal hält, ein Antisemit
ist—dann *welcome to the club*," *Wir Antisemiten*, January 4, 2013, accessed
March 20, 2018, http://www.taz.de/1/archiv/digitaz/artikel/?ressort
=me&dig=2013%2F01%2F04%2Fa0080&cHash=98c63ffofc967e8c1a01da
c1a3686948, own translation.

56. See Betzler and Glittenberg, *Antisemitismus im deutschen
Mediendiskurs*, 205.

57. "In aller Welt kritisieren Atomwaffengegner Atomwaffen. Wer aber
Bedenken gegen israelische Atomwaffen vorträgt, die einzigen in der

Region, der muss Antisemit sein!" Drieschner, "Wer hasst da wen?" own translation.

58. It must come as no surprise that, in 2015, Augstein spoke out only against Israel's supposed nuclear capability but welcomed Iran's ambitions to become a nuclear power, because this would end an "anomaly: in the foreseeable future Israel will no longer be the only nuclear power in the region. . . . Those who want to deny Iran the right to possess nuclear arms, should take away Israel's nuclear arms." Jakob Augstein, "Die iranische Bombe kommt sowieso," *Spiegel Online*, April 9, 2015, accessed March 20, 2018, http://www.spiegel.de/politik/ausland/jakob-augstein-ueber-den-atomvertrag-mit-iran-und-benjamin-netanyahu-a-1027654.html, own translation.

59. Drieschner writes: "Im publizistischen Nahostkonflikt ist ein eher leichtfertiger Umgang mit dem Vorwurf des Antisemitismus üblich. Was gerade geschehen ist, sprengt allerdings diesen Rahmen. Die Frage ist, ob sie womöglich gemeinsam durchdrehen: Israel, das Land, das sich anschickt, eine Zwei-Staaten-Lösung durch neue Siedlungen endgültig zu verhindern, während zwei Drittel seiner jüdischen Bewohner nach einer aktuellen Umfrage den Palästinensern in einem gemeinsamen Staat die Bürgerrechte verweigern wollen. Und seine Lobby, die soeben in Gestalt des renommierten Simon-Wiesenthal-Zentrums den deutschen Journalisten Jakob Augstein zu einem der schlimmsten Antisemiten der Welt erklärt hat." In short, Drieschner claims that the state of Israel and Israeli citizens and their lobby, the SWC, are silencing a German journalist by making him one of the world's worst antisemites. Drieschner's defense of Augstein itself incorporates images of Jewish conspiracy and power. See Drieschner, "Wer hasst da wen?" own translation.

60. "Anstatt sich einem rationalen argumentativen Wettbewerb zu stellen, greift das Wiesenthal-Center zur Waffe der Denunzination. Schon die nun ventilierte Frage, ob Augstein ein Antisemit ist (vielleicht doch ein ganz kleines bisschen), hat etwas Diffamierendes. Denn an wem dieses Etikett klebt, der ist im öffentlichen Diskursgeschäft erledigt. Diese Stigmatisierung dient also auch als Warnschuss. Wer Israel kritisiert, wird mit der Antisemitismus-Schrotflinte beschossen." Stefan Reinicke, *Wir Antisemiten*, January 4, 2013, accessed March 20, 2018, http://www.taz.de/1/archiv/digitaz/artikel/?ressort=me&dig=2013%2F01%2F04%2Fa0080&cHash=98c63ff0fc967e8c1a01dac1a3686948, own translation.

61. Matthias Küntzel, "Jakob Augstein und der Israelkomplex," *Welt*, January 14, 2013, http://www.welt.de/kultur/article112761041/Jakob-Augstein-und-der-Israelkomplex.html; Malte Lehming, "Was im 21.

Jahrhundert antisemitisch ist," *Der Tagesspiegel*, January 9, 2013, accessed March 20, 2018, http://www.tagesspiegel.de/meinung/debatte-um-jakob -augstein-was-im-21-jahrhundert-antisemitisch-ist/7602976.html; Denis Yüzel, "Mit fettarsciger Selbstzufriedenheit," *Taz*, January 15, 2013, http:// www.taz.de/!5075375/.

62. Josef Joffe, "Es ist heute schlimmer, jemanden einen Antisemiten zu nennen, als einer zu sein," *Antisemitismus-Knüppel*, January 13, 2013, accessed March 20, 2018, http://www.zeit.de/2013/03/Zeitgeist -Antisemitismus-Adorno, own translation.

63. "Hier finden sich die klassischen AS-Topoi wieder; bloß gelten sie nicht dem Juden, sondern dem jüdischen Staat: Allmacht, Verschwörung, das Böse schlechthin. Das ist nicht Kritik, sondern Dämonisierung." Josef Joffe, "Antisemitismus-Knüppel," *Zeit Online*, January 13, 2013, accessed March 20, 2018, http://www.zeit.de/2013/03/Zeitgeist-Antisemitismus -Adorno, own translation.

64. See Joffe, "Antisemitismus-Knüppel," own translation.

65. Spiegel-Streitgespräch, "Was ist Antisemitismus?" *Spiegel Online*, January 14, 2013, accessed March 20, 2018, http://www.spiegel.de/spiegel /print/d-90535659.html.

66. See Betzler and Glittenberg, *Antisemitismus im deutschen Mediendiskurs*, 261.

67. See Matthias Küntzel, "Auffällige Emotionalität," Texte, January 31, 2013, http://www.matthiaskuentzel.de /contents/auffaellige-emotionalitaet.

68. See Betzler and Glittenberg, *Antisemitismus im deutschen Mediendiskurs*, 267.

69. Few had criticized Augstein before the SWC put him on the list. Broder and Mense had published their articles online and Trampert in a small Communist magazine. Thorsten Mense, "Augstein, Pirker und die 'Cui bono?'-Frage," *Publikative*, September 24, 2012, accessed March 20, 2018, http://publikative.org/2012/09/24/deutsches-abc-augstein-birker -und-die-cui-bono-frage/. See also Rainer Trampert, "Freitagsgebete," *Konkret*, November 2012, accessed March 20, 2018, http://www.konkret -magazin.de/aktuelles/aus-aktuellem-anlass/aus-aktuellem-anlass -beitrag/items/333.html; and Henryk Broder, "Jakob und seine Brüder," *Henryk M. Broder*, April 8, 2012, accessed March 20, 2018, http://henryk -broder.com/hmb.php/blog/article/5671.

70. Several media studies identify one-sided pro-Palestinian reporting on Israel that fails to acknowledge the Israeli perspective. To name only

the latest case, see Vijeta Uniyal, "Germany's State-Run Broadcaster Peddles Anti-Israel Water Libel as News," *Legal Insurrection*, August 16, 2016, accessed March 20, 2018,http://legalinsurrection.com/2016/08 /germanys-state-run-broadcaster-peddles-anti-israel-water-libel-as-news/.

71. Hagemann and Nathanson, *Deutschland und Israel heute*, 35.
72. Hagemann and Nathanson, *Deutschland und Israel heute*, 55.
73. Hagemann and Nathanson, *Deutschland und Israel heute*, 54.
74. Simon Wiesenthal Center, *2012 Top Ten Anti-Semitic/Anti-Israel Slurs*.

MARC GRIMM is an academic researcher at the Centre for Prevention and Intervention in Childhood and Adolescence at Bielefeld University. His work focuses on empirical social research, critical theory, racism, and antisemitism.

The Roots of Anti-Zionism in South Africa and the Delegitimization of Israel

MILTON SHAIN

ALTHOUGH A PEW poll based on an urban population study conducted in 2007 indicated that 28 percent of South Africans sided with Israel in the Israeli-Palestinian conflict as opposed to 19 percent with the Palestinians,[1] and although the African National Congress (ANC)-led government currently accepts the two-state solution to the Israeli-Palestinian conflict, when it comes to the "chattering classes" (white and black) and the ANC as a political party, as well as the largest trade union federation, the Congress of South African Trade Unions (COSATU), Zionism is now demonized as signifying oppression, expansion, and illegitimacy.[2] Why has this hostility gained such traction in the new and democratic South Africa, and to what extent has classic antisemitism penetrated anti-Zionist discourse?

It would seem that four major factors underpin this hostility: (1) the radicalization from the early 1970s of a new Muslim generation that is more educated and more influential despite comprising less than 2 percent of the total South African population; (2) a "third worldist" and pro-Palestinian ANC-led sentiment fueled by close ties between the South African apartheid regime and Israel during the 1970s and 1980s coupled with a visceral suspicion of ethnicity; (3) a discourse among intellectuals—white and black—framing the Israeli-Palestinian struggle through a South African prism; and (4) antisemitism.

RADICALIZATION AMONG EDUCATED
AND INFLUENTIAL MUSLIMS

Although the tiny Muslim community had long been hostile to the Zionist enterprise (the Israeli war of independence in 1948 was described at the time in the Muslim press as a catastrophe or Nakba), Jews in predemocratic South Africa experienced a sense of quiescence on the part of Muslims—no doubt a product of apartheid's hermetic separation.[3] However, a new Muslim militancy was evident in the wake of the United Nations resolution of 1975 equating Zionism with racism that was hailed in the national Muslim weekly *Muslim News* as a victory for the Palestine Liberation Organization (PLO) and a defeat for the United States and Israel.[4]

This new generation of Muslims began to challenge its more conservative elders through, for example, the formation of the Muslim Youth Movement in 1970 and the Muslim Students Association in 1974.[5] Inspired by radical teachings and by the African student uprising in Soweto in 1976, younger Muslims rejected the more accommodating behavior of the Muslim establishment. In calling for an "Islamic way of life," groups such as the Muslim Youth Movement, writes Abdulkader Tayob, "reflected the black consciousness movement's appeal to an authentic black identity in South Africa."[6]

While substantial opposition to the new Islamism persisted among conservative Muslims, these new radical forces began to gain momentum and influence. Study programs and camps were initiated, and manuals were printed. Much of the material was provided by Islamic groups abroad that targeted Zionism, secularism, capitalism, and communism as the major threats to Islam.[7] In searching for a "socially relevant Islam," South African Muslims increasingly became acquainted with the antistate writings of Abdul A'la Mawdudi (1903–79) and Sayyid Qutb (1906–66). Added impetus was provided by the success of the Iranian revolution in 1979. In its wake, the writings of Ali Shari'ati (1933–77) and Ayatollah Khomeini were included on Muslim Youth Movement reading lists.[8]

Although Iran was not perceived as a model for South African Muslims, Qibla, an Islamist movement founded in 1980, was patently inspired by the overthrow of the shah. Three years later, this movement objected to the creation of the United Democratic Front, an anti-apartheid umbrella movement that included progressive Jewish organizations. Accusing it of being Zionist-controlled and operating at the behest of the international Jewish financial conspiracy, Qibla was able to tap into a deep-rooted anger that identified Zionism as the "citadel of imperialism."[9] Indeed, for some, apartheid was even perceived as a product of Jewish and Zionist manipulation.[10]

Although Qibla remained a minority movement and was in essence a front for marginalized religious figures and a few small organizations who accepted the preeminence of Qibla and its leader, Ahmed Cassiem, its ideas were widely shared.[11] The Muslim press regularly wrote about Zionist-inspired international financial machinations and accused Jews of supporting and influencing the apartheid state. Even those Jews committed to the struggle against apartheid were never fully trusted. Radicalization was evident in well-organized Al Quds Day events. The Jewish state was described as a focus of evil and a conspiratorial center that was rooted in the Zionist movement, and its record on human rights abuse was condemned.[12]

A Qibla-inspired vigilante movement called PAGAD (People against Gangsterism and Drugs), which emerged amid the breakdown of law and order in the aftermath of apartheid's demise and the loosening of the police state, was touted as an answer to social evils.[13] Islam was the preferred solution.[14] Muslim writings now reflected an increasingly paranoid cast of mind, with Jews being portrayed as pulling all the strings.[15] Global events and identification with Muslims in the Middle East and Near East

sharpened boundaries between the South African Muslim community and "others," which, of course, included Jews. Relations
with the South African Jewish community were further strained
by PAGAD's flaunting of its links with Hamas and Hizballah.

The Muslim community became increasingly "hot-wired" to
events in the Middle East. Thus, the infamous "pig poster" incident
in Hebron, Israel, led to heated protests in Pretoria and Cape Town
and the firebombing of a Jewish book center.[16] The hostile mood was
exacerbated by the breakdown in the Israeli-Palestinian Oslo peace
process. In this atmosphere, even an invitation to the mayor of the
Cape Metropolitan Council, the Reverend William Bantom, to attend an international mayoral conference in Israel in May 1998 led to
fierce debate and heavy pressure on the mayor from Muslim organizations (supported by the ANC provincial caucus) not to accept.[17]

In the context of such tensions, Qibla led protests at the 1998 Israeli Jubilee celebrations in Cape Town, and the secretary general
of the Muslim Judicial Council, Sheikh Achmat Sedick, claimed
that it was unthinkable for any South African to share in these
Jewish and Zionist celebrations.[18] The mood was further inflamed
when the South African government refused to issue a visa to
Sheik Ahmed Yassin, spiritual leader of Hamas, who nevertheless
conducted a telephone interview that was broadcast on a Cape
Town Muslim radio station.[19] Protests followed, with marchers
outside parliament chanting the usual "death to Israel" and "one
Zionist, one bullet" while an Israeli flag was burned.[20] It thus
came as no surprise that *The Protocols of the Elders of Zion* went
on sale at the 2001 World Conference against Racism in Durban,
where South African Muslims joined their coreligionists from
abroad and others hostile to Israel in what turned out to be an
anti-Zionist and antisemitic hate fest.[21] Muslims were prominent
in driving the anti-Israel agenda. Relatively well educated and
well placed in the corridors of power in post-apartheid South
Africa, this tiny minority—punching well above its weight—has
managed to keep the Palestinian question uppermost in popular

and party-political discourse while enjoying substantial support among the black and white intelligentsia.

THIRD WORLDIST AND
PRO-PALESTINIAN SENTIMENT

The ANC (together with the Indian Congress, the Coloured People's Organisation, and the Congress of Democrats) had already formulated a hostile view of "tribalism" or ethnicity in its Freedom Charter of 1955, which stressed the unity of South Africa and opposed the politics of ethnic or tribal division.[22] Intellectually, these positions were underpinned by a critique of the dangers of ethnic mobilization as evident in the Afrikaner national movement. These ideas were reinforced from the 1960s by Marxian currents within the academy, both in South Africa and abroad. Scholars deconstructed ethnicity while demonstrating how it was being manipulated and used in South Africa as a means to divide and rule, so clearly evident in the apartheid project with its proposed puppet ethnic "homelands."[23]

A broadly third worldist and anticolonial *weltanschauung* evolved among local and exiled domestic activists who took a decidedly dyspeptic view of the West and its support for the apartheid state, as well as the Pretoria-Jerusalem axis that evolved in the years before and after the Yom Kippur War of 1973, when sub-Saharan states cut links with Israel.[24] With such views came a growing identification with third world liberation movements and with the PLO. By the late 1980s, an increasingly radicalized left was describing Israel as an exclusivist apartheid state. At the United Nations, Dr. Neo Mnumzama, the chief representative of the ANC—still in exile at the time—put it bluntly: "The South African people have never approved of Zionism. They see parallels of apartheid in Zionism and therefore their struggle against apartheid automatically has overtones of anti-Zionism which is not the same thing as being anti-Jewish."[25]

These views were shared by Aubrey Mokoena, a senior member of the local United Democratic Front, which was effectively an internal wing of the ANC. Zionism, he maintained, was simply racism "because Zionism says we close our ranks on an ethnic basis. We take care of the Jewish interests. If you are Jewish it's okay, if you are not Jewish, *out*."[26] A former president of the "Africanist" Azanian Political Organization, Ishmael Mkhabela, took a similar view, claiming that Zionism was a form of religious discrimination that, in his view, was the same as the racial discrimination faced by blacks in South Africa.[27]

This alleged Jewish exclusivity ran counter to the nonracial and inclusivist outlook of the ANC liberation movement and invoked an easy sympathy for the PLO.[28] There is no doubt, said the prominent Soweto civic leader Dr. Nthato Motlana, "that Black Africans tend to identify with the PLO. . . . Let's be clear about this, there is a perception of the Israeli-Arab conflict as one of almost colonialism of a white race coming out of Europe."[29]

With the release of Nelson Mandela in 1990 and the unbanning of the ANC and other proscribed movements, a broad hostility toward Zionism appeared in public discourse. Indeed, within weeks of Mandela's release, the Jewish community was jolted when photographs were published of Mandela warmly embracing Yasser Arafat at their meeting in Lusaka. A day later, Mandela was quoted as saying that if his meeting with Arafat and his statements equating the struggle of the Palestinians with that of the blacks were to alienate "South Africa's influential Jewish community," that was just "too bad."[30]

INTELLECTUAL DISCOURSE FRAMING
THE ISRAEL-PALESTINIAN STRUGGLE
THROUGH A SOUTH AFRICAN PRISM

Hostility toward the Jewish state has become deeply entrenched in intellectual circles. The English-language press, most of which was owned by Irish Tony O'Reilly's Independent Group from 1994 to 2014, took an anti-Israel stance that has been amplified by the new owners, an ANC-connected consortium chaired by Iqbal Surve. Under O'Reilly's Independent Group, a previously benign view of Israel shifted to one of hostility. Robert Fisk and John Pilger were regular columnists, poisoning an already antagonistic atmosphere. Even 9/11 did not temper hostility. Some of it was driven by Ronnie Kasrils, who was a communist Jew, a member of the ANC underground for thirty years, and a senior commander of its military wing, Umkhonto We Sizwe. Until 2009, as a cabinet minister, Kasrils consistently compared Israel with apartheid South Africa and portrayed Jews as having much in common with the Afrikaners, including the idea of "chosenness," which he argued is used to advance the cause of a particular people. "It is an exclusivity which gives rise to racism and all sorts of negative things," he explained.[31] Of course, the notion of exclusivity—manifest in the ethnonational state—has often raised problems for the radical left (albeit selectively) in that it challenged a deep-seated universalism and hostility to nationalism.

In addition to these theoretical challenges, South Africa's so-called miracle transition further undermines the Jewish state with commentators frequently questioning why Israelis and Palestinians cannot follow the South African example and establish a single constitutional state that includes Jews and Palestinians. An exemplar of this reasoning is Allister Sparks, the influential journalist and former editor of the liberal *Rand Daily Mail*. In his articles, Sparks has repeatedly drawn parallels between South Africa and Israel, arguing that the Jewish state has to negotiate with its enemies, including Hamas and Islamic Jihad. Israel's refusal to do so, he maintains, is reminiscent of the old National Party in South Africa.[32]

According to Sparks, the two-state solution is dead. Israel's lack of will to remove the settlements coupled with demographic realities has precluded this option. "Like South Africa's bantustan policy," he writes, "it was a nice idea in theory: to separate rival groups living in one country so that each can have its own national homeland sounds like a moral solution—provided the separation is fair and the homelands are viable." In building his case, Sparks recalls how the apartheid planners had also denied demographic realities in their dream of a white South Africa. But eventually, he reminds us, they had to face the truth.[33]

Sparks always frames the Israeli-Palestinian conflict through a South African prism. The fact remains, he argues, "that many ethno-nationalisms grapple with the problem of other ethnic groups in their midst.... The new South Africa has not required the forfeiture of the 'Afrikaner homeland.' I well remember the dark warnings, uttered from pulpit and platform, over half my working life, that 'one man one vote' would mean the 'national suicide' of the Afrikaner *volk* and that they would never, ever contemplate it."[34]

In a series of articles resulting from a visit to the region, Sparks reinforced the South African paradigm. After meeting in Damascus with Musa Abu Marzook, deputy to Hamas's Damascus-based Khalid Mashaal, Sparks reported that he found the Hamas man to be a pragmatist. Hamas's call for a *hudna*, or truce, which could prepare the way for a settlement, made great sense to Sparks. "The mutual recognition of a stalemate," he wrote, "or what we South Africans back in the 1980s called a 'violent equilibrium,' has been identified by political analysts as a crucial first step toward resolving national conflicts of this kind. Thereafter, as the South African experience showed, events can sometimes start generating their own momentum."[35]

Underpinning Sparks's critique is a comparison of Palestinian life with that of blacks under apartheid. "The whole matrix is vividly reminiscent of South Africa's Bantustan dispensation, although Israelis vigorously resist any such comparison," he explained. "I travelled extensively through the West Bank, talking to Palestinians and experiencing what they go through every day, and I am convinced it is neither a viable homeland nor a bearable existence for them."[36]

The mantra of nonracism in the "new South Africa," its opposition to ethnic politics, its powerful anticolonialism, its support for the underdog, historic ties between the ANC and the PLO, and the success of South Africa's so-called miracle all add popular weight to the Sparks view. If South Africa could pull itself back from the chasm and avoid a racial conflagration, why can't the Jews and Palestinians do the same? After all, South Africans negotiated a constitution that was inclusive but respectful of cultural and religious diversity. Surely this can be replicated by Israelis and Palestinians.

What we have in Israel, then, is—to use Tony Judt's term—an anachronistic ethnic state. At least this is the way many South Africans, including some leftist Jews, see it. The ethnic state evokes echoes of failed Afrikaner dreams. Like the apartheid state, Israel builds on exploited cheap Palestinian labor. In this paradigm, the Palestinian struggle represents anticolonial resistance. But the parallels are taken even further. South Africans believe that the Palestinians were offered "Bantustans" at Camp David, akin to what the "homeland" leaders were offered under apartheid and would replicate the historic migrant labor system that looms large in South African consciousness.[37] And so it follows that those resisting Zionism should learn from the South African experience. As Blade Nzimande, the minister of higher education, told a mass meeting in Johannesburg recently, the conflict was one of "western imperialism in partnership with Zionism" against the indigenous Palestinians.

> Let us use people's sanctions against Israel as effectively as the international anti-apartheid movement did so against apartheid South Africa. The Palestinians will resist oppression in any way that they can. However, it is the duty of democratic forces across the world to support them in any way that we can. Let us campaign to persuade South Africans not to buy Israeli consumer goods and South African businesses not to import Israeli products of any kind. Let us research ways in which the Israeli economy can be compromised through legal means. We should cooperate with anti-Zionist forces in all countries to get international financial, trade and cultural sanctions against Israel.[38]

ANTISEMITISM

At least some of the hostility toward Israel is informed by blatant hostility toward Jews. The telltale signs emerge from time to time, as in Holocaust denial on a Muslim radio station in the 1990s,[39] in hate mail, social media abuse, verbal abuse, mass email postings, demonstrations and pamphlets, graffiti, and violence and vandalism.[40] Invariably, it tracks the ebb and flow of the Israeli-Palestinian conflict. But antisemitism is also evident at the highest levels. At the time of Operation Cast Lead, Israel's incursion into the Gaza Strip in early January 2009 in response to the rocketing of nearby Israeli population centers, South Africa's then foreign minister told a mainly Muslim audience that the United States and the West were controlled by "Jewish money power."[41] COSATU even raised the possibility of trade unions targeting specifically Jewish business.[42] On another occasion, COSATU's spokesperson described the South African Zionist Federation as having hands "dripping with blood," while Israel was said to be a "legalisation of Jewish supremacy to further dehumanise everyone outside the scope of Zionist purity."[43] The pressure persisted well after the Gaza incursion, with Nobel Laureate Archbishop Emeritus Desmond Tutu and other prominent figures regularly castigating Israel's actions.[44] In 2011, the University of Johannesburg severed ties with Ben-Gurion University of the Negev, and in 2012, Deputy Foreign Minister Ebrahim called on South Africans not to visit Israel.[45] During Israel Apartheid Week in 2013, protestors, led by the South African chapter of the international Boycott, Divestment, Sanctions (BDS) movement, disrupted a concert at the University of the Witwatersrand, Johannesburg, featuring a visiting Israeli pianist.[46] Later in the year, demonstrators chanted "Dubula e Juda" ("Shoot the Jews" in Zulu) outside a concert intended to compensate for the earlier disruption.[47] All the old canards were heard once again during Operation Protective Edge in August 2014.

In a particularly ugly communication at the time, Tony Ehren-reich, a one-time trade unionist and now a senior ANC politician in the Western Cape opposition, called on those Jews support-ing Zionism to leave the country.[48] As R. W. Johnson, a former Oxford don, wrote, this was a "blood libel."[49] Social media has displayed even worse outrages recently. "Kill the Jew"; "May you burn in Hell"; "You must get out of South Africa and don't come back, you Jewish bastards," all reflect the tone. Posters held aloft during marches show no distinction between opposition to Israel policies and simple, crude Jew hatred. "Keep calm and Kill the Jews" was posted on the ANC Youth League website.[50] More disturbingly, ANC secretary general Gwede Mantashe issued a statement describing the establishment of the state of Israel as a "crime against humanity."[51] Amid such discourse has even been talk (albeit denied) of the ANC considering making far-reaching changes to South African citizenship laws, the specific purpose of which was to place restrictions on ties between South Africans and Israel and impose punitive sanctions against South African companies that do business with Israel.[52]

It is in this context that the BDS movement has had such reso-nance in South Africa. Fully aware that it is the linchpin in an international movement, BDS South Africa enhances the "apart-heid Israel" critiques, doing its best to keep the issue alive, with apartheid Israel central to its efforts because it resonates so eas-ily with those who struggled for liberation in South Africa. Jews are accused of siding with the apartheid regime and now with apartheid Israel. Some of the actions of the BDS movement are driven by simple hatred of Jews—but this will be denied. Instead, a human rights discourse is employed; it is an easy sell. Driven largely by Muslims and well placed in the corridors of power, BDS effectively calls for a single-state solution. Local activists connect internationally, appear to be well funded, employ so-phisticated methods, and make good use of the electronic media. At the highest levels of state, Israel has been marginalized, and those wishing to plead her case find little access. University administrations encourage and often support BDS activism, albeit informally—and in one case at least, it would seem that material support was provided for Israeli Apartheid Week.

Put simply, among the human-rights-oriented elites, Zionism is considered a nineteenth-century ethnonational movement, and the new South Africa has little empathy for ethnic concerns. As Hermann Giliomee, a leading historian, explains, South Africa today is informed by "a dogmatic or intransigent universalism." "Its point of departure is that race or ethnicity as a principle of social organization is essentially irrational and ephemeral and that there is no need to make any concessions to it. What this boils down to is the unshakeable conviction that there is not much more to racial or ethnic identification than the legacy of apartheid classification."[53]

This mind-set, of course, runs counter to the notion of a Jewish state. Zionism as a liberation movement is forgotten; the term has become associated with exclusivism, oppression, and expansionism. "It's a policy that to me looks like it has very many parallels with racism," explains Desmond Tutu.[54] Jewish suffering in the diaspora and the dramatic rebirth of the Jewish state are not acknowledged. Indeed, the anti-Zionist critique employs simplistic comparisons, bypassing the failure of Jewish emancipation in nineteenth- and early twentieth-century Europe, and ignoring international support for Zionist efforts, beginning with the Balfour Declaration of 1917 and concluding with the decision of the United Nations in 1947 to partition British Mandate Palestine into a Jewish and Arab state. Historic ties between Jews and the land of Israel are of no consequence. Attempts on the part of Jewish leaders in the Yishuv to compromise are skipped over, and no attention is given to Israel's Declaration of Independence, which declares all its citizens equal, without distinction of race. Analogies between the apartheid state of South Africa and Israel are, to be sure, crude and devoid of historical context.[55] Even South

Africa's celebration of cultural diversity—enshrined in its much-vaunted constitution—seemingly cannot entertain space for a minority community that overwhelmingly shares the Zionist dream. Historic ties between Jews and the land of Israel are of no consequence. Put simply, an important dimension of Jewish identity is fundamentally challenged.

NOTES

1. Pew Global Attitudes Project: Spring 2007 Survey of 47 Publics—FINAL 2007 TRENDS TOPLINE, http:www.pewglobal.org/files/pdf/256topline.pdf (p.96).

2. Statistic from Milton Shain, "South Africa," in *American Jewish Year Book, 2008*, ed. David Singer and Ruth Seldin (New York: American Jewish Committee, 2008), 559.

3. Muslims at the time protested outside Cape Town against the "occupation of Palestine by the Zionists." See Muhammed Haron, "The Muslim News (1960–1986): Expression of an Islamic Identity in South Africa," in *Muslim Identity and Social Change in Sub-Saharan Africa*, ed. Louis Brenner (London: Hurst, 1993), 222.

South African Muslims, mostly Sunni, numbered 654,064, or 1.5 percent of the total population, in the 2001 census—the most recent that included religious identification. Muslims were considered part of the "colored" population in the old apartheid categories. They are descendants of seventeenth-century political prisoners brought to the Cape from Indonesia—ex-slaves, nineteenth-century immigrants, and the offspring of black/white miscegenation. See Ebrahim Moosa, "Islam in South Africa," in *Living Faiths in South Africa*, ed. Martin Prozesky and John de Gruchy (Cape Town: David Philip, 1975).

4. See "UN Verdict on Zionist Racism," *Muslim News*, November 28, 1975, and interview with Ibraheem Mousa in *The Jews in South Africa: What Future?* ed. Tzippi Hoffman and Alan Fischer (Johannesburg: Southern Book Publishers, 1988), 171–74.

5. Farid Esack, "Three Islamic Strands in the South African Struggle for Justice," *Third World Quarterly* 10, no. 2 (1988): 33.

6. See Abdulkader Tayob, *Islamic Resurgence in South Africa* (Cape Town: University of Cape Town Press, 1995), 122.

7. Tayob, *Islamic Resurgence*, 140; Haron, "The Muslim News," 223.

8. See Tayob, *Islamic Resurgence*, chap. 3; Desmond Charles Rice, "Islamic Fundamentalism as a Major Religiopolitical Movement and Its Impact on South Africa" (MA diss., University of Cape Town, 1987), 438–52. The writings of Mawdudi and Qubt were serialized in *Islamic Mission*, a newsletter started by the Claremont Muslim Youth Association. See *Islamic Mirror*.

9. Interview with Ebrahim Rasool in Hoffman and Fischer, *Jews in South Africa*, 118.

10. Hoffman and Fischer, *Jews in South Africa*, 118–20.

11. See Farid Esack, "Pagad and Islamic Radicalism: Taking on the State?" *Indicator SA* 13, no. 14 (Spring 1996): 357.

12. For a general overview of these developments, see Margo Bastos, "Muslim Anti-Zionism and Antisemitism since the Second World War, with Special Reference to Muslim News/Views" (MA diss., University of Cape Town, 2002).

13. For more on PAGAD, see Esack, "Pagad and Islamic Radicalism," 9.

14. For a critique of reporting on PAGAD, see Gabeda Baderoon, *Regarding Muslims from Slavery to Post-Apartheid* (Johannesburg: Wits University Press, 2014), chap. 5.

15. See, e.g., *Muslim Views*, March 1997. See also "How the Media Manipulates the Truth about Terrorism," *Muslim Views*, April 1997, for evidence of conspiracy theories explaining how the West demonizes Islam. Similarly, see "Israel's Attack on Christianity," *Muslim Views*, August 1997, in which the Western media are accused of helping to establish Zionism.

16. See Milton Shain, "South Africa," in *American Jewish Year Book, 1998*, ed. David Singer and Ruth Seldin (New York: American Jewish Committee, 1998), 402–4.

17. Shain, "South Africa," 413.

18. See Allister Sparks, "Two-State Solution in Israel Is Already Dead," *Cape Times*, May 5, 1998.

19. Minister of Justice Dullah Omar and Minister of Provincial and Constitutional Affairs Valli Moosa met with Hamas spiritual leader Sheik Ahmed Yassin while in Saudi Arabia in April 1998.

20. Farid Esack, *Qur'an, Liberation and Pluralism* (Oxford: Oneworld, 1997), 225.

21. For firsthand accounts, see Benjamin Pogrund, *Drawing Fire: Investigating the Accusation of Apartheid in Israel* (Lanham, MD: Rowman and Littlefield, 2014), 157–60; Tova Herzl, *Madame Ambassador: Behind the Scenes with a Candid Israeli Diplomat* (Lanham, MD: Rowman and Littlefield, 2015), 187–96.

22. See Raymond Suttner and Jeremy Cronin, eds., *50 Years of the Freedom Charter* (Pretoria: University of South Africa, 2006), 132–37.

23. See Merle Lipton, *Liberals, Marxists, and Nationalists: Competing Interpretations of South African History* (New York: Palgrave Macmillan, 2007), 19–22, 42–44, 51–53.

24. See Sasha Polakow-Suransky, *The Unspoken Alliance: Israel's Secret Relationship with Apartheid South Africa* (New York: Pantheon Books, 2010).

25. Interview with Neo Mnumzama in Hoffman and Fischer, *Jews in South Africa*, 72.

26. Interview with Aubrey Mokoena in Hoffman and Fischer, *Jews in South Africa*, 34.

27. Interview with Ishmael Mkhabela in Hoffman and Fischer, *Jews in South Africa*, 46.

28. See Interview with Frank Chikane, Secretary General of the South African Council of Churches, in Hoffman and Fischer, *Jews in South Africa*, 20–22.

29. Interview with Dr. Ntatho Motlane in Hoffman and Fischer, *Jews in South Africa*, 61.

30. See Richard Mendelsohn and Milton Shain, *The Jews in South Africa: An Illustrated History* (Cape Town: Jonathan Ball, 2014), 195–97. In 2014, Mandela's old comrade, Ahmed Kathrada, confirmed his friend's sentiments during an interview on BBC's *Hard Talk*, episode 72, April 27, 2014.

31. Immanuel Suttner, ed., *Cutting through the Mountain: Interviews with South African Jewish Activists* (London: Viking, 1997), 281.

32. See, e.g., Allister Sparks, "Cutting a Peace Deal Easier Now," *Cape Times*, November 16, 2004.

33. "Israel's Two State Solution Is Dead," *Star*, September 21, 2005. See also "The Boys Who Cried 'Anti-Semite,'" *Star*, October 6, 2006.

34. *Cape Times*, October 5, 2005.

35. Allister Sparks, "We're Ready to Talk with Israel," *Star*, July 12, 2006.

36. Allister Sparks, "Israel's Two State Solution Is Dead," *Star*, September 21, 2005. See also Allister Sparks, *The Sword and the Pen: Six Decades on the Political Frontier* (Cape Town: Jonathan Ball, 2016), 558–59.

37. Ronnie Kasrils, "Israel Wall of Shame Will Create Poor Palestinian Bantustans," *Sunday Times* (South Africa), February 22, 2004.

38. Blade Nzimande, "Zionism a Form of Settler Colonialism," *Politicsweb*, August 7, 2014, http://www.politicsweb.co.za/documents /zionism-a-form-of-settler-colonialism--blade-nzima.

39. Interview with Dr. Yacub Zaki, *Prime Talk*, Radio 786, May 8, 1998.

40. See, e.g., "Antisemitism Report: South Africa 2014," SA Rochlin Archive, South African Jewish Board of Deputies, Johannesburg, unpublished report.

41. See Mendelsohn and Shain, *Jews in South Africa*, 216.

42. See "Cosatu to Intensify Israeli Goods Boycott," *News24*, August 24, 2016, https://www.news24.com/SouthAfrica/News/Cosatu-to-intensify-Israeli-goods-boycott-20140826.

43. "Trends and Responses to Antisemitism in South Africa 2012," SA Rochlin Archive: South African Jewish Board of Deputies, Johannesburg, unpublished report.

44. Congress of South African Trade Unions, "COSATU Condemns South African Zionist Federation's Abuse of Blacks under Religious Guise to Legitimise Apartheid in Israel," June 27, 2012, http://www.cosatu.org.za/show.php?ID=6247.

45. Ilham Rawoot and David Macfarlane, "UJ Severs Ties with Israel's Ben Gurion," *Mail and Guardian*, March 23, 2011; Raphael Ahren, "South Africa's Deputy Minister 'Don't Visit Israel,'" *Times of Israel*, August 12, 2012.

46. "Antisemitism Report," South African Jewish Board of Deputies, Johannesburg, 2013.

47. See Rebecca Hodes, "'Dubul' ijuda/Shoot the Jew' and the Local Architecture of Anti-Semitism," *Daily Maverick*, September 12, 2013, http://www.dailymaverick.co.za/opinionista/2013-09-12-dibul-ijudashoot-the-jew-and-the-local-architecture-of-anti-semitism/#.VDzhfaIaKM8.

48. Tony Ehrenreich, "If the SAJBD Wants to Advance a Zionist Agenda It Should Leave SA–COSATU WCape," *Politicsweb*, July 30, 2014, http://www.politicsweb.co.za/news-and-analysis/if-the-sajbd-wants-to-advance-a-zionist-agenda-it-.

49. R. W. Johnson, "Tony Ehrenreich's Blood Libel," *Politicsweb*, July 31, 2014, http://www.politicsweb.co.za/news-and-analysis/tony-ehrenreichs-blood-libel.

50. "Antisemitic Incidents in South Africa." I am indebted to David Saks, Associate Director, South African Jewish Board of Deputies, for providing me with this information. See https://muslimcaucus.wordpress.com/. It should be noted that the posting was questioned and denied by the ANC.

51. See Raphael Ahren, "Israel's Founding a 'Crime against Humanity,' Says South Africa's ANC," *Times of Israel*, September 14, 2014.

52. See Mary Kluk, "Board Denounces Bapela's 'Undemocratic Proposals,'" *South African Jewish Report*, September 9, 2015.

53. Hermann Giliomee, "Manipulating the Past," in *Political Correctness in South Africa*, ed. Rainer Erkens and John Kane-Berman (Johannesburg: South African Institute for Race Relations, 2000), 93–94.

54. Interview with Archbishop Desmond Tutu in Hoffman and Fischer, *Jews in South Africa*, 15.

55. For a full analysis, see Benjamin Pogrund, *Drawing Fire: Investigating the Accusation of Apartheid in Israel* (Lanham, MD: Rowman and Littlefield, 2014).

MILTON SHAIN is Emeritus Professor in the Department of Historical Studies at the University of Cape Town. He has written and edited several books on South African Jewish history, South African politics, and the history of antisemitism. He is author of *A Perfect Storm: Antisemitism in South Africa, 1930–1948*, which won the Recht Malan Prize (Media 24) for English and Afrikaans Non-Fiction for 2016.

From Donetsk to Tel Aviv

*Czech Antisemitic Movements Respond to the
Russian-Ukrainian War*

ZBYNĚK TARANT

THE CRISIS IN Ukraine began in late 2013. What started as a political revolt, symbolized by large gatherings of people on Kiev's Maidan Square in opposition to the pro-Russian policies of president Yanukovich, later developed into a violent revolution. This was followed by the covert annexation of Crimea by the Russian special forces and by insurgencies on the part of Russian-backed rebels in the industrial regions of eastern Ukraine. Today, the events are referred to by the Russian media as the "Ukrainian civil war" and by the Western media as the "Ukrainian crisis" or the "Russian-Ukrainian war" or the "war in eastern Ukraine." Whatever the name, the violence has cost thousands of lives and created hundreds of thousands of internally displaced persons. As a result, Ukraine, the former agricultural and industrial heart of Eastern Europe, has become a failed state, hovering on the verge of financial collapse and unable to control its own territory.

Ukraine may appear to be fairly distant from the Czech Republic, but Kiev is closer to Prague than one might think. Ukraine is a neighbor of the former Czechoslovakia, with the latter even controlling the region of Ruthenia between 1918 and 1938. Ukrainians represent the largest national minority in the contemporary Czech Republic, and the various responses to the Ukrainian crisis have uncovered the continuing polarization within Czech society along pro-Western and pro-Russian lines. Finally, the crisis has become an important topic for Czech extremist and antisemitic elements. This chapter explores the responses of Czech antisemitic movements and individuals to provide a better understanding of their worldviews and policy making. What can we learn about the nature of Czech antisemitism from the way it responds to one particular political crisis?

THE CHANGING FACE OF CZECH ANTISEMITISM

The so-called Velvet Revolution of 1989 not only brought down the Communist government but also ended the official state-sanctioned anti-Zionist rhetoric. The new democratic government denounced antisemitism, quickly reestablished diplomatic ties with Israel, and it enacted legislation against hate speech and genocide incitement and denial. Following this, antisemitism became a domain of the radical fringes of Czech society—that is, those who were dissatisfied with the post-1989 course of events. Most of these groups were concentrated either on the far right of the political spectrum or around the radical core of the Communist Party. Some of the post-1989 antisemitic actors have quite complex personal histories, including the tendency to switch between the Communist Party and far-right movements.[1] This was also because Communist parties in Central and Eastern Europe adopted the role of conservative champions, promising a return to a simple and idealized past when rules were set, borders were closed, and the American capitalists were kept away. Their rhetoric locates them much closer to the "reactionary" far right than even they would be willing to admit. The issue of Russia and Ukraine presents an interesting case study in relation to this phenomenon.

Today's Czech Republic is a parliamentary democracy and a member of the European Union and the North Atlantic Treaty Organization (NATO); it is generally considered to be one of the most determined allies of Israel in the region as well as a very safe country for Jews, with only a small level of antisemitism and largely indifferent societal attitudes to the small Jewish minority. A recent survey by the Czech Sociological Institute, based on a representative sample of 1,069 respondents, describes Czech attitudes toward Jews as mostly neutral. In the survey, respondents were asked to express their attitudes toward various groups by using "school grades" from 1 (most sympathetic) to 5 (most unsympathetic). Respondents gave Jews an average grade of 2.83 on a scale of popularity. Jews placed directly after Germans (2.82), Greeks (2.72), Poles (2.47), Slovaks (1.79), and Czechs (1.59). At the other end of the scale were Arabs (4.02) and Roma (4.30).[2] In 2014, the Anti-Defamation League concluded that about 13 percent of the public probably held some form of antisemitic views based on stereotypes, making the Czech Republic one of the best ranked countries in this survey, with levels of antisemitism far below the Eastern European average.[3]

To some extent, the mostly indifferent attitudes of Czechs toward Jews are confirmed by reports of the Federation of Jewish Communities—an umbrella organization of Czech Jews. According to these reports, based on statistics relating to antisemitic incidents recorded by the federation's security department, the rate of antisemitism remains rather low. Only four isolated physical attacks against Jewish individuals were recorded from 2006 to 2014.[4] There have been some cases of vandalism, but the problem is generally less serious than it is in other Western or Eastern European countries. According to the same report, Jewish communities recorded an increased incidence of harassment in 2014 (about half a dozen events), probably due to the impact of Operation Protective Edge. Reports by the Federation of Jewish Communities have pointed to a significant increase in the number of verbal incidents, such as pamphlets, websites, blogs, pictures, videos, and remarks on social networks. In 2015, the Jewish community concluded, there was a leveling out in the intensity of cyberhate, with three cases of threat and five cases of harassment. The majority of verbal incidents took place in the electronic realm.[5]

Reports on extremism by the Czech Ministry of Interior reveal that there were 175 hate crimes reported and investigated in 2015, marking the lowest number since 2005. About 120 of these constituted verbal crimes, such as genocide denial, racist incitement, and expressions of support for movements aimed at curbing human rights. Out of the 175 hate crimes in 2015, 114 were successfully investigated, and 154 perpetrators were convicted. Crimes motivated by antisemitism represented a small portion of these crimes, because most of them targeted Romanies or foreigners. The report contains no estimate on the numbers of unreported hate crimes.[6]

It is difficult to ascertain the size and potential of the activist antisemitic scene in the Czech Republic, but judging from the election results, antisemitic political parties remain on the fringe in the country. There are two antisemitic political parties in the Czech Republic: the neo-Nazi Workers' Party of Social Justice (abbreviated as DSSS in Czech and WPSJ in English) and the fascist National Democracy. Both parties have been receiving less than 1.0 percent in the elections. For example, in the last parliamentary elections in 2013, the WPSJ received 42,906 votes, or 0.84 percent. That is far below the threshold required for entering the parliament and puts the party on the political fringe. In the 2014 elections for the European Parliament, the WPSJ, running in a coalition with another nationalist subject, received 7,902 votes, or 0.52 percent. National Democracy, established only months before these elections, had been mobilizing its supporters by using explicitly antisemitic television advertisements. Yet the party has received only 0.46 percent, which equals 7,109 votes.[7] The parties are somewhat more successful in the elections to local municipalities, where especially the Workers' Party acquired several mandates thanks to its anti-Romany rhetoric.[8] Its focus on populist, anti-Romany, and anti-immigration rhetoric also means that it might attract supporters who might not be antisemitic despite their otherwise racist convictions.

Since the Czech Jewish population has declined to only a few thousand, the Jews are simply not a topic for some of the far-right movements.[9] Where antisemitism does exist, the decline of the Czech Jewish population makes it an interesting example of the phenomenon of "antisemitism without Jews." A typical manifestation of this phenomenon is the various "lists of Jews" that ascribe Jewish descent to many non-Jews.[10] Among new and emerging threats are antisemitism in response to the refugee crisis, the introduction of antisemitism into anti-Muslim and anti-Romany rhetoric, antisemitism in popular esotericism, Salafist propaganda that seeks to target the otherwise small and nonconfrontational Czech Muslim community, and the introduction of antisemitic conspiracy theories into antiglobalist discourse (a "New World Order," which represents an alleged globalist metaconspiracy led by the Jews).[11] On the other hand, Muslim extremism and the Boycott, Divestment, Sanctions (BDS) movement have been, at least so far, significantly weaker in the Czech Republic than in Western Europe and the United States.[12]

Rallies and gatherings of antisemitic movements in the Czech Republic are rarely presented openly as antisemitic (doing so would enable the municipality to ban the gathering) and are usually given a different title, such as "protest against immigration" or "protest against the criminality of 'unadaptable persons,'" meaning the Romanies. Because of the broader targeting and populist rhetoric, not everyone who participates in such rallies is necessarily an antisemite. The WPSJ speakers are especially careful not to provoke with explicit antisemitic remarks. The rallies are usually attended by three hundred to six hundred people, but there are exceptions; on November 17, 2015, National Democracy managed to attract more than thirty-five hundred protesters by cleverly appealing to attendees of multiple anti-immigration and anti-Muslim gatherings that were held earlier the same day.[13]

In sum, the Czech antisemitic movement may vary in size from thousands to tens of thousands. While such numbers are a tiny percentage of the 10.5 million Czech population, several thousand violent activists are still enough to justify further monitoring as well as increased security measures in and around the Jewish community institutions, because the radical core is large and determined enough to cause occasional disruptions and security incidents. There has been no significant terrorist attack in the country so far, yet the Czech Police has recorded several dozen isolated "criminal acts that contained certain marks of terrorism" since 1989. None of these acts were motivated by antisemitism.[14] The recent terrorist attacks in Europe, however, perpetrated by so-called lone wolves (radicalized individuals), show that numbers do not always tell the whole story.

CZECH ANTISEMITIC CYBERSPACE

Because most of the antisemitic content in the Czech language is located on the web, the main part of this analysis focuses on the electronic realm.[15] Surveying Czech cyberspace by using a combination of keyword search and snowball sampling method revealed that in 2015, there were eighty-seven dedicated antisemitic websites in the Czech language, ranging from large portals with more than one hundred thousand monthly readers to very small blogs with negligible traffic. Inspired by similar surveys on the Arabic and Iranian blogospheres, I have adopted the social network analysis method to gain a comprehensive picture of the nature and composition of Czech antisemitic cyberspace.[16] Social network analysis facilitates the visualization of the entire network of antisemitic websites as a web chart, where the sites are represented as nodes of the web and the links between them as threads. The creation of such a map is possible because of the relatively small size of the scene (see table 16.1) and because of the very clear linguistic borders of the Czech antisemites, who usually prefer the Czech language. The computer software tool Visone can then calculate the nodes with the highest authority, according to the percentage of links the particular node receives and from which nodes it receives them. This makes it possible to determine the relative influence of each website. Once the map is created, it can be easily distilled into lists and samples for further content analysis. Websites and blogs can then be systematically explored and sorted according to their political affiliation, the nature and intensity of the antisemitic attitudes expressed, and attitudes about other particular topics—in this case, the Ukrainian crisis.

Periodic mapping of Czech antisemitic cyberspace via the method described above reveals that their composition underwent an important transformation between 2010 and 2015 (see table 16.1). In 2010, most of the antisemitic websites in the Czech language were hosted by neo-Nazis and far-right movements. In 2015, the main sources of Czech antisemitism were the esoterica and conspiracy theories scenes, combined with strong antiliberal, anti-American, and antiglobalist attitudes. For simplicity, they are referred to as "conspiracy debunkers," although in 2017, two years after the core of this article was finished, the term "fake news" became popular in America in connection to the role of such websites in the 2016 American presidential elections. This newly established term "fake news" cannot be used in all cases, however, because some of these websites of conspiracy debunkers are not "fake" in terms of conscious effort to mislead the readers—some are sincere manifestations of genuine beliefs and convictions of their authors, who think that they are sharing the truth and who themselves act in accordance with such beliefs. Our dismissal of all such websites as mere intentional fakes could lead to a dangerous underestimation of the determination of their authors.

TABLE 16.1. ANTISEMITIC WEBSITES IN THE CZECH LANGUAGE ACCORDING TO POLITICAL AFFILIATION, AS OF MARCH 15, 2015

	Conspiracy debunkers	Christian traditionalists	Neo-Nazi	Workers' Party (political party)	National Democracy (political party)	Total
February 2010	8	2	57	9	0	76
August 2011	22	4	44	8	2	80
2012 (no data)						
2013 (no data)						
November 2014	33	5	24	13	5	80
August 2015	55	4	17	8	3	87

These websites usually acquire the role of false opposition by portraying themselves as sources of "alternative" information. With names such as Czech Free Press, Outsidermedia, Free Press, The Curious Fellow, New World Order Opposition, and Against the Current, they claim to provide "different" information for those who seek "alternative" lifestyles and worldviews.[17] Many of them combine antisemitic conspiracy theories with mainstream commercial esoterica. From these beginnings, it is only a short step from convincing a reader that the US government conceals UFO kidnappings to the belief that the US government is seeking to deny Mossad's involvement in the 9/11 attacks.

This new generation of antisemitic websites is capable of targeting a much wider audience than those of the old school. While the visitor counters previously showed numbers on the neo-Nazi websites in units of thousands, one of the most authoritative conspiracy theory websites, Zvědavec ("The Curious Fellow"), claims to have around 160,000 unique monthly readers (which represents about 1.5 percent of the Czech population).[18] Some other antisemitic websites, while marginal, are hosted and linked by the server Parlamentní listy. This server, co-owned by the Czech senator and financial tycoon Ivo Valenta, belongs, in general terms, to the top fifty most influential websites in the Czech language according to Alexa ratings, which could mean that there are hundreds of thousands of monthly readers.[19] At least 15 percent of the traffic directed to this website then heads to its antisemitic subdomain—the website Protiproud ("Against the Current"), run by Petr Hájek, the former advisor to the Czech president Václav Klaus.[20]

A content analysis of attitudes toward Russia and Ukraine in 2015, as expressed in the specific websites, reveals that, whereas the neo-Nazis seem to be split over the issue of Ukraine, the conspiracy debunker websites are almost unequivocally pro-Putin, leaving only several ambivalent or neutral voices (see table 16.2). This trend becomes even more apparent when only the first twenty websites that were identified as most influential out of

TABLE 16.2. ATTITUDES OF CZECH ANTISEMITIC WEBSITES TOWARD UKRAINE AND THE PUTIN REGIME IN RUSSIA ACCORDING TO POLITICAL AFFILIATION, AS OF MARCH 15, 2016

	No. of Czech antisemitic websites that actively published their content in 2014 and 2015			The top twenty most influential active antisemitic websites in the Czech language		
	Pro-Ukrainian	Neutral/ambivalent	Pro-Putin	Pro-Ukrainian	Neutral/ambivalent	Pro-Putin
Conspiracy debunkers	0	9	41	0	0	18
Christian traditionalists	0	2	2	0	0	0
National Democracy	0	0	2	0	0	1
Neo-Nazis	2	10	3	0	0	1
Workers' Party	2	3	2	0	0	0

TABLE 16.3. LIST OF THE TWENTY MOST INFLUENTIAL ANTISEMITIC
WEBSITES IN THE CZECH LANGUAGE IN 2015 ACCORDING TO THE
VISONE SOFTWARE'S AUTHORITY RANKING

Rank	URL	Main theme
1	http://www.zvedavec.org/	Conspiracy theories
2	http://www.nwoo.org	Conspiracy theories
3	http://www.ac24.cz/	Conspiracy theories
4	http://www.czechfreepress.cz/	Conspiracy theories
5	http://wertyzreport.com/	Conspiracy theories
6	http://protiproud.parlamentnilisty.cz	Conspiracy theories
7	http://www.outsidermedia.cz/	Conspiracy theories
8	http://svobodnenoviny.eu/	Conspiracy theories
9	http://www.freepub.cz/	Conspiracy theories
10	http://freeglobe.cz/	Conspiracy theories
11	http://leva-net.webnode.cz/	Conspiracy theories
12	http://orgo-net.blogspot.com/	Conspiracy theories
13	http://www.stripkyzesveta.cz	Conspiracy theories
14	http://cz.sputniknews.com	Conspiracy theories
15	http://www.novarepublika.cz	Conspiracy theories
16	http://www.osud.cz/	Conspiracy theories
17	http://aeronet.cz	Conspiracy theories
18	http://narodnidemokracie.cz	National Democracy
19	http://www.mustwatch.cz/	Conspiracy theories
20	http://deliandiver.org	Neo-Nazis

the total list of eighty-seven by the method of social network
analysis are taken into account (see table 16.3). Such a narrow
list would contain only one neo-Nazi website; the rest would be
conspiracy theory websites. All of these top twenty most influential antisemitic websites in the Czech language appear to express pro-Putin attitudes. Combined with the previous finding
that these conspiracy theory websites are also the loudest voices
on the Czech antisemitic scene, one can reach the preliminary
conclusion that Czech antisemitic cyberspace is dominated by
pro-Russian voices. Finding a voice on the Czech Internet or even

social media that is both antisemitic and anti-Putin has become quite a challenging task.

The proclamations made by organized antisemitic movements, expressed both online and in the streets, appear to be mostly pro-Putin. This includes the fascist National Democracy, the influential Catholic traditionalist platform DOST, the tiny clero-fascist party National Unification (Národní sjednocení), as well as the Czech branch of the neo-Nazi organization Generation of Identity (Generace identity), formed by the former Autonomous nationalists (Autonomní nacionalisté). Other neo-Nazi movements appeared to be split over the issue of Russia and Ukraine, but they later chose to side with the Putin regime; a case study of the neo-Nazi Workers' Party of Social Justice (Dělnická strana sociální spravedlnosti) is presented below. Traditionally, some of the far-left movements and parties are pro-Putin, including the Communist Youth Union (Komunistický svaz mládeže) and the Communist Party of Bohemia and Moravia, whose radical fringes may also be associated with the antisemitic scene despite their formal denunciation of antisemitism. However, most of those involved in the conspiracy debunkers scene do not align themselves along the left–right political spectrum, and their thoughts and ideas are often appropriated by both the far left and the far right, as the same conspiracy theories can be found on both of the radical fringes of the Czech political spectrum.

THE NEO-NAZI LOYALTY DILEMMA: THE CASE OF THE WORKERS' PARTY

Being a Czech neo-Nazi presents one with a difficult dilemma when it comes to Russia and Ukraine. Before the 2014 Maidan events, the Czech and Ukrainian neo-Nazis used to meet at White Power music concerts and occasionally participated in each other's rallies and events. But adopting a pro-Russian position after the Maidan revolt is likely to entail abandoning past friendships and relationships, even committing an act of treason. Furthermore, most neo-Nazis prefer to refer to themselves as "nationalists," calling for the preservation of one's own national identity. Such a position is difficult to defend, however, while simultaneously supporting an invader. There is also the issue of anticommunism—that is, how does one reconcile neo-Nazi anticommunism with the nostalgia for the Soviet past that currently drives the Russian establishment? And, finally, how should one react to the "war on fascism" that has become the key element in anti-Ukrainian rhetoric? Some of these dilemmas can be resolved by recourse to antisemitic conspiracy theories; others remain unresolved and are simply not spoken about.

The neo-Nazi cyberspace has been host to a number of quarrels and discussions in relation to Russia and Ukraine. When the Maidan revolt started in the winter of 2014, Czech neo-Nazi activists began sharing images of pro-Ukrainian graffiti, and on February 24, 2014, the neo-Nazi Workers' Party manifested its support for the Ukrainian neo-Nazi movement, Right Sector, which played a significant role during the violent stages of the revolt; its representatives were even invited to Prague.[21] Following the rhetoric of the Ukrainian Right Sector, these pro-Ukrainian voices were both anti-Putin and anti-Western, citing the Maidan revolt as a chance for the Ukrainian nation to find its own path, independently of the wishes of both Russia and the West.

A more skeptical voice was that of party member Martin Kněžický, who claimed that those who supported the Maidan were putting themselves on the wrong side of the barricade and warned that the Czech Republic was about to be swamped by a massive influx of Ukrainian refugees.[22] About a month after the Maidan events, which brought the pro-Western government of Petro Poroshenko to power, the Workers' Party expressed its support for the Russian annexation of Crimea, this endorsement coming from its vice chairman, Jiří Štěpánek.[23] The vice chairman leveled accusations against several Czech and European nongovernmental organizations, which he claimed were trying to systematically destabilize the Russian Federation and had selected Prague as their main base of operations for this purpose.[24]

Some of the activists were not satisfied with this trend, and there was a perceivable disagreement between the party's core and the representatives of its youth organization, Workers' Youth (Dělnická mládež), which appeared to have adopted an anti-Putin position. In his polemic targeted at fellow comrades, Jan Kuřec, chief editor of the party's youth magazine, *Hlas mládeže*, criticized what he saw as a disturbing trend: "The uprising in Ukraine has fully uncovered one of the negative phenomena of the last era. In recent years, the nationalist structures have been infiltrated with an attitude of servility towards Putin's Russia." Kuřec labeled the Russian Federation as "Jewish plutocracy" and continued:

> The economic system of Russia is capitalism, even further deformed by the interests of a small group of mostly Jewish entrepreneurs around the Russian president. Putin is never going to stand unequivocally with the Palestinian people against Israel, because he is limited by the people around him. Among the exploiters around Putin, there are people such as: Vitaliy Malkin, Piotr Aven, Leonid Michelson, Viktor Vekselberg, German Khan, Michail Fridman and the Rotenberg brothers. All of them are Jews and many of them have Israeli citizenship. Such people hold the real power in today's Russian Federation and it is utterly misleading to say that Putin stands again Zionism. Because of the powerful people around him, Putin is a direct part of 21st century Zionism. If they speak of the Wall Street bankers as having Jews behind them, one can also openly say the same about the Russian oligarchs.[25]

Despite these dissenting voices, the Workers' Party line started to adopt a pro-Russian direction. Erik Lamprecht, vice chairman of the party, explained that, in the conflict between Ukrainian natives and pro-Russian separatists, the sympathies should lie with the Ukrainians. However, "one must look at the conflict from the wider geopolitical perspective," stated Lamprecht, and

ANTI-ZIONISM AND ANTISEMITISM

from that perspective, despite Russia's imperfections, it is still the least problematic alternative in a world dominated by a global conspiracy, where there are no good alternatives: "Putin's Russia, where the strings are being pulled by almost the same people as in its imaginary Western antipole, is far from being an ideal for us, yet it becomes a somewhat more acceptable choice between the two Molochs."[26]

Meanwhile, the bulletin of the Workers' Youth was discontinued, together with its website, which silenced at least some of these dissenting voices.[27] A small island of anti-Russian voices can be found on the discussion forums of neo-Nazi hooligans;[28] however, the rest of the scene, including its most prominent websites and movements, gravitated toward a pro-Russian stance. The top leaders of the Workers' Party strongly criticized the sanctions imposed on Russia after the downing of Malaysia Airlines Flight 17 and has repeated this criticism on multiple occasions.[29] When Russia began its air strikes in Syria, the party, usually very critical about "war on terror" rhetoric, wrote that "Russia has started the true war on terror."[30]

The existence and subsequent disappearance of such dissenting voices does not necessarily mean a significant shift in rhetoric about Russia, because these voices were always on the margin of the scene. As for the rhetoric vis-á-vis Ukraine, it is the political reality in Ukraine that has changed, not the mainstream attitude of the Czech antisemitic movements to Russia. What we may see as a shift is actually a logical result of the network of alliances as it is seen by the movements. The Czech antisemitic movement is anti-American, anti-European, and antiglobalist. Russia has managed to present itself as the main antiglobalist and anti-American force. As long as the Ukrainian government was pro-Russian, Ukraine was not an issue. Under the pro-Russian president Yanukovich, Ukraine was simply seen a part of the same block. After the Maidan revolt brought a "pro-Western" government to power, Ukraine was no longer part of the perceived anti-Western block and was now seen as the ground zero of American interference. The Russian-Ukrainian war also fully uncovered the anti-Russian attitudes of the Ukrainian far right, which had existed previously but were not a significant issue for mutual relations with the Czechs—not until 2014. Once the Russian-Ukrainian war started, however, the Czech antisemitic movement had to choose sides. It chose not to abandon its former pro-Russian position, even at the cost of abandoning its Ukrainian comrades.

If there had in fact been a loyalty dilemma in early 2014, it seems to have disappeared by 2015. As for the relationship with Ukrainian neo-Nazi organizations, the most influential neo-Nazi website, Deliandiver, has published a series of translated articles by Western neo-Nazi and antisemitic thinkers, accusing the Ukrainian far-right movements of being supported by the Israeli secret service. These articles included Max Blumenthal's piece "How the Israel Lobby Protected Ukrainian Neo-Nazis" and Kevin MacDonald's text "The Unstable Alliance of Nationalists and 'Mainly Jewish Oligarchs' in Ukraine."[31]

By playing the Jewish conspiracy card in relation to Ukrainian nationalist organizations, the Czech neo-Nazi movements were free to align themselves with Putin's "war against Ukrainian fascism" rhetoric. After all, if Ukrainian nationalist movements are funded by the Jews, they can no longer be regarded as "true" nationalists, which solves the loyalty dilemma. On the Polish antisemitic scene, one can even find explicit references accusing Ukrainian nationalist movements of being funded by "Judeo-Bandera money."[32]

PRO-PUTIN ANTISEMITIC MOVEMENTS: THE CASE OF NATIONAL DEMOCRACY

If there is one explicitly antisemitic party that has never experienced a loyalty dilemma vis-à-vis the Russian-Ukrainian war, it is National Democracy (Národní demokracie, or ND). Both the party and its members have a long and complex history, a description of which is outside the scope of this chapter. Its leader, Adam Benjamin Bartoš, is a young activist who started out as a philosemite and a pro-Israeli hawk but has since evolved into the loudest Czech antisemite.[33] The party was officially established in late 2014, making use of the empty shell of a previously existing, yet inactive, political party, Law and Justice (Právo a spravedlnost). National Democracy is a relatively small party, and it has never received more than 1.5 percent in elections, which indicates that it has several thousand supporters.[34] To complicate matters, the party competes with the neo-Nazi Workers' Party for a very similar electorate. Thus, the reason for closely watching the activities of this rather small party is not because of its actual influence but because of its radicalism.

The party can be characterized as nationalist, fascist, and antisemitic. Conspiracy theories, especially anti-Jewish ones, play a dominant role in its program and ideology. Despite its far-right fascist orientation, former Communists can be found in the ranks of National Democracy. A former vice chairman of the party, Ladislav Zemánek, for example, has been a member of the Communist Youth. Leading Czech conspiracy debunkers, such as Daniel Solis and the founder of the Zvědavec website, Vladimír Stwora, have appeared in prominent posts in the party's leadership structure. The party's leader, Adam Bartoš, has established his own publishing house, which specializes in antisemitic literature, the latest piece being a new edition of *The Protocols of the Elders of Zion*, translated by Vít Skácel—a former vice chairman of the disbanded National Party and frequent speaker at National Democracy rallies.[35]

The former vice chairman of National Democracy, Ladislav Zemánek, participated in the mission of European far-right parties to the Donetsk region of eastern Ukraine, where he acted as one of the "observers" of the elections in the self-proclaimed Donetsk People's Republic in November 2014. After his return,

FIGURE 16.1. NATIONAL DEMOCRACY RALLY IN PRAGUE ON MARCH
26, 2016. THE FLAG OF DONETSK PEOPLE'S REPUBLIC IS DISPLAYED
(TO THE LEFT). IN THE MIDDLE IS A BANNER WITH SLOGANS: "NO TO
ISLAM, NWO, TTIP, EU AND NATO!" (PHOTO BY ZBYNĔK TARANT)

Zemánek publicly admitted that the journey had been organized
and paid for by the Russian government.[36] He was blacklisted
for this activity by the Ukrainian government and banned from
entering the country.[37] When the convoy of American military
vehicles, sent from the Baltic countries through Eastern and
Central Europe as an expression of support for the NATO allies, was passing through the republic in March 2015, the party
allowed far-left, neo-Stalinist movements, such as the Czech
Borderlands Club (Klub českého pohraničí)—a nostalgia club
made up of former Communist soldiers who were responsible for
patrolling the Iron Curtain—to join its rallies and fly their flags
at the head of its protest march.[38] In reaction to such events and
activities of National Democracy, the Czech Security Information Service warned against Russian attempts to establish a "New

FIGURE 16.2. MEMBER OF PARLIAMENT TOMIO OKAMURA SPEAKS
AT A NATIONAL DEMOCRACY RALLY ON SEPTEMBER 8, 2015. A
FLAG WITH ORANGE AND BLACK STRIPES OF THE RIBBON OF
SAINT GEORGE IS VISIBLE ON THE RIGHT-HAND SIDE ALONG WITH
THE FLAG OF NATIONAL DEMOCRACY. BEHIND THE STAGE (NOT
VISIBLE IN THIS PHOTO), THERE WAS A STAND WITH ANTISEMITIC
LITERATURE FOR SALE. (PHOTO BY ZBYNĚK TARANT)

International" (in reference to the Socialist International), this
time by using a network of nationalist, populist, and far-right
parties as proxies and spearheads of propaganda in the West.[39]

The party's supporters express their pro-Russian stance by
flying the flags of the self-proclaimed Donetsk People's Republic (see Fig. 16.1) and wearing the Ribbon of Saint George at all
their events and gatherings, even if they are not thematically
connected to the issue of Ukraine.[40] One can frequently see the
orange and black stripes at anti-immigration and anti-Muslim
gatherings of the party, for example.[41] It does appear in the form
of flags as well (see Fig. 16.2). From personal observation, it seems

that the Ribbon of Saint George appears much more at National Democracy rallies than at neo-Nazi Worker's Party rallies, where, as described above, attitudes toward Russia seem to be more complex. Tomáš Vandas, the leader of the Workers' Party, does not wear the ribbon when speaking publicly, while all the speakers at National Democracy rallies do.

As for National Democracy, the pro-Russian attitude is fully in line with its obsession with conspiracy theories. The party's leadership sees Russia as the last stronghold against the almighty New World Order, governed by the Jews, who are seeding revolution around the world: the Velvet Revolution in Czechoslovakia, the Orange Revolution in Ukraine, the Green Revolution in Iran, the Arab Spring, the Maidan, and so on. The party follows Putin's claims that the West is preparing for a new "color revolution" against the Russian leader.

These beliefs were probably best summarized by Vít Skalský, a member of the party's Control Committee and one of the prominent speakers at its rallies. Skalský presented a six-point plan, by which the global conspiracy is allegedly attempting to attack Russia through Ukraine: (1) the destabilization of Ukraine and the installation of a puppet government; (2) the instigation of a civil war; (3) the crushing of the resistance of the Russian minority by the massive use of force; (4) the launching of ethnic violence with the assistance of "Western Nazi forces" in order to instigate massive levels of migration to Russia; (5) the use of a Russian counterattack as the pretext for an invasion of Russian territory; and, finally, (6) the installation of a puppet government in Russia and the use of the financial debts of both parties, Russia and Europe, as a means of depriving national states of all their property in order to concentrate financial and political power in the hands of the "Western superelites."[42] Skalský does not mention Jews directly, but he provides several hints within his text and he also precedes his vision with a reference to the *Analysis of November 17* by Miroslav Dolejší—a constitutional document

FIGURE 16.3. FLAG "STOP PRAGUE MAIDAN #SAVE DONBASS PEOPLE"
IN THE BLACK AND ORANGE COLORS OF THE RIBBON OF SAINT
GEORGE FLIES IN FRONT OF THE MUNICIPAL HOUSE IN PRAGUE.
THE NOVEMBER 17, 2015, RALLY WAS ORGANIZED BY THE NATIONAL
DEMOCRACY. EUROPEAN UNION FLAGS WERE BURNED AT THE SAME
EVENT. (PHOTO BY ZBYNĚK TARANT)

of the Czech far right that describes the 1989 Velvet Revolution
as stemming from a worldwide Jewish conspiracy to establish
Greater Israel.[43]

For National Democracy, the Maidan revolt is not only about
Ukraine. The party sees this as merely a symptom of the worldwide conspiracy that infiltrates everywhere, including the Czech
Republic. This is how one should interpret slogans such as "Stop
the Prague Maidan" (see Fig. 16.3), which can be seen at the
party's rallies. On November 17, a public holiday in the Czech
Republic titled the International Day of the Student Struggle
for Freedom and Democracy, Adam Bartoš delivered a speech

in front of the Municipal House (Obecní dům) in Prague. In this speech, he referred to the events of November 17, 1989, that sparked the anti-Communist Velvet Revolution, likening it to a conspiracy of foreign secret service agencies against the Czech nation. He continued by connecting the Velvet Revolution to Maidan: "The secret services of the United States and Israel want to force a new change upon us. . . . Their goal is to divide the nation, induce conflicts and disturbances, civil war. Their tactic is Maidan, their goal is disintegration similar to the one they have managed to achieve in Ukraine."[44]

THE CASE OF THE MALAYSIAN PLANES

The year 2014 was a black one for Malaysia Airlines. In a short span of time, the company suffered two large disasters, which saw the loss of hundreds of lives. The first accident involved flight MH3370, a Malaysia Airlines Boeing 777, which disappeared from the radar on March 8, 2014, for reasons that still have not been fully explained; however, the crew and all the passengers are presumed dead. The second flight, MH17, also involving a Malaysia Airlines Boeing 777, was shot down on June 17, 2014, over the Donetsk region in eastern Ukraine, near the village of Hrabove, by a ground-to-air missile.

Aviation disasters, especially those involving missing airplanes, are magnets for conspiracy debunkers. They represent mysterious stories that ignite the human imagination, which finds it difficult to accept the lack of clear answers. Suffice it to mention the Bermuda triangle myth, which continues to inspire the human imagination. The facts that both accidents took place shortly after each other, that they involved the same company, and that the planes were of the same type has absolutely no scientific relevance. The application of Occam's razor theory suggests that a coincidence is still more probable than conspiracy.[45] But for the conspiracy debunkers, who place the reification of numerical patterns at the core of their "methodology," this is still too much of a coincidence. Coincidences simply do not find a place in the thought processes of conspiracy debunkers. And once somebody is convinced that there is a conspiracy, linking the two accidents together, the door is left wide open for the injection of an antisemitic dimension into such a myth.

The immediate reaction of the antisemitic movement to the MH17 disaster was chaotic and unorganized, yet still in line with the multiple and frequently parallel Russian versions of the events leading up to the disaster.[46] It took only hours for the first antisemitic conspiracy theories to pop up as well. One of them referred to the disaster as "a trap, set for Russia and Vladimir Putin." The piece contains all the typical esoteric methodology, including numerology and reification, to demonstrate an immensely complex conspiracy on the part of US and Israeli secret services, directed against the Russian Federation. The conspiracy theory claims that the lost flight MH3370 was actually found in one of the hangars at Ben Gurion airport in Tel Aviv, the intention being to use it in "a new 9/11" event that would serve as a pretext for inciting World War III directed against Russia. As for flight MH17, the conspiracy debunkers cite alleged numerological evidence: "The Malaysian Airlines plane was shot down on 17 July 2014, at 17 hours and 17 minutes local time (other sources, however, speak about 15 hours and 21 minutes CEST). The plane was numbered MH17, the plane type a Boeing 777. The plane had flown for the first time on 17 July 1997 and crashed exactly 17 years afterwards. . . . The three sevens from the plane type designation are similar to the three sixes standing for Divinity in Zionism."[47] Unfortunately, the author does not explain how he reached the conclusion about the meaning of the three sevens in Zionist ideology. Several days after the disaster, the esoterica website Osud.cz came up with a report, according to which the airplane had been shot down by an Israeli air-to-air missile.[48] In the following weeks, conspiracy theorists accused Israel of causing the disaster to divert attention from its ground operations in Gaza, as part of Operation Protective Edge, which began on the same day—yet another example of how an unfortunate coincidence has helped perpetuate antisemitic myths. Additional examples would include theories put out by the Osud.cz and the Catholic activist Michael Winkler on the prominent Czech antisemitic website Freeglobe.cz.[49]

The Czech antisemitic movement has paid significant attention to the MH17 case and expressed its full support for the Russian version of events. Only a small part of its coverage actually contained direct antisemitic accusations. Not every article on an antisemitic website includes antisemitic content; only about one in ten of the reports on flight MH17 appearing on antisemitic websites contained antisemitic statements. Most stories about MH17 that appeared on Czech antisemitic websites were simply reports taken directly from the Russian media. These non-antisemitic yet still radically pro-Russian expressions emanating from the otherwise antisemitic websites are still noteworthy. They illustrate how Czech antisemitic groups have participated in the creation of a fog of disinformation by publishing multiple versions of the MH17 incident and have been instrumental in creating a notion that the truth cannot actually be found in the vast amounts of alternative explanations. These alternative versions include a report that the passengers on MH17 were already dead at the time of the strike,[50] that the plane was shot down by a Ukrainian jet fighter, SU-25,[51] that the plane was intentionally directed over the conflict region by the Ukrainians,[52] and that the navigation software of the plane was intentionally reprogrammed.[53] In this context, the explanation of an antisemitic conspiracy theory is just one of many "alternative versions," possibly meant to divert the focus of the investigation. The Jews, in fact, are the victims, but not the primary targets, of this propaganda warfare. It should be noted that the Dutch Safety Board—the committee that investigated the crash—rigorously tested all the alternative hypotheses but found them to be unlikely.[54]

Possibly the most complex conspiracy theory that has appeared in connection with the Russian-Ukrainian war is the myth of a New Israel. According to this myth, Zionists have begun to search for a reserve homeland in case their project in occupied Palestine fails, and they have found it in Ukraine. The myth claims that preparations for the transfer of millions of Jews have already begun and that all recent events in Russia and Ukraine constitute a part of this complex conspiracy.[55] Judging from the amount of attention paid to it (only a handful of articles per year), the impact of this myth seems to be marginal, even among those who believe in conspiracy theories. It can, however, provide an interesting case study on how contemporary antisemitic myths are born and perpetuated.

In the context of the Russian-Ukrainian war, the myth was revived in 2014, when James Wald, a researcher on antisemitism, posted a parody for Purim on his blog, which is hosted by the *Times of Israel.* In it, Wald described alleged leaks of top-secret information that were supposed to prove that the Jews were preparing themselves for a massive and organized colonization of Ukraine.[56] At the time of writing this parody, Wald was working on a study of the role of the Khazar myth in Russian thought and was careful to insert clear signs into his text that this was a fiction.

Wald's piece was discovered nine months later by the American conspiracy theorist Wayne Madsen, who republished it on the websites of the pro-Russian think tank Strategic Culture Foundation.[57] However, he presented the piece not as a parody but as fact—that is, as if the Jews were really admitting to the existence of Ukraine colonization plans. He also "forgot" to mention that his source text was a post by an independent blogger and instead presented it as a regular report by the *Times of Is-rael*. Madsen ended his "investigative" report with the following: "Thanks to the *Times of Israel* exposé of the secret Israeli report on the Khazars and modern-day Israel, the machinations behind the American and European Union destabilization of Ukraine become all the more apparent."[58] Madsen's distorted piece was picked up by other antisemitic media outlets across the globe, including the influential Czech antisemitic website AC24 Vědomí.[59]

James Wald was clearly surprised by the amount of attention his parodic post received. In a personal conversation, he commented sarcastically, "this was possibly the most successful piece I have ever written."[60] However, he managed to hit a sensitive spot with his Purim parody. Claims that Jews intended to yank Ukraine from the embrace of Mother Russia to create a new Jewish state in Ukraine were circulating within Eastern European antisemitic circles for quite some time before the 2014 Maidan revolt and before the subsequent war had even started. A particular case involving this myth involves accusations made against the Hassidic movement Chabad. In 2012, the influential Czech antisemitic website The Curious Fellow (Zvědavec) translated a series of articles by a certain Ales Bolinskyi from the Russian think tank Foundation for Strategic Culture (*Fond Strategicheskoy Kultury*). The articles connected the establishment of the so-called European Jewish Parliament with the alleged Chabad conspiracy to establish a second Israel in Ukraine, or "the Third Khazariya" as they put it in a reference to Arthur Koestler's *Thirteenth Tribe*.[61] An interesting tactic is involved in this particular take on the "second Israel" myth: by singling out the Chabad movement for attack, identifying it as the alleged "extremist" anti-Russian force within global Jewry, Bolinskyi managed to construct his anti-Jewish conspiracy theory while claiming to be sincerely concerned about the fate of the rest of the Jews, who "suffer for someone else's Messianic ambitions."[62]

As this older example shows, the Russian-Ukrainian war has only brought a new dimension to the recurring myth of New Israel. The first incidence of this during the war occurred in mid-2014—that is, before Madsen's discovery of the James Wald Purim parody. By June 2014, direct accusations were appearing, according to which Jewish organizations were trying to cleanse eastern Ukraine by means of war in order to prepare the ground for Jewish settlement. All the pieces associated with an antisemitic myth are present, including vague references to a reliable source and a presentation style that makes it difficult to verify the claims:

> The Ukrainian national newspaper—the press agency UNN, has published the revelations of a well-known expert, a veteran of the Israeli organization Shin Bet ("Shabak"), and a person responsible for internal security, Alex Groissman, who believes that in the context of recent events in the Middle East, more and more Israelis are considering the option of moving to Ukraine. They have put their faith in Kolomoyskyi as the agent to protect them against the Islamic militants. They believe that they have done their job, by having expelled the Soviet Union and China from the region and having kept their Arab neighbors, who have been in revolt, under control. And now, Washington is going to utilize this controlled chaos to prepare a way for the creation of a new quasi-state under their control. [This state] will take over new oil and natural gas deposits so that Israel, with its special vision of the Middle East, will be able to expand.[63]

The myth circulated not only in Czech antisemitic circles but also within the Polish antisemitic movement at the same time.[64] The case study of the "second Israel" myth documents how the antisemitic movement works with sources by twisting and bending the original to fit the fantasy, sometimes clearly ignoring the difference between truth and apparent mystification. Once a core report is published, it is immediately picked up and republished by other antisemitic websites in a way that makes it very difficult to trace back to the original source. Instead of providing a clear source, the websites link with one another, thus creating citation circles of their own.

Obviously, no such Jewish exodus to Ukraine is taking place. The opposite is actually the case in a war situation where both sides have occasionally resorted to anti-Jewish violence, be it to attack Jews directly or to use a false-flag antisemitic incident to blame the other party. According to the Jewish Agency, more than fifty-five hundred Jews made *aliyah* to Israel in 2014.[65] In 2015, an additional seven thousand Jews, "a staggering 11 percent of the Ukrainian Jewish population," emigrated to the Jewish state according to preliminary numbers from the Jewish agency, achieving a 230 percent growth rate when compared with 2013.[66] This made Ukraine the second largest source of Jewish *aliyah*, right after the widely discussed issue of France. The third largest source has been Russia, from which about twelve thousand people emigrated to Israel in 2014 and 2015. "The depreciation of the Russian ruble and the erosion of civil liberties under the government of Vladimir Putin" are quoted as the main reasons for this new wave of Russian Jewish migration to Israel, according to Natan Sharansky.[67] In the same report, Sharansky explains that Israel is the only country with a Western style of democracy that is actually willing to take in Ukrainian Jews, as both the United States and the European Union countries put barriers on Ukrainian immigration.[68]

CONCLUSION

The pro-Russian orientation of the antisemitic scene has deep roots, and the takeover of the Czech antisemitic movement by pro-Russian voices is the result of a much longer process, with the Russian-Ukrainian war fully exposing these attitudes. The consolidation of the pro-Russian position continued during 2014, and the symbolic takeover was completed in 2015. Antisemitic and anti-Putin voices still existed in 2014 but have since fallen silent.

Today the vast majority of Czech antisemitic movements—including the neo-Stalinist, Catholic traditionalist, fascist—and the majority of neo-Nazi movements sincerely admire Putin's Russia to the extent that the neo-Nazis, for example, have been willing to abandon their former friendships with the Ukrainian neo-Nazis. Czech antisemitic groups express this attitude both online, by carefully selecting content that presents the Russian point of view, as well as in the streets in their speeches, flags, banners, and, very symbolically, by wearing the orange and black Ribbon of Saint George.

Russia has jumped on the train of conspiracy debunking combined with antiglobalist and anti-European sentiments, even though it meant tolerating the antisemitism that comes in the same package. In a world of conspiracy debunkers, Russia is portrayed as the last stronghold against the alleged New World Order, represented by almighty Jewish/American forces. The Ukrainian Maidan is then depicted as an event in which the worldwide Jewish conspiracy attempted to pull Ukraine away from its Russian embrace and redirect its course toward the "wicked" West.

Conspiracy theories have truly become an important weapon in the propaganda war that surrounds the Russian-Ukrainian war. As the Czech Security Information Service aptly noted in its report, the goal of current Russian propaganda is not to present "a better truth" but to create a fog of disinformation, in which "there is no truth"—nothing can be verified, everything can be forged, manipulated, and speculated about, and thus, no claims about Russia (such as its interference in Crimea or eastern Ukraine) can be proven.[69] The methods of conspiracy debunkers and "9/11 truthers" provide excellent source material for such a disinformation fog. Antisemitism is just one more piece that helps make the whole set of conflicting stories and reports even more confusing. The case of hoaxes disseminated after the MH17 disaster is an excellent example of this method.

By analyzing some of the myths and propaganda pieces, one can sometimes arrive at the conclusion that Jews and Israel are not necessarily always the primary target but are rather the victims and scapegoats in somebody else's propaganda war. In such a propaganda war, the image of the Jew is used as an important component in the bestiary of conspiracies—after all, what kind of conspiracy would it be if there were no Jews involved? The Russian-Ukrainian war is being fought in Donbas and Donetsk, with the headquarters of the main adversaries located in Kiev and Moscow, yet there is a still a belief that there must be some sort of link to Tel Aviv as well; there must be something more to it that might explain the alienation that has arisen between two Slavic "brother nations." In that sense, Israel has become collateral damage in the propaganda war, not because of anything it has or has not done in relation to the conflict but simply because of its Jewish status. As such, the case of anti-Jewish rhetoric in the propaganda that surrounds the unfortunate Russian-Ukrainian conflict can be taken as a clear textbook case of new antisemitism. No matter who wins the war in Ukraine, Israel, as the perceived representative of a global Jewish conspiracy, will be blamed for it.

The Czech antisemitic movement offers four main types of conspiracy theories in relation to the Russian-Ukrainian war. The most common is the accusation that the secret service organizations of the United States and Israel directly participated in the Maidan revolt; that the revolt was a carefully prepared provocation meant to remove the pro-Russian president Yanukovwich and set Ukraine against mother Russia. The second type of conspiracy theory elaborates on the Russian "war against fascism" rhetoric, blaming the Jews and Israel for supporting Ukrainian neo-Nazi organizations. These two myths appear to be the most common ones. The third myth is directly connected to the fog of disinformation spread by the Russian media after the downing of Malaysia Airlines Flight 17 over the eastern Donetsk region in eastern Ukraine, where the involvement of the Russian "Buk" land-to-air missile system is believed to have played a crucial role. Last but not least, the war in eastern Ukraine has seen the revival of some of the older myths about the alleged Jewish plan to create a new Jewish state in Ukraine.

However absurd some of these conspiracy theories may appear to be, they influence the actions of the movements that plan their strategies and choose their partners according to these beliefs. Analyses such as the one presented in this essay are thus crucial for documenting this phenomenon and for gaining a better understanding of how particular movements might react in the case of increased tension between NATO countries and Russia. In such a scenario, it seems likely that Czech antisemitic elements would side with Russia, which could lead to a spate of domestic protests, incidents, or even violent riots and insurgencies against the Czech state and the obligations it has to its NATO allies. With up to tens of thousands of supporters, these movements are not sizable at the moment, yet they could still cause security incidents or provide a basis for anti-NATO incitement. Contrary to their "nationalist" ethos, these forces would, very likely, be willing to abandon the local nationalists of Latvia, Lithuania, and Estonia in favor of Russian revisionism. It is not clear, though, how they would react should an incident occur between Poland and Russia.

While this particular analysis has been limited to the Czech context, much of the content published by Czech elements did not originate in the Czech Republic. On many occasions, antisemitic conspiracy theories about the Russian-Ukrainian war have been translated into Czech from foreign languages—mainly English, Russian, and Polish. This suggests that we would expect to see the similar myths and attitudes of antisemitic movements and individuals expressed in other parts of Europe and America. The question is not about whether we can expect to see such manifestations but to what extent they may have penetrated antisemitic thinking in Western countries.

This research was made possible thanks to the scholarship of the Jan Hus Educational Foundation (Vzdělávací nadace Jana Husa), Czech Republic.

NOTES

1. The most notorious case relates to the leader of the antisemitic Republican Party of Bohemia and Moravia, Miroslav Sládek, who is a former Communist censor. Another example is the former vice chairman of the antisemitic National Democracy, Ladislav Zemánek, who started his career as a board member of the Youth Communist Union. Finally, the publisher of the notorious antisemitic far-right journal, *Týdeník Politika*, banned for antisemitic incitement in 1994, appeared for a short time as press speaker for the Communist Party of Bohemia and Moravia.

2. Jan Červenka, "Tisková zpráva: Vztah české veřejnosti k národnostním skupinám žijícím v ČR—únor 2015," *Centrum pro výzkum veřejného mínění*, March 6, 2015, https://cvvm.soc.cas.cz/media/com _form2content/documents/c2/a1868/f9/ov150306.pdf.

3. Anti-Defamation League, "ADL Global 100—An Index of Anti-Semitism," http://global100.adl.org/public/ADL-Global-100-Executive -Summary.pdf.

4. *Annual Report on Antisemitic Manifestations in 2014*, Security Center of the Jewish Community of Prague (Prague, 2015), 8.

5. *Annual Report on Antisemitic Manifestations in 2015*, Security Center of the Jewish Community of Prague (Prague, 2016), 6, https://www.fzo .cz/3031/vyrocni-zprava-o-projevech-antisemitismu-v-cr-za-rok-2015/.

6. Report on Extremism in the Territory of Czech Republic in 2015. *Ministry of Interior–Department of Security Policy and Crime Preventionkriminality* (2016), http://www.mvcr.cz/clanek/extremismus -vyrocni-zpravy-o-extremismu-a-strategie-boje-proti-extremismu.aspx.

7. Volby do Evropského parlamentu konané na území České republiky ve dnech 23.05– 24.05.2014. *Volby.cz—Official Election Portal of the Czech Statistical Office*, http://volby.cz/pls/ep2014/ep11?xjazyk=CZ.

8. Volby do zastupitelstev obcí, *Volby.cz—Official Election Portal of the Czech Statistical Office*, http://volby.cz/pls/kv2014/kv1111?xjazyk=CZ&xid =0&xdz=2&xnumnuts=4206&xobec=567515&xstat=0&xvyber=0.

9. The estimated Jewish population in the Czech Republic is no higher than thirty-nine hundred. See Sergio DellaPergola, *World Jewish*

Population, 2013 (New York: Berman Jewish DataBank, 2013), appendix A, http://www.jewishdatabank.org/studies/downloadFile.cfm?FileID=3113.

10. One of these lists has been created by the National Democracy leader Adam B. Bartoš on his blog *Čechy Čechům*, accessed March 15, 2016, https://cechycechum.wordpress.com/category/slavni-zide-mezi-nami/; but there are older examples as well, with the most notorious one being published in the 1990s by the bulletin *Týdeník Politika* 96/1992.

11. For more on antisemitism in response to the refugee crisis, see Zbyněk Tarant, "Antisemitism in Response to the 2015 Refugee Wave— Case of the Czech Republic," *Flashpoint* 13 (December 2015), http://isgap .org/flashpoint/antisemitism-in-response-to-the-2015-refugee-wave-the -case-of-the-czech-republic/.

12. It was possible to hear BDS rhetoric from the representatives of the International Solidarity Movement (ISM), supported by the former Czech diplomat Jan Kavan at an ISM rally in Prague in August 2014. Attempts to popularize BDS have been made by Charles University professor Pavel Barša, but without much success. There have also been attempts by the ISM to call for a boycott of the Days of Jerusalem, organized by the city of Pilsen in cooperation with the Israeli embassy. The city of Pilsen, however, refused to succumb to the ideological pressure.

13. Personal observation of the rally. November 17 marks the beginning of the Velvet Revolution that brought down the Communist regime in 1989. The day has become a feast of street politics with dozens of diverse rallies and protests taking place only in Prague.

14. For the list of incidents from 1989 to 2002, see the Ministry of Interior's website: Ministry of Interior, "Terrorism and Its Manifestations in Czechoslovakia and the Czech Republic," http://www.mvcr.cz/clanek /terorismus-a-jeho-projevy-v-nekdejsim-ceskoslovensku-a-dnesni-ceske -republice.aspx.

15. Printed antisemitic journals and bulletins were available in the past—namely, the infamous *Týdeník Politika*, which was banned in 1994 by court order. In 2017, there were three antisemitic publishing houses: Guidemedia (led by Pavel Kamas), Bodyartbook (led by Radek Fiksa) and Nakladatelství Adam Bartoš (a private publishing enterprise associated with Adam B. Bartoš). In 2016, these publishing houses increased their output, but most of the content is published online. Their activity has somewhat decreased in 2018. The several antisemitic books represent a tiny fraction in the tens of thousands book titles, published in the Czech language every year.

16. Independently of my survey, Avukatu and Lupač used a similar method to analyze Czech far-right websites as well. Their results were published in Czech. See Jiřina Avukatu and Petr Lupač, "Analýza on-line sítě české krajní pravice," *Rexter*, January 2014, http://www.google .co.il/url?sa=t&rct=j&q=&esrc=s&source=web&cd=1&ved=0CB4QF jAA&url=http%3A%2F%2Fwww.ceeol.com%2Faspx%2Fgetdocument .aspx%3Flogid%3D5%26id%3D93bf8d16-1ccf-4345-afc4- 7ac48f7ceb44&ei=OcanVNqqAcnsUs-0g9AC&usg=AFQjCNEY3Rky8z hkqIlpjsnufUsptbxnSA&bvm=bv.82001339,d.d24. For more on the Arabic blogosphere, see Bruce Etling, John Kelly, Robert Faris, and John Palfrey, "Mapping the Arabic Blogosphere: Politics, Culture, and Dissent" (Berkman Center Research Publication no. 2009-06, June 2009), http://cyber.law .harvard.edu/sites/cyber.law.harvard.edu/files/Mapping_the_Arabic _Blogosphere_0.pdf. For more on the Iranian blogosphere, see John Kelly and Bruce Etling, "Mapping Iran's Online Public: Politics and Culture in the Persian Blogosphere" (Berkman Center Research Publication no. 2008-01, April 2008), http://cyber.law.harvard.edu/sites/cyber.law.harvard.edu /files/Kelly&Etling_Mapping_Irans_Online_Public_2008.pdf.

17. See http://www.czechfreepress.cz; http://outsidermedia.cz; http:// svobodnenoviny.eu; http://www.zvedavec.org; http://www.nwoo.org; http://protiproud.parlamentnilisty.cz.

18. http://www.zvedavec.org/inzerce.htm.

19. Alexa Internet is a private company based in California and owned by Amazon. It provides commercial web traffic data and analysis. The data are collected by the (rather controversial) Alexa browser toolbar, which tracks user browsing habits and visited websites. The data are collected and used for global statistics and traffic analysis. A publicly accessible portion of the data allows sorting of websites according to their traffic both on the national and global level. The ratings become less reliable in smaller countries but are still somewhat useful for distinguishing between less and more influential websites in a given scene or location. See http:// www.alexa.com.

20. Alexa, site overview for "parlamentnilisty.cz." The data are valid for April 28, 2016.

21. WPSJ will invite representatives of the Right Sector to the Czech Republic. Dělnická strana sociální spravedlnosti, February 24, 2014, http://old.dsss.cz/dsss-pozve-zastupce-praveho-sektoru-do-cr. For more on neo-Nazi activists sharing pro-Ukrainian graffiti, see *Svobodný odpor*, February 3, 2015, http://www.svobodnyodpor.info/image/109963900820.

22. Martin Kněžický, "Ukrajinská válka," *Dělnická strana sociální spravedlnosti*, February 20, 2014, http://old.dsss.cz/ukrajinska-valka.

23. J. Štěpánek, "KOMENTÁŘ: Rusko ukazuje svoji sílu," *Dělnická strana sociální spravedlnosti*, March 10, 2014, http://old.dsss.cz /komentar_-rusko-ukazuje-svoji-silu?newspage39=10.

24. "Sídlo budoucích pučistů je v Praze," *Dělnická strana*, February 27, 2014, http://www.dsss.cz/stepanek-_dsss__-sidlo-budoucich-pucistu -je-v-praze.

25. Jan Kuřec, "Obrazy z Rus," *Hlas mládeže*, April 7, 2014, http://hlas .delnickamladez.cz/uvaha_-obrazy-z-rus.

26. Erik Lamprecht, "Mocenský zápas o Ukrajinu," *Dělnická strana sociální spravedlnosti*, July 18, 2014, http://www.dsss.cz /lamprecht-_dsss__-mocensky-zapas-o-ukrajinu.

27. "Hlas mládeže končí svou publikační činnost," *Hlas mládeže*, November 2014, http://hlas.delnickamladez.cz.

28. *Hooligans.cz*, forum.hooligans.cz.

29. Tomáš Vandas, "Sankce proti Rusku poškozují ČR," *Dělnická strana*, July 31, 2014, http://www.dsss.cz/dsss_-sankce-vuci-rusku-poskozuji-cr. For more on repetitions of this criticism, see Jiří Štěpánek, "Nevyšetřené sestřelení a úloha USA," *Dělnická strana*, August 22, 2016, http://www .dsss.cz/stepanek-_dsss__-nevysetrene-sestreleni-a-uloha-usa.

30. Jiří Štěpánek, "Rusko zahájilo skutečný boj proti teroristům," *Dělnická strana*, October 15, 2015, http://www.dsss.cz /stepanek-_dsss__-rusko-zahajilo-skutecny-boj-proti-teroristum.

31. "Křehké spojenectví nacionalistů a 'z větší části židovských oligarchů' na Ukrajině," *Deliandiver*, May 4, 2015, http://deliandiver .org/2015/05/krehke-spojenectvi-nacionalistu-a-z-vetsi-casti-zidovskych -oligarchu-na-ukrajine.html.

32. "Ukraina—Żydo-banderowskie krwawe pieniądze," *Wolna Polska*, March 14, 2016, http://wolna-polska.pl/wiadomosci/ukraina-krwawe -pieniadze-zydo-banderowcy-organizuja-wycieczki-do-strefy-ato-za-1700 -hrywien-2016-03.

33. I describe the complex personal story of the party's leader, Adam Bartoš, in Zbyněk Tarant, "From Philosemitism to Antisemitism—A Case Study of the 'Mladá Pravice' Movement in the Czech Republic," in *Faces of Hatred: Contemporary Antisemitism in Its Historical Context*, ed. Zbyněk Tarant and Věra Tydlitátová (Pilsen, Czech Republic: University of West Bohemia, 2013), 114–52.

34. Czech election results can be seen in full detail at http://volby.cz.

35. Personal observation of rallies in Prague on November 17, 2015, and February 6, 2016.

"Po devadesáti letech vycházejí Protokoly sionských mudrců tiskem v novém českém překladu," Personal website of Adam B. Bartoš, January 22, 2015, https://abbartos.wordpress.com/2015/11/22/po-devadesati-letech -vychazeji-protokoly-sionskych-mudrcu-tiskem-v-novem-ceskem -prekladu/.

36. Ladislav Zemánek's post on Facebook, November 4, 2014: "The action was organized by Russia, and it was obvious who paid for it, . . . I recognize the recent elections in the Donetsk region . . . I can state with a clear conscience that I did not notice any mistakes during these elections, they were held in a very friendly atmosphere and with great enthusiasm. We could learn from their success."

37. "Мвс встановило особи 'спостерігачів' на так званих 'виборах ДНР,' готуються санкції (список)," *Ukrainian National Police*, November 3, 2014, http://www.npu.gov.ua/uk/publish/article/1210405.

38. Personal observation. Prague, March 28, 2015.

39. *Annual report of the Security Information Service—2014* (Security Information Service, 2014), https://www.bis.cz/vyrocni-zprava6c8d .html?ArticleID=1096. The Security Information Service is a civilian state security service with authorities somewhat comparable to the US Federal Bureau of Investigation. "Under Act No. 153/1994 Coll., on the Intelligence Services of the Czech Republic, the Security Information Service (BIS) is responsible for acquiring, collecting and evaluating information concerning: terrorist threats, activities jeopardizing the security or major economic interests of the State, activities of foreign intelligence services in the territory of the Czech Republic, intents or acts aimed at undermining democratic foundations, sovereignty or territorial integrity of the Czech Republic, organized crime and activities posing a threat to classified information." "What We Do," Security Information Service (BIS), https:// www.bis.cz/cim-se-zabyvameEN.html.

40. The so-called Saint George's Ribbon or Ribbon of Saint George (*Georgiyevskaya lenta*) is a relatively new Russian military symbol. It is a long rectangular ribbon with three black and two orange stripes" (Wikipedia, "Ribbon of Saint George"), originally used to hold Soviet military medals. It became a symbol of Soviet military veterans and, later, a symbol meant to counter the symbolism of the 2004 Ukrainian Orange Revolution. It became notorious as a symbol of the Russian military during the annexation of Crimea, and it is a symbol of the Russian-backed

separatists in eastern Ukraine. Wearing the ribbon has become an expression of pro-Putin opinion.

41. Personal observations in Prague, September 8, 2015; November 17, 2015; February 6, 2016; March 26, 2016.

42. Vít Skalký, "Na východě Ukrajiny sledujeme triumf síly lidského ducha," Národní demokracie, March 1, 2015, http://narodnidemokracie.cz /na-vychode-ukrajiny-sledujeme-triumf-sily-lidskeho-ducha/.

43. For the role of Miroslav Dolejší's Analysis of November 17 in the thought of the Czech far right, see Zbyněk Tarant, "Neo-Nazis on the Nation's Boulevard: The Role of the 'International Students' Struggle for Freedom Day' (November 17th) in the Ideology of Antisemitic Movements," in History of Hatred—Hatred of History: Encounters between Antisemitism and Historical Memory, ed. Zbyněk Tarant and Věra Tydlitátová (Pilsen, Czech Republic: University of West Bohemia, 2013), 66–108.

44. Author's own recording, Prague 2015. The full text of the speech can be found in Czech at "Listopad byl podvod, ale litovat se nebudeme. Chceme změnu, chceme národní stat," Národní demokracie, November 18, 2015, http://narodnidemokracie.cz/listopad-byl-podvod-ale-litovat-se -nebudeme-chceme-zmenu-chceme-narodni-stat/.

45. Occam's razor provides us with one of the basic methodological laws: "Among competing hypotheses, the one with the fewest assumptions should be selected." The rule was defined by William of Ockham (1287–1347).

46. Věra Tydlitátová, "Malajská letadla a zneužité tragédie," in "Spiknutí!" Úloha antisemitských konspiračních teorií ve veřejném a politickém diskurzu, ed. Zbyněk Tarant and Věra Tydlitátová (Pilsen, Czech Republic: University of West Bohemia, 2014).

47. "Sestřelení malajského letounu zřejmě léčkou na Rusko, záminka k třetí světové válce?" Osud.cz, July 17, 2014, http://www.osud.cz/sestreleni -malajskeho-letounu-zrejme-leckou-na-rusko-zaminka-k-treti-svetove -valce.

48. "Obrat: podle skupiny expertů sestřelila let MH17 izraelská raketa," Osud.cz, July 19, 2014, http://www.osud.cz/obrat-podle-skupiny-expertu -sestrelila-let-mh17-izraelska-raketa.

49. "Sestřel je jen náhoda, jednou jsi dole, pak zas nahoře," Osud.cz, July 28, 2014, http://www.osud.cz/sestrel-je-jen-nahoda-jednou-jsi-dole -pak-zas-nahore;

Michael Winkler, "Malajsijské letadlo nad Ukrajinou a Obamovo sluchátko," Freeglobe, August 20, 2014, http://freeglobe.parlamentnilisty

.cz/Articles/14230-malajsijske-letadlo-nad-ukrajinou-a-obamovo
-sluchatko.aspx.

50. "Zpráva očitého svědka: Cestující z letu MH 17 byli mrtví dávno
před sestřelením u Doněcka. S teorií o 'fingovaných mrtvolách' přišel už
Strelkov. Neblížíme se náhodou i k odpovědi na záhadu letu MH 370?"
Protiproud, September 3, 2014, http://protiproud.parlamentnilisty.cz
/politika/1205-zprava-ociteho-svedka-cestujici-z-letu-mh-17-byli-mrtvi
-davno-pred-sestrelenim-u-donecka-s-teorii-o-fingovanych-mrtvolach
-prisel-uz-strelkov-neblizime-se-nahodou-i-k-odpovedi-na-zahadu
-letu-mh-370.htm.

51. "Ukrajinský SU-25, který sestřelil 'Boeing,' pilotoval Dmitrij
Jakacud," *New World Order Opposition*, December 1, 2014, http://
www.nwoo.org/2014/12/01/ukrajinsky-su-25-ktery-sestrelil-boeing
-pilotoval-dmitrij-jakacud/.

52. "Důkladný rozbor Zprávy o MH-17: Případ 'kontrolovaného úniku,'
který má zakrýt zjištění pravdy. Náhodou 'osleply' všechny radary. Co a
proč vynechali holandští vyšetřovatelé?" *Protiproud*, October 20, 2015,
http://protiproud.parlamentnilisty.cz/politika/2014-dukladny-rozbor
-zpravy-o-mh17-pripad-kontrolovaneho-uniku-ktery-ma-zakryt-zjisteni
-pravdy-nahodou-osleply-vsechny-radary-co-a-proc-vynechali-holandsti
-vysetrovatele.htm.

53. "Sestřelený Boeing 777 letu MH17 má otevřít cestu k vyhlášení
'bezletové' zóny nad Ukrajinou, kterou by zajišťovalo NATO!" *AE News*,
July 17, 2014, http://aeronet.cz/news/sestreleny-boeing-777-letu-mh17
-ma-otevrit-cestu-k-vyhlaseni-bezletove-zony-nad-ukrajinou-kterou-by
-zajistovalo-nato/.

54. For the official report, see "Investigation Crash MH17, 17 July 2014
Donetsk," Dutch Safety Board, esp. chap. 3 "Analysis," section 3.5 "Possible
Sources of Damage," and chap. 10 "Conclusions," section 10.3 "Excluding
Other Causes of the Crash" as well as the relevant appendices, https://
www.onderzoeksraad.nl/en/onderzoek/2049/investigation-crash
-mh17-17-july-2014.

55. For additional, older examples of this myth, see also Věra
Tydlitátová, "The Influence of Russian Anti-Semitism in the Czech
Republic," in *Faces of Hatred—Contemporary Antisemitism in Its Historical
Context*, ed. Věra Tydlitátová (Pilsen, Czech Republic: University of West
Bohemia, 2013), 153–78.

56. James Wald, "Leaked Report: Israel Acknowledges Jews in Fact
Khazars; Secret Plan for Reverse Migration to Ukraine," James Wald's

blog on the *Times of Israel,* March 18, 2014, http://blogs.timesofisrael.com/leaked-report-israel-acknowledges-jews-in-fact-khazars-secret-plan-for-reverse-migration-to-ukraine/.

57. "Israel's Secret Plan for a 'Second Israel' in Ukraine," Strategic Culture Foundation, December 3, 2014, http://www.strategic-culture.org/news/2014/12/03/israel-secret-plan-for-second-israel-in-ukraine.html.

58. "Israel's Secret Plan for a 'Second Israel' in Ukraine."

59. Wayne Madsen, "Secret Plan for 'Second Israel' in Ukraine," *AC24,* December 5, 2014, http://www.ac24.cz/zpravy-ze-sveta/5186-wayne-madsen-tajny-plan-na-druhy-izrael-na-ukrajine.

60. Personal conversation with James Wald, Bloomington, Indiana, April 3, 2016.

61. The so-called European Jewish Parliament can be described as a lobbyist nongovernmental organization that is meant to unify and represent the interests of European Jewish communities vis-à-vis the EU Parliament in Strasbourg. The activities of the EJP, established by the Ukrainian billionaire Vadim Rabinovich, were met with mixed feelings by European Jewish communities. See the EJP's website at http://ejp.eu. For more on "The Third Khazariya," see Ales Bolinskyj, "K čemu je Evropě dobrý vlastní Kneset?" *Zvědavec,* June 28, 2012, http://www.zvedavec.org/komentare/2012/06/5023-k-cemu-je-evrope-dobry-vlastni-knesset-ii.htm; originally published as Ales Volinskyj, "Зачем Европе собственный Кнессет? (II)," *Fond Strategicheskoy Kultury,* June 19, 2012, http://www.fondsk.ru/news/2012/06/19/zachem-evrope-sobstvennyj-knesset-ii-14938.html.

62. Volinskyj, "Зачем Европе собственный Кнессет?"

63. "Ukrajinský mocenský boj Kolomojskij versus Porošenko," *AC24,* July 14, 2014, http://www.ac24.cz/zpravy-ze-sveta/4394-ukrajinsky-mocensky-boj-kolomojskij-versus-porosenko.

64. See, for example, "Antychryst już tu jest—Ukraina nowym Izraelem," *Talbot,* July 14, 2014, http://talbot.nowyekran.pl.neon24.pl/post/111014,antychryst-juz-tu-jest-ukraina-nowym-izraelem. See also "Nowa Chazaria. Ekspert—Kołomojski przygotowuje na Ukrainie miejsce na 'ziemię obiecaną,'" Gloria.tv, July 12, 2014, https://gloria.tv/?media=635383&language=YiwzPCkSG6u.

65. "Aliyah Hits Ten-Year High: Approximately 26,500 New Immigrants Arrived in Israel in 2014," Jewish Agency for Israel, January 2, 2015, http://www.jewishagency.org/blog/1/article/31301.

66. Eylon Aslan-Levy, "Aliyah Numbers Rise, but the Majority Coming from Just Three Countries," *Tablet,* April 22, 2016,

http://www.tabletmag.com/scroll/196250/aliyah-numbers-rise-but
-majority-coming-from-just-three-countries; "30,000 Immigrants Arrived
in Israel in 2015," Jewish Agency for Israel, http://www.jewishagency.org
/reports-israel/30000-immigrants-arrived-israel-2015.

67. "France Is Israel's Largest Source of Aliyah for the 2nd Straight
Year," *Jewish Telegraphic Agency*, December 22, 2015, http://www.jta.org
/2015/12/22/news-opinion/israel-middle-east/france-is-israels-largest
-source-of-aliyah-for-2nd-straight-year.

68. The inclusion of Ukraine into the visa waiver program is under
discussion in the EU at the time of writing this chapter.

69. *Výroční zpráva Bezpečnostní informační služby za rok 2015* [Annual
report of the Security Information Service—2015] (Security Information
Service, 2015), https://www.bis.cz/vyrocni-zprava890a.html?ArticleID
=1104.

ZBYNĚK TARANT is Assistant Professor in the Department of
Middle Eastern Studies at the University of West Bohemia in
Pilsen, Czech Republic. While his main topic of research is the
history of Holocaust memory and its institutions in the state of
Israel and the United States, he has been actively involved in research on contemporary antisemitism since 2006. He specializes in the monitoring of cyberhate and the analysis of emerging
threats in contemporary Central European political extremism.

Muslim Antisemitism and Anti-Zionism in South Asia

A Case Study of Lucknow

NAVRAS JAAT AAFREEDI

STUDIES THAT FOCUS on Muslim antisemitism have tended to overlook South Asia despite the region's great importance. Twenty-two percent of the world's population is Muslim, and one-third of Muslims live in the countries of the South Asian Association for Regional Cooperation, where they have a thousand-year history of relations with Jews.[1] South Asia is home to some of the largest Islamic movements in the world, such as Tablighi Jama'at, the largest Sunni Muslim revivalist (daw'a) movement in the world; Jama'at-i-Islami, a prototype of political Islam in South Asia; Darul Uloom Deoband, the alleged source of ideological inspiration to the Taliban; and Nadwātul Ulamā of Lucknow.

A degree of antipathy toward Jews has almost always existed among the Muslims in this region, but it never expressed itself through violence until the creation of the state of Israel in 1948. The intertwining of antisemitism and anti-Zionism among South Asian Muslims has manifested itself on more than one occasion, such as the attacks on Jews in Karachi, Pakistan, coinciding with the Arab-Israel wars in 1948, 1956, and 1967; the murder of Daniel Pearl in Pakistan in 2002; the Pakistani attack on Beit Chabad in Mumbai, India, in 2008; and the explosion of an Israeli diplomat's wife's car in Delhi, India, in 2012 by Iranians with local logistical support. Muslim institutions of religious learning have regularly produced hate literature against Jews, and Muslim seminaries worldwide subscribe to the curricula they prescribe. Many of these seminaries are attended by Muslims in the diaspora in the West, where they are often inspired to either wage or support a holy war against the Judeo-Christian West. This is evident from the many instances of Muslims going to Iraq to join the Islamic State and from Muslim involvement in terrorist attacks in Europe and America.

The South Asian Muslim diaspora is numerically larger and geographically more widespread than that of Muslims from any other region of the world, giving them significant power to influence Muslim opinion globally. The migration of South Asian Muslims to all corners of the world means that their views can be highly influential within the wider diaspora Muslim communities, and indeed beyond. Diasporic South Asian Muslims have their strongest presence in the United Kingdom, where they form 3 percent of the total British population. A 2009 survey of 166 full-time Muslim schools in the United Kingdom, most of which subscribe to the curricula of the major Islamic institutions in India, found that they teach "the rejection of Western values and hatred of Jews."[2]

An example of the impact of South Asian Muslims is that in the 1920s, the South Asian Muslim sect Ahmadiya reached out to African American Muslims and influenced them to organize on the basis of religion rather than nationality or culture. It was a novel approach, because the Arab diaspora had previously been organized along the lines of common national origin, culture, and language rather than religion. Today African American Muslims constitute 30 percent to 40 percent of the American Muslim population, South Asians constitute 24.4 percent, and Arabs constitute 12.4 percent. Yet despite the significant global influence of South Asian Muslims, their attitudes toward Jews have attracted little attention.[3]

LUCKNOW

Muslims make up 14.2 percent of India's total population of
1.2 billion (17.05 percent of the world's population); 172 million
Indian Muslims comprise the world's third largest Muslim population. As estimated in 1911, the 742,529 Muslims in Lucknow
constituted only 26.36 percent of the city's total population of
2.8 million. However, Lucknow, the administrative capital
of India's most populous state, Uttar Pradesh, is a major center of
Muslim scholarship, with two prestigious institutions of Islamic
studies: Firangi Mahal and Nadwātul Ulamā. Lucknow continues to be a place of active Muslim politics. The collection of
texts that came to be taught as the madrasā curriculum throughout Muslim India was standardized by Maulana Nizam al-din
Muhammad (d. 1748), the leading scholar of Firangi Mahal at
the time. With the leadership of Islamic scholars in Lucknow,
Delhi, and Hyderabad, India attained prominence in the Islamic
world, leading Albert Hourani to label the eighteenth century
the "Indian century" in Islamic history. Maulana Tariq Rasheed
Firangi Mahali, director of the Islamic Society of Greater Orlando, Florida, is a ninth-generation direct descendant of Mulla
Nizamuddin Firangi Mahali, who framed what is known as the
dars-e nizami, the basic syllabus that continues to be followed by
the vast majority of Islamic madrasas in South Asia even today.

Nadwātul Ulamā (established in 1898) educates four thousand
students in Lucknow and has 111 affiliated madāris (Islamic seminaries) in Bihar, Madhya Pradesh, Uttar Pradesh, Maharashtra,
West Bengal, Haryana, Andhra Pradesh, Karnataka, and Nepal.[4] Many madāris in Africa and the United Kingdom follow its
curriculum. Its graduates have positions as teachers around the
world.[5]

Lucknow has been home to generations of eminent Shia Muslim scholars and clerics and is the biggest Shia cultural center
outside Iran and Iraq. It has several prestigious Shia seminaries,

such as Jamiā Nazimiā (established in 1890), Sultan ul-Madāris (established in 1892), Madrasātul Waizeen (established in 1919), and Tanzeemul Mukātib (established in 1968).[6]

From 1906 to 1947, Lucknow served as the headquarters for the All India Muslim League, the political organization that success-fully led the movement for the partition of India for the creation of Pakistan (an independent state for the Muslims of preindepen-dence India) by uniting those areas of British-ruled India that had Muslim majority. Lucknow continues to be a place of active Mus-lim politics, and the city influences South Asian Muslim attitudes more than any other city in this part of the world. An example of how it influences Muslim politics far and wide is the massacre of Shia Muslims in Pakistan since 2002 as a result of the anti-Shia edicts (*fatwās*) issued by Manzur Numani, the then head of Nadwātul Ulamā, Lucknow, that were printed in a series in the Lucknow-based journal *Al-Furqān* from December 1987 to July 1988. The distribution of these fatwas in Quetta, Pakistan, trig-gered the massacre of the Shia Hazara community there in 2003.[7]

Except for a Jewish writer from Ahmedabad, Sheela Rohekar, who publishes in Hindi and has settled in Lucknow, and a few American and Israeli Jewish converts to Hinduism, there are no Jews in the city. Yet Jews are frequently mentioned, almost always negatively, in the Muslim discourse there. Anti-Israel protests are common in the city. During the US-led military operation in Iraq, for example, flags of Israel and the United States were drawn on the floor at the entrance to the biggest tourist attraction, the Shia Muslim monument Asafi Imambara (also called Bara Imam-bara), so that the flags were trampled on by all who entered.

The attitudes of the Lucknow Muslims toward Jews, as is the case elsewhere in India (except Mumbai, which has a Jewish population), are shaped by secondary sources of information, not as a result of any direct contact. Several factors shape these perceptions: bias and prejudice in the press, religious narratives, and intellectual discourse.

YELLOW JOURNALISM OF THE MUSLIM PRESS

The Muslim press in Lucknow is openly prejudiced against Jews. Its bias can be illustrated by several examples of Holocaust denial and antisemitic caricature.

Holocaust Denial

The anti-Jewish posture of the Muslim press negatively affects Indian Muslims' perceptions of Jews in general. Many South Asian Muslims deny that the Holocaust took place or raise doubts about its magnitude and scale.[8] This Holocaust denial emanates from the Middle East/West Asia and then spreads to South Asia and farther east. Any writing or documentary film aimed at denying the Holocaust that appears in Arabic or Farsi (Persian) eventually finds its way into the Urdu language (the lingua franca of almost all South Asian Muslims even if it is not their first language). Muslim Holocaust deniers apparently believe, according to Meir Litvak, "that the memory of the Holocaust was the foundation of Western support for the establishment of the State of Israel. Therefore, refuting it would severely undermine Israel's legitimacy in the West and help in its eradication."[9]

As an example, the first ever Holocaust film retrospective in South Asia was held at two universities—the Bābāsāhéb Bhīmrāo Ambédkar University, Lucknow, and the University of Lucknow—in September–October 2009. During the event, the largest-circulation Urdu daily newspapers in Lucknow, *Rāshtriya Sahāra* and *Aag*, published stories denying the Holocaust. The articles were largely based on the arguments made by well-known Holocaust deniers, such as Arthur R. Butz, David Irving, Harry Elmer Barnes, David Hoggan, and Paul Ressinier. Qutbullah, author of the article in *Rāshtriya Sahāra*, said in an interview he gave me: "Jews as a nation have a long history of defying God's commandments and betraying the prophets. Considering their long record of betrayal, no European nation was ready to tolerate them in their midst. Hence they targeted the weakest in the Arab world, Palestine, and partitioned it to establish a state for them, Israel. . . . They defile the sanctity of Masjid Al Aqsa by going inside with their shoes on. Young Israelis indulge in physical intimacy there. . . . They have falsified the sacred texts."[10] Qutbullah possesses reliable knowledge of the Arabic language, regularly reads the antisemitic Arabic language press, and often publishes articles in Urdu based on those Arabic sources.

Ahmad Ibrahim Alvi (a Sunni), editor of *Aag*, the other Urdu newspaper in Lucknow that carried an article denying the Holocaust with the aim of sabotaging the Holocaust Films Retrospective in the city, when asked about his opinion of Jews, said, "As a Muslim I don't have a good opinion of Jews. . . . It is a historical fact that Israel is actually Palestine. . . . Jews believe they are the chosen people and everybody else should be subservient to them. It is for this reason that they do not proselytize and take converts." Even the nonproselytizing nature of Judaism is a cause for indictment of Jews in his opinion.[11]

The famous Shia cleric of Lucknow, Maulānā Kalbé Sādiq, one of the shareholders of True Media Indian Communication Limited, the company that owns *Aag*, once said in an interview, "The Bush administration certainly is anti-Islam. This owes, in large measure, to the power of the Zionist lobby in America. Pro-Zionist Jews control large banks, many industries and much of the media in America, and if they leave America, the country will collapse. And it is this lobby, in addition to the extreme right-wing Christian lobby, that is behind the clearly anti-Islamic and anti-Muslim policies of the Bush government."[12]

Hasan Ejaz, a freelance Shia Muslim journalist in Lucknow, joined the chorus when he said in an interview he gave me, "It is clearly mentioned in the Qur'an that the Jews can never think in the interest of Muslims. Although there is a great diversity of the interpretations of the Qur'an, yet there is no conflict among the well-known established commentaries on the references to

Jews. . . . It is a historical fact that the country where the State of Israel was established did not belong to the Jews."[13]

Eminent analyst of South Asian Muslim politics Tufail Ahmad is of the view that the Urdu press is turning Muslims into terrorists. According to him, "The feelings of persecution, siege mentality and exclusion from the mainstream among Indian Muslims as well as hospitable intellectual environments that nurture jihadist attitudes are created not by the internet but by Islamic clerics and Urdu publications."[14] He draws attention to a point made by social reformer Sultan Shahin: "Nearly a century ago when there was no internet, about 18,000 Muslims left their homes and jobs in India to fight for the Ottoman Caliphate in Turkey."[15] To illustrate his point, Ahmad gives the example of how, on June 23, 2016, several Urdu daily newspapers commemorated *Ghazwa-e-Badr*, the first war of Islam against *Kufr* (unbelief) led by Prophet Muhammad on the 17th of Ramadan in the second year of Hijri, corresponding to March 13, 624 CE. Particularly worth mentioning is the Urdu daily *Roznama Sahafat*, published in Lucknow along with editions from Delhi and Mumbai (formerly Bombay). Allama Pir Muhammad Tabassum Bashir Owaisi, in a half-page article, cites "Islamic jurists as arguing that for Muslims the 'most legitimate halal' source of income is *maal-e-ghanimat* (goods seized from non-Muslims), followed by profits from trade, farming, and income from work done by one's own hand—the last being the lowest in importance."[16] Ahmad notes that "while Prophet Muhammad was fighting against the Meccans partially in response to their mistreatment of Muslims, Allama Pir Muhammad Tabassum Bashir Owaisi nevertheless argued that fighting against non-Muslims is mandated by Allah. He observed, 'Otherwise too, the infidels are enemies of Allah and their properties . . . are *halāl* (permissible as per Shariah) for Allah's friends, in other words, for Muslims.' To radicalise Muslims, he wrote an Urdu couplet: 'Create the environment of Badr, because the angels for your aid will come down, in rows after rows even now.'"[17]

An Antisemitic Caricature

In December 2012, the feature editor of the English weekly the *Lucknow Tribune* Mehru Jaffer, a Muslim who had lived in Vienna (once a center of European antisemitism) for a number of years, published an article of mine on Jews in Lucknow that was given a different title from the one that had originally been submitted, and he illustrated it with an antisemitic caricature. In response to letters of protest from myself and several scholars, the *Lucknow Tribune* republished the article without the illustration but did not publish an apology or the letters of protest. It also did not publish the article on its website. It is worth quoting what Dr. Myer Samra, an eminent scholar of Jewish studies, wrote to the editor of the *Lucknow Tribune*, criticizing the publication of the caricature:

> What otherwise might have been an interesting article about Jews and people reputed to have Israelite backgrounds who have been associated with Lucknow over the centuries has instead turned into an offensive, anti-semitic piece, which in some countries could lead to either disciplinary measures against the paper, or to prosecution for publishing something likely to incite hatred and violence against a minority population group. The title itself is a cause of concern. In relatively small letters you have the words "JEWS IN LUCKNOW" . . . Below that, and in very large writing, the use of an exclamation mark after "Moneylender and the Watchmaker" makes the "revelation" of such a community in Lucknow appear extraordinary, but more disturbing is the use of the term "Moneylender," appearing in such large, bold red letters, making this appear to be the most significant aspect of the article. Moneylenders are never popular, and presenting this designation as a stereotype of a Jew, coupled with a cartoon sketch which has a long history as a hateful, antisemitic depiction of an avaricious Jew, taking up almost as much space as the article itself, makes for a strong statement that renders the article itself insignificant by comparison. . . . I believe you owe an apology to your readership, and an assurance that such hateful material would never again be published in your newspaper.[18]

ANTISEMITIC DISCOURSES BY CLERICS

Muslims who do not have a chance to interact directly with Jews over any considerable period of time easily develop prejudices and biases against them based on the many antisemitic stereotypes propagated by the *ulama*. The discourses are now spread more widely and rapidly than ever before through modern technology. What is most surprising is that an antisemitic theologian, Syed Abul Hasan Ali Nadwi,[19] former rector of the Darul Uloom Nadaw-tul Ulama in Lucknow, came to enjoy the position of the founding chairman of the trustees of the highly prestigious Oxford Centre for Islamic Studies. This appointment did far more to make anti-semitic rhetoric respectable than anything that had come before.

He was also the person who translated the Urdu writings of the founder of the Islamic revivalist movement Jama'at-i-Islami, Mau-lana Abul Ala Maududi (also spelled Mawdudi), into Arabic, which were read by Sayid Qutb, the figurehead of Muslim Brotherhood of Egypt; Qutb embraced Maududi's antisemitic concept of jihad against the Judeo-Christian West and popularized it across the Arab world, leading to the emergence of global Islamist terrorism. The following are some examples of Nadwi's antisemitic statements:

> They [Jews] were destined always to live in subjection to other na-tions and ever to be exposed to injustice, oppression, chastisement, extradition, troubles and hardships. Political serfdom, oppression and anguish suffered indefinitely had produced in them a typical racial character. They were notorious all over the world for exces-sive pride of blood and greed. Meek and submissive in distress, they were tyrannical and mean when they had the upper hand. Hypocrisy, deceit, treachery, selfishness, cruelty and usuriousness had become the normal traits of their nature. In the Qur'an we find repeated references to the extent to which they had sunk into degradation in the sixth and the seventh centuries.[20]

> Intrigue and crime, violence and high-handed tactics have been the essential ingredients of the Jewish heritage, their inborn tendencies which could clearly be discerned at any time or place where they

have happened to reside, like a pivot on which their entire intelligence and endeavours have always revolved for the satisfaction
of their ulterior motives. Theirs has been the master mind and the
secret hand behind every insurrection and revolution, conspiracy
and intrigue, lawlessness and anarchy, and every movement
designed to foment social, political, economic and moral disintegration of the non-Jewish people. An eminent Jew, Dr Oscar Levy,
exultingly summed up the characteristics of Jews when he claimed
that in fact they are the rulers of the world; mischief mongers who
foment every trouble and turmoil, wherever it might be.[21]

He has even attacked the nonproselytizing nature of Judaism:

> The Jews have never had any message of salvation for the human-
> ity. The reason for this is that the ideas bound up with superiority
> of Jewish race, and its predetermined salvation simply by virtue of
> birth, no matter what one believes or what one does, are signally
> incompatible with the spirit of any universal message of brotherhood
> and equality of mankind.... Such an idea, naturally, delimits even
> the scope of divine guidance and salvation and places restriction on
> its dissemination beyond the closed circle of one's blood kin. And
> this is the reason why Judaism could never become a universal reli-
> gion, and why the Jews were not required by their own scriptures to
> preach and convert other people to their faith. On the contrary, the
> scriptures of the Jews expressly prohibit missionary endeavour. The
> logical result of such an attitude was that the Jews should discrimi-
> nate against other nations and evolve such norms of virtue and vice,
> right and wrong which should make allowance for the superiority
> of one race over the other. And, then, nothing more is required to
> justify and persist in the cruelest injustice against the non-Jewish
> people. The holy Quran alludes to this very attitude of the Jews when
> it says: "That is because they say: We have no duty to the Gentiles."[22]

In fact, Jews could live in peace and complete harmony with
their non-Jewish neighbors in India and China in part because of
the nonproselytizing nature of the predominant religions there
(Hinduism in India and Confucianism in China), in contrast to
Christian Europe and the Muslim Middle East and North Africa.
The nonproselytizing nature of Judaism helped in this regard. But

unlike the Muslims who are neighbors to Jews in cities such as Mumbai, Kolkata, Cochin, Thane, and Ahmedabad, the Muslims who never have any direct contact with them tend to develop antipathy and antagonism toward them based on what they hear and read; and so is the case with most of the Muslims in South Asia.

Another example of how Nadwātul Ulamā contributes to the spread of antisemitism among Muslims is its publication *Western Media and Its Impact on Society*, authored by one of its graduates, Nazrul Hafeez Nadvi. He writes, "Towards the end of the nineteenth century the Zionists contrived a global government. This was the League of Nations.... In 1897 CE the Jewish thinkers, in a conference in the city of Basel in Switzerland, prepared documents consisting of as many as nineteen chapters. Whereas the eleventh and the nineteenth chapters gave the idea of a world order, the twelfth dealt with controlling the press and the sixteenth with the process of brain washing through education. However, these things are now being denied to exist anywhere."[23] Elsewhere in the same book, Nadvi adds:

> In order to control media and ideological, social and economic fields in addition to the fundamental institutions of American set up, the Jewish policy makers schemed to establish an American institution for world affairs. Its name was later on changed to the "Council of Foreign Relations" (C.F.R.) with the Jews at the helm of its affairs. Many sub institutions were later on established to work under its authority.... Through the institution of CFR the Jews dominated all the quarters of American government.... In America the Jews who dominate American media publish more than 60 million daily newspapers. A single family New House Family [*sic*] possesses 48 dailies, 20 weekly magazines, 120 radio stations, 140 TV cables and 1735 publishing houses. In twenty American universities Jews constitute 50% of the teachers. In Harvard University alone, the percentage of the Jewish lecturers amounts to 75. In American political system 92% of the voters are Jews whereas 54% of the whole American population is eligible to exercise their franchise (1997 census report).[24]

Alluding to a Jewish/Zionist conspiracy in partnership with the West to prevent the Muslims from obtaining nuclear armament, Nadvi writes: "Since 1950 onwards, the Israeli intelligence agency MOSAD [*sic*] has killed all the Muslim scientists working in the research centers of modern weaponry in America, France, Germany, Holland, Egypt, Iraq, Libya, Pakistan and India. These Muslim scientists were working on Atom bomb, anti-missile system and Torpedo war ships."[25]

With regard to the "War on Terror" declared by G. W. Bush Jr. after the September 11, 2001, attacks, Nadvi writes: "G. W. Bush himself admitted the fact that different Jewish organization had faxed anti-Muslim messages to him to such a great extent that they overpowered him. Even the American deputy Defence Minister (a Jew) played a wicked role in this respect."[26]

Maulana Saeed ur Rahman, rector of Nadwātul Ulamā, Lucknow, maintains that, "Since the advent of Islam, Judaism and Christianity have had no relevance for the world. Islam has covered all the teachings of Judaism. Therefore, we invite Jews to join our ranks as Muslims. . . . Qur'an mentions as to how they falsified the sacred texts."[27]

The radical anti-Israel and anti-Zionist position of Iran is well known. The essence of Iran's enmity with Israel is religious, for the two nations neither share a border nor have conflicting strategic or economic interests. What is generally not realized, though, is how Iran's antagonism toward Israel and Zionism influences Shias across the world. Lucknow, a major center of Shia culture, is a prominent example. The Nawabs of Lucknow used to spend a million rupees annually for the upkeep of the Shia shrines in Iraq.[28] The patronage of intellectual pursuits provided by its Shia Muslim rulers of Iranian origin (1722–1858) attracted Shia Muslim scholars from around the world, including the ancestors of the founder of the Islamic Revolution of Iran (1979), Ayatollah Ruhollah Mussaui Khomeini (1902–89). A direct lineal ancestor of his migrated from Nishapur, Iran, to Kintoor, District Barabanki, next to Lucknow, in the late eighteenth century and stayed there until 1830, when his grandfather, Seyed Ahmad Musavi Hindi (1790–1869), left for Iran. This connection with India has been deliberately downplayed by the Iranian regime. Saeed Naqvi, a prominent Shia Muslim journalist from Lucknow, writes:

> Last year, addressing a group of foreign policy analysts in New Delhi, the ambassador of Iran to India, Gholamreza Ansari, made an important admission. He admitted that Ayatullah Ruhollah Khomeini, leader of Iran's Islamic Revolution, came from an important family of divines from Kuntoor, in the Awadh region of Uttar Pradesh, not far from Lucknow.
>
> It was an important admission, because this very fact had been de-nied at the time of the Iranian revolution in 1979 by the Ayatullah's office in Gumran, outside Tehran. In fact, "denial" is too emphatic a term. The fact was not denied, but Ayatullah Khomeini expressed great anger that this connection had been raised so soon after the revolution succeeded.
>
> At the receiving end of this angry outburst was a goodwill delega-tion, hurriedly put together by Atal Bihari Vajpayee, then foreign minister in the Janata government led by Morarji Desai. His foreign secretary, Jagat Mehta, was even more enthusiastic about establishing contacts with the new regime in Tehran.
>
> The delegation was led by the former vice chairman of the Planning Commission, Ashoke Mehta. The impressive Shia per-sona of former ICS Badruddin Tayabji, with his distinctive head-gear, was mobilized too. But the pièce de résistance in the group was a young Shia cleric, Agha Ruhi Abaqati, scion of the family of Saiyyid Nasir Hussain Qibla, a theological scholar of great distinc-tion. He was enlisted as the guide for the delegation.
>
> Before returning to Iran, leading the revolution, Ayatullah Khomeini had spent years in exile, among other places, at Neauphle-le-Chateau, outside Paris. Among those who attended him in France, was Maulana Agha Ruhi. The families of Khomeini and Abaqati are, in fact, linked by relationships.

This fact alone qualified the cleric from Lucknow to be a key player in the Vajpayee–Jagat Mehta initiative to establish links with the new regime in Tehran.

A bright Indian Foreign Service officer, first secretary in the embassy, Kuldip Sahdev, escorted the delegation to the Gumran headquarters. But before they could be ushered into the Supreme Leader's presence, they were halted by the leader himself, with a wave of his hand. He then gestured to Abaqati to come closer. Just when it appeared Khomeini might share a confidence with Abaqati, it dawned on everyone that the cleric from Lucknow was being given an earful by the leader of the Islamic revolution.

He was angry that not only had Abaqati claimed a relationship with the Iranian leader, he had in fact encouraged the government of India to take a diplomatic initiative on that basis. The poor man was not guilty at all. The government of India had contacted him on a tip off.

During a conversation in Qom a year later, Ayatollah Montazari, nominated as deputy to Khomeini in the earlier days of the revolution, explained to me the secret of the diplomatic debacle. "It was a young, insecure revolution. We were afraid ultra nationalists might snipe at the India link."

The ambassador's admission was important because it demonstrated how secure the Islamic revolution now was.

The second, and more important message was one which the audience, typically, did not register. Even by the admission of the Iranian ambassador, Lucknow and Awadh have always been at the very heart of world's Shia culture.[29]

It was Ayatollah Ruhollah Mussaui Khomeini who made antisemitism the central component of Iran's Islamic ideology, followed by Shias across the world. On the first page of his major work, *Velayat-e Faqih: Hukumat-e Islami* (The governance of the jurist: Islamic government), Khomeini accused the Jews of afflicting Islam with their anti-Islamic propaganda and engaging "in various stratagems" against the Muslims. The Jews, "may God curse them," writes Khomeini, "are opposed to the very foundations of Islam and wish to establish Jewish domination throughout the world."[30] The terms *Jews*, *Israelis*, and *Zionists* are often used interchangeably in Iran, as in most of the Muslim world. Considering all this, it is not surprising that a Shia cleric, Maulana Kalb-e-Jawad, is at the forefront of all anti-Israel and anti-Zionist demonstrations and agitations in Lucknow. During one such agitation, he said:

> The source of all terrorism are three countries, America, Israel and Saudi Arabia. Weapons come from America and Israel and the funding from Saudi Arabia. The Imam of Bait ul-Muqaddas has been denied visa by India, whereas the clerics from Saudi Arabia, which is slave to America, have visited India innumerable times. Visa is not given to the clerics from Iraq and Iran, because they will speak against America and Israel. It only implies that the Indian State too has submitted to America and Israel. It is a matter of great shame to all Indians that a country as large and great as India has become a slave to these countries. Earlier India was a slave to Britain, now it is a slave of America and Israel. All policies in India are made with the consent and approval of America and Israel. It is our politicians who are responsible for this. They are bribed. They get huge funds. They are selling away India to America and Israel. Iran has been boycotted and now oil is not being purchased from there. As a result petrol and diesel have become so costly. Gas is Rupees Nine Hundred per cylinder. It is all because of American pressure. Our politicians are getting money from America and Israel. Had we got gas from Iran through the planned pipeline a gas cylinder would have cost merely Rupees One Hundred.[31]

FREEMASON TEMPLE

Muslims believe that the Freemason Temple in Hazratganj in Lucknow is Jewish-owned, and that is how it is represented by the Muslim journalists in Lucknow. A movement has been initiated to liberate the building, which used to be an *imāmbārā* before being leased to the Freemasons, from the alleged Jewish control.

This is a manifestation of the spread of many features of European antisemitism to the Muslim world. In Germany in the 1860s, Jews and Freemasons began to be perceived as working hand in glove to undermine traditional society. This combined criticism of the two groups shifted to France, where a string of books emphasized it. The notion of a sinister alliance between the two played a conspicuous part in the Dreyfus Affair, and it became a prominent feature of European antisemitism. *The Protocols of the Elders of Zion* (first published in Russia in 1904) includes the idea of a Jewish-Masonic plot to control the world. Up to this time, Freemasonry had been thought of as a conservative and partly antisemitic association in Germany, but as soon as the Protocols appeared in German and English in the 1920s, Jews and Freemasons began to be identified as the sinister agents responsible for the outbreak of World War I and the German defeat. The slogan *"Juden und Freimaurer"* emerged as a battle cry of the German right wing and was utilized by Hitler during his ascent to power. During World War II, the Nazis under the leadership of Hitler persecuted Freemasons together with Bolsheviks and Jews.

According to cleric Maulana Kalb-e-Jawad, the leader of this Shia movement, which aims to regain control of the structure that houses the Freemason Temple, "Freemason is a Jewish organization. However, it also has some Christians as its members. Unfortunately, some opportunists among Muslims are also a part of this movement that is a conspiracy against Islam." Jawad, for whom Freemasons are worshippers of Satan, adds, "You should read the Jewish book Talmud. It is a very dangerous book. I call it dangerous because it states that only Jews have the right to live. If given a choice between saving a non-Jewish human life and a life of the dog, the Jew should save the dog. This is the kind of religious instruction given to Jews in their book. Now you can understand yourself."[32]

DEMAND FOR SEVERING DIPLOMATIC
TIES WITH ISRAEL

Anti-Israel sentiment is one of the few things that unite all Muslims in Lucknow, a city notorious for its Shia-Sunni clashes. Although the two sects do not pray together, they did exactly that on March 30, 2012, when Maulana Khalid Rasheed Firangi Mahali, the *Imam-e-Jummah* (Imam of the Friday Prayer) of the highly regarded Shahi Asafi Mosque of Lucknow, led the prayer service at the request of the Shia cleric Maulana Kalb-e-Jawad. It was attended by both Shia and Sunni congregations, after which anti-Israel statements were given by both Shia and Sunni leaders asking for severing diplomatic ties with Israel.[33]

BOYCOTT OF ISRAELI GOODS

In response to the Israeli military action in Gaza in 2009, the most respected and important Sunni cleric in Lucknow, Maulana Khalid Rasheed Firangi Mahali, issued a fatwa calling for a boycott of Israeli products, without any mention of Hamas's attacks on Israeli civilians. He said, "The companies which fund Israel or support it economically, such companies and their products should be boycotted so that Israel can be weakened. So that such attacks do not take place in future against Palestinians or any innocent." He added, "Following its non-aligned movement, India should strongly condemn such act of Israel and help Palestinians on humanitarian grounds. Strong action should be taken against Israeli Embassy in India, and New Delhi should voice its concern on the issue in the international fora like the UN."[34]

The director of the Islamic Society of Greater Orlando, Florida, Maulana Tariq Rasheed (also spelled Rashid) Firangi Mahali, mentioned above, is Maulana Khalid Rasheed Firangi Mahali's brother. According to the former, "misconceptions about Muslims are created by the Jewish lobby and by western countries and their media. The Jewish lobby's target is to malign Islam. . . . We've tried to dispel misconceptions about Islam but we are a victim of conspiracy by the Jewish community. Because Islam is spreading very fast they are threatened by it and have conspired against it."[35] The fact that no distinction is made between Israelis and Jews and that the two terms are often used interchangeably is illustrated by a report in an online Muslim magazine about a call given in Lucknow to boycott Israeli products in response to Israel's military action in Gaza that represents even non-Israeli products as Israeli because they are owned or perceived to be owned by Jews: "The citizens of Lucknow have taken pledge not to use any Israeli products like CocaCola, McDonalds, Maggi, Nestle and JohnsonAndJohnson etc."[36]

PATHAN RESISTANCE TO THE ACADEMIC STUDY OF THE TRADITION OF THEIR ISRAELITE DESCENT

In a 2005 estimate, the township of Malihabad in Lucknow district was found to be the home of a small community of 600 people of Israelite descent, primarily from the Afridi tribe, among the 1,200 Pathans there in a total population of 16,850. Famous as the mango capital of India and as the birthplace of great Urdu poets such as Josh Malihabadi, Faqeer Muhammad Khan Goya, and Anwar Nadeem, the area has recently attracted international attention because of the putative Israelite origins of its six hundred Afridi Pathans. There is an age-old tradition among certain Pathan tribes, including Afridi, that they descended from the lost tribes of Israel. Most of the Pathans in the new generation are unaware of it, but those who do know insist on making a clear distinction between Israelite and Jewish; they take offense at being connected to Jews—a term that has acquired a pejorative connotation because of the Arab-Israeli conflict. They also fear that being connected to Jews might put their allegiance to Islam in doubt.

According to the narrative of the trilogy of Semitic religions of Judaism, Christianity, and Islam, the twelve tribes of Israel sprang from the prophet Jacob's twelve sons, which were later divided into two kingdoms, Israel and Judea, in the ancient land of Canaan in the modern Jewish state of Israel. Modern Jews are believed to have descended from the two southern tribes that lived in Judea and not the ten northern tribes that lived in Israel, which were exiled by the Assyrians and disappeared into oblivion, known today as the lost tribes of Israel. Hence, those of the older generation emphasize that, even if there is a connection, they should be called Israelites and not Jewish.

The often interchangeable use of the two terms by the press has made the Afridi Pathans suspect the academic attempts to ascertain the historic authenticity of the tradition at research institutes in India and abroad as Zionist conspiracies against Islam, aimed at convincing its bravest followers (as they see themselves), the Pathans, of their Israelite roots and then persuading them to convert to Judaism and migrate to Israel. Their DNA samples have been analyzed by geneticists in the United Kingdom and Israel, but the results have largely been neutral because of the small sample sizes.

PALESTINIAN RESISTANCE
THEATRE'S LUCKNOW VISIT

In December 2015, Freedom Theatre Palestine in collaboration with Jana Natya Manch (People's Dramatic Stage/Forum), an Indian theatrical organization, staged shows in nine Indian cities, starting with Lucknow. The following is from a report by correspondent Yusra Husain, a Shia Muslim from Lucknow, in the *Times of India* Lucknow edition:

> The Indian government should revisit its own values of freedom struggle and speak up against Israel's stand towards Palestine and its blatant repression of Palestinians. This was the joint appeal made by Indian and Palestinian artists, theatre persons

and activists in Lucknow on Friday when the first-ever Indo-Palestinian theatre collaboration was performed in the city. . . .
It was also a take on the political stand of the governments of India, Israel and America. "India is the largest customer for Israel-made weapons, and hence, is financing the political aims of the two governments. It is time India amended its policy towards Palestine," said Moloyashree Hashmi, president, Janam [Hindi acronym for Jan Natya Manch, which sounds like the Hindi word for birth].[37]

PERCEPTIONS OF JEWS, ISRAEL, AND ZIONISM

As noted at the beginning of this chapter, most Muslims in Lucknow have no direct contact with Jews because of the almost complete absence of Jews in the city and their small numbers in South Asia in general. This is true of other South Asians, irrespective of their religious persuasions. Hence the perceptions that the Muslims in Lucknow have of Jews, Israel, and Zionism are largely formed by their religious narrative, their press and their intellectual discourse, which are generally biased and prejudiced.

Professor Khan Muhammad Atif, a Sunni Muslim and a retired professor of the department of Persian at the University of Lucknow, who is also active in local politics in Lucknow and a well-known face of the local Muslim elite, maintains as follows:

America would have never attacked Muslims across the world the way it has been doing had it not been controlled by Jews. . . . The State of Israel is illegitimate. It exists only because of the American support. The day American support comes to an end the Jews will be driven out of there in merely five or six hours by the Arabs. Jews are also aware of this. It is for this reason that they maintain homes also in Europe. USSR ceased to exist. USA too will decline. It is for Jews to think what would happen to them then.[38]

He adds, "Israelis, Jews, Zionists are not any different from each other. They are, in fact, all the same. Merely the names are different. . . . The Jews are not in conflict with Muslims, but with God, for they are guilty of the falsification of sacred texts. They have suffered through-out their history only because of the wrath of God." He goes on to deny the Holocaust, clearly influenced by the antisemitic propaganda produced in his language of study, Persian (Farsi), by the Iranian regime: "The number of those who perished at the hands of the Nazis is projected to be way too high for it to be possible, for the Jews were never in such large numbers in Germany. Holocaust is undoubtedly a big lie."[39] The expression of views such as these is also a strategy for gaining quick popularity among the Muslim masses in Lucknow. The antisemitic rhetoric indulged in by academics such as Atif is extremely dangerous, because they are in a strong position to influence and shape the perception of Jews, Israel, and Zionism held by the Muslims there.

Another example of this type of rhetoric comes from the former head of the department of Urdu at the University of Lucknow, Professor Anis Ashfaq, who holds the following view:

> The Palestinians were made homeless as a result of the creation of the State of Israel . . . and were further persecuted after that when they were deprived of their civil rights. . . . Although as Muslims, we recognise both Moses and Jesus as prophets, yet Jews and Christians do not recognise Muhammad as a prophet. It only testifies to the broadmindedness of Muslims. . . . There is this perception that the theory of deconstruction is either a Jewish invention or has been formulated to basically benefit the Jews as its application would imply that the Qur'anic verses can be interpreted in various ways. This perception actually gains strength from the accusation against Jews that they falsified the sacred texts.[40]

POSSIBILITIES FOR POSITIVE CHANGE

It might be utopian to imagine that there could ever be a time when Muslim antisemitism no longer exists, but this realization should not discourage us from our efforts to combat it, for it is only by such efforts that we keep it from increasing in scale and magnitude. Between 2008 and 2010, when I was a fellow of the Centre for Communication and Development Studies, Pune, under its youth outreach program Open Space, I organized fifty-six events, most of them focused on bringing about a positive change in Muslim attitudes toward Jews, Israel, and Zionism. The events aimed to eliminate ignorance and break stereotypes through the spread of information by various means, such as film screenings, lectures, book readings, discussions, and musical evenings. One of the events in this series was a Holocaust Films Retrospective, the first ever in South Asia, which was discussed above.

A couple of comments posted on the blog that I created to document my efforts are worth highlighting,[41] because they pro-vide some hope for the future and testify to the fact that efforts made in this direction are not in vain:

> The movie *A Mighty Heart* is such an interseting [sic] work and touching for people that i went to watch it the third time. Having seen this movie before, i was quite aware of Daniel Pearl's life and the incident with him in Pakistan. But this evening was special because i got to know some real facts about his life and much more through the distribution of booklet on Daniel Pearl. This event changed my thinkings about Jews all around the world which was a mistake by people like me belonging to Islamic religion and culture.[42]

Another comment worth repeating is as follows:

> Thank you for inviting me to such an enlightening program and the discussions that followed. I must say the program did succeed in considerably influencing me by its content and forced me to see beyond my misconceptions. It's true but I always looked upon Hitler as a person driven by the patriotic zeal. Having read "Main Kamph" also forced me always to see things from his point of view, though I never seconded on his views and the atrocities against a certain sect, but I always thought that he wanted to pull Germany out of the misfortunes that it fell into after the WW1. The program educated

me about his absurd ideas and the level of his crime against
humanity. It forced me to read and know about the other side of
the picture as well. He definitely pushed Germany further into
misfortunes with his actions. I now have realized that no zeal can
be taken up as an excuse to commit a crime such hinenious [*sic*] as
the one done by Adolf Hitler and any other group also who thinks
idolizing.[43]

Hatred thrives on falsehood. The only way to fight it is by eliminating ignorance and raising awareness.

NOTES

1. Member countries of the South Asian Association for Regional
Cooperation are Afghanistan, Bangladesh, Bhutan, India, Maldives,
Nepal, Pakistan, and Sri Lanka.
2. Gunther Jikeli, "Antisemitism among Young European Muslims,"
in *Resurgent Antisemitism: Global Perspectives*, ed. Alvin H. Rosenfeld
(Bloomington: Indiana University Press, 2013), 271.
3. Karen Leonard, "American Muslims: South Asian Contributions
to the Mix" (paper, Conference on French and US Approaches to
Understanding Islam, Stanford University, September 2004), http://www
.wkconline.org/resources/pdf/2005muslim_SAsian_Muslims.pdf.
4. Website of Nadwātul Ulamā: http://www.nadwatululama.org
/am.pdf.
5. Mohammad Akram Nadwi, a graduate of Nadwātul Ulamā,
Lucknow, is the principal of Al Salam Institute and an honorary
visiting fellow at the Markfield Institute of Higher Education in the
United Kingdom. Another alumnus of Nadwātul Ulamā, Dr. Saeed
Faizi Nadwi, is the founder and president of the Al-Nadwa Educational
Islamic Centre in Richmond, Ontario, Canada. He is also the secretary
of the Canadian Council of Imams and a member of the board of
directors of the Crescent Committee of Canada. Yet another alumnus
of Nadwatul Ulama, Dr. Iqbal Masood Al-Nadvi, is the emir (president)
of the Islamic Circle of North America, Canada. Prior to this, he was
the imam of the Muslim Association of Calgary Islamic Centre
(1998–2004) and director of Al-Falah Islamic School in Oakville,
Ontario (2004–11).

6. Nadeem Hasnain, *The Other Lucknow: An Ethnographic Portrait of a City of Undying Memories and Nostalgia* (New Delhi: Vani Prakashan, 2016), 76–77.

7. Khaled Ahmed, "The Lucknow Connection," *Indian Express*, May 12, 2014, http://indianexpress.com/article/opinion/columns/the-lucknow-connection/.

8. Fawad Javaid, "Holocaust Denial in Pakistan: An Appraisal," in "Jewish-Muslim Relations in South Asia," ed. Navras Jaat Aafreedi, special issue, *Café Dissensus*, no. 21 (January 7, 2016), https://cafedissensus.com/2016/01/07/holocaust-denial-in-pakistan-an-appraisal/;
Ambreen Agha, "Indian Muslim Denial of the Holocaust: Who Are These Muslims?" in "India's Response to the Holocaust and Its Perception of Hitler," ed. Navras Jaat Aafreedi, special issue, *Café Dissensus*, no. 31 (January 20, 2017), https://cafedissensus.com/2017/01/20/indian-muslim-denial-of-the-holocaust-who-are-these-muslims/; Md. Muddassir Quamar, "Holocaust in the Indian Urdu Press," in "India's Response to the Holocaust and Its Perception of Hitler," ed. Navras Jaat Aafreedi, special issue, *Café Dissensus*, no. 31 (January 20, 2017), https://cafedissensus.com/2017/01/20/holocaust-in-the-indian-urdu-press/.

9. Meir Litvak, "The Islamic Republic of Iran and the Holocaust: Anti-Semitism and Anti-Zionism," in *Anti-Semitism and Anti-Zionism in Historical Perspective: Convergence and Divergence*, ed. Jeffrey Herf (New York: Routledge, 2006), 251.

10. Qutbullah, interview by the author at the *Rāshtriya Sahāra* Lucknow office, December 29, 2010.

11. Ahmad Ibrahim Alvi, interview by the author at Alvi's office at the *Aag* headquarters in Lucknow, December 28, 2010.

12. Yoginder Sikand, "Interview with Maulānā Kalbé Sādiq, Shia scholar," TwoCircles.net, August 9, 2007, accessed on July 14, 2018, http://twocircles.net/2007aug08/interview_maulana_kalbe_sadiq_shia_scholar.html.

13. Hasan Ejaz, interview by the author at Ejaz's residence in Lucknow, December 29, 2010.

14. Tufail Ahmad, "It's Urdu Dailies Not Internet Alone That's Turning Muslims into Terrorists," *Daily O*, July 7, 2016, http://www.dailyo.in/politics/muslims-radicalisation-isis-hyderabad-ramzan-internet-war-of-badr-prophet-muhammad-orlando-shooting/story/1/11599.html.

15. Ahmad, "It's Urdu Dailies Not Internet Alone."

16. Ahmad, "It's Urdu Dailies Not Internet Alone."

17. Ahmad, "It's Urdu Dailies Not Internet Alone."

18. Myer Samra, email to the editor of the *Lucknow Tribune*, December 20, 2012.

19. His grandson, Maulana Salman Nadwi, a graduate of Nadwatul Ulama and a renowned Islamic scholar in his own right, reportedly congratulated Abu Bakr Baghdadi of the Islamic State when he declared the establishment of the caliphate and called himself the caliph. See Sultan Shahin, "Indian Maulana Salman Nadwi Congratulates Abu Bakr Baghdadi, Accepts Him as Caliph of Muslims, Writes Him a Letter Expressing His Excitement at the Establishment of the Islamic Caliphate," New Age Islam, July 17, 2014, http://www.newageislam.com/the-war-within-islam /indian-maulana-salman-nadwi-congratulates-abu-bakr-baghdadi,-accepts -him-as-caliph-of-muslims,-writes-him-a-letter-expressing-his-excitement -at-the-establishment-of-islamic-caliphate/d/98142. He also wrote an open letter to the government of Saudi Arabia asking it to raise an army of Indian Sunni Muslims to fight against the Shia militias in Iraq and elsewhere, as reported in "Nadwa Cleric Asks Saudi Govt to Prepare an Army of Sunni Youth for Iraq," *Times of India*, July 26, 2014, http://timesofindia.indiatimes .com/india/Nadwa-cleric-asks-Saudi-govt-to-prepare-an-army-of-Sunni -youth-for-Iraq/articleshow/39012903.cms.

20. Syed Abul Hasan Ali Nadwi, *Islam and the World* (Lucknow, India: Academy of Islamic Research and Publications, 2003), 22–23.

21. Syed Abul Hasan Ali Nadwi, *The Arabs Must Win* (Lucknow, India: Academy of Islamic Research and Publications, 1967), 8–9, http://www .nadwatululama.org/english/books/arabsmustwin.pdf.

22. Nadwi, *The Arabs Must Win*, 9–10.

23. Nazrul Hafeez Nadvi, *Western Media and Its Impact on Society*, English 1st ed., Series 318, trans. Nazir Ahmad Zargar (2000; repr., Lucknow, India: Academy of Islamic Research and Publications, 2006), 159.

24. Nadvi, *Western Media and Its Impact*, 160.

25. Nadvi, *Western Media and Its Impact*, 153.

26. Nadvi, *Western Media and Its Impact*, 156.

27. Maulana Saeed ur Rahman, interview by the author at Rahman's office in Lucknow, July 10, 2011.

28. Ahmed, "The Lucknow Connection."

29. Saeed Naqvi, "Centrality of Lucknow in World's Shia Culture," *Two Circles*, May 15, 2015, http://twocircles.net/2015may15/1431700266.html #.VyaR5nrXmJc.

30. Litvak, "Islamic Republic of Iran," 252.

31. See a video at "Molana Kalbe Jawad Interview Israel Amrika ke khila Report by Mr Roomi, Asian TV News," *Youtube.com*, April 12, 2013, https://www.youtube.com/watch?v=I7v4coUmWjk.

32. Ambreen Agha, "A Tale of Two Brothers: History of Estrangement and the Birth of Two Religions," in "Jewish-Muslim Relations in South Asia," ed. Navras Jaat Aafreedi, special issue, *Café Dissensus*, no. 21 (January 7, 2016), https://cafedissensus.com/2016/01/07/a-tale-of-two-brothers-history-of-estrangement-and-the-birth-of-two-religions/.

33. Mohsin Habib, "Indian Shia and Sunni Unite in Hating Israel," Gatestone Institute International Policy Council, August 10, 2012, https://www.gatestoneinstitute.org/3267/indian-shia-sunni.

34. ANI, "Fatwa in India to Boycott Israeli Goods," *DNA*, January 20, 2009, http://www.dnaindia.com/india/report-fatwa-in-india-to-boycott-israeli-goods-1223180.

35. Rachel Aspden, "Changing Islam: A Journey through Egypt, Sudan and India," Winston Churchill Memorial Trust Fellowship, 2010, http://www.wcmt.org.uk/sites/default/files/migrated-reports/755_1.pdf.

36. Anonymous, "Nationwide Protest against Israel Continues," *Muslim Mirror News*, July 19, 2014, accessed on July 14, 2018, http://muslimmirror.com/eng/nationwide-protest-against-israel/.

37. Yusra Husain, "Rights of Palestinians a Public Responsibility," *Times of India* (Lucknow), December 19, 2015, http://timesofindia.indiatimes.com/city/lucknow/Rights-of-Palestinians-a-public-responsibility/articleshow/50239829.cms.

38. Khan Muhammad Atif, interviewed by the author at Atif's residence in Lucknow, December 28, 2010.

39. Khan Muhammad Atif, interview by the author at Atif's residence in Lucknow, December 28, 2010.

40. Anis Ashfaq, interview by the author at Ashfaq's office at the University of Lucknow, December 27, 2010.

41. *Dr. Navras Jaat Aafreedi's Social Activism*, http://openspacelucknow.blogspot.in/.

42. Read the comment at "An Evening Dedicated to Jewish-Muslim Relations in Memory of Daniel Pearl," *Dr. Navras Jaat Aafreedi's Social Activism*, June 21, 2009, accessed on July 14, 2018, openspacelucknow.blogspot.com/2009/06/evening-dedicated-to-jewish-muslim.html.

43. Read the full comment at "In Dark Times," *Dr. Navras Jaat Aafreedi's Social Activism*, April 16, 2009, accessed on July 14, 2018, http://openspacelucknow.blogspot.in/2009/04/in-dark-times.html.

NAVRAS JAAT AAFREEDI is Assistant Professor of History at Presidency University, Kolkata, India. He is an Indo-Judaic studies scholar who specializes in study of the Holocaust, antisemitism, mass violence, and intercommunal relations. Among his numerous publications is *Jews, Judaizing Movements and the Traditions of Israelite Descent in South Asia.*

Index

CPSIA information can be obtained
at www.ICGtesting.com
Printed in the USA
BVHW040003060220
571540BV00015B/110